THE MYTH OF
ARAB PIRACY
IN THE GULF

THE MYTH OF ARAB PIRACY IN THE GULF

SULṬĀN MUḤAMMAD AL-QĀSIMĪ BSc, PhD

CROOM HELM

London • Sydney • Dover, New Hampshire

© 1986 Sultān Muhammad Al-Qāsimi
Croom Helm Ltd, Provident House, Burrell Row,
Beckenham, Kent BR3 1AT
Croom Helm Australia Pty Ltd, Suite 4, 6th Floor,
64–76 Kippax Street, Surry Hills, NSW 2010, Australia

British Library Cataloguing in Publication Data

Al-Qāsimi, Muhammad
    The myth of Arab piracy in the Gulf.
    1. Pirates — Persian Gulf — History — 18th
    century   2. Pirates — Persian Gulf — History
    — 19th century
    I. Title
    364.1'64   DS326

    ISBN 0-7099-2106-3

Croom Helm, 51 Washington Street, Dover,
New Hampshire 03820, USA

Library of Congress Cataloging in Publication Data

Qasimi, Sultan Muhammad.
    The myth of Arab piracy in the Gulf.

    Bibliography: p.
    Includes index.
    1. Persian Gulf Region—History, Naval.
2. Pirates—Persian Gulf Region.   I. Title.
DS326.Q38   1985   364.1'64   85-22411
ISBN 0-7099-2106-3

Filmset by Mayhew Typesetting, Bristol, England
Printed and bound in Great Britain by Mackays of Chatham Ltd, Kent

Contents

Colour Plates

Between pages 116 and 117.

Plates are labelled with the original description made by the artist at the scene.

1. The Fleet under convoy of HMS Chiffone, Capt. Wainwright leaving Bombay Sept. 14th 1809. From the Apollo Gate (R. Temple HM 65th Regt)
2. Muscat Harbour/from the Fisher-men's Rock (R. Temple HM 65th Regt)
3. Rus ul Khyma, with the attack of the H C-s Cruisers/on the evening of the 11th Nov. 1809 (R. Temple HM 65th Regt)
4. The wall and beach near Rus ul Khyma, with the troops preparing to land/on the morning of the 13th Nov. 1809 (R. Temple HM 65th Regt)
5. The troops landing at Rus ul Khyma/at Sun-rise — 13th Nov. 1809 (R. Temple HM 65th Regt)
6. The storming of a large storehouse near Rus ul Khyma, where Capt. Dancey, of HM 65th Regt was killed/Nov. 13th 1809 (R. Temple HM 65th Regt)
7. Rus ul Khyma, from the S.W. and the situation of the troops/at ½ past 2pm Nov. 13th 1809 (R. Temple HM 65th Regt)
8. A view of Linga or Lung, from the sea/during the destruction of the dows 6c Nov. 16th 1809 (R. Temple HM 65th Regt)
9. A view of Luft, 26th Nov. 1809 (R. Temple HM 65th Regt)
10. The attack on the Fort of Luft, Nov. 27th 1809 (R. Temple HM 65th Regt)
11. A view of Mutra from the East (R. Temple HM 65th Regt)
12. Schinaass from the sea (R. Temple HM 65th Regt)
13. The attack of the enemy's cavalry at Schinaass, Jan. 2nd 1810 (R. Temple HM 65th Regt)
14. Schinaass from the right of the encampment, on the morning of the 3rd Jan. 1810 (R. Temple HM 65th Regt)
15. The storming of Schinaass, Jan. 3rd 1810 (R. Temple HM 65th Regt)
16. Ras ul Khyma, Persian Gulf — 1809 (J. Thirtle)
17. Khorfakkan
18. Bushire (Lieutenant-Colonel Charles Hamilton Smith)
19. Ras el Kyma, chief port of the Wahabee pirates (Lieutenant-Colonel Charles Hamilton Smith)

Colour Plates

Plates 16 and 17 are from the author's private collection. All other plates are reproduced by courtesy of the National Maritime Museum, London.

To my wife Jawāhir

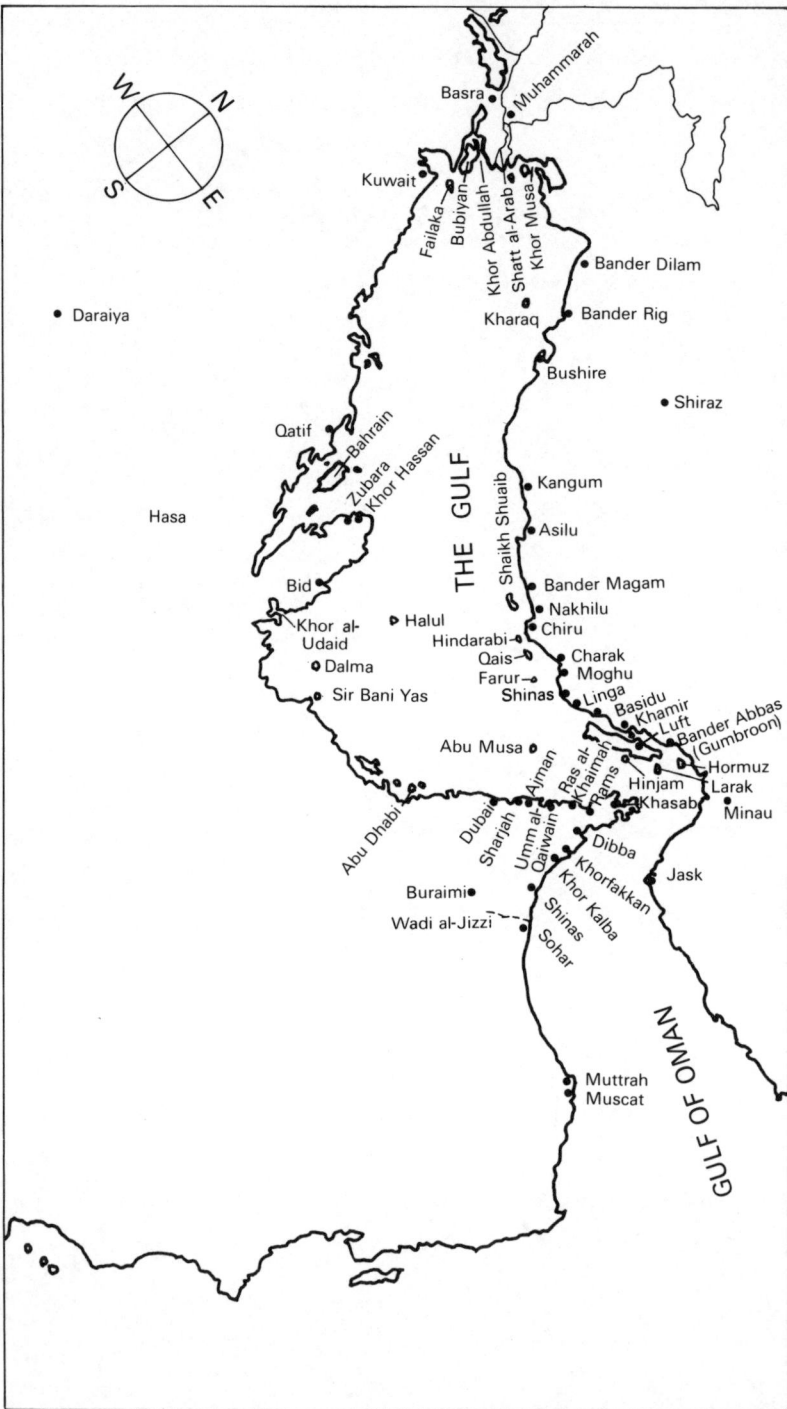

W N S E

Basra
Muhammarah
Kuwait
Failaka
Bubiyan
Khor Abdullah
Shatt al-Arab
Khor Musa
Bander Dilam
Daraiya
Kharaq
Bander Rig
Bushire
Shiraz
Qatif
Bahrain
Zubara
Khor Hassan
Hasa
Kangum
THE GULF
Shaikh Shuaib
Asilu
Bid
Bander Magam
Nakhilu
Khor al-
Udaid
Halul
Chiru
Hindarabi
Dalma
Qais
Charak
Farur
Moghu
Sir Bani Yas
Shinas
Linga
Khamir
Basidu
Luft
Bander Abbas
(Gumbroon)
Abu Musa
Ras al-
Khaimah
Hormuz
Rams
Hinjam
Larak
Abu Dhabi
Dubai
Ajman
Shariah
Umm al-
Qaiwain
Khasab
Minau
Dibba
Jask
Buraimi
Khorfakkan
Khor Kalba
Wadi al-Jizzi
Shinas
Sohar
Muttrah
Muscat
GULF OF OMAN

Trigonometrical Plan of the Backwater at Sharjah

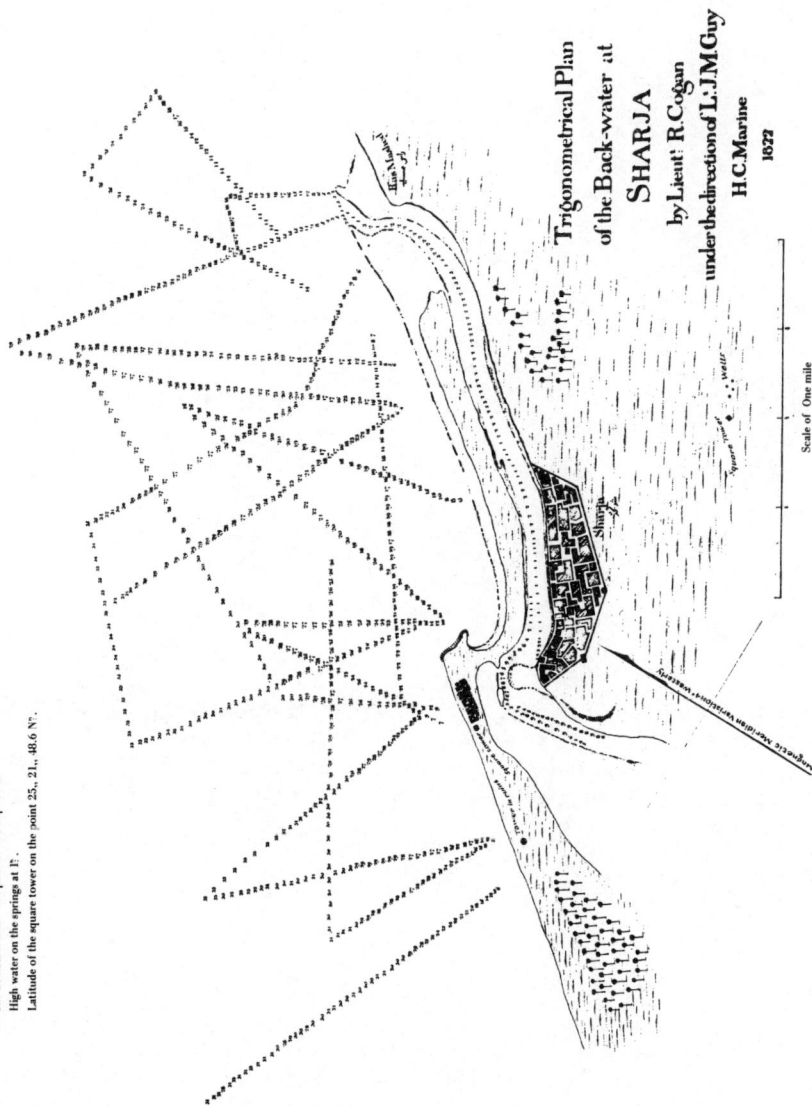

Remarks

The soundings are in feet, & for low water. Rise and fall six feet.

The bottom is sand with patches of sharp rocks.

High water on the springs at 1ʰ.

Latitude of the square tower on the point 25, 21, 48.6 Nº.

Trigonometrical Plan
of the Back-water at
SHARJA
by Lieutᵗ R.Cogan
under the direction of LᵗᵗJMGuy
H.C.Marine
1822

Scale of One mile

Introduction

For three quarters of a century, since J.G. Lorimer compiled his *magnum opus*, his deliberate misrepresentation of the history of the Arabian Peninsula and the Gulf has prevailed, and has never been challenged. The fact that his work was commissioned by Lord Curzon, the Viceroy of India, as an apologia for the long history of British colonialism in the Gulf has been forgotten. As a civil servant in the British Imperial Government of India, Lorimer could not be expected to be an impartial student of the affairs of his government. The prominence of his *Gazeteer* is due to the fact that he had access to all the relevant documents, but the flaw in his work is that he did not use this advantage properly. Indeed, with the authority derived from his access to the documents, he was able to present falsehoods and rumours as irrefutable facts. His method of compilation was highly selective and so designed to serve his purpose as to render his work apocryphal. It is not difficult to understand the effort put into translating it into Arabic because this effort has helped to propagate the British imperial point of view.

It is also curious that in his study, *Britain and the Persian Gulf 1775-1880* Dr J.B. Kelly includes Lorimer's work in his 'printed documentary sources'. Kelly admits:[1]

a number of documentary collections and precis put together in the Foreign Department of the Government of India, most of them by J.A. Saldanha, in preparation for the compilation of the historical volume of the *Gazeteer*. Although they contain a generous selection of correspondence from the records of both the Government of India and the Government of Bombay, concerning the affairs of the Gulf there are serious omissions in them, and their historical accuracy cannot always be relied upon.

It is difficult to reconcile this admission with Kelly's classification and use of Lorimer's work as a documentary source. However, Kelly's purpose was to support rather than to challenge Lorimer's work. In a sense he was more royalist than the king and his adoption of the imperialistic point of view was almost more unquestioning than that of the imperialist functionaries themselves. Francis Warden, the Secretary of the Bombay Government, stated in his famous Minute written in 1819 that piracy was not indigenous to the Gulf.[2] Kelly made the generalisation that, 'over the centuries the tribes of the southern shore of the Gulf had acquired notoriety as pirates'.[3] In my view, there is no truth whatsoever in Kelly's statement. On the contrary, the Gulf was always a peaceful waterway that served more as a connecting link between the peoples living on its shores than a divider; and with the exception of Raḥma b. Jābir, pirates were not known in the Gulf.

Although Kelly follows Lorimer in recounting the incidents of piracy and attributing them almost totally to the Qawāsim (and this without providing us with any evidence), he seems in two minds and almost contradicts himself. He asserts:[4]

> It was largely due to the exploits of the Qawasim that the coast of al-Shamal from Rams southwards became known to Europeans as the 'Pirate Coast', though it must be said in their defence that their reputation was largely earned as a result of incidents arising out of their protracted struggles with successive Al Bu Said rulers of Muscat.

Strangely enough, Kelly stresses the continued resistance of the Qawāsim to the attempts at domination by the rulers of Muscat; yet almost in the same breath he continues to quote John Malcolm who was reporting the remarks of his Persian servant in 1808 about the Qawāsim:[5]

> their occupation is piracy, and their delight murder; and to make it worse they give you the most pious reasons for every villainy they commit . . . If you are their captive, and offer all you possess to save your life, they say 'No! It is written in the Koran that it is unlawful to plunder the living, but we are not prohibited in that sacred work from stripping the dead'; so saying they knock you on the head. But then . . . that is not so much their fault, for they are descended from a Ghoul or monster.'

To Kelly it was not only the Qawāsim who were abnormal; the whole situation in the Gulf, especially when it came to piracy, was beyond explanation. Thus he argues:[6]

> Piracy is generally thought to have a depressing effect upon trade, though this was not the case in the Gulf before 1820. Nor did the normal corollary that the reduction of piracy is followed by a resurgence of trade apply after 1820. It may be that the relationship that seemed to exist between pirates and merchants, such as that between the Qawasim and the Al Khalifah before 1820, operated to exempt the Gulf from the normal laws of commerce.

This kind of explanation only helps to emphasise the complete misunderstanding of the history of the area and the factors involved. The indigenous people of the Gulf were normal people with normal human ambitions. Although poor, they were skilful. They were people practising normal human activities, in particular trade, in which they had been involved for millennia. The only abnormal factor was the introduction of a foreign people whose aim was to dominate and exploit. The intruders were the forces of British imperialism, who knew very well and often testified that the indigenous people of the Gulf were only interested in the peaceful pursuits of pearl diving and trade.

Advocates of British imperialism have managed to propagate the notion that towards the end of the eighteenth century and during the first two decades of the nineteenth the Arabs of the Gulf, particularly the Qawāsim, were zealously

involved in a great scheme of piracy against international trade, not only in the
Gulf, but also in the Red Sea, the Arabian Sea and the Indian Ocean. They argued
that this sudden change on the part of the Gulf Arabs came about because these
'pirates' were encouraged and supported by the rising power of the Saudis whose
creed the Gulf Arabs, particularly the Qawāsim, had accepted with fervour.

Supporters of this argument want us to believe that the Arabs of the Gulf were
saved from this nefarious occupation by the benevolent efforts of the British East
India Company, whose intervention in the Gulf was for the sole purpose of preserving law and order. The resulting British domination of the Gulf for almost two
centuries was a responsibility thrust upon the British almost against their will.

In my view, however, the East India Company was determined to increase
its share of the trade of the Gulf by all possible means. Any increase in the Company's share would be at the expense of the Arab natives of the Gulf: the 'Utūb,
the Omanis and the Qawāsim. The 'Utūb in the upper Gulf managed to establish
a prosperous trade with India directly, by-passing altogether the Arabs of the lower
Gulf — the Omanis and the Qawāsim. The Omanis wanted to institute themselves
as the dominant Arab power in the Gulf, but their attempts to destroy the 'Utūb
and occupy their base in Bahrain were doomed to failure and they did not have
sufficient naval strength to destroy the Qawāsim. This persuaded them to attempt
an alliance with the British against the Qawāsim. For their part, the British, i.e.
the Company, were willing to go along with this attempted alliance, but only
half-heartedly in spite of the efforts of men like David Seton, the British Resident in Muscat, to convince his superiors of the advantages of such a policy.

The Company's Government of Bombay realised that any real opposition to
their plans in the Gulf would come from the Qawāsim. But they were also well
aware that they did not themselves possess the necessary warships to defeat the
powerful navy of the Qawāsim. The Omanis might not have been much help,
but there was certainly no harm in using Muscat against Rās al-Khaimah, at least
until such time as the Company could muster sufficient strength to conquer the
Qawāsim. In order to achieve this goal the decision-making bodies of the Governments of Bombay and of India, and indeed of the Empire itself, needed to be
mobilised against the enemy. Accordingly, a concerted campaign was mounted
by Company officials to present, or rather misrepresent, the Qawāsim as pirates
whose depredations posed a serious threat to all maritime activities in the Indian
Ocean and adjacent waters. Any misfortune that happened to any ship in the area
was capriciously attributed to the 'Joasmee pirates'. In this way the strategy of
the 'Big Lie' was contrived; almost overnight the term 'Joasmees' became
synonymous with 'pirates', and even the home of the Qawāsim became the 'Pirate
Coast' instead of the 'Arabian Coast' or its less frequently used name 'Seer'.
The fight against 'piracy' became the Company's battle cry. If accidents did not
occur, incidents were invented and attributed to these imaginary 'pirates'. Indeed, Philip Francis, Member of Parliament at the time, commented in the House
of Commons during a debate on the affairs of the Company that, 'whenever the
Governor General and Council were disposed to make war upon their neighbours
they could at all times fabricate a case to suit their purpose'.[7] Finally, in 1820

a situation was created in the Gulf which was not unlike that of Suez in 1956, the only difference, perhaps, being that the Gulf operation destroyed the Qawāsim.

To designate the Qawāsim as pirates was injustice enough thrust upon them, though it could perhaps be understood in the circumstances of the time. However, for this false designation to become an accepted fact propagated by later historians is a sad comment on the research into the history of the Gulf.

Perhaps the least guilty was C.R. Low, the author of *History of the Indian Navy*, whose book was published in 1877 at the height of British imperialism to glorify it and to celebrate the triumphs of its forces. Lorimer was essentially part of the same school and he copied a good deal of fictitious narrative from Low's book. In his almost thirty years' tenure in Bahrain, Charles Belgrave was not a popular figure in the Gulf. His book *The Pirate Coast* has done little to bolster his reputation and credibility. Although one cannot accuse him of plagiarism, his work is largely based on the memoirs of Captain Francis Loch, one of the most reckless naval officers in the Gulf in 1819, with a generous portion taken haphazardly from Lorimer's work. To add to the confusion, Belgrave also added his own tendentious observations.

Lieut.-Colonel H. Moyse Bartlett gave his book the misleading title *The Pirates of Trucial Oman*. In it he confined himself to the incidental issue of the action and trial of Captain T. Thompson whose main claim to fame was his blunder in the expedition against Āl Bu 'Alī in 1820. Even with this limited scope, the book adds very little to our knowledge of the subject.

Donald Hawley's study *The Trucial States* was followed by a number of books whose main contribution was to sum up what had previously been written about the Gulf States, mainly by Lorimer and Kelly.

It is the aim of the present study to offer a more objective and logical explanation for the developments in the Gulf in the first two decades of the nineteenth century. It was these developments that established Britain as the dominant power in the Gulf, a situation which lasted for one hundred and fifty years and was certainly the major feature of the history of the Gulf until very recent times.

Notes

1. J.B. Kelly, *Britain and the Persian Gulf, 1795-1880*, (Oxford University Press, 1968), a comment in the Bibliography.
2. Bombay Archives, Summary of the Proceedings relative to the boats captured in the Persian Gulf, vol. 77/1819-20, Minute by Mr Warden, p. 12.
3. Kelly, *Britain and the Persian Gulf*, p. 19.
4. Ibid.
5. Ibid.
6. Ibid., p. 251.
7. C.H. Philips, *The East India Company 1784-1834*, (Manchester University Press, 1940), pp. 32-3.

Sources

By far the most important documentary sources for this study are the Bombay Archives.

It comes as a surprise to learn that, though they were opened in 1954, to our knowledge they have never been used by Western scholars interested in this subject: indeed, their existence is hardly known. The overwhelming reputation of the documents preserved in the India Office Library has completely overshadowed the documents in the Bombay Archives. Admittedly the Bombay documents are in a sad state of repair and organisation, and, indeed, in some cases are falling apart, which makes them sometimes difficult to use. But the fact remains that they are richer and more complete than those of the India Office Library, especially as regards documents relating to the early period with which this study is concerned. These are the complete files of the East India Company Government of India. Copies of all records and incoming and outgoing correspondence were kept. Many of these were not necessarily sent to London and thus exist only in Bombay. In Bombay also, there are copies of Arabic and Persian letters which were received or sent out from the Governor's Office. These were not sent to London, and only a few of their translations are to be found in the documents of the India Office Library.

The system of recording was changed in 1821, but as we are concerned here with the documents up to 1820, we shall confine our remarks to the pre-1821 documents. These are contained in about 7,000 volumes consisting of:

 (i)   Factory and Residency records;
 (ii) Bombay Presidency records;
 (iii) Records of special missions and committees;
 (iv) Despatches from and to the court of Directors; and
 (v)   Miscellaneous records, such as Selections compiled for a particular person or purpose.

The earliest records in Bombay go back to 1630, in the form of copies of letters from the Surat Factory which was at that time the headquarters of the East India Company. The accumulation of records starting in 1650 continued during the rest of the seventeenth century, mainly in the form of the Surat Factory Diaries. Indian researchers in the Bombay Archives state:[1]

the proceedings of the Government of Bombay from 1720 are complete, with the exception of those for the years 1721–3, 1725–7, 1729, 1730 and 1732. They are recorded in 'Diaries' in which every business transacted in the Secretary's Office, as also information received in his Office and letters received in and issued from the Secretariat and Minutes and orders of the Board, used to be recorded in the order of the date of consultations at Council meetings. By 'Consultations' is meant the meetings of the President and his Council. The word was also used to denote the minutes of such meetings.

The compiling of these Diaries continued to improve and applied to all Factories and Residencies. Obviously the Diaries of Factories and Residencies that are preserved in Bombay are of importance to this study; those of Basra and Gumbroon were also of some use.

The Bombay Castle Diaries began in 1720. They included at first abstracts and eventually complete copies of all outgoing and incoming letters, all memoranda between officials, records of Consultations about matters arising at meetings of Council, their decisions and often detailed reasons for these decisions, indeed sometimes even the reasons for certain individuals' opposition to these decisions. These records of Consultations became almost a complete chronicle of events, and resemble the combination of a log book, minute book and correspondence book.

In 1755 the records of the Bombay Government were divided between two newly created departments, the 'Secret and Political' and the 'Public' Departments. In the present study we are more concerned with the Diaries of the Secret and Political Department, since it dealt with political matters and relations with foreign countries through correspondence with Residents and Agents; issues of negotiations and military expeditions were also discused and the decisions taken were fully recorded. From 1809 until 1820 these Diaries were divided into the 'Political' and the 'Secret' Department Diaries; we are fortunate that the Diaries from 1755 to 1820 have been catalogued and that this catalogue was published in 1954.

From 1779 onwards new departments were created in the Government of Bombay and they also started their own Diaries. The Marine and Forest Department Diaries were begun in 1818, and by 1820 24 volumes of records had accumulated. However, as these Diaries were concerned with the principal work of the Department, namely the building, maintenance and manning of ships, they are not as important for the present study as the records of its chief officer, the Marine Superintendent. This official was the main link between Government and its naval power, and the 186 volumes of the Diaries of the Marine Superintendent contain some very valuable information, especially about naval expeditions and movements of British warships in the Gulf.

The Diaries of the Marine Superintendent are only one item out of 58 important groups of records which the organisers of the Bombay Archives preferred to classify under 'Miscellaneous Records'. This classification is perhaps a little unfortunate, as it gives the researcher the impression that these documents are of less value than the others and thus might be overlooked or at least left as a last resort. Be that as it may, these Miscellaneous Records 'consist of the proceedings of many interesting old bodies and institutions, Political Missions, Committees appointed for administrative matters, records of subordinate offices and a few miscellaneous registers and returns'.[2] It is ironic that the Indian organisers and researchers should label this collection miscellaneous and then use the same term to describe what they themselves classified as 'Selections', because in these 'Miscellaneous Records' at least three 'Selections' are officially recognised. One is composed of 184 volumes containing some 'original papers of subjects brought before Government',[3] many of which are of great significance to the present study. Another set of 'Selected Compilations', also in 184 volumes, are in the same pattern as the above 'Selections'. Then we find the 'Mr Warden Selections', in 19 volumes. As the Chief Secretary of the Bombay Government for practically the whole period covered in this study, these special selections were made to enable him to defend and explain his point of view, and, indeed, to establish in writing in his own words his famous Minute, covering the history of the period from the point of view of a top British official. These selections are invaluable to the present research.

One of the most exciting experiences during the course of our research was the discovery, in the stacks of the Bombay Archives, of a bundle containing seven volumes of obviously long-forgotten documents, also labelled 'Selections' on pirates in the Persian Gulf. It goes without saying that these had never been used before by any researcher and were of great value, especially as they include Arabic documents which are appended to the thesis version of this study.[4]

I was also very fortunate to have found and purchased in London a collection of 59 original documents relating to the subject which are all listed in the appendices to the thesis. Particular attention should be drawn to the Journal of David Seton, one of the major actors in the Gulf during this period, and to his observations on his negotiations with the Qawāsim and his plans for the Empire. The views of another empire builder, John Malcolm, are also reflected in a detailed letter to the Governor of India, the Earl of Mornington, in 1800 in which Malcolm outlined his plan for the establishment of a British base in the Gulf.

The rest of the items in this private collection are also concerned with the events of the period under review and are edited and appended to the thesis. In addition, the appendices include copies of letters in Arabic exchanged between Arab leaders and officials of the Company. The rest of the documentary material used in the research is indicated in the bibliography of this book.

Finally, the reader will notice that in this book there is more than one system of transliteration of names of persons and places; indeed it has been impossible to follow any particular system throughout. The early nineteenth century transliterations varied from one person to the other, and sometimes the same writer would even spell the same name differently in the same letter. Modern writers also differ widely in transliterating names, and some of the established names of leading persons and famous places are nowadays wrongly transliterated. In all these cases, and especially in quotations, no attempt has been made here to correct even obvious mistakes and the original transliteration has been followed precisely. For the rest of the work, an attempt has been made to offer a correct and unified system of transliteration. Attention must also be drawn to the fact that the English language, grammar and spelling were different in the eighteenth and nineteenth centuries from what they are today. Furthermore, the standard of literacy, particularly among the naval officers of the British Empire, does not seem to have been very high; and, perhaps because of the volume of work, secretaries making copies of documents etc. were bound to compound the mistakes of the originals. These literary idiosyncrasies have been left in order to avoid further mistakes.

Notes

1. *The Handbook of the Bombay Archives*, compiled by Sanjiv P. Dasai, (Bombay, 1978), p. 19.
2. Ibid., p. 105.
3. Ibid., p. 107.
4. Sultān Muhammad Al-Qāsimi, 'Arab "Piracy" and the East India Company Encroachment in the Gulf 1797–1820', Ph.D. thesis, University of Exeter, 1985.

1 The Arabian Gulf in the Eighteenth Century

Our immediate object here is to describe the Gulf as it was in the eighteenth century. On the right at the entrance of the straits of Hormuz lies the Island of Hormuz which 'was once the emporium of all the riches of India, the receptacle for the gems of Samarkand and Bokhara, and for the manufacture of Europe and Asia'.[1] This island is 12 miles in circumference and is formed of volcanic rock. Salt and red mud were produced from the mines there.

To the east of Hormuz extends the coast of Makrān beginning with the town of Minau where a stream of the same name enters the sea. Further down the coast, near the Cape of Jask, was situated Jask harbour where the English East India Company had been granted permission to trade into Persia by Shah Abbas I in 1616; accordingly it had established a factory there in 1619. The coast of Makrān was studded with many other towns and harbours that traded with the interior, from which crops of vegetables and fruits were brought to the coast. Along this coast lived the Balūch, who were wrongly described by Niebuhr as Arabs.[2] These people had a considerable number of ships and carried on a sizeable trade with places as far away as Baṣra and the coast of Malabar.

To the south of Hormuz lies the island of Larak, 11 km long and 5.6 km wide and also formed of volcanic rock. In the eighteenth century it had a small population of close on 200 people, living by fishing and pearling.

On the Persian coast, and only about 19 km away, stood the town of Gumbroon (later known as Bander 'Abbās), which served as a sea port for Kirmān, although landing there was too difficult for ships of more than 4 metres draft. Accordingly the anchorage was 3–5 km offshore. Niebuhr described Gumbroon as the most remarkable place on the Persian coast.[3] It was a commercial town with a mixed population composed of Persians, Arabs, Kurds, a few Armenians and some Balūch,[4] totalling 4,000–5,000 in number. The Dutch, English and French had factories there. The French factory closed first in the 1720s; the Dutch was the second to close in 1759, followed by the English in 1763.[5] In 1784 the port of Gumbroon was leased from Persia by the Imām of Muscat.

To the west of Gumbroon there were only three small villages: Khāmir, Bander Hallām and Kung, before Linga about 100 km away. In the vicinity of Khāmir there were sulphur mines, which were extensively worked and exported large quantities of sulphur to Muscat. In Kung, there had been a Portuguese factory to control the copper mines around it.[6]

To the south of Gumbroon lies the island of Qishm, the largest in the Gulf, 108 km long and on average 18 km wide. Its north-eastern edge is 22 km from Gumbroon and its south-western edge is 36 km from Linga. It is separated from the coast by the Khoriyāt Strait which extends from Gumbroon to Linga. The depth of this strait permitted navigation only to ships of not more than 6 metres draft, and even that required a pilot to guide the sailing among the small islands covered with mangrove trees. There were 36 different villages on the island of Qishm and there had been more, but many had fallen into decay and become uninhabited.[7] By the eighteenth century the population numbered about 5,000, concentrated mainly in the three small towns: Bāsīdū, Luft and Qishm. Bāsīdū was at the western end of the island and Qishm at the eastern end; the latter was an important source of wood for boats from all parts of the Gulf.[8] The town of Luft was the closest port to the Persian coast and was opposite the village of Khāmīr. On the other side of the island, only 2 km to the south-east is the small island of Hinjām, 9 km wide and 9 km long.

The next important town on the Persian coast was Linga, which was then a port with a considerable trade.[9] Captain Robert Budden of the East India Company's Marines described it in 1809 as follows:[10]

> Linguy on the Persian side of the western entrance of Kishma channel is still more contemptible, being a smaller town without fortifications and completely exposed. It has neither creek nor harbour, only a kind of wet dock formed by a pier not capable of containing more than 8 or 10 dows, which may with care be taken out and destroyed. The roadstead is entirely clear of danger, has good anchorage and is sheltered from the N. Westers.

However, there were rock plates parallel to the coast, extending some 200 metres alongside it. The eastern side of the town was more suitable for landing because the shore was sandy. Boats of 7 metres draft could anchor 1,200 metres from the coast and larger ships of 9 metres draft could anchor 1,800 metres from the coast.

Close to Linga to the west was the village of Shinās which offered a safe shelter for boats from the northern and eastern winds and in addition it had a wharf for off-loading cargo and passengers. Next to it was another small village, Bostānah, which was suitable only for anchorage of small boats. Further on was the small town of Chārak at the bottom of the bay of the same name. It was inhabited by 900 men of the Al ‘Alī tribe who worked at fishing as well as trading; they had six *baghalahs*, from 60 to 120 tons, and twenty smaller trading vessels. Chiru, at the bottom of a bay formed by Rās Chīrū, was populated by 150 men from the ‘Abābdah tribe; they also had a few trading boats, but most important was the fact that they could offer supplies and water in addition to one of the best anchorages in the Gulf.[11] Moghu, a nearby village, was considered a good shelter from the cold north-eastern winds, although its coast was rocky. Nakhīlū was an important small town with a population of 800.

There are a few small islands opposite this part of the coast: Farūr, Qais, Hindārābī and Shaikh Shu‘aib. Farūr and Hindārābī are too small to be of any significance; the island of Qais is a little bigger — 15 km long and 7 km wide — and it also allows its inhabitants some agriculture. It is 17 km away from the coast and its people made their living mainly from fishing and pearling. The island of Shaikh Shu‘aib is a little closer to the coast, only 7 km away. It is 24 km long and 5 km wide, and its inhabitants depended completely on fishing for their living.

Close to the town of Nakhīlū was the town of Bander Maqām. Then came the village of 'Asīlū and further on the town of Kangūn, the point where the jurisdiction of Bushire began.[12]

Bushire was on a peninsula connected to the mainland by 4 km-long lagoons which were very difficult to cross during the rainy season. On the north side of the town was an anchorage named Deira Creek, off which ships of 6 metres draft could anchor 3 km away, while larger ships anchored 7 km away. There was a jetty at Khor Sultān for ships of the high seas. In 1762 the East India Company's agent, after reconnoitring all the ports of the Gulf, considered Bushire the best because three parts of the town were surrounded by water, and thus the factory there could be easily defended against attack. There was considerable freedom and it was also not necessary to gratify anyone but the Shaikh. Another advantage from his point of view was the fact that it was full of inland merchants to whom good sales of woollens and metals could be made.[13]

Niebuhr recorded that the deep anchorage of Bushire, which was also close to the town, enabled Nādir Shāh to have big ships built there and to gather his whole fleet in the port. He added that, although Bushire was the port of Shīrāz, it was in fact an Arab colony; the town's most important families were those of the three Arab tribes Za'āb, Bū-Muhair and Matārish.[14] In the eighteenth century the town was three miles in circumference and was surrounded by stone walls, with two gates on the land side. There was neither castle nor battery in the town or near it.[15]

From Bushire the coast runs north-west until it reaches a low plain where the port of Bander Rīg was located below heights that reached 200 metres. This had been an important port and the East India Company had had a factory there, but by the eighteenth century the troubled situation in Persia caused it to decline. It was observed that most of the houses there were built of mats and the population was completely Arab.[16] Opposite the coast of Bander Rīg and 30 km out to sea is Khāraq island, which was then 8 km long with an average width of 4 km.

From Khāraq island ships sailed to the west, passing by Bander Dilam and Khor Mūsā until they reached Shatt al-'Arab. On the right bank was Muhammarah, dominated by Banū Ka'b. On the left bank, 150 km inland was Basra. The town itself was built 5 km from the river from which a creek ran into it, and vessels of 50–60 tons could navigate it at high water. Basra was described by an eighteenth century traveller as 'very large and extremely populous. The Bazaar or Market Place is nearly two miles long and appears to be well supplied'.[17] Of course the East India Company had an establishment at Basra, but the importance of the town to the British in India far exceeded the activities of this establishment, because it was a most important link in communications with London.

Leaving Shatt al-'Arab behind and passing by Khor 'Abdullah and Būbiyān and Failaka islands on the left, the sailing ships reached Kuwait Bay. The town of Kuwait was situated on the left side of the bay. Its population numbered about 25,000, and they possessed 31 *baghalahs* and *bateels* of from 150 to 300 tons, which traded mainly with India.[18] The country inland was sandy desert, and the water was salty and bad.

From Kuwait to the Bay of Qaṭīf there was nothing of note. The port of Qaṭīf stood on the bay, where the shallow water extends to Bahrain Island. The bay was unsafe for large ships, although Qaṭīf had been a big trading centre for the surrounding region which consisted of dense groves of date palms. One day's sailing to the south of Qaṭīf and right opposite Bahrain was the ancient port of 'Uqair, another outlet for the Hasā region. This port naturally had extensive trade with Bahrain and across to Persia.[19]

The main island of Bahrain was 30 miles long and 9 miles wide and was blessed with a well-sheltered harbour and numerous springs of fresh water. Manāmah and Muharraq were the main towns on the islands and we know that the former's population was estimated at 25,000 people.[20] Bahrain was well-known for its pearl industry which employed some 500–600 boats; also between 30 and 40 *baghalahs* were busy carrying trade all over the Gulf and the shores of the Indian Ocean.

Within sight of Bahrain is the Qatar Peninsula with Zubāra and Khor Hassan at its northern tip; the latter was the centre of the Jalāhima and their notorious naval power. Bid' was a port on the eastern coast of the peninsula, inhabited by members of the Dawāsir and Sūdān tribes. Its bay was formed by two dangerous reefs; inside anchorage was safe for small ships but large ones had to anchor within a mile offshore. Kelly explained that Bid' was once a large town; 'its development was hastened by the siege of Basra by the Persians in 1775–6, which diverted much of the trade of the upper Gulf to the new settlement and caused several merchants to move there'.[22]

The pearl bank starts at the island of Halul to the east of Qatar and extends to Shārjah. Khor al-'Udaid marks the bottom end of the coast of the Qatar Peninsula after which the coast runs north-east off the main Arab coast of the Gulf. Sir Banī Yās is separated from the coast by a passage of water and not far to the west of it is Dālma at the centre of the pearl bank. In the eighteenth century Abu Dhabi was an island with creeks on both sides and inshore anchorage. Water was discovered in 1761 and members of the tribe of Banī Yās moved in, increasing the population considerably.

One hundred miles inland to the east of Abu Dhabi was the town of Būraimi. Kelly described it as[23]

> the inland key to Oman. It was the only well-watered locality in the hundreds of miles of desert that stretched between it and Hasa and it stood at the crossroads of the routes between Oman and the Pirate Coast. A dozen miles or so to the east rose the foothills of the western Hajar, through which the Wadi-al Jizzi wound its way to the coast of the Gulf of Oman at Sauhar. Northwards and westwards ran the tracks to Sharjah, Ras al-Khaima and Abu Dhabi. Southwards ran the tracks to Dhank and Ibri, and beyond them to Nizwa, Jabrin and Izki, in the very heart of Oman. Buraimi's appearance was as singular as its situation.

The coast from Abu Dhabi to Rās al-Khaimah was barren with the exception of date groves near the towns, but the fresh water on the coast was good except for the part of the coast close to Abu Dhabi. Each town had a bay of the same name and good anchorage a mile or so offshore. The towns were: Dubai, Khān, Shārjah, 'Ajmān, Umm al-Qaiwain, Jazīrat al-Ḥamra, Rās al-Khaimah and Rams.

Dubai stood, like most other towns, on the coast. It was inhabited by about 700–800 of the Bani Yās tribe. The town was defended by several towers, and there were a number of trading and pearl fishing boats. The anchorage was about a mile and a half offshore. There was a creek where Dubai stood on the south bank. Abū Heyle village was situated on one side of Khān creek, and Khān village on the northern bank. The two villages jointly contained about 250 inhabitants of various tribes, who were mostly fishermen.

Shārjah town was situated on Shārjah creek, which was shallow and about 150 yards wide. The town was long, narrow and open, defended by a fort and cannons and some detached towers. It was inhabited by Qawāsim, al-'Alī, Shewaiḥain, and some mixed tribes, amounting to about 3,500–3,800 inhabitants in all. Three or four hundred boats of various sizes plied the pearl fishery. The Shaikh received a lakh (100,000) Maria Theresa dollars from the taxes collected from the boats at the rate of 1–2½ dollars per boat. Banyans (Indian brokers) settled there as pearl merchants, goldsmiths and cloth and grain dealers. Fresh water was procurable; the anchorage was 5 fathoms for one and a quarter miles, and 2–3 fathoms close to the beach. Fasht village was one mile north of the entrance to Shārjah creek.

The town of 'Ajmān lay to the north of the town of Shārjah on the south bank of the 'Ajmān creek. The creek, which was one of the best on the coast, had 5 ft depth of water at low tide and 10 ft at high tide, and a good entrance. The town was small, and inhabited by 1,500 men of the N'aim tribe. The anchorage was 5 fathoms, about a mile and a quarter offshore. To the north of 'Ajmān, the town of Ḥamria stood on the north side of the Ḥamria creek.

Umm al-Qaiwain town with its extensive creek was to the north of Ḥamria. The creek, which ran several miles, had 7 fathoms of water in some parts, but the entrance was blocked by a very extensive reef. Between the creek to the north of Umm al-Qaiwain and the sea there is an island on which the town of Libīnī was situated.[24]

The report on the situation of the Arab tribes in the Gulf in 1756, written by the residents in Khāraq island, T.F. van Kniphausen and J. van der Hulst, states:[25]

Between Kateef and Seer (Ras el-Khaimah) there are three places on the coast, 'Ajīr, Qatar and Shārjah, each of which only had few houses, where from Basrah dates and rice were brought to sell to the Arabs of the desert or to pearl-divers.

The report describes Jazīrat al-Ḥamra as a large piece of land which extended into the sea near Sīr and became an island at high tide; it was inhabited by a tribe of Arabs called Za'āb, who lived from pearl-diving. They had to obey the Shaikh of the 'Qassim' and pay him a considerable tribute. The report also described Rās al-Khaimah:

The town was according to the local manner fairly well fortified and had some artillery. It was inhabited by Qassim and their Shaikh called Kaiyd or Rahmah bin Matter.

Rās al-Khaimah stood upon a sandy point from which a spit of land ran in a north-easterly direction, forming a snug harbour for its boats and affording complete shelter from all winds. The inlet from the sea extended in a south-westerly direction to the back of the town where the dhows were anchored; it then turned south-easterly inland. In the harbour of Rās al-Khaimah there was generally, at spring tides 4 ft of water at low tide and 9 ft at high tide. The harbour was a sandy bed and the ground shifted about once every six months as a result, for one half of the year the anchorage might be on one side of the harbour and for the other half, on the opposite side. In the passage to Rās al-Khaimah round by Dehān, there was usually 11 ft of water at high tide and 6 ft at low tide. Rās al-Khaimah could not be approached nearer than 1½–2 miles by ships drawing 13–14 ft of water, on account of a bank almost that distance from the shore and running parallel to it. Smaller vessels were able to go within 500 metres of the shore. Rams with its long fort and shallow creek was 10 km to the north of Rās al-Khaimah.

From Rams to Khaṣab northwards the mountains came closer to the sea. There were six villages on the seashore, three of which could be approached by land and the others at coves. The people there lived on fishing and cultivation, and onions, sweet potatoes and date palms grew extensively. Khaṣab was a small village located at one of the coves of Musandam, and it grew crops of wheat, barley, and onions as well as dates. The depth of water in the coves was about 30 fathoms. Passing these mountains and the rocky inlet one reaches Rās Musandam, the northern-most extremity of the Arabian coast. Opposite Rās Musandam there are two rocky islets called the Quoins. Passing them one leaves the Arabian Gulf and enters the Gulf of Oman which is part of the Arabian Sea.

Moving south, and following the edge of the mountains and the coves on the east side of Musandam, one reaches Dibbā. This part, from Dibbā to Kalbā in the south, was described in the report of the travels of the Dutch ship *Meerkat*, in 1666. Dibbā was a small village of 300 houses built from date-palm leaves, and the largest of the four fortresses built by the Portuguese was still standing. The place had fresh water from wells and there was a multitude of date trees. On the northern side of the village there was a stream. From the southern corner of Dibbā to Albediā, the course was south for 2½ miles, at a depth of 19–22 fathoms with a sandy bottom. Albediā consisted of 200 houses built of date-palm leaves near the beach. Fresh water could be obtained from its wells. There were a great many date palms and some fig trees, also melons and water melons. At this place one could obtain cows, goats and chickens. The anchorage was a quarter of a mile from the shore and the depth was 10–12 fathoms with a sandy bottom. From the southern corner of Albediā up to the southern corner of the Bay of Khor Fakkān the course was south. Khor Fakkān overlooked a deep bay with a sandy bottom at depths of between 16 and 35 fathoms. The town had about 200 houses built of date palm leaves.

On the north side of the bay there was still a triangular fortress, built by the Portuguese, but it was in ruins. Another fortress was built on a mountain on the southern side of the bay and it also was in ruins. The valley of Khor Fakkān was a beautiful place with date, lemon, orange and fig trees. Melons and water melons also grew there. Fresh well-water was used for irrigation. Behind the valley of Khor Fakkān the countryside was rocky barren mountain land. The people were poor and lived on subsistence cultivation; there was no trade. Cows and goats, chickens and fruit were available in Khor Fakkān. The bay of Khor Fakkān was half a mile wide with a small island on its southern corner, 100 metres out to sea. From the southern corner of Khor Fakkān to Kalbā the course was south, with no cliffs or rocks offshore. The depths of the anchorage four miles from the coast were 20, 18, 22, 25, 30, 40, 45 and 57 fathoms on black sand.[26]

From Khor Kalbā southwards to Muscat the land between the mountains and the sea was called the Bātinah coast. This coast was sandy and many villages along it were surrounded by dense groves of date palms. Shinās was a town at the north, and Sohār another town 27 miles to the south. Shinās did a good deal of coastal trade and the inhabitants lived from fishing and cultivation. Sohār was an ancient trade centre on this part of the coast, with 4,000 inhabitants; fruit, vegetables, cattle, poultry and fish were abundant. Matrah was a large wealthy town two-and-a-half miles north of Muscat, inhabited by 15,000–18,000 people, 1,000 of them Banyans. Matrah possessed about 50 trading boats, of between 300 and 30 tons.[27]

Muscat was situated at a cove of the same name, formed by Rās Muscat on the east and Rās Seerah on the west. There was a large fort on each side, one called Merani, and the smaller one Jelalee. The population of Muscat amounted to nearly 12,000 souls, 1,700 of them Banyans, who were merchants, brokers to Arab merchants and agents of any European ships that traded with Muscat. The town was surrounded by a wall with fortified gates. A church built by the Portuguese in 1530 was still standing. Muscat was a very important commercial port, with nearly 200 large trading boats of its own. It was the warehouse and centre of the transit trade for Persia, the Euphrates and India. There, the exchange of the products of Oman and the African coast took place.[28] As Kelly stated:[29]

> Muscat's location, at the crossroads of the trade routes from the Red Sea and the Persian Gulf to India and Africa, and its possession of the only harbour deserving of the name in South Eastern Arabia, made it the natural entrepot of the trade of the Arabian and Persian Gulfs.

The Main Ports in the Arabian Gulf and Their Trade

Basra: This was the only outlet for 'Irāq and the principal port for commerce between the Turkish dominions and India. The main articles imported into Basra were piece-goods, chintz, long-cloth, cotton yarn, muslins, fine cotton cloth and coarser cloth, English woollens, silks, Arabian coffee, sugar and sugar-candy, spices, condiments, perfumes, indigo, drugs, chinaware and metals. Some of these goods were delivered to the Turkish dominions and the rest were destined for Persia. From Persia came horses, pearls, silks, brocades, carpets, sword blades, spear heads, gun barrels, glass, rose-water, attar of roses, cotton cloth, shawls, skins, raw silks, some indigo, tobacco, rhubarb, drugs of different sorts, dried fruits, iron and copper, Caramania wool, wines and small quantities of silver, gold and coins. From the Turkish dominions came gold and silver coins, brassware, Angora shawls, piece-goods, silks, satins, gold and silver lace, French broadcloth, Venetian jewellery and glassware, cochineal and tobacco. The exports from Baṣra were dates, old and new copper, gall-nuts, tobacco, opium, gum, catgut and pen-reeds. Horses were also exported to India. Kelly stated that the Muscat coffee fleet loaded the Baṣra date crop every year, estimated at that time at about £100,000; the pearl trade at the same time was valued at £112,500. Goods were carried to Iraq and Arabistan by river boats. The rates per bale (300–400 lb (English) weight) from Baṣra were 12 Bombay rupees to Baghdād by the Tigris, 15 Bombay rupees to Hillah by the Euphrates, and 4 Bombay rupees to Shushtar by the Karun. From Kuwait or Baṣra to Aleppo by camel, the rates were 130 Bombay rupees per camel-load of 700 lb for piece-goods and 90 Bombay rupees for heavier weights. The East India Company charged 6 per cent duty and consulage on all goods imported in English ships. Customs duties at Baṣra were levied at 3 per cent on Europeans and 8 per cent on other merchants. Another duty had to be paid on goods carried directly from Baṣra to Aleppo, and goods transferred from Baṣra to Baghdād had to pay a further duty at Baghdād. Kelly stated that the non-Europeans paid 7½ per cent, and the second round of duties was charged at 3 per cent for Europeans and 5½ per cent for the Asiatic merchants. The accounts were kept in Mamoodies or 100 Fils. 100 Mamoodies equalled 1 Toman, which was valued at 15 Rupees. The weights were in *mann* and *ookia*, 25 *ookias* being equal to one *mann*. the 'Irāqi *mann* was equal to 28 lb 8 oz.[30]

Bander 'Abbās: The old name for Bander 'Abbās was Gumbroon, a fishing town of little importance. Commerce was transferred to this port in 1622, and goods from India and Africa were landed and carried by caravan to the interior of Persia. The English, Dutch and French had factories here, and merchants from many places resorted to it. Until the close of the seventeenth century, Bander 'Abbas was the emporium of Persia.[31] The kind of goods, quantities and prices can be noted from the following lists of merchandise:

A quantity of merchandise sent to Persia by the Dutch East India Company in 1714 for a total amount of 515,564 guilders:[32]

20,009	lb tin	6,503	guilders
40,139	" cloves	12,543	"
24,000	" cinnamon	7,200	"
25,169	" nutmeg	1,573	"
1,000,000	" black pepper	132,000	"

20,433	lb benzoin	10,723	guilders
6,061	" Japanese camphor	5,387	"
5,000	" elephants teeth	8,757	"
250,056	" candy sugar	34,831	"
800,222	" powdered sugar	57,791	"
60,000	" zapon wood	1,735	"
39,040	pieces of sundry kinds of Indian cotton cloth	221,000	"

The weights here are measured in Amsterdam lb; 1 lb equalled 494 grams metric.

Another consignment was sold in 1757 in Bander 'Abbās[33]

5,277	lb cloves	2,150	guilders
4,675	" nutmeg	953	"
15,914	" tin		
28,524	" pepper	21,000	"
189,171	" powdered sugar	17,702	"
105,094	" candy sugar	14,450	"
2,800	" coffee (Java)	365	"
5,000	pieces Indian cotton cloth	15,094	"
3,500	pieces Dutch woollen cloth	12,175	"

The ship *Mamoody* arrived at Bander 'Abbās from India on 17 July 1751, and delivered 188 bales of broadcloth, 62 bales of perpets (velveteen), 7 pieces of brocade, 6 of satin, 12 tons of iron, and 3 tons of lead.[34] The Dutch warehouses were full of goods, particularly sugar, sugar-candy, pepper, rice, leather, spices of all kinds, lead, iron, perpets of a double breadth, and broadcloth of different kinds.[35] The Bander 'Abbās trade consisted of both Indian and European goods, carpets, tobacco, dried fruits, Kirmān wool, and salt. In 1784 the Al Bū Sa'id Sultāns of Muscat leased the port from the Persians and collected an annual revenue of 8,600–10,000 Maria Theresa dollars. Imports into Bander 'Abbās in the 1820s were valued at about three lakhs of Rupees (about £30,000 sterling) annually.[36] Accounts were kept in Mamoodie currency. Gold and silver and other valuable commodities were weighed in *mithqal*. 2½ *mithqal* = 1 Surat *tola* = the weight of one rupee. Sugar, copper and other commodities were weighed in *mann*. The Persian *mann* = 7½ lb. The length measure was *guz*: 93 *guz* = 100 English yds.[37]

Bushire: This was a town of considerable importance, being the centre of the British and other foreign trade with Persia. Bushire became the principal seaport of Persia, from which merchants supplied the country with a considerable trade in Indian and European commodities. From India and Muscat, cotton, cotton yarn, cardamoms, cloves, cinnamon, chinaware, lead, musk, nutmegs, pepper, red lead, sugar, sugar-candy, steel, shawls, silk goods, turmeric, tobacco, tin, and woollen goods were imported. Part of the importation was for Turkey and Arabia, as well as for Persia. From Bushire, drugs of various kinds, carpets, rose-water, and Shiraz wine were exported to India. The balance of trade was about 20 per cent in favour of imports and against exports of Persian goods.[38] Kelly stated that imports from India were valued at about 20 lakhs of Rupees annually, and exports amounted to only a third of that.[39] The Shaikh of Bushire collected a lakh of Rupees (about £10,000 sterling) annually from pearling.[40] A 3 per cent duty was levied on all goods imported and exported by those trading under the East India Company's protection. The President and Council at Bombay also permitted the collection of a consulage of 1 per cent on all English trade. Half of this went to the Resident and the other half was credited to the Agent of Bushire.[41] Lorimer mentioned that the 2 per cent consulage collected at Bushire and Basra was divided between the local Resident and the Governor of Bombay, but that from 1784 it had been credited to the Company's own receipts.[42] Kelly stated that the principal import duties were 5 per cent on piece goods, 10 per cent on metals, 15 Rupees per chest of indigo, 6 per bag of spices, and 2 per bag of coffee.[43] At Bushire, the weight unit was the Tabriz *mann*, which was overrated at 6⅔ lb. The Resident fixed the Tabriz *mann* at 7 lb; and the Agency received and delivered by English weights.[44] Coins of European and Asiatic currency were used at Bushire. Accounts were kept in *Floose, Mamoodies* and *Tomans* (100 *Mamoodies* making 1 *Toman*).

Khāraq Island: This had no trading importance except during the period from 1753, when the Dutch, who had left Basra in 1752, opened their factory there, until December 1765, when it was taken by Mīr Muhannā. No list of merchandise sold by the Dutch in Khāraq could be found except the following list for 1760:

Sugar, cloves, nutmeg, Siamese tin, Dutch lead, iron hoops, iron bars, black Banten pepper, Manilla zapan wood, Java coffee, Dutch vermilion, Chinese musk, Malacca cardamom, pewter, Chinese silk, Chinese sewing yarn, Dutch woollen cloth, cotton cloth from several places (India, Vietnam, Java, China) and chinaware.

Total amount	Buying price (guilders)	Selling price (guilders)
Fine spices (cloves and nutmegs)	10,337	135,364
Other merchandise sold by weight (pound-goods)	141,747	254,960
Cloth	17,627	20,859[45]

Bahrain: Because of its situation, surrounded by small ports like 'Uqair, Qatif, Zubāra and Bid', Bahrain carried on a considerable trade. Its most important export was pearls. Lorimer mentioned that in 1790 the annual value of this trade was estimated at half a million Bombay Rupees; and Captain John Malcolm, ten years later, estimated the annual export of pearls at one million Rupees.[46] In 1790 Bahrain's export of pearls to Basra averaged 5 lakhs of Rupees (about £50,000 sterling) annually.[47] In 1818 the value of the pearl trade was 100,000 Tomans (about £187,500 sterling).[48] In the 1820s about 2,500 boats were engaged in pearl fishing.[49] The Shaikh levied a tax of £10,000 sterling a year for his protection.[50] Kelly mentioned that the total annual value of Bahrain's trade was $MT 2,459,200 (about £490,000 sterling), one-third in imports and two-thirds in exports.[51] Bahrain's large *baghalas* brought rice, sugar, cloth, indigo, iron, brass, ghee and timber from the Malabar Coast twice a year. From the Gulf ports Bahrain imported dates, sugar, ghee, cloth, gunpowder, swords and matchlocks, and from the Ḥasā region and Qatīf, goats, sheep, bullocks, cows, dates, donkeys and horses.[52]

Trade of Bahrain[53]

Exports	German Crowns	Imports	German Crowns
Pearls to India	1,200,000	(from India)	
Ditto to Arabia, Turkey		Rice from Mangalore	
and Basra	300,000	60,000 morahs	65,000
Ditto to Persia	100,000	Rice from Bengal,	
Various articles to India,		8000 bags	24,000
Sind, etc:		Sugar, 600 bags	12,000
Dry dates	15,000	Sugar candy, 500 tubs	5,000
Tortoiseshell	3,500	Pepper, 400 morahs	10,000
Bahrain canvas	3,000	Solder or block tin	2,000
Shark-fins	2,000	Iron, 5,000 bars	10,000
		Lead, 2,000 pigs	2,400
To Persia:		Steel, 100 tubs	1,000
Bahrain canvas	3,000	Plank & ship timber	17,000
Mats	1,200	Coins	5,000
Date syrup	2,000	Cloth, blue & white	
Dry dates	1,200	common & dungaree,	
		600 bales	100,000
To Basra:		Cinnamon	600
Bahrain canvas	5,000	Other spices	4,000
Mats	1,200	Musk	2,000
Coarse coloured cloth	1,000	Indigo	5,000
		Turmeric, 400 bags	4,500
To Kuwait:		Camphor	4,000
Bahrain canvas	5,000	Sandalwood	2,000
Mats	800	Drugs of various	
		descriptions	5,000
To various places:		Tamarinds	2,000
Sundries to the amount:	5,000	Sundries	1,800
Total	1,651,900	Total from India	284,300

Imports	German Crowns
From the Red Sea and Muscat:	
Coffee, 1,520 guntras	93,000
From Muscat and the Persian Coast:	
Dry fruit, grain and Indian produce	200,000
From Baṣra:	
Dates, grain, etc.	200,000
From various places:	
Sundries	30,000
Total	807,300

Towards the end of the eighteenth century Bahrain robbed Muscat of its pre-eminence as the centre of the trade of the Arabian Gulf. This came about for several reasons: the decline of trade at Baṣra, the location of Bahrain in the Gulf, and the skill of the rulers of Bahrain as traders and shipowners.[54]

Rās al-Khaimah: The old name for Rās al-Khaimah was Julfār, which was known as a trading place; it was mentioned in the Dutch records at Baṣra in 1646, when a ship was recorded as arriving from Julfār on the Arab Coast carrying 100 boxes of sugar loaves.[55] From a report of the Governor General in Batavia to the Directors of the Dutch East India Company in Holland of 11 November 1654, concerning the pearl trade in the Arabian Gulf, Julfār was mentioned as follows:[55]

We are of the opinion that if Your Honours wish to proceed with this trade, there should be sent two clever and expert merchants some time before the start of the ordinary fishery season to Bahrain or Julfār island where this jewel is being fished. They must be ordered to stay there from the first until the last fisheries and so personally observe the way trade is done.

Julfār was again mentioned in a report sent from the Head of the Dutch establishment in Gumbroon to the Governor General of the Dutch East Indies, dated 27 January 1702, concerning the ship *Devet Salamett* going from India to Julfār. He related an oral report by a native sailor, Ismael, who had been on board the ship:[57]

A year and three months ago he departed from Cochine (Malabar Coast) to Muscat. On the way they encountered bad weather and thunderstorms. Because of this the Nakhuda decided to return and to call at Basalore where they unloaded the ship and put the merchandise in the building of the Dutch East India Company to wait for the good monsoon. They put the merchandise on board again and they took in other merchandise, from an Arab and from two inhabitants of Cannora, to sail to a place called Julfar situated in the Persian Gulf on the Arab Coast to carry a quantity of cargo. In order to do this we left two months ago from Basaloor.

The Qawāsim of Rās al-Khaimah and their tributaries were engaged in commercial enterprises, in the cultivation of extensive groves of date palms, and in the pursuit of a lucrative pearl fishery. The sale of the annual produce of their date groves put the proprietors in possession of an amount equivalent to 80,000 Rupees, of which the Shaikh received a tenth. Their fleet of large boats visited the ports of India, Yemen, Africa, Sind, Cutch, Muscat and also Baṣra, and in each of three different voyages the value of the share of a single seaman was as follows:

India	50–80 Rupees
Yemen	80 Rupees
Africa	40 Rupees
Sind and Cutch	25–30 Rupees
Muscat	12 Rupees

In the voyage to Baṣra the seamen earned nothing but they shipped a cargo of fresh and dried dates which they sold at the other ports. The smaller vessels traded generally with Bahrain and Qaṭif, but they also used to visit Baṣra and load with grain for Rās al-Khaimah and its adjacent tributaries, and this paid each seaman 10 Rupees, similarly the voyages to the ports of Congoon, 'Asilū, Linga and Qishm paid 2–3 Rupees. From the profit of each of these voyages, the Shaikh was entitled to a share equal to that of a seaman, at a time when there were 60 large vessels and 200 smaller ones. Their pearl banks, which were famous for the excellent quality of their produce, lay a few miles offshore in 6–7 fathoms of water, and 400 boats of different sizes, 200 large, 100 intermediate and 100 small, were annually involved in the fishing. The sale of the whole annual produce of the fishery amounted to about 40,000 Tomans.[58] The tax levied on each diver and his attendant varied under the different Arab chieftains, from 1½ to 7 MT dollars. The amount also fluctuated each season, at the will of the Shaikh.

Whitelock stated that Rās al-Khaimah and its dependencies in the Gulf could fit out nearly 100 boats, many of them from 300 to 400 tons. The Shaikh of each place received a tax of from 1 to 2 dollars according to the size of the boat. The crews of the pearl-fishing boats were not hired for wages but shared the profits. The Shaikh received a tax on all goods landed and also 10 per cent of the sale of dates.[59]

Trade was extensive with the other ports of the Arabian coast and was also carried on with many other countries. Imports were as follows:

From Baṣra and Bahrain:	dates, horses, donkeys
From Persia:	gunpowder, tobacco, carpets, cloth, sugar, swords and matchlocks
From Makrān:	iron, ghee, sugar, oil, carpets
From Muscat:	rice, ghee, sugar, cloth, indigo
From Bātinah:	dates and ghee
From Bombay:	iron, rice, brass, steel, thread and needles,

	cotton and yarns
From Yemen:	coffee and slaves
From Zanzibar:	slaves[60]

Muscat: Because of its location on the route between Baṣra and India, Muscat carried an extensive trade between India and the Arabian Gulf. The volume of its trade in the eighteenth century is clearly illustrated by the list of ships which arrived at Baṣra between September 1735 and September 1736; five from Muscat, five from Bushire, two from Rig, three from Indian Muslims, two Dutch, three French and four British.[61] Muscat merchants in the late eighteenth century had 15 ships of 400–700 tons, three brigs, 50 large dhows, and 50 smaller ones. Some ships sailed for India, and others for Zanzibar, East Africa and the Red Sea. To India, Muscat ships carried drugs, pearls, copper, arsensic, and salt, and brought back spices, indigo, rice, sugar, timber, sandalwood, cotton piece-goods, chinaware, metals and goods of European manufacture. To the Red Sea the ships carried dates, pearls, piece-goods and spices, which were exchanged at Mocha and Hodeida for coffee, drugs, and Abyssinian slaves. From Zanzibar and East Africa the ships brought back gold dust, ivory and slaves.[62]

The Imām of Muscat had mercantile communications with Cutch and the Afghans to the north.[63] Muscat became a place of storage and transit for goods coming from India, East Africa and the Red Sea, which were distributed over the interior of Oman, the Arabian Coast, the Persian Coast, Bahrain and Baṣra. Trade between Muscat and the interior of Oman consisted of almonds, cattle, drugs of all sorts, various gums, hides, honey, skins, sheep, wax, pearl shells, horses and raisins. The merchants of the interior took back Indian commodities, principally ginger, grain, opium, piece-goods, pepper, sugar, spices, turmeric and European cutlery, glassware, looking-glasses and broad cloth.[64] The coffee fleet sailed to Baṣra with coffee beans for the surrounding countries and parts of Europe. Muscat trade was estimated at £1,000,000 sterling; most of it was re-exported, and a rebate of 2½ per cent was usually allowed on the original customs duties.[65]

The customs of Muscat were farmed out to a rich Banyan at a rent of 180,000 dollars annually. Duties were levied at 5 per cent for foreigners, while Muslims paid 2½ per cent.[66] Kelly mentioned that 'in Ahmed Ibn Said's day the Europeans paid 5 per cent, while Muslims paid 6 per cent; and Banyans and Jews 9 per cent. In 1790 the duty was 6½ per cent for all traders'.[67] A duty on slaves was also collected at Muscat; a dollar per head for every African and Abyssinian, and 2 dollars for Georgians or Armenians.[68] Muscat revenues amounted to 300,000 Rupees, in addition to 40,000 Rupees for salt from Bander 'Abbās.[69] All coins of Persian, Turkish and Indian currency were used at Muscat: 1 Surat Rupee equalled 3½ Mamoodies; 1 Bombay Rupee equalled 4 Mamoodies; 1 Spanish dollar equalled 7½ Mamoodies.

An idea of the trade of the Gulf, the type of goods, quantities, places of delivery and ships' owners can be gained from the following lists:

List of shipping in Khāraq for the accounting year 1755/6[70]

— British ship *St George* from Bengal to Gumbroon and Baṣra: rice, sugar, Bengali cotton and gum-lacquer

— French ship *Le Moore* from Bengal to Baṣra: 300 parcels Bengali cotton cloth (mostly for Armenian merchants)
    50 same for its own account
    600 bags sugar
    60 tons rice

— Wrecked near Cape Verdistan in 1756 a British ship from Bombay destined for Bander Rīg:
    750 boxes of chinaware
    80 packs Surat cotton cloth (all this was carried away by local inhabitants)
    50 packs indigo

— (Passed by Khāraq) British ship *Ganges* to Baṣra had sold rice in Muscat:
    600 bags sugar
    12,000 lb gum-lacquer
    25,000 lb iron
    6,000 lb tin
    350 packs cotton cloth for Armenians and 40–50 packs for its own account

— British ship *Elizabeth* from Bengal sold part of its cargo in Muscat and Gumbroon:
    6,000 lb pepper
    5,000 lb cardamom
    40 packs Bengali cotton cloth
    sold in Gumbroon 370 packs cotton cloth
    10,000 lb tin from England but cast into ingots of the same shape as used for Malay tin

— *Tegenepatnam*, French ship from Bengal sold rice in Muscat:
    400 packs of Bengali cotton cloth
    700 packs of sugar
    30,000 lb iron

— British ship *Success* to Bushire:
    rice, pepper, cardamom, china. It could not sell its cargo in Bushire and went on to Gumbroon

— Two ships from Surat to Baṣra, owned by the Muslim merchant Celebi, with cargo for Muslim and Armenian merchants:
    1,000 packs Surat cotton cloth
    130 packs indigo

— British ship *Experiment* from Malabar to Rīg:
rice
10,000 lb pepper
5,000 lb cardamom
4 boxes cloves
2 boxes nutmeg and mace
was only able to sell its rice in Rīg, and took on wheat there and sailed on
to Baṣra

— French ship *Sainte Catherine* from Mahe sold rice in Muscat and 30,000 lb
of iron in Bushire:
carried to Baṣra 50,000 lb pepper
10,000 lb cardamom
10,000 lb tin
6,000 lb ginger
5,000 lb curcuma
1,000 lb false cinnamon
50 lb benzoin
18 boxes chinaware
1,000 ropes
2 packs French fine woollen cloth

— British ship *Warren* (belonging to the British Governor of Bombay) from Bombay to Bander Rīg:
100 boxes chinaware
250 packs cotton cloth
(to Bander Rīg but was unable to sell them there, but, out of friendship for
the Bombay Governor, was allowed to sell its cargo in Khāraq)

List of shipping in Khāraq for the accounting year 1756/7[1]

— British ships *Dragon* and *Swallow* sent empty for repair by the establishment
in Bander Rīg

— arrived at Khāraq the captain of the wrecked British ship *Phoenix*

— British ship *Dragon* from Bombay to Baṣra
150 packs of Surat cotton cloth
24,000 lb iron
30,000 lb pewter
13,000 lb lead
20,000 lb pepper
400 packs indigo
150 packs Surat and 100 packs coastal cotton cloth for the account of Armenian merchants

— the Moorish ship *Leifde* from Surat owned by the brother of Saleh Celebi
sent to Baṣra 400 pieces Surat cotton cloth
300 packs indigo

— British ship *Success* from Bengal to Baṣra
sold 2,000–3,000 bags of rice in Muscat
sold 500 packs of Guinea cotton cloth in Khāraq and 61 packs of sundry other
kinds of cotton cloth
200 lb cardamom

— *Armandien*, native ship from Surat in the service of the British East India Company, destined for Baṣra
200 pieces Surat cotton cloth
80 packs indigo

— (passed by) a Surat grab carrying coffee from Mocha

— British sloop *Phoenix* carrying letters and the news about the fall of Chander-
nagore but no cargo

List of shipping in the season 1757/8[72]

— 3 British ships sent to Muscat carried only rice and did not enter the Gulf
(The British brought much woollen cloth and Indian manufactures to Bander
'Abbās which were carried to Baṣra by native ships)

— British ship *Triumvirate* brought to Bander Kong and Ṭāhirī Malabar cinnamon,
Bengali ginger, gum-lacquer, curcuma and rhubarb

— French frigate *Bristol* from Mahe to Baṣra
200 lb pepper
150 packs sugar
took in wheat at Khāraq which had been brought there by native ships from
Ginora and Bander Rīg

— British ship *Hibernia* from Bengal
rice, iron, gum-lacquer, lead
400 large packs of 200 pieces each Bengal mulmul, most of it for Moorish
merchant

— British ship *Dragon* belonging to the Governor of Bombay
200 packs Surat cotton cloth
800 packs capok
indigo, rice, gum-lacquer
chinaware, Chinese rhubarb
also carrying parcels to Baṣra for native merchants

— ship of Celebi from Surat to Baṣra
rice, indigo, cotton cloth

— Dutch private ship owned by the broker of the Company in Surat
indigo, rice, Surat cotton cloth

— *St John Baptist*, private ship of the Armenian Tarkhan in Surat, carrying Dutch
flag
iron, lead, sugar, Malabar cinnamon, pepper, chinaware, rhubarb

— British grab *Katti* from Malacca and Malabar
sugar (sold in Muscat)
rice, curcuma, ginger, chinaware

Shipping list of Khāraq 1758/9[73]

— Private Dutch ship *Phoenix* from Bengal
400 packs cotton cloth
5,000 lb gum-lacquer
rice

— British private ship *Neptune Galley* from Bombay to Baṣra
rice and copperware

— British East India Company ship *Swallow*
European manufactures to Baṣra

— British grab *Monmouth* from Bengal
gum-lacquer, Malabar cinnamon, capok, cardamom
6 packs Bengal cotton cloth, sold rice in Muscat

— *Tass* private British ship from Bombay
curcuma, ginger, pepper, cardamom, rice

— British private ship *Dragon* to Baṣra carrying merchandise belonging to its
captain.

— Ship *Soliman* belonging to Celebi of Baṣra.

— (passed to Baṣra) British ketch *Ketti*
400 packs British woollen cloth

— British ship *Rose Galley*
sold capok and rice to Bander Rīg

— British ship *Welcome* from Bengal
200 packs cotton cloth for natives in Baṣra
sold rice in Muscat

Shipping list of Khāraq, March-August 1760[74]

— British grab *Speedwell* from Bengal to Baṣra carried 85 packs of Bengal cotton cloth, also iron, pepper, ginger, cardamom, curcuma, lead

— British private ship *William* from Bengal to Baṣra
200 packs Bengali cotton cloth, tin and iron

— British private ship *Defence* from Bengal to Baṣra carried 300 packs of Bengali cotton cloth, iron, pepper, tin, cardamom, curcuma, gum-lacquer and sugar

— (passed by) British private ship *Admiral Pocock* from Bombay to Baṣra carried 300 packs Surat cotton cloth
800 packs European woollen cloth and 150 churls indigo

— British private ship *Dudley* from Bengal to Baṣra
300 packs Bengali cotton cloth (of which 200 were for Armenian merchants)
200 goeries sugar, gum-lacquer, lead, rice

— British Company ship *Swallow* from Bombay carried only letters

— Danish private ship *Success Galley* from Bengal to Baṣra
450 packs Bengali cotton cloth (mostly for Armenian merchants)
200 boxed cardamom
60 boxes chinaware
100 packs gum-lacquer
iron, lead, tin

— British private ship *Dragon* from Bengal to Baṣra
250 packs Bengali cotton cloth
150 churls indigo
100 packs pepper
iron

— Small ship of the Muslim merchant Celebi from Surat to Baṣra
60 packs Surat cotton cloth
woodwork, pepper, cinnamon, indigo

— British ship *Prince Edward* from Bengal to Baṣra
120 packs Bengali cotton cloth, rice, false cinnamon

— Danish sloop *Eleanora Adriana* from Bengal to Baṣra
120 packs Bengali cotton cloth, iron

— Ship of Adi Radja of Malabar, from Malabar to Baṣra
300 packs pepper
20 packs false cinnamon
cardamom, woodwork

— British ship *Rose Galley*
60 packs capok
10 packs Surat cotton cloth
500 packs pepper
iron, tin, lead, cardamom, chinaware

— British grab carrying only letters from Bombay to Baṣra

Shipping during the accounting year 1761 (1 September 1760–31 August 1761)[75]

— British private ship *Prince Edward* from Baṣra to Bengal carrying cash and a little merchandise

— Danish ship *Eleanora* from Baṣra to Bengal carrying cash

— Moorish ship of Celebi from Baṣra to Surat
cash and a little merchandise

— Moorish private ship of Ali Radje from Baṣra to Cananor
cash and a little merchandise

— British private ship *Dragon* from Baṣra to Bombay
cash and a little merchandise

— Moorish ship *Soliman* of Celebi from Baṣra to Surat
cash and a little merchandise

— British private ship *Monmouth* from Bengal to Madras to Baṣra
40 packs cotton cloth
tin, lead, dry ginger

— Moorish ship *Santa Catharina* of Hadji Yusuf from Baṣra
dates and wheat to Muscat and Diwel

— British ship *Monmouth* from Baṣra to Bombay and Bengal
cash

— British Company ship *Swallow*
carrying new British residents to Baṣra

— British private ship *Admiral Pocock* from Bengal to Bombay
200 packs Bengali cotton cloth
150 packs Surat cotton cloth
300 churls indigo

— 2 British private ships *Fort William* and *Dudley*
500 packs Bengali cotton cloth (mostly for Armenian merchants)
iron

— Moorish ship of Celebi from Malabar to Baṣra
500 packs pepper
30 packs false cinnamon
cardamom

— Danish ship *Eleanora Adriana* from Bengal to Baṣra
180 packs Bengali cotton cloth (mostly for Armenian merchants)
dry ginger

— Moorish ship *Solimani* of Celebi from Surat to Baṣra
200 packs Bengli cotton cloth
400 churls indigo

— The same ship returning to Malabar with cash

— British private ship *Admiral Pocock* from Baṣra to Bombay
cash and a little merchandise

— Danish ship *Eleanora Adriana* from Baṣra to Bengal
cash and a little merchandise

Merchandise received in Batavia from Persia in 1703[76]

Two ships:
First ship, cargo valued at £210,991 sterling cost price all cash (gold and mostly
Iranian silver coinage) and bullion except:
4,759 lb gold cloth
1,837 lb woollen cloth, and
11 lb melon seed

Second ship, total cargo valued at £23,411 sterling, carried the equivalent of
£11,698 in gold, 6 camels.
The remainder: small quantities of carpets, velvet, leather, almonds, kismis prunes,
rosewater, Shiraz wine, seeds, drugs.

Two ships from Persia delivered merchandise to Batavia in 1715. *Kockenge*, arrived 21 March 1715.[77] Total value carried £217,178.

	£ sterling
100 boxes Shiraz claret	2,008
1 box tarragon vinegar	22
620 lb red raisins	113
800 lb kismis	135
250 lb pistachios	174
200 lb almonds	163
792 lb drugs	1,694
10 charges red earth	95
750 pieces Kirmān pottery	256
Remainder in cash or bullion	

Merchandise received in Batavia from Persia in 1735[78]

Received from Persia, two ships: first valued at £250,960, second valued at £61,735.
First ship: all in cash and bullion except:

	£ sterling
44,063 lb Kerman wool	78,050
100 boxes rosewater	5,256.14
81 charges red earth	2,926
Tools	2,009

Second ship: *Prins Eugenius*, arrived 17 May 1735
Cargo valued at £12,766 sterling:
  50 ps cloth
  200 lb prunes
  300 lb Salmiac
  400 lb gum
  11,160 lb dye roots

These shopping lists make it clear that the bulk of the trade in the Gulf was transit trade involving the produce of South and South-East Asia, the Middle East and Europe. Of course, there was some trade involving the local produce of the partners in this trade, such as rice and coffee, and Indian spices and cloth which were consumed in the Gulf area. In this respect Persia and Turkish 'Irāq were major importers as well as consumers. But by the nature of things the Arabs of the Gulf were less involved as consumers than as active participants in the transit trade itself. In the fifteenth century before the arrival of the European powers in the Gulf, this vast transit trade was in the hands of the indigenous population, Arab and Indian merchants and shipowners.

Both sides traded and settled freely in each other's territory without any hindrance. The arrival of the Portuguese at the beginning of the eighteenth century changed this situation completely: they relied on brute force to dominate the Gulf and its trade.

The arrival of the British, Dutch and French changed the situation yet further. Although it allowed for competition for a greater share in the transit trade, it tended to continue to exclude the local people from participating in this trade. The European competitors concentrated first on Persia, the biggest local market. In 1616 the English East India Company was permitted by Shāh Abbas I to trade into Persia, and the first consignment of goods from India was landed at Jask one year later. In the same year factories were established at Shiraz and Ispahan, and in 1619 a third factory was established in Jask.[79] Soon after, in 1623, the Dutch received trading privileges from the Shah and they also established a factory of Gumbroon.[80] The French were also allowed to trade in Persia after a French delegation arrived in Ispahan in 1666.[81]

So far the Arabs of the Gulf were left alone and no attempt was made to replace the Portuguese occupation of Arab ports by any other European power. But the Indians, especially the Muslims of Surat, were stimulated to compete with the European intruders. In 1655 they sent 40 ships of their own into the Gulf carrying their own goods.[82] Furthermore, and in the same year, they shipped goods on the British ship *Seahorse*.[83] In 1656 a Surat ship arrived at Gumbroon carrying goods to the value of 2.1 million guilders, which was more than the entire Dutch trade.[84] However, this success of the Indians of Surat were short-lived and custom privileges granted to the Dutch and the British made the decline of the Surat trade inevitable.[85]

Early in the eighteenth century the Surat merchants suffered a noticeable decline in their trade and the number of their vessels fell from 112 in 1701 to about 20 in 1750.[86] Meanwhile, competition increased between the European powers themselves. The first to suffer were the French who closed their factory in Gumbroon in the 1720s. The French attempts to establish themselves in Baṣra and Muscat were no more successful. Although they were allowed to trade in Muscat in 1785, they had to stop trading in Baṣra in 1765.[87]

The Dutch persevered in their competition with the British to the extent that they occupied the Island of Hormuz for a short period, but they soon had to evacuate it.[88] The following figures clearly show the decline of Dutch trade in the Gulf in the eighteenth century.[89]

1700–10 the average profit was 581,027 guilders
1710–20 the average profit was 475,344 guilders
1720–30 the average profit was 219,868 guilders
1730–40 the average profit was 102,565 guilders
1740–50 the average profit was 46,592 guilders
1750–57 the average profit was 47,956 guilders

These figures speak for themselves. In 1752 the Dutch left Baṣra and in 1759 they closed their factory in Gumbroon. After twelve years of operation in Khāraq Island they were expelled by the Persians in 1765.[90]

The British Ascendancy

The British ascendancy was perhaps marked by the transfer of their principal establishment in the Gulf from Gumbroon to Bushire in 1763,[91] and the arrival soon afterwards in April of Mr William Andrew Price, Agent for Affairs of the British Nation there.[92] He signed an agreement with Shaikh Sa'dūn of Bushire (wrongly identified by Kelly as Shaikh Nāṣir).[93] This commercial agreement between the East India Company and Shaikh Sa'dūn is reproduced below.[94]

Articles of Agreement made and concluded this 12th day of April 1763 between the Right Honourable William Andrew Price Esq., Agent for Affairs of the British Nation in the Gulf of Persia, on behalf of the Honourable United English East India Company on the one part, and Shaikh Sadun of Bushire on the other part.

1st — no customs or duties to be collected on goods imported or exported by the English and in like manner only 3 per cent to be taken from the merchants who buy from or sell to the English.

2nd — the importation and sale of woollen goods to be solely in the hands of the English, and if any person whatever attempts to bring in woollen goods clandestinely it shall be lawful for the English to sue them, this article to take place in four months from the date hereof.

3rd — no European national whatever is to be permitted to settle at Bushire so long as the English continue a factory here.

4th — the Broker's Linguists, servants and others of the English, are to be entirely under the protection and Government of the English, nor is the Shaikh or his people in any shape to molest them, or to interfere in their affairs.

5th — in case any of the inhabitants become truly indebted to the English and refuse payment, the Shaikh shall oblige them to give the English satisfaction.

6th — the English to have such a plot of ground as they may pitch upon for erecting a factory, and proper conveniences for carrying on their commerce to be built at the Shaikh's expense, they are to hoist the colours upon it, and have twenty-one guns for saluting.

7th — a proper plot of ground to be allotted the English for a garden and another for a burial ground.

8th — the English and those under their protection not to be impeded in their religion.

9th — soldiers, sailors, servants, slaves and others belonging to the English who may desert, are not to be protected, or entertained by the Shaikh or his people, but bona fide secured and returned.

10th — in case any English ship sell to or buy from the country merchants apart from the factory, a due account thereof is to be rendered to the English Chief for the time being, for which purpose one of his people is to attend at the weight and delivery of all goods so sold, which is to be done at the public Custom House.

11th — if through any accident an English vessel should be driven on shore, in the country belonging to the Shaikh, they shall not in any respect be plundered, but on the contrary, the Shaikh shall afford the English all the assistance in his power for saving them and their effects, the English paying them for their trouble.

12th — the Shaikh shall not permit his subjects to purchase any goods from the English vessels in the Road, but only on shore.

Commercial relations between the English and the Turkish Government in 'Irāq started in 1640, and in 1723 a factory was established by the East India Company at Basra. The Residency at Basra was recognised by the Porte in 1764 as a Consulate under capitulation.

Because of the difficulties in Persia during the reign of Karim Khan, the factory at Bushire was closed in February 1769, but was re-established in 1775.[95] The involvement of the Resident in Basra in political matters gave the British a bad reputation.[96] The trade in Basra during the period 1773–9 was not profitable, owing to the Persian occupation of the town and the plague which broke out there. In 1793 the Residency was moved temporarily to Kuwait.[97] In Muscat, where a Residency was not permitted, the East India Company had a Native Agency.[98]

On the whole, the trade in the Arabian Gulf during the last quarter of the eighteenth century was shared by the East India Company, with its establishments, the Basra and Bushire Residencies, and the Agency at Muscat, and Persian, Armenian, but mostly Arab and Indian, merchants and shipowners.[99] Merchandise was carried between India and the Gulf by very few vessels belonging to the East India Company, and by more vessels belonging to the Indian merchants, but mostly by vessels belonging to the Arabs.[100] However, the increasing share of the East India Company was at the expense of both the Indians and the Arabs.

As could be expected, the Indians were dealt with effectively by the East India Company. The Arabs were not so easy to handle, although they were not united and their interests were at variance. However, for almost all the first thirty years of the eighteenth century Oman was beset by civil war and a struggle for power among the members of the ruling family. Some of the neighbouring Arab tribes were inevitably dragged into this civil war. Nevertheless, other tribesmen stayed out of the conflict and tried to take advantage of the sudden weakness of the two major powers in the Gulf: Persia and Oman.

It is almost misleading to write about the Persian side of the Gulf in contrast to the Arab side, because the Persian coast had a considerable Arab population.[101] The tribe of Ka'b in the north was a major source of trouble to the Ottomans in Basra, but this does not concern us here. On the other hand, we are concerned with the Ma'in tribe whose members lived on the southern part of the coast. It was the alliances and the conflicts in which this tribe was involved that had a considerable impact on the course of events in the second half of the century.

Before we go any further we must recognise two important facts. Strange as it may seem, it is an inexplicable fact that the Persians, throughout their history, had never had a strong navy nor had they been able to develop the manpower necessary for this purpose. This is the more inexplicable because Persia has a very long coast indeed. This strange fact forced the Persians to rely on the Arabs of the Gulf whenever they thought of getting involved in any seafaring adventures[102] and, as we shall see, this need created unexpected alliances. The second important fact in the history of the period is that the Persian central Government, even at a time when it was strong, had never exercised full control over the local Persian chiefs of the Persian coast. These chiefs were practically autonomous rulers of their regions or towns and apparently felt free to enter into any alliances which they deemed useful. These two factors, in addition to the chronic weakness of the Persian central Government, created a situation where local Arab-Persian alliances almost inevitably resulted in local conflicts. It also gave the Qawāsim the opportunity to gain a stronghold on the Persian side of the Gulf.

In the chaos that followed the assassination of Nādir Shāh in 1747, the major actors on the Persian coast were, first, Nāṣir Khān, the hereditary ruler of the region of Lar adjacent to the Gulf, who had ambitions to be the major figure in the area,[103] and second, Mullā 'Alī Shāh, a naval commander of the now non-existent navy of Nādir Shāh, who took the opportunity after the latter's fall to seize Bander 'Abbās.[104] Mullā 'Alī Shāh knew that Shaikh Rāshid b. Maṭar, the hereditary chief of the Qawāsim, could be tempted to help him establish his power. In 1751 an alliance was born between the two.[105] Nāṣir Khān was naturally not happy at these developments and tried in vain to dislodge Mullā 'Alī Shāh from Bander 'Abbas.[106] Meanwhile, the latter, with his allies the Qawāsim, attacked and occupied Qishm and Luft in 1755, which were then in the hands of the Ma'in tribe.[107] The Ma'in turned to Nāṣir Khān for help and another alliance was born between Persians and Arabs. There is no need here to go into the details of the prolonged fighting that took place between the partners in the two alliances.[108] The net result was a victory for the Qawāsim who were able to continue to maintain their stronghold in Qishm and Linga. Furthermore,[109] in 1777 the new chief of the Qawāsim, Ṣaqr b. Rāshid, married the daughter of the chief of the tribe of Ma'in; they naturally became good allies, a fact which could only add to the strength of the Qawāsim and their control of both sides of the entrance to the Gulf.[110]

Writing in 1807, David Seton, then British Resident in Muscat, stated that the Qawāsim possessed not only the Arab coast known as Sīr, but also the islands of Qishm and Qais near the Persian coast. They also possessed the towns of Chārak, Linga and Shinās on the Persian side. The ships of these places added greatly to the formidable fleet of the Qawāsim which in itself numbered as many as 500 vessels. He also asserted that the Qawāsim, with the help of their allies in the interior, could muster as many as 20,000 men. To the British these were all considered 'Qawasim', although they included many members of other tribes inhabiting Sīr who acknowledged the authority of the Qāsimī chief of Rās al-

Khaimah.[111]

Under the vigorous leadership of Shaikh Ṣaqr the Qawāsim were able to expand their trade,[112] but this in itself aroused the fears of the Omani rulers, the Al Bū-Saʿīd, and a new conflict between them and the Qawāsim came into being. The more important conflict which confronted the Qawāsim, however, was with the British, who also soon became the allies of the Omanis.

It is an acknowledged fact that towards the end of the century the trade of the East India Company in the Gulf was declining and running at a loss. Lorimer explained this as being due to temporary reasons, i.e. the rise of piracy by the tribe of Kaʿb and the petty chiefs of the Persian coast, the threatening behaviour and activity of the Qawāsim, the spreading plague in ʿIraq in 1773, the Persian occupation of Basra 1776–9, and the civil war in Persia in 1779.[113] While agreeing with Lorimer, Kelly explained that[114]

what was happening, in effect, was that the Company's role in the trade of the Gulf was fast changing from one of active participation to one of mere protection of the 'country' trade from India which by now was dominated by Persian, Armenian, Arab and Indian merchants and ship-owners.

It is difficult to see who else should 'dominate' this trade; was it the natural right of the East India Company to dominate it instead of the indigenous population of the region? The Indian state of Mysore gives us a good example of the Indian traders competing with the Company. Haider ʿAlī, the ruler of Mysore, and his son Tipū Sulṭān, who succeeded him in 1782, established relationships with the Turks, Persians and Omanis by sending missions and ambassadors to their countries.[115] Tipū Sulṭān started many commercial projects by arranging for warehouses to be set up for small merchants all over his domains, thus increasing the volume of local trade. He also established many state enterprises where he supplied capital to the citizens at a rate of interest of 12 per cent. The Indian merchants of Mysore, for their part, co-operated with the freighters of their own communities. The common language and customs made co-operation easy and, as a result, competition with the Company increased. The Indian merchants were not accustomed to the official European documentation. Although the Company's ships were better equipped and defended, the expenditures of the Indian ships were less; accordingly their freight rates were cheaper and the Indian shipowners were satisfied with a small profit. Furthermore, the Indian freighters distributed their freight among ships on the spot to divide up the risk. It is for these reasons that the trade of the East India Company declined.[116]

The competition that the Company faced became increasingly tougher and a way had to be found if the Company was to continue trading in the Gulf. The Company did not protect Tipū Sulṭān; instead it attacked and defeated him, putting an end to his imaginative enterprises. The Company did not protect the 'country' trade of Mysore; it destroyed it. While ignoring all these developments, Kelly states that 'the burden of protecting the ''country'' trade was borne principally by the Bombay Marine, the armed branch of the Company's maritime service'.[117]

It is now clear that the Company had no intention of protecting anybody's trade. Its obvious intention, in face of the increasing competition, was to use 'protection' as an excuse to employ the force of the Bombay Marine to squash the competitors. Instead of peaceful trade, it became gun-boat trade. In the following chapter the process of this change will be elaborated.

Notes

1. G.B. Kempthorne, 'Notes made on a Survey along the Eastern Shores of the Persian Gulf in 1828', *Journal of the Royal Geographical Society*, v (1835), p. 275.
2. Carsten Niebuhr, *Description de l'Arabie*, (Copenhagen, 1773); *Voyage en Arabie et en d'autres pays circonvoisins* (2 vols., Utrecht, 1775-9), p. 296.
3. Niebuhr, *Description de l'Arabie*, p. 296.
4. Kempthorne, 'Notes', p. 176.
5. Ibid., p. 175.
6. J.B. Kelly, *Britain and the Persian Gulf, 1795-1880*, (Oxford at the Clarendon Press, 1968), p. 51.
7. H. Whitelock, 'Notes taken during a journey in Oman along the East Coast of Arabia', *Trans. Bombay Geog. Soc.*, i (1836-8), pp. 51-2.
8. Kempthorne, 'Notes', pp. 177, 277.
9. Whitelock, 'Notes', p. 34.
10. Collection of original documents in the possession of the author; extract from a letter from Captain Robert Budden of the Honourable Company's Marine to W.C. Bunce, dated 31 August 1809. See Sultān Muhammad, Al-Qāsimi, 'Arab ''Piracy'' and the East India Company Encroachment in the Gulf 1797-1820', Ph.D. thesis, University of Exeter, 1985, appendix no. 29.
11. *Selections from the Records of the Bombay Government*, New Series, no. XXIV: *Historical and other information connected with the Province of Oman, Muskat, Bahrain, and other places in the Persian Gulf*, compiled and edited by R. Hughes Thomas, (Bombay, 1856), pp. 596-7.
12. V. Maurizi, ('Shaik Mansur'), *History of Seyd Said, Sultan of Muscat*, (London, 1819), pp. 34-5.
13. Bombay Archives (BA), Political Department Diary (PDD), no. 38 of 1762, p. 73.
14. Niebuhr, *Description*, p. 299.
15. W. Milburn and J. Thornton, *Oriental Commerce*, (London, 1825), p. 92.
16. Ibid., pp. 91-2.
17. J. Jackson, *Journey from India towards England in 1797*, (London, 1799), pp. 29-30.
18. *Sel. from Records of Bombay Gov.*, p. 109.
19. Whitelock, 'Notes', p. 53.
20. C.R. Low, *History of the Indian Navy*, (2 vols, London, 1877), p. 349.
21. *Sel. from Records of Bombay Gov.*, pp. 104-5, 107.
22. Kelly, *Britain and the Persian Gulf*, p. 26.
23. Ibid., p. 102.
24. *Sel. from Records of Bombay Gov.*, pp. 542-6.
25. Algemeen Rijks Archief (ARA), (General State Archives) in the Hague, Adnwinste le Afdeling, 1889-23B.
26. ARA (General State Archives) in the Hague, Van de Oostindische Compagnie (VOC), vol. 1259, pp. 3371-3. (Report on the travels of the Dutch ship *Meerkat*.)
27. *Sel. from Records of Bombay Gov.*, p. 629.
28. Documentation Centre, Abu Dhabi, collection of French documents, *Revue d'Histoire Diplomatique: la France et Muscate*, Auzouk, A. Muscat, p. 524; Kelly, *Britain and the Persian Gulf*, p. 13; Maurizi, *History of Seyd Said*, pp. 18-22.
29. Kelly, *Britain and the Persian Gulf*, p. 14.
30. J.G. Lorimer, *Gazetteer of the Persian Gulf*, 'Oman and Central Arabia*, (2 vols, Calcutta, 1908-15), pp. 164-7; Kelly, *Britain and the Persian Gulf*, pp. 36-7; Milburn and Thornton, *Oriental Commerce*, pp. 164-7.
31. Kempthorne, 'Notes', pp. 174-5.
32. ARA, Koloniaa Archief (KA), vol. 11,838, pp. 462-3.

33. ARA, VOC, vol. 2937, (p. Gumbroon 14–15).
34. India Office Library (IO), London, Gumbroon Diary, vol. 7, p. 160.
35. *Selection from State Papers, Bombay, (Sel. SP) regarding the East India Company's connection with the Persian Gulf, with a Summary of Events, 1600–1800*, ed. J.A. Saldanha, (Calcutta, 1908), p. 99.
36. Kelly, *Britain and the Persian Gulf*, pp. 44–5.
37. Milburn and Thornton, *Oriental Commerce*, pp. 95–6.
38. Ibid., pp. 93–4.
39. Kelly, *Britain and the Persian Gulf*, p. 44.
40. Ibid., p. 29 (cf. Niebuhr, *Description*, p. 286).
41. BA, Bussorah Diary, no. 193, pp. 31–4.
42. Lorimer, *Gazetteer*, p. 168.
43. Kelly, *Britain and the Persian Gulf*, p. 44.
44. *Sel. SP*, p. 177.
45. ARA, VOC, vol. 3027, pp. 10–11.
46. Lorimer, *Gazetteer*, p. 164.
47. Kelly, *Britain and the Persian Gulf*, p. 29.
48. Ibid., p. 29 (cf. IO, Bombay Selections).
49. Ibid. (cf. Enclosure to Bombay Secret Proceedings, vol. 36).
50. Charles Belgrave, *The Pirate Coast*, (London, 1966), p. 166.
51. Kelly, *Britain and the Persian Gulf*, p. 30.
52. Whitelock, 'Notes', p. 52.
53. *Sel. from Records of Bombay Gov.*, pp. 568–9.
54. Kelly, *Britain and the Persian Gulf*, p. 29.
55. ARA (General State Archives) in the Hague, Family Archive, Geleynssen Jongh, nr. 260e, (Travel to Basra), pp. 1645–6.
56. ARA, VOC, vol. 1208, p. 91.
57. Ibid., vol. 1667, pp. 418–19.
58. IO, Residency Records, Bushire, ref. R/15/1/20, p. 13.
59. Whitelock, 'Notes', pp. 34, 45, 46, 49.
60. Ibid., p. 48.
61. ARA, VOC, vol. 3795, pp. 2953–4.
62. Kelly, *Britain and the Persian Gulf*, pp. 15–16.
63. *Sel. SP*, Part II, p. 25.
64. Milburn and Thornton, *Oriental Commerce*, pp. 81–2.
65. Kelly, *Britain and the Persian Gulf*, p. 14.
66. Maurizi, *History of Seyd Said*, pp. 29–30.
67. Kelly, *Britain and the Persian Gulf*, p. 14.
68. Whitelock, 'Notes', pp. 48–9.
69. *Sel. SP*, Part II, p. 25.
70. ARA, VOC, vol. 2909, Kharaq, p. 55.
71. Ibid., vol. 2937, p. 29.
72. Ibid., vol. 2968, p. 29.
73. Ibid., vol. 2996, pp. 20–2.
74. Ibid., vol. 3027, pp. 20–1.
75. Ibid., vol. 3064 (Kharaq, Part I), pp. 50–4.
76. ARA, KA, Vol. 10753, p. 53.
77. Ibid., vol. 10760, p. 207.
78. Ibid., vol. 10769, p. 51.
79. Kelly, *Britain and the Persian Gulf*, p. 50.
80. Pieter Van Dam, *Beschryving, Van de Osstindiche Compagnie*, (ed. F.W. Stapped), (The Hague, 1939), vol. II, Part 3, pp. 279, 330, 331, 334, 338.
81. ARA, VOC, vol. 1255, pp. 855–70.
82. Ibid., vol. 1209, pp. 101–2.
83. Ibid., pp. 123–4.
84. Van Dam, *Beschryving*, vol. 83, p. 315.
85. Ibid., pp. 278–9, 318–19; ARA, VOC, vol. 1,562, p. 256.
86. T. Raychaudhuri, I. Habib, D. Kumar, M. Desai, *The Cambridge Economic History of India*, (2 vols. Cambridge, 1982–3), vol. I, p. 412.

87. Kelly, *Britain and the Persian Gulf*, p. 54; *Revue d'Histoire Diplomatique*, p. 530; *Sel. SP*, p. 319.

88. ARA, VOC, vol. 2105, pp. 148–94, 671–705; vol. 2,138, pp. 38–277.

89. G.C. Klerk de Reus, *Geschichtlicher Ueberblick der administrativen, rechtlichen und finanziellen Entwicklung der Niederlandisch Ostindischen Compagnie*, (Batavia, S-Nage, 1894), Appendix IX.

90. ARA, VOC, vol. 3179, pp. 405–22; vol. 3184, part Kharaq, pp. 1–90.

91. Lorimer, *Gazetteer*, p. 138.

92. BA, Bussorah Diary, no. 193, pp. 22–3.

93. Kelly, *Britain and the Persian Gulf*, pp. 51–2.

94. BA, Bussorah Diary, no. 193, pp. 26–30.

95. Kelly, *Britain and the Persian Gulf*, p. 53.

96. *Sel. of Records of Bombay Gov.*, pp. 56–7.

97. Kelly, *Britain and the Persian Gulf*, pp. 53, 55.

98. Lorimer, *Gazetteer*, p. 157.

99. Kelly, *Britain and the Persian Gulf*, p. 57.

100. Lorimer, *Gazetteer*, p. 166.

101. Niebuhr, *Description*, pp. 298–300.

102. *Sel. SP*, p. 54.

103. Ibid., p. 76.

104. Ibid., p. 95.

105. IO, Gumbroon Diary, vol. 8, May 13–29, 1751.

106. Sel. SP, p. 76.

107. Ibid., p. 75.

108. Ibid., p. 139.

109. Ibid., pp. 152, 158.

110. BA, *Summary of the Proceedings relative to the boats captured in the Persian Gulf*, vol. 77/1819–20, Minute by Mr Warden, pp. 81–2.

111. BA, Secret and Political Department Diary, no. 208/1807, pp. 4937–50.

112. BA, Minute by Mr Warden, p. 82.

113. Lorimer, *Gazetteer*, p. 163.

114. Kelly, *Britain and the Persian Gulf*, p. 57.

115. Lorimer, *Gazetteer*, p. 156.

116. *Cambridge Economic History of India*, vol. I, pp. 417, 428; vol. II, p. 354.

117. Kelly, *Britain and the Persian Gulf*, p. 56.

2 Accusations of 'Piracy', 1797–1806

The defeat of Tipū Sultān allowed the British to occupy Mysore and put an end to all the trading activities of this dangerous competitor. Any hopes he might have entertained of cultivating a relationship with the governor of the Ile de France vanished with his death in 1799. The Agency of Mysore at Muscat that was intended to improve trade between the two states was closed down.[1] The Imām of Muscat did not endear himself to the British by his dealings with Tipū Sultān, and they saw an increasing threat to their trade in the continued trade between Muscat and the Dutch and the French, who were actually at war with the British at that time.[2] After getting rid of Tipū Sultān, the British asked the Imām to prevent the French and Dutch ships from trading to and from Muscat.[3]

In order to help persuade the Imām to comply with their demands, the British took two steps. To show the flag, British ships were dispatched to cruise the Gulf.[4] On the other hand, Mehdī 'Alī Khān, the East India Company's Resident at Bushire, was vested with full powers from the Bombay Government and dispatched to Muscat in September 1798. Soon after his arrival, he succeeded in obtaining an agreement between the Company and the Imām. Accordingly a factory for the Company was set up at Muscat and the Imām agreed to the expulsion of the French and all other Europeans from his domain. Having succeeded in his mission to Muscat, Mehdī 'Alī Khān then went to Persia, where he met the Shāh and persuaded him to issue orders to all Persian sea ports to seize the French wherever they made an appearance by sea or land.[5]

Having secured the co-operation of the Persians and the Omanis, the British then turned their attention to their more persistent competitors; the Qawāsim who had been carrying on a vigorous and profitable trade by sea. Their fleet at this time consisted of 63 large and 669 small ships, with a complement of 18,760 men.[6] To the Qawāsim, trade was practically the only source of livelihood in their arid lands. And trade with Indian ports in particular was of the utmost importance to them because it was from there that they could acquire the two most important commodities, food for themselves and wood for their ships. They saw the British as serious competitors who could deprive them of their livelihood. Foreign competition for trade in the Gulf had been a feature of life there for a long time, and the indigenous population of the area had learned to live with it. But the British seem to have introduced a new element into this competition. Their eventual demand that all ships trading in the Gulf should have British 'passes' suggests that they considered themselves the masters of the Gulf waters and were of the opinion that trade should be conducted there solely for their benefit and that nobody else had the right to trade there without their approval. Indeed, to the British the French ships that attempted to approach the Gulf were 'privateers', while the Arabs there were 'pirates' whose ships could only be involved in acts of 'piracy' even if they were simply floating in the Gulf waters.

31

Because of their far-reaching trading activities in and out of the Gulf, the Qawāsim were a main target of these false accusations of piracy. Every misfortune
that befell a British ship inside the Gulf — and sometimes outside it — was attributed to the 'piracy' of the Qawāsim. Every incident, even when the Qawāsim
could not conceivably have been involved, was regarded, with absolute certainty,
as the result of the aggression of the Qawāsim 'pirates'. Rumours were taken
as facts and compounded by other dubious hearsay, and were submitted as reports
by various British agents who tried to trace every event and prove it to be the
work of the mischievous Qawāsim 'pirates'. When the culprits could not be identified, it was reported without a shade of doubt that it was the Qawāsim who
were responsible. When Agents and Residents wanted to justify a certain action
or to defend their policy or behaviour regarding an incident, the Qawāsim provided
a convenient scapegoat and the blame was laid on them. All these accusations
were part of a deliberate policy which can only be described as the 'Big Lie'.
The British East India Company set this policy in motion and 'cried wolf'. Their
Agents and Residents in the Gulf repeated the cry with alacrity and helped to
substantiate the Big Lie in order to find an excuse to use their marines and gun-
boats to 'protect' their trade. As we shall see, in all the incidents that were attributed to the Qawāsim as acts of 'piracy' it can be proved that they were not
involved, or, if they were, that they were involved only to defend themselves
against British 'piracy'.

The first incident described as an act of 'piracy' by the Qawāsim was related
by Lorimer. He stated that in 1778 the Qawāsim captured a vessel belonging to
the East India Company, adding for good measure that the crew and passengers
were sold as slaves.[7] From the correspondence between John Beaumont, the British
Resident at Bushire at the time, and Shaikh Rāshid the ruler of Julfār, the base
of the Qawāsim, it transpires that, while it is true that the Qawāsim captured the
ship, the circumstances justified their action. Shaikh Rāshid explained that his
fleet 'having fallen in with the vessel taken, she showed the Imam's colours with
whom we being at war, we attacked her and while we were boarding her, and
in a manner had her in our possession, her crew hauled down these colours and
hoisted the English colours'.[8] Therefore the Qawāsim captured a ship that was
sailing under enemy colours, an enemy with whom they were then at war. The
Beaumont correspondence discussed payments to Shaikh Rāshid to release the
ship, but we do not know whether it was released or not. Certainly there was
no mention of passengers and crew having been sold as slaves and they seem
to have been only a figment of Lorimer's imagination.

Kelly repeats the same accusation, but with a difference. 'As far back as
December 1778 a brig carrying company dispatches had fought a running battle
for three days with six Qasimi vessels from Ras al-Khaima before being captured
and held to ransom for Rs. 4,000.' Obviously Kelly thought better of repeating
the false accusation of crew and passengers being sold as slaves. However, he
added another rumour, doubtless hoping that the accumulation of accusations might
help to prove at least one of them true: 'In January 1779 the *Success* ketch, en
route from Basra to Muscat, was set upon by eight to ten dhows but beat them

off. A month later the *Assistance* snow beat off an attack by Qawasim on its way up the Gulf'.[9]

John Beaumont put the whole episode in a better perspective when he reported to the Board that in November 1778 the Qawāsim had seized some small craft belonging to Bushire because they believed that their cargo was Muscat property. Subsequently Shaikh Khalfān, the long-time and well-known Governor of Muscat, sailed to Julfār and settled the matter peacefully, although the Imām of Muscat and Shaikh Rāshid of Julfār had been at war for some time.[10] The same John Beaumont also reported the rumour that eight to ten ships of the Julfār fleet had attacked the ketch *Success* and that the *Success* had beaten them off. There was also another rumour that two Julfār ships had attacked the *Assistance* snow but were driven off after an engagement lasting 25 minutes. However, in neither case could the aggressors be identified with any certainty.[11]

What had been started as a rumour about an attack by unidentified parties was eventually reported as an actual act of piracy by the Qawāsim and exaggerated into an act of enslavement of British subjects. Perhaps the testimony that best vindicates the Qawāsim, at least in respect of this incident, is that of Francis Warden, Chief Secretary to the Government, who clearly stated that 'until the year 1796 I was unable to trace a single act of aggression on the part of the Joasmee against the British flag'.[12] Indeed, the attitude of the Qawāsim is best illustrated by an event that happened in 1782. The Ottoman authorities in Baṣra seized a quantity of coffee unloaded there by the Qawāsim on the pretext that the Qawāsim had captured a boat belonging to Bushire. Subsequently the son of Shaikh Rāshid of Julfār arrived at Baṣra with several armed boats, demanded the coffee, and threatened to seize a large boat loaded with goods belonging to the Baṣra merchants if it was not released. On the other hand, he acknowledged that his father had engaged with the Ottoman authorities to be answerable for the restitution of such Baṣra property as might be taken by any of the people at the southern end of the Gulf. He therefore gave his word that, if the coffee was released, all the goods captured in the Bushire boat would be brought back by the group who had taken them. The Ottoman governor of Baṣra was all the more alarmed at the threat of the Qawāsim, since he found that they were supported by most of the boats from different parts of the Gulf which were then at the port. Shaikh Rāshid's son was cordially invited to land at Baṣra and Mr William Digger, then British Resident there, helped to solve the problem peacefully.[13] This was not the behaviour of people who either thought of themselves as pirates or were seen as such by others. The Qawāsim were certainly at that time responsible traders who were respected by the various powers in the Gulf.

The British were not the only party busy carrying out plans to control the Gulf and its trade. Sayyid Sultān, the Imām of Muscat, also entertained similar ambitions, albeit with much less success because of his lack of gun-boats and manpower.[14] He must have grossly overestimated his power, because in 1797, while he was at war with the Qawāsim, he sailed north with his fleet to attack Baṣra. Realising that he could not afford to fight on two fronts, he negotiated peace with the Qawāsim. When he could make no advance in his attack against Baṣra, he was only too happy to accept the intercession of the British resident at Baṣra and the Chief of the Qawāsim, Shaikh Ṣaqr. But when peace was restored with the Ottomans, the Imām sailed with a large fleet in 1799 to attack Bahrain, seizing three Bahraini ships in the process. Bahrain, which had recently been made a tributary of the Persians, applied for help to Shaikh Nāṣir, the representative of the Persian Government at Bushire. The Imām was forced to satisfy himself with a temporary possession of Khāraq Island only and return to Muscat.[15]

The Bassein and Viper Incidents

During the war between the Qawāsim and the Imām of Muscat two incidents occurred in 1797 that were recounted by Lorimer as heinous acts of piracy. Kelly repeated these accusations unquestioningly:[16]

> On 18 May 1797 the *Bassein* snow, carrying Company dispatches, was attacked and taken by twenty-two dhows off Qais Island, carried to Ras al-Khaima, and released a few days later. In October of the same year the Company's cruiser *Viper*, lying in Bushire Roads, was suddenly attacked by some Qasimi dhows, apparently in an effort to seize the cruiser's store of powder and shot. With the commander and many of the crew ashore, there seemed little hope that the Qawasim would be beaten off, but those on board, with great presence of mind, frustrated the pirates' attempts to board by cutting the cable and putting to sea. When they had enough sea-room they drove off the dhows with several well-aimed broadsides. A protest was sent to Shaikh Saqr ibn Rashid, who replied that the dhows involved were from Lingah, not Ras al-Khaima.

To be fair to Lorimer, it should be stated that he claimed that the *Bassein* snow was attacked and captured off Rams and detained at Rās al-Khaimah for only two days, in contrast to Kelly's 'several' days. Kelly's exaggeration also boosted the number of dhows attacking the *Bassein* to twenty-two.

The commander of the *Bassein* wrote to Samuel Manesty, the Resident at Baṣra, detailing the circumstances which attended the detention of the vessel. He informed Manesty that in meeting near Kishm, in the *Bassein*, the fleet of Sheikh Abdulla — the brother of Sheikh Saqr — certain dhows belonging to it bore down towards her with evil intention, that on their near approach he hailed them acquainting them in friendly language that the *Bassein* snow was a vessel belonging to the British nation, that declining to pay requisite deference and attention to this communication, the commander of the dhows caused near two hundred and fifty people in boats, belonging to them, to board the *Bassein* and to take possession of her, that Sheikh Abdulla on being made acquainted with the capture of the *Bassein* came himself on board her, directed his people to quit her and carried him, her commander, on shore with him at Kishm and subsequently on board his own vessel. Sheikh Abdulla made some reparation for the *Bassein* snow by allowing the *Bassein* to prosecute its voyage to Basra without further delay. It is true that there had not arisen any very serious detriment from the detention of the *Bassein* by Sheikh Abdullah but it was an event that detained the *Bassein* for more than twenty-four hours.

Manesty sent a letter to Shaikh Saqr bin-Rāshid, the Shaikh of Rās al-Khaimah, protesting against the incident. Shaikh Saqr answered Manesty's protestation in October 1797:[18]

After compliments, I have received your gracious and honoured letter, and I rejoice in your health and felicity . . . In respect to your vessel which some little time ago fell in with my vessels cruising on the Persian shore of the Gulf, and which you suspect them of wishing to capture, let me declare conscientiously 'God forbid I should think of capturing your vessels'.

To this day the British nation and my tribe have been honourable friends and we have entertained wishes respecting them similar to those we have entertained respecting ourselves; you may put faith in my assurances and in the security of your vessels navigating the Gulf. They will ever experience from my vessels when they meet them, friendship, and if necessary, assistance and service. Think of me with kindness and confidence and on all occasions express your wishes to me in the certainty of their entire accomplishment.

I must however observe on the subject of the detention of your vessel by my cruisers near the Island of Qishm that in all our wars we only fear the Supreme Being, opposing our enemies in all places. When my cruiser meets the vessel of my friends such as those belonging to you, to the Arabs in alliance with me, and to the Basra Government, they behave to them with amity, but when they meet the vessels of my enemies they attack and destroy them, placing confidence in God.

It is now clear that the *Bassein* incident was a minor misunderstanding that resulted in the Qawāsim detaining the ship for only 24 hours. The Qāsimī leader tried to rectify the error on the spot, to the best of his ability, and his chief reasserted his peaceful intentions. No piracy was involved and no crimes were committed. Indeed, Manesty himself confirmed in a letter to his Directors in Bombay that the prominent Qāsimī leader Shaikh Saqr had instructed his cruisers in the most 'forcible and liberal expression' to respect the British flag.[19]

The *Viper* incident was another where piracy can definitely be ruled out, but the circumstances as described by some of the participants indicate no small amount of confusion. Captain Smith, the Resident at Bushire, wrote to Manesty at Basra and reported:[20]

On the 14th of September the Viper arrived at Bushire. On the morning of her arrival Captain Edward Stephenson came ashore in her own boat . . . The next morning while we were at breakfast, we were alarmed by a report of guns and on going up on the terrace observed the vessel surrounded by four large dhows and a patel. The Captain wished to go on board but I could not consent to his going from the certainty of his being cut off from the vessel. The Sheikh of Bushire himself was not on the spot but his brother in charge pretended to do a great deal, but in fact did nothing, nor could I either by offers or any other means get a boat to go off with provisions which she stood in need of . . . Thus the vessel was left to fight for herself. Her men and officers were at breakfast when the largest dhow first came upon them and she immediately cut her anchor and got underway, at the same instant her crew flew to arms when Mr Caruthers (chief officer of the ship) was unfortunately shot through the body but refused to quit his station till another ball put an end to his existence and Mr Salter, a young volunteer and the only remaining officer, nobly continued the engagement till the dhows sheered off. The Captain then went on board, and I sent pilots in order if he conceived it requisite from the state of the vessel, as the dhows were still hanging about, to bring her into the creek which he accordingly did, from finding her ammunition expended, the chief officer and one sepoy killed, one European and four natives wounded, and one supposed mortally so. The dhows had arrived at Bushire about six days previous to the Viper, and were commanded by Sheikh Saleh, nephew to Sheikh Saqr, Chief of Joasmee Arabs in a state of hostilities with Sultan of Muscat. The intention of their pursuit was the interception of the Suree fleet at Basra at that time, and the day before the arrival of the Viper, Sheikh Saleh had asked one of my servants if we had any lead in the factory, to which he replied in the negative and reported to me the circumstances.

On the evening of the arrival of the Viper, Sheikh Saleh expressed to the Broker that he wished to have an interview with me, which was accordingly granted, when after the utmost professions of friendship he informed me he was going to attack the Suree dhows on their leaving Basra, and begged me to direct Captain Stephenson not to protect them if they should come near the Viper for protection, and he also hoped that neither the Resident at Basra nor myself would ship any goods in those dhows, but if we did, to send somebody with it who would inform him of its being the British property and it should be sacred from plunder. After that Sheikh Saleh requested a few balls and powder from the Viper and I got an order from Captain Stephenson for the delivery of forty three-pounders but no powder.

The following account from the Company's Broker at Muscat explains these circumstances differently. He said:[21]

that day letters had been received there from the merchants at Bushire announcing that after one of the Company's vessels had come to anchor at Bushire, the captain went on shore subsequent to which five dhows belonging to Julfar, with 250 men on board, came in with the intention of attacking the vessel, on observing which the chief officer cut her cable and got under weigh, and engaged the dhows from morning until evening when a great number of people belonging to the dhow had been killed. The chief officer of the Viper and one man were also killed, and four wounded.

Manesty sent a letter to Sheikh Ṣaqr demanding from him an explanation of the incident.[22] Sheikh Ṣaqr replied to this demand by a letter of November 1797:[23]

After compliments. I have received your gracious and honoured letter and the intelligence of your health has afforded me satisfaction.

I clearly understood the information which you have communicated to me and the nature of the unfortunate circumstances which with the permission of God have attended the meeting of Sheikh Saleh Ibn Mohamed and your vessel.

You must know that Saleh some time ago left Ras al-Khaimah and separating himself from us repaired to the Persian shore of the Gulf and there established himself among the Beni Maeen Arabs, marrying a woman of that tribe which is one of a villanous nature and character.

You must also know that since the commencement of hostilities between the Jausimee Arabs and the people of Oman, Saleh accompanied by the Banu Maeen Arabs and holding himself distinct from us, has united with certain vessels committing depredation according to his inclinations.

Saleh, as you justly related, visited the Resident at Bushire and solicited a supply of powder and balls, but without evil intentions. Your vessel was first attacked by a dhow belonging to the Arabs of Sohar and other vessels in company with Saleh, an engagement ensuing in which they suffered considerably and lost many men and subsequently Saleh, wishing to prevent further mischief and to separate the combatants, approached your vessel in his own dhow and received her fire of round and grape shot and musketry. These are the events which happened. God forbid that Saleh our relation should entertain evil intentions towards our friends, and indeed it is evident that had he meant to attack your vessel, accuse him of improper conduct on his visit at the factory. If they can, with justice, he is guilty.

We have not any dispute with the English, they are our friends; our enemies are the people of Oman. As we have absolutely informed you, we are as friendly in our disposition towards you as you can wish. We will not injure you nor are we willing that others should do so. We will do you every good that may be in our power, but not the least harm.

On the receipt of your letter we dispatched orders and vessels to bring Saleh to our presence and we are equal to the eligible and equitable settlement of the accident which has occurred, and even of more important ones. Your reputation with us and with all the Arabs in the Gulf is extensive and your wishes must be accomplished; with God's permission our friendship will enrich. You may entirely confide in our friendship towards you which we will manifest by words and deeds. May God give you health.

Manesty then wrote a letter to Jonathan Duncan, President and Governor in Council in Bombay, informing him that he had received a reply to his letter to

Shaikh Saqr b. Rāshid, the nature of which was very satisfactory. He was himself convinced that neither Shaikh Saleh nor the Qawāsim Arabs would again molest British vessels. He was also of the opinion that Shaikh Saqr, notwithstanding his politic endeavour to palliate the conduct of his nephew, which, justly considered, apparently reflected discredit on himself, would manifest in his behaviour towards him the highest displeasure and possibly punish him himself for his crimes in such a manner as his family connections might permit.[24]

Francis Warden corroborated the testimony of the Resident of Bushire and, to some extent, that of Shaikh Saqr b. Rāshid that the incident of the cruiser *Viper* in 1797 was supposed to have been the action of Arabs in the interest of the deposed Prince of Oman, the elder brother of Sayyid Sultān.[25] Again there was no piracy. Moreover, it was the *Viper* that fired first because its chief officer was under the impression that he was going to come under attack from ships that were concerned with a completely different mission against the Sūri fleet of Oman. The Qawāsim involved were a faction acting independently in a purely Arab fight. The British stepped in clumsily and actually got away with killing more Arabs than the two men they themselves lost. Yet Shaikh Saqr was still willing to make 'the eligible and equitable settlement of the accident'.

The turn of the century witnessed the appearance of the Saudis as a major threat to the minor powers of the Gulf. In 1800 the Saudis not only captured the port of Qatif and occupied the district of al-Hasā, but also advanced east and occupied the strategic Būraimi Oasis, thus threatening both Oman and Rās al-Khaimah.[26] This threat persuaded Sayyid Sultān of Muscat to drop his hostility to Shaikh Saqr and seek an alliance with the Qawāsim against the Saudis. But when the Imām proceeded to Rās al-Khaimah to join Shaikh Saqr the Saudis quickly agreed to restore peace with him.[27]

The Arrival of Captain Malcolm

The British were no less alarmed by the appearance of the Saudis in the Gulf. They reacted by sending Captain John Malcolm to carry out an exhaustive plan to establish British influence and trade in the Gulf once and for all. Malcolm's career was to prove that he was one of the most ambitious empire-builders of all time. His plan was no less ambitious. First he was to restore and strengthen the treaty of 1798 with Oman.[28] His second objective logically was to establish British representation in Muscat.[29] Not surprisingly his third objective was to conclude a commercial and a political agreement with Persia.[30] Having secured a grip on the trade with Muscat and Persia, Malcolm's task was then to examine the possible locations for the establishment of a British commercial base in the Gulf.[31]

On 8 January 1800 Malcolm arrived at Muscat and was met by its governor, Saif b. Muhammad, in the absence of the Imām who was then on his way to attack Qishm. However, we soon find Malcolm joining the Imām on the quarterdeck of his ship the *Gunjava*, where an agreement was signed and sealed between Sayyid

Sultān, the Imām of the State of Oman and Captain John Malcolm Bahadur, Envoy of the Right Honourable the Governor General the Earl of Mornington.[32] We are fortunate to have a copy of the draft of this agreement,[33] an extract from which is given here:

> Translation of a draft agreement between Syed Sultan, Imaum of the State of Oman and Captain John Malcolm Bahadur, Envoy of the Right Honble the Governor General the Earl of Mornington K.P.
> Dated
> Article 1st   The Caulnamah dated the
> Formerly entered into by this State with Mehedy Aly Khan Bahadur remains fixed and unaltered.
> Article 2nd. As a number of contrary reports have been spread and have come to the hearing of the Governor General Earl of Mornington K.P., which have had a tendency to disturb the harmony and good understanding that subsists between the two States to prevent the baneful effects of such cases in future I agree that an English Gentleman shall always reside at the Port of Muscat on the part of the Company and that he shall act as the medium of communication between the two States so that the actions of both governments may be fairly and honble represented by such person and no opportunity afforded to designing of men who are ever endeavouring to excite commotions and the friendship between the States may exist uninterrupted to the end of time and till the sun and moon have finished their revolving career.

As we can see, Malcolm succeeded very easily in achieving his first and second objectives. The treaty of 1798 which obliged the Imām to put an end to his dealings with the French and the Dutch was reinstated and a British representative was installed in Muscat. Lorimer recorded that a certain Dr Bogle who had joined Malcolm in his mission established himself in the Imām's confidence and undertook the position of British Political Agent at Muscat.[34] Soon after and with the same ease Captain Malcolm, having arrived at Shiraz, signed an agreement with Persia whereby he secured a commercial concession from the Persians, who also undertook to forbid the French from entering their country.[35]

As to the choice of a port most suitable for the establishment of a British commercial base in the Gulf, Malcolm's views have been preserved in a letter from him to the Earl of Mornington. This letter also throws considerable light on the British plans for trade in the Gulf. After reviewing the conditions of every port on the Persian side of the Gulf, Captain Malcolm recommended the Island of Qishm as the most suitable site from the point of view of water, food supplies, climate, and strategic position and as having the best harbour. Furthermore, a British base on an island away from the Persian mainland would help the British avoid involvement in internal Persian affairs. The main points in Malcolm's letter concerned the control and expansion of trade between India, Persia and Arabia. But perhaps the most astounding part of the letter is paragraph 83, which reveals British plans to deprive Oman of its trade with India only a few days after the conclusion of a commercial agreement with the Imām. Malcolm suggested that the British could undercut the Muscat authorities by charging only half the custom duties they imposed on trade that stopped at Muscat when this trade was diverted to the British base in the Gulf. He wrote:[36]

> The harbour between Kishm and Anjam is at most seasons of the year as short a run from Bombay as Muscat and indeed when the difficulty of getting into Muscat Cove, and the favourable winds which vessels generally secure by keeping to the northward and close in with the shore is considered, the voyage I am inclined to believe will be performed sooner and certainly with much more ease and confidence by the ships and small craft of natives who fear going out of sight of land. It is to be further considered that when goods from Bombay reach Muscat, they have to perform a voyage of at least four and probably six days in the most favourable season before they reach the length of this Port in their passage up the Gulph. When we add to this circumstance that the collections at this settlement would not probably be above one half of that of Muscat and the confidence of the merchants for obvious reasons tenfold, we cannot hesitate in concluding that this port would immediately become the medium of that commerce between the Gulph and Bombay, which has hitherto been carried to Muscat. The trade with the coast of Malabar would, for nearly similar reasons, soon find the same channels as well as that from the Coast of Coromandel and Bengal. This change might in some articles be more slow than in others from the Muscat merchants, being at present the chief traders, and their vessels being mostly employed in freight, but it is impossible they could long support a competition with other merchants and ship owners who conveyed their goods at less expense and navigating their vessels by a less circuitous track. This remark applies most pointedly to that considerable trade which I have stated to be carried on between Surat, Bombay and Guzerat with the Gulph, which could not but find its mart in the port proposed.

In December 1800 Captain David Seton made his appearance at Muscat where he was appointed Resident.[37] He firmly believed in a close alliance with Sayyid Sultān, with whom he established a personal friendship.[38] Nevertheless, Seton's orders were not to involve the British in any hostilities that might occur between Oman and any other Arabs in the Gulf. Seton seems to have gone beyond these orders, as there is evidence that he accompanied the Imām on some of his expeditions.[39]

Perhaps encouraged by his developing friendship with the British, the Imām embarked in 1801 on one of his favourite ambitions: the conquest of Bahrain. But, as usual, his ambitions exceeded his military power and after a few months of occupying Bahrain the 'Utūb were able to drive him out.[40]

Meanwhile, the Saudis made their presence felt in the vicinity of Oman where they were joined by the nomadic tribes who were only too happy to free themselves from the authority of the Imām. Faced with this dangerous situation, the Imām tried to form an alliance with the Qawāsim against the Saudis. But the two sides were unable to overcome their old mutual enmity. Very soon the Saudis managed to extend their influence and reduce to, at least, nominal submission the whole of the Arab coast from Baṣra to Dibbā, leaving only Rās al-Khaimah, the seat of the Qawāsim, the only tribe who had not yet submitted to their influence or doctrine.⁴¹ Unable to check their progress, in spite of offers of assistance from the Turks and the Persians, the Imām in 1803 acceded to a three-year truce with the Saudis. Nevertheless, this truce did not deter the Saudis from helping and encouraging an attempt by Sayyid Badr, a nephew of the Imām, to overthrow his government. The Saudis went as far as invading Oman and advancing in support of their protégé, but this operation came to a halt on the assassination of 'Abdul'azīz, the Saudi leader, in November 1803.⁴² A year later in November 1804 Sayyid Sulṭān was also assassinated while he was going ashore on the Island of Qishm. Many parties, the Qawāsim included, were accused of this assassination, but there was no evidence that could determine who the murderers were and Sayyid Sulṭān had made many enemies who would have wished for his elimination. However, the struggle for power that followed his death involved not only his cousins, sons, and nephews, but also their supporters from outside Oman. The end result was the accession to power of the Saudis' client Sayyid Badr, a move which brought the government of Oman almost completely under their control.

During this struggle the British stayed neutral, though apprehensive about the growing influence of the Saudis in Oman. Their concern was for the preservation of their interests at Muscat and the security of their trade in the Gulf, which could be threatened by the establishment of a government at Muscat less favourable to those interests than that of the late Imām. The Governor General furnished guidelines in that event, namely that the existing engagements between the East India Company and Muscat did not impose on the former any obligation to support any particular person in the struggle for the succession:⁴³

but the nature of the connection existing between the Company and the Imam and cemented by the engagements concluded with that Prince in the year 1798 and 1800 justified the interference of the British Government in support of that candidate whose pretensions should appear to be founded on justice, provided that support could be afforded without the hazard of involving the British Government in hostilities with the State of Muscat. Secondly, the British would be desirable that the engagements concluded by Mahdee Ali Khan and Major Malcolm with the late Imam should be formally recognised by the person who should ultimately succeed to the Government of Muscat, and thirdly, with a view to the maintenance of the British influence at Muscat under any issue of the expected consent, it was the British desire that agreeable to the engagements concluded by Major Malcolm in the year 1800, a residency on the part of the Company should be permanently established at that station under the superintendence of a civil or military servant of the Company of the establishment of Bombay.

On the whole the Qawāsim, though tempted to interfere, stayed out of the struggle in Oman. But events were moving in a direction that would eventually force their hand. In 1803 Shaikh Sulṭān b. Ṣaqr succeeded his father in the leadership of the Qawāsim. His long and controversial career shows all the signs of a vigorous ruler who did not hesitate to take the initiative when he deemed it necessary. Although sometimes adventurous, he had all the determination of a leader who knew what he and his people wanted. On the other hand, he could change course and even seem unscrupulous when it was to the advantage of his objective.

Less than a year after his succession, Shaikh Sulṭān led the Qawāsim in accepting Saudism; of course, this meant an alliance with the Saudis, a move that in itself would indicate hostility to Oman. The worse fears of the British thus materialised and their allies, the Omanis, were isolated and under attack from the Saudis and their allies. The hysteria that prevailed in British circles concerned with the Gulf is echoed by Kelly.[44]

Within weeks of Sultan's death the Gulf was up in arms, as the Qawasim strove to usurp the maritime supremacy held by Muscat. Together with their kinsmen from Lingah, on the Persian shore, and the Bani Main from Qishm and Hormuz, they overran those two islands in February 1805, and went on to capture Bander Abbas and lay siege to Minab, a few miles away. Masters now of the Straits of Hormuz, they could strike at any vessel making for or leaving the Gulf.

These erroneous conclusions are easy to refute. To begin with 'the maritime supremacy held by Muscat' in the Gulf is certainly wishful thinking on the part of Kelly, to say the least. And how could the Bani Ma'in capture Qishm and Hormuz, islands they already possessed and occupied? And from whom did they capture them? There was no sign of the Qawāsim either from Linga or from Rās al-Khaimah taking part in these alleged attacks. While it is true that Bander 'Abbās was taken by Bani Ma'in, the Qawāsim themselves had nothing to do with this operation. To add strength to his arguments Kelly raises the spectre of the 'religious fanaticism' of the Qawāsim and states that their 'recent conversion to Wahhabism had inflamed their naturally warlike disposition'.[45] He then proceeds to accuse the Qawāsim of successive acts of piracy and in many cases does no more than repeat the unfounded accusation first reported by Lorimer.

Lorimer reports that 'In 1804 the crew and passengers of the Fly, which had been captured by a French privateer, were piratically attacked while on their way to India in a native vessel that they had purchased at Bushire and were carried off by the Qawāsim, who did not readily restore them to liberty'.[46] If we look at the report of William Bruce, the Resident at Bushire, to Manesty, the Resident at Basra, written on 5 January 1805, we find that, although Bruce accused the Qawāsim of capturing the crew of the Fly, he reported that the latter were taken to Bokha where they were kept for a month before delivering them to Shaikh Raḥma of Nakhīlū, who treated them well and procured their passage to Bushire.[47] It all sounds credible until one realises that Bokha was under the control of the Imām of Oman; the contradictions in Bruce's report then become evident. Another report by Mullā Ḥussain of Qishm to Captain Seton confirmed that the crew and their ship were taken to Sayyid Majid, a person of some distinction on the part of the government of Oman.[48] In all cases the Qawāsim had nothing to do with the *Fly* and its crew.

The Trimmer and Shannon Incidents

Then comes the celebrated case of the seizure of the two British brigs. As Lorimer reports 'In 1805 the Shannon and Trimmer, two merchant vessels owned by Mr Manesty, the British Resident at Basrah, were taken by Qasimi pirates', and, as if to reconfirm this report, he adds, 'and in the same year a fleet of Qasimi vessels attempted to seize the East India Company's large cruiser Mornington, but were beaten off with loss'.[49] Had the two brigs not belonged to the notorious Manesty, the Baṣra Resident, the whole episode would not have taken on such exaggerated proportions. And had Seton not been the Resident at Muscat, the aggressive moves of the cruiser *Mornington* in the Gulf would not have occurred, and no excuse would have been sought for its presence in the area.

To understand what happened to the two brigs it is best to let the reports of the British individuals involved speak for themselves. The Commander of the *Trimmer* wrote to Manesty immediately after the event in December 1804:[50]

To Samuel Manesty Esqre.
Resident Bussore

Sir,
The Brig Trimmer under my command, having been captured by a fleet of pirate dows and battilas, I think it necessary to state the particulars to you.

On the 1st of December 1804 at day break in the morning, Cape Ceret bearing 6 B.S. distance five or six miles, we saw two dows close under the Cape, the other within half a mile of us. About 7 a.m. shelving our water to three and half fathoms halled in shore and deepened to nine fathoms when it fell. Little wind and the nearest dow there being a quarter of a mile from us we hoisted our colours and the dow did the same. Supposing it to be a trading boat I sent our jolly boat with the serang who speaks the Arabic language for intelligence and to enquire if there was any place in shore where we could water quick at. After the boat had been quarter of an hour alongside of the dow we fired a gun to seaward as a signal for the serang to return which they seemed to take no notice of. In 10 minutes afterwards we fired another gun, and then perceived two men that were in the jolly boat go up on board the dow at the same time she made sail and stood inshore, which gave me the first suspicion of his being a pirate, we immediately made sail after her firing shot at first wide and afterwards right at her. She seemed to wish to draw us inshore. At 9 a.m. we could see a number of dows coming out of Charik Bay besides others from the east and westward to join him, we then steered wide of him by which I expected he would think better of detaining an English boat and let her go in the stead of which he kept towards us. We then set all sail and he came right after us. We got a four pounder over our stern and played on the dow as fast as we would and began to lighten ship by heaving overboard some chests of soft sugar in order to escape, we continued firing pound double head and grape shot and our small arms (which they returned with their matchlocks) till they struck us on the larboard quarter, when they threw a shower of spears on board and instantly filled our quarter deck with men sword in hand which was in vain for us to resist. They immediately began to plunder having wounded the chief mate in the hand. We were all presently stripped of the clothes we had on and insulted by spitting at us and pushing us from place to place and after threatening putting me to death (by holding a dagger to my breast) I did not discover where treasure was hid. In a very short space of time there was as many dows alongside as could come at us taking out the cargo and robbing the ship's stores. Our packet was shot and thrown overboard on their boarding.

About 12 o'clock the Shannon Captain Babcock hove in sight and several dows gave him chase. They continued plundering till 5 p.m. when they towed us in shore and came to anchor, not one of us was allowed to go below all day, in the evening one of the captains of the dows came on board the Trimmer who told me they only intended to take our cargo that was the property of the merchants at Bushire and that in a day or two the brig would be given up and all the stores taken out returned. This man took me, my servants, two helmsmen and an Armenian passenger on board his dow (my officer having lost so much blood could not be removed) under pretence of looking for our clothes. When on board the dow they gave us an old sail to lay on and all we had to eat was a few dates and sometimes a small piece of salt fish, all the time we were with them.

On the 2nd December in the morning we found the Shannon brought into the fleet seemingly treated as we had been. I requested to go on board her but was not allowed. About 8 a.m. the whole fleet of dows, twenty-nine in number (carrying each between one hundred fifty and two hundred men) got under sail, the Trimmer and Shannon in company, and steered westward and about 10 a.m. fell in with two trading dows which the pirates captured. One of them making some resistance, the crew was put to death. On the same day at 11 p.m. they fell in with and engaged two large dows and two battilas, the whole four in the action took fire and were burnt. The crews that were obliged to jump into the water, I had the shocking sight to see murdered begging for mercy.

On the 3rd in the morning the Captain of the dow I was on said in two days at farthest both vessels would be given up and kept promising day after day we should be let go. I could never get permission to go and see either Captain Babcock or my officer till the 8th December when I and my people were ordered to a boat and sent on board the Shannon where I found Captain Babcock laying covered with wounds and his left hand cut off and his vessel torn to pieces.

Now, I came to understand that the Shaiks of Linja and Rusulkima were the head of these pirates. Captain Babcock also informed me that they did not intend to give up the Trimmer and that they promised daily to let the Shannon go. On the 11th December about 3 a.m. a boat came on board the Shannon bringing my officer gunner, a helmsman, two washermen and woman. She kept a young woman and a little girl. These washing people were passengers for Bussora. After putting these people on board, they told Captain Babcock we might go only giving us one trail of dates for our subsistence and no water. We immediately weighed and made sail with the wind at N.6 for Bushire. On the 18th December we saw the Honourable Companies Cruiser Mornington and Captain Babcock went on board her for assistance, and the 19th we anchored in Bushire Roads.

Bussora   I have the honor to be &ca
December 19th, 1804   Signed/Ins. Cumming

Here also is the report of the Captain of the *Shannon*:[51]

To
Samuel Manesty Esqre
Resident at Basra

Sir

It is with regret I address you on this occasion stating the melancholy circumstance that occurred on board the brig Shannon under my command in the Persian Gulf on the 1st inst.

At about half an hour after noon on the aforementioned day when the Island of Polior bore south with the wind at east south east having all sails set we descried a square rigged vessel bearing west north west and shortly after several dows around her, the vessel appearing much like the brig Trimmer, Captain Cumming made me conclude it was her and that she had been captured by the pirate dows about her. Every person on board also concurring in opinion that such a circumstance had been effected made me resolve (being of the west extreme of Polior) to alter my course from west by north to south west with the intention of avoiding them. Quarter of an hour before 2 o'clock I perceived that fifteen dows, and other country boats, were in chase of us and every preparation was made to defend ourselves should they attack us. The chase continued till between two and three o'clock. When they were within musket distance I hoisted my ensign and hailed in Arabic to which they did not make any reply but continued to approach nearer. I hailed a second time desiring them to come no nearer when they immediately fired a musketon and shot on board us and which determined me to repel the attack they were about making. I consequently ordered a broadside of four guns to be discharged at them, which was repeated with the small arms. We had eight of the dows being there but a short distance off, one of which was obliged to haul her wind from us for a short time. However soon after being three o'clock the whole of them bore down and boarded us sword in hand taking possession of the vessel and treating myself and crew most severely. I am sorry to inform you that on the occasion we had one man killed and four badly wounded, besides myself being most cruelly treated, they having cut off my left hand by the wrist and wounded me in nine other places about the head and body, plundered us of everything we possessed to the very covering we had on at that time leaving us naked and destitute of anything to eat or drink. In this inhuman manner did they oblige me to remain on the deck unable to stir from the loss of blood I had sustained and really should have perished, was it not for a little wine and biscuit that I saved (for eight days).

The cargo that we had on was all plundered and taken away also several stores belonging to the vessel, her guns, light sails, one anchor, one grapnel, a new gallant and aft mainsail, one lower and three top studding sails, and otherwise damaged her much. The packet that I received at Bombay was also taken by them and all the letters torn, a few of which I have been able to save.

On the 11th about 3 a.m. a boat was sent on board to tell us we were at liberty to proceed to where we chose, at the same time giving us one bag of dates only for our subsistence, a compass, a part of our old ensign and two guns with their carriages. They also sent us all the Christians that were taken in the Trimmer with three washermen for Mr Donald at Busora, and in this unprovided state we set sail for Charack bay with a light breeze from the north east up the Gulf for Bushire.

During our detention I had opportunities of conversing twice with the Shaik, the first time was four days after we were captured when I represented the very treatment we had received and complained of our being left in a starving state to which he made no reply. I then requested him to furnish me with a small boat that sailed well to land us at either Bushire or Bussorah and that I would be answerable for his boat being safe and pay him five thousand piasters to which he replied that he could not part with me without the vessel went; also as he was not at war with the English, but wanted the property that belonged to Bushire, Muscat and Bussora. However, after questioning his reason for allowing us and the vessel to be plundered he would make no reply. The second time we met I renewed my request for the boat and was answered as before with promises that our cargo and other property should be restored, all of which proved false as he not only sent us away without an article of provision and utensils to cook in but I understand has kept the Trimmer for himself.

On the 18th I went on board the Mornington, Captain Gilmour from whom I received great civilities, and politeness, and for his attention I return him my sincere thanks also to the doctor on board her. I gave Captain Gilmour every intelligence informing him that the fleet was commanded by Shaik Greab of Linge-Lung and Shaik Sultan Ben Sugger of Rossalkima or Joasmees, the latter appeared to be the principal man. On the 19th we arrived at Bushire and on the same day the Shannon anchored in the evening.

Bussora   I have the honor to be &ca.
29th December 1804   Signed/R. Babcock

Reporting to headquarters, Manesty wrote:[52]

To
His Excellency
The Most Noble the Marques Wellesley
Governor General & ca. in Council
at Fort William
In the Political Department

It is with infinite concern that I respectfully report to your Excellency, of further and more serious interruption to the communication between Bussora and India than that lately occasioned by the visit to the Gulf of the French Privateer La Fortune.

Late on the 17th instant I received intelligence of the capture, to the northward of the Island of Kishmee about the 1st ultimo of the brigs Shannon and Trimmer, employed with conveyance of public advices for Europe from the Presidency, by the Gausemee Arabs which intelligence has been confirmed by letters from Bushire and on the importation on the 29th ultim of the Shannon liberated on the 11th preceeding in a much injured state by order of Shaik Sultan bin Sugger, the Jausemee Shaik. The enclosed copies of the reports made to me by the Commanders of the Shannon and Trimmer who are now here will make known to your Excellency the dreadful circumstances which attended their capture and subsequent captivity.

The Jausemee tribe, have been latterly subjected to the authority of the Whahabee Shaik and in consequence of the recent fall of Syed Sultan in a sea engagement, on his late returning voyage from Bussora to Muscat they have commenced hostilities against many destructive piratical depredations.

The only possible immediate mode of attempting to check the inimical proceedings of the Jausemee Arabs towards English vessels by negotiation is through the medium of their new master, Shaik Sood bin Abdul Aziz the present Whahabee Shaik and I have consequently determined to dispatch a confidential person to Drauah charged with a letter to the Shaik explanatory of the unfortunate events which have taken place, and of the necessity of his causing immediate restitution of the Trimmer, of his issuing positive orders to the Jausemee Arabs, whose chief residence is at Rasel Khima to observe a friendly conduct towards British vessels in future, and his declaring the nature of his own sentiments towards the British nation.

I have much reason to believe that Shaik Sood is favourably inclined towards us but it is very difficult to form an opinion on the subject of his effecting the restitution of the Trimmer, and his taking decided measures preventative for future insults and injuries.

Your Excellency will duly estimate the expediency of finally compelling the offenders to respect the British Flag I can only respectfully hint that if admission to the British ports in India be refused to all Arab vessels belonging to the Gulf indiscriminately, that single demonstration of British resentment must operate almost instantaneously the desirable effect of reducing the Jausimee and the other Arabian maritime tribes to the necessity of cultivating British friendship, for subsistence and of making such arrangements amongst themselves as would attone for present injuries and prevent inimica operations. To suffer further insults from men who depend on the ports of Calcutta and Mangalore, for the rice they eat, and on the Malabar Coast for the timber with which they construct their vessels, would be a circumstance extremely derogatory to the honor and dignity of the British Government.

I am of the opinion that it will be absolutely requisite that merchant vessels be for a time prohibited visiting the Gulf, unless extremely well armed, or under powerful convoy, and that the public packets be transmitted from Bussora to Bombay and from Bombay to Bussora, in cruisers of real and considerable force.

Such is the strength and number of the dows and boats belonging to the Jausemee tribe that I dare not in the present moment not withstand the opportune arrival and continuance on a cruise in the Gulf of the Honble Company ship the Mornington venture to despatch a single vessel with my present advices for government and I therefore direct the Queen and Antelope to sail together on the plan of their proceeding in company to the entrance of it and there separating the Queen in prosecution of her voyage to the Presidency and the Antelope on her return to Bussora attended to a certain point of latitude and longitude by the Mornington.

I flatter myself that you will approve of the tenor of the accompanying copies of my letters of this date to the Commanders of the Queen, Antelope and Mornington and I have again the power to subscribe myself with the greatest respect.

Bussora	Your Excellency
the 2nd January 1805	and obedient humble sevt.
	Signed/Samuel Manesty

Here we have three reports about the same incidents all written at Baṣra obviously after much consultation. They all agree that the incidents took place near Chārak on the Persian coast to the north of Qishm island. But there is some uncertainty about the identity of the attackers. Captain Cumming of the *Trimmer*, writing from Baṣra on 19 December said, 'Now, I came to understand that the Shaiks of Linja and Rusulkima were the head of the pirates'. There is no doubt that he acquired this understanding in Baṣra; he probably combined two rumours in order to sound convincing. Captain Babcock of the *Shannon* tried harder and actually put down in his report the name of 'Shaik Sultan Ben Sugger of Rossalkima or Joasmees', though he did not know the name of the Shaikh of Linga with whom he claimed to have conversed on two occasions, on one of which he assured the

Captain that 'he was not at war with the English, but wanted the property that belonged to Bushire, Muscat and Bussora'. Captain Babcock also took it upon himself to put down in his report to Manesty that 'I understand (the Shaikh) has kept the Trimmer for himself'. Of course, Captain Babcock acquired this information from the same source as Captain Cumming, and at the time of writing their reports they were both regurgitating some of the information they had been given by Manesty. When the latter reported to his seniors in Bombay he was more careful in his allegations just in case head office might get different information elsewhere. Manesty reported that the attacks were 'by order of Shaikh Sultan bin Sugger the Jausemee Shaik'. It seems like a deliberate attempt somehow to implicate the leader of the Qawāsim without regard to the truth of his being there or not. It is really surprising that Captain Babcock would know the name of the Shaikh of Rās al-Khaimah who had not yet completed a year in office. But the Captain, who claimed that he had conversed twice with the 'Shaik', did not tell us to which of the two he had spoken, nor in what language they spoke to each other. It could not have been Arabic, and English was not yet the *Lingua Franca* in the Gulf.

It is clear from Captain Cumming's report that it was not obvious to him at first sight whether the approaching Arab ships were pirates and his suspicions were aroused a few minutes later when the Arab ship 'made sail and stood in-shore'. There was no attack, there was no sign of threatening behaviour and there was no communication that indicated any bad intentions. Yet Captain Cumming took only at most half an hour to start firing 'right at her', and he expected the Arab ship to accept this behaviour as peaceful and remain passive in the face of the fact that he fired first. From the Arabs' point of view, the *Trimmer* was the aggressor and its crew were the pirates. Having been in the wrong, Captain Cumming was anxious to have any excuse to justify his folly that had ended in disaster, and Manesty was only too willing to supply the name of Sultān b. Ṣaqr and the Qawāsim as the culprits. Manesty had another reason for blaming the whole thing on the Qawāsim. The two brigs belonged to him and the Qawāsim, and particularly the newly installed Shaikh Sultān, were a better target for his accusation, since he certainly wanted to demand compensation for damages, than any other of the small Arab groups in the Gulf. It was not beyond Manesty's scruples to invent a story, indeed he was a rather unscrupulous man. Saldhana mentioned him as the restless and fussy Resident at Baṣra.[53] Kelly explained how he resorted to mysterious ways to promote his own personal interests.[54] These interests were intricate and widespread over India, the Gulf, Persia and 'Iraq. It was difficult to differentiate his personal interests from those of the Company. In fact, it was more than likely that he believed that what was good for Manesty was good for the Company. The Basra Diaries reveal a great deal about his vast operations and devious dealings.[55] His seniors, his colleagues, his subordinates and all his acquaintances and enemies had nothing good to say about him and a great deal to say about his dishonest, deceitful and underhand dealings. His contemporary, Sir Harford Jones, the Resident at Baghdad, had a great deal to complain about in respect of his intrigues, meddling and pomposity.[56]

The Activities of Captain Seton

While Manesty was directing his own independent politics in the area, another man was also embarking on his own plan for what he thought was good for the Company in the Gulf. Captain David Seton, whom we already met as the Resident in Muscat, was not the wheeler-dealer Manesty was; he was perhaps a rather naive young officer with too much confidence in his own judgement and ability. He had left Muscat in 1803 as a result of ill-health, but from Surat where he was recuperating he kept in touch with the Government in Bombay about events in Oman. On 26 February 1805 he wrote to the governor of Bombay, Jonathan Duncan, suggesting 'this government assisting that of Muscat in chastising the Joasmees by affording the assistance of the cruisers in the Gulf.[57] Duncan replied by ordering Seton back to Muscat to reopen the Residency and giving him clear instructions about the British policy and objectives in Oman and the Gulf:[58]

> To
> Captain David Seton
> Resident at Muscat
> Sir,
>   The communication made to you previously to your recent return from Surat will have apprised you of the circumstances which render it desirable that you should resume your duties as Resident in Muscat, as speedily as may be practicable; and I am now instructed to convey to you instructions founded in orders from His Excellency the Most Noble the Governor General, for the regulation of your conduct under the recent change in the Government occasioned by the premature death of Seyud Sultan, an event requiring that measures should be adopted for the preservation of the interests of the British Government at Muscat; and for the security of our trade in the Gulf of Persia, objects which (independently of the events of the intermediate period) might be exposed to increased hazard by the establishment of power at Muscat less favourable to those interests than the Government of the late Imaum.
>
> 2nd. The existing engagements between the Company and the Imaum of Muscat do not impose on the former any obligation to support the successor of the sons of the late Imaum to the right and power of their father; but the nature of the co-operation existing between the company and the Imaum and cemented by the engagements created with that Prince in the year 1798 and 1800 justify the interference of the British Government in support of what interest whose pretensions shall appear to be forwarded on justice, provided that support can be afforded without hazard of involving the British government in hostilities with the State of Muscat.
>
> 3rd. It is, therefore, the desire of the Supreme Govt. of India that every degree of countenance and support be afforded to the sons of the late Seyud Sultan which can be effected through the means of the British influence at Muscat,

and without engaging in hostilities with the opposing party.

4th. Should the interests of the Brothers of Seyud Sultan prevail against those of their nephews, it is nevertheless the wish of the Company's Government to maintain with the ruling party at Muscat the same relations of amity which subsisted with the former Government and in the event supposed, it is accordingly desired that you cultivate harmony with the successful candidates and endeavour by every means consistent with the dignity of the British Government to consolidate their good will.

5th. It will be desirable that the engagements concluded by Mehdi Ali Khan and Major Malcolm with the late Imaum, should be formally recognised by the person who shall ultimately succeed to the Government of Muscat. In view of which copies of both in English and Persian are enclosed, the first, of that negotiated by Mehdi Ali Khan dated the 12th October 1798 and the second, of that by Major Malcolm the 18th of January 1800.

6th. With a view to the maintenance of the British influence at Muscat under any issue of the contest for power among the relations of Seyud Sultan, it is intended that, agreeable to the engagement concluded by Major Malcolm in 1800, a Residency on the part of the company shall be permanently established at that station, but, notwithstanding this intention it is not meant, under the already experienced deleterious effect of the climate of Muscat on European constitutions, to restrict you from returing to Bombay in the month of August next or even sooner should the state of your health require it.

7th. The most recent account from Muscat rendering it highly probable that you'll find the late Imaum's son Salim in the exercise of the powers of Govt. on your arrival there a letter to his address is in this expectation enclosed accompanied by a translation for your own information. Should, however, intermediate circumstances have placed the powers of the Muscat Government in other hands, you will abstain from delivering the letter to Salim. In such case it will become your duty to conduct yourself towards the ruling party for the time being in the spirit of that part of the preceeding instructions which apply to such a contingency.

8th. The suggestion contained in your letter of the 26th ultimo in favour of this Government assisting that of Muscat in chastising the Joasmees, by affording the assistance of the cruisers on the Gulf (as may now be conveniently done through the means of the Mornington already there) appears very desirable, in so far it may be found free of objection in respect to the Wahabee, who from your report would appear to have been formerly the protector though now said to have quarrelled with that tribe. Provided, therefore, that you shall on your arrival at Muscat have every reason to believe that the Wahabee will not take offence at the intended coercion it may (all other local circumstances continuing in your view of them on your arrival, to render the same urgently advisable) be pursued or otherwise as Mr Manesty has intimated his intention to depute a proper person to Deryah to demand the restitution of the captured vessels and property; you may await the result of that intervention of which Mr Manesty has been instructed to advise you, with all practicable dispatch.

9th. In view to it being thus eventually determined to act against the Joasmees, a letter under flying seal to the commander of the Hon'ble Company's Cruiser Mornington is now enclosed in which he is instructed to comply with all your requisitions and to remain in the Gulf, while you may require his presence.

10th. On the ground of the suggestion contained in the concluding paragraph of your letter of the 26th ultimo, the Superintendent of the Marine has been instructed to prepare a small vessel as there is proposed, or if there be none such to arm the Queen in the mode desired; upon which she is after delivering her packet, to be employed in concert with the Mornington under your direction in the protection of the British navigation, by suppressing the pirates in the Gulf. The Queen is, in this view, to have 11 artillery men under a good sergeant, put on board of her, and to be victualled till the end of August, and also the Mornington, the supplies necessary for this purpose being as far as there may not be room for them in the Queen, sent on board of the dinghy engaged by you.

11th. As the Queen must in the first instance proceed up the Gulf to Bushire and Bussora, with the Basha of Baghdad ships and the packet to Bussora, you should by the same opportunity write to Mr Manesty for the purpose of advising that gentleman of the views in relation to the suppression of the pirates, if still requiring to be hostility course and desire his advice as to the effect which any active proceedings against the Joasmees or any other tribe may probably have on our national interests with the Wahabee or other power on either coast of the Gulf, such as it may perhaps be in Mr Manesty's power (thro' his local influence particularly in the upper part of the Gulf) to avert. As you will accordingly request of him and wait to answer, before our vessels enter in any offensive plan of hostility against the pirates, unless as above observed the urgency of circumstance should for the protection of our trade and nagivation call for a speedier course.

12th. In your proceedings towards the pirates, you are to be particularly cautious to act with the greatest moderation to aim at pacification by means of negotiation and to avoid hostilities, at all cost with any classes of the armed boats or vessels belonging to either side of the Gulf which may have respected the British Flag, so as that we may not prove the aggressors in any instance.

13th. You are likewise to correspond with, and to act generally in concurrence with views and advice of Mr Bruce at Bushire, with a view to keep clear of all disputes with the Wahabee, or either of the two Governments of Turkey or Persia.

I have the honour to be

Bombay Castle
3rd March 1805

& ca & ca & ca
Signed/Jo. Duncan

The following letter was written on 3 March to Lieutenant Charles Gilmour, Officer Commanding the Hon'ble Company's cruiser *Mornington*:[59]

To
Lieutenant Charles Gilmour
Officer Commanding the Hon'ble Company's Cruiser Mornington.
Sir,
   The continuous instances of depredation by the piratical chieftains in the Gulf of Persia as recently restated in the case of the plunder of the Zepher (sic) having appeared to the Govt. in Council to render it expedient to instruct Captain Seton, the Resident at Muscat to adopt such measures as may on his arrival there be found most advisable for repressing future similar excesses, and it being thence probable that he may have occasion to call for the services of the Hon'ble Company's Cruiser Mornington, I am, in consequence, instructed to desire that you comply with all requisition from that Officer whilst he may require the continuance of the Mornington in the Gulf of Persia and consider you will (sic) as generally, subject to that Resident's orders, for the purpose thus intimated, as well as in respect to the period of your return to the Presidency and in case Captain Seton shall think fit, to embark at any time on your vessel, you will be careful to afford him very suitable accommodation and to conduct you will (sic) in all respects with that becoming spirit of knowing so essential to the advancement of the public service.

2nd. Inview of this probable prolongation of your cruise the Superintendent of the Marine has been instructed to forward to you such supplies as he may judge the Mornington to be most in want of, as to which he will by this opportunity separately write to you.

Bombay Castle
3rd March 1805

I have &ca.
Signed/J. Duncan

The following letter was also written to the Commander of the Hon'ble Company's Cruiser *Queen*:[60]

To
Lieutenant Daniel Ross,
Commander of the Hon'ble Company's Crusier Queen.

Sir,
   1st. Having received on board the dispatches intended to be forwarded to the

Gulf of Persia by the Hon'ble Company's Cruiser Queen, the Governor in Council is pleased to direct that you enter on your voyage, observing the following instructions for your guidance . . .

3rd. Captain Seton with his servants and baggages will embark on the Queen for Muscat, whence you are, under his orders, as Resident at that place, to prosecute your voyage into the Persian Gulf. Receiving also in charge (in addition to those from Government and from the Superintendent of the Marine) such despatches as he may commit to your care for the commander of the Mornington, the acting Resident at Bushire and Resident at Bussore.

4th. In case of being attacked and in danger of being captured you must destroy the packets committed to your care, but not till the last extremity; and as independently of the chance of falling in with European enemies, you may be exposed to the attacks of the pirates who now infest the Gulf of Persia, the greatest caution and vigilance become necesary for the security of the vessel and dispatches under your charge, you are accordingly not only to abstain from aggression, but to avoid putting yourself in way of interruption by any of them; at the same time, that if attacked, you will use your utmost endeavour for the annoyance of the enemy.

5th. When you shall have delivered the dispatches as above pointed out, and received the orders of the Resident at Bussora, for your return, you will do so, accordingly, standing already apprised through the communication of the Superintendent of the Marine under whose instructions you will have made the necessary preparations for that purpose, and there is a likelihood of your being employed under the orders of the Resident at Muscat in measures against the pirates in the Gulf of Persia, as to which Captain Seton will determine, after he shall have heard by the Queen from the officers in charge of the Residencies of Bussora and Bushire. Should you be thus employed, the Governor in Council relies on receiving from Captain Seton a favourable report of your exertions in the execution of the orders which he may have occasion to issue to you, understanding, as indeed the Superintendent will have already informed you, that you are to remain in the Gulf of Persia as long as that officer may desire, the strength of the Queen having in this view, been materially augmented by the addition of a detachment of European Artillery men.

Bombay Castle   I am & ca.
3rd March 1805   Signed/J. Duncan

Duncan's instructions to Seton were clear, logical and forceful. Seton's proposal to form an alliance with the Imām against the Qawāsim was accepted and he was empowered to put it into effect. It is not clear why the Imām chose to chastise the Qawāsim, although it is clear why the Company chose to assist him in this task. Obviously the Governor in Bombay believed that the Company and Oman had common interests that should be supported by the Company's gunboats. Seton was clearly instructed to consult with Manesty in Baṣra and Bruce in Bushire before taking any action. Apparently Bombay expected its agents to work together for the good of the Company, but such optimism was absolutely misplaced, especially in the case of Manesty whom the governors in Bombay knew they could not control. As it turned out, Seton, confident of Duncan's support, went far beyond his instructions and certainly did not bother to consult his colleagues, as we shall presently explain. But one thing we cannot explain is a curious mistake in Duncan's letter to Lieutenant Charles Gilmour, Captain of the *Mornington*. It speaks very clearly and without any doubt about the plunder of the *Zepher*, and not the *Shannon* or the *Trimmer* in this context. The governor in Bombay could not possibly have confused the *Trimmer* or the *Shannon* with the *Zepher*. This kind of mistake in such an important letter leaves us in real doubt as to the accuracy of the information exchanged between the higher authorities of the Company and their numerous agents. If they did not know whether it was the *Trimmer* or the *Zepher* that was involved, how could they be certain whether any ship had really been plundered?

Captain Seton arrived at Muscat on the *Queen* in May 1805 and on 6 June we find him on the *Mornington*, accompanying Sayyid Badr in an attack on Bander 'Abbās which was then in the hands of Mullā Ḥussain, the leader of the Banū Maʿīn. It was a strange move on the part of the Imām and Seton who was suppoed to 'chastise the Qawāsim' to turn around and attack Bander 'Abbās, and all of a sudden, to justify this attack, we are told that Mullā Ḥussain was an ally of the Qawāsim.[61] Even if this was true, and there is no evidence whatever that it was, it shows that Seton had no intention of obeying his instructions. It should be noted that these instructions warned him against any involvement against the Persians and the Turks. Furthermore, the lack of full consultation with Manesty and Bruce brought upon his head the wrath of both, in addition to that of the Persian authorities who considered Bander 'Abbās to be part of their own domains.

On 4 May 1805 David Seton wrote the following letter to William Bruce:[62]

Mr Wm. Bruce
Acting Resident, Bushire

Sir,
I have pleasure to apprise you of my return to this Residency.

I am directed by Government to receive your information in how far acting hostilely to the pirates in the Gulph would be agreeable to the Court of Persia, and whether I am to consider in that light, their tributaries, the Bani Main and the Shaiks of Lingua and Chinas who were very active in plundering the Shannon and Trimmer.

The Queen will call for your answer, on her return from Bussora and by which time you have been able to . . . from Shiraz.

Muscat   I am Sir & ca.
4th May 1805   Signed/David Seton
                                       Resident

This letter was about the only move Seton performed in accordance with his instructions, for he did not wait to receive an answer from Bruce. This answer was written in Bushire on 30 June 1805:

To
Captain David Seton
Resident of Muscat

Sir,
    I have the honor to acknowledge the receipt of your letter dated 4th May and which reached me on the 20th instant pr. the Queen. On the same day I waited on His Excellency the Persian Ambassador and enquired of him whether the Beni Main, the Shaiks of Linga and Shinas were under the protection of the Persian government, and whether our acting hostilely against them would be agreeable to the latter. He at that time answered they were subjects of Persia, but this allegiance was very precarious in general, and entirely depended on the state the country was in at the time, and he did not suppose there would be any objection to our prosecuting them, if they had acted in any manner deserving of it.
    In your application to me you mention that I shall have time enough the return of the Queen, to get answer to any application I might make to Shiraz, of the propriety of our acting hostilely against the above mentioned tribes I should agreeable to your wish have made an application on the subject to the Shiraz Government but being too well acquainted from experience of the dilatoriness of the Persians in answering any application on matters relating to the redress of grievance on our part (for instance the unfortunate Nackheloo business) and knowing that it must be referred to Court before the Shiraz Govt. would presume to give an answer and which would occupy more . . . month at least 3 or 4, I thought it advisable not to do it, but merely to know the opinion of the Persian Ambassador on the subject, which I before mentioned, but I have to observe to you that his opinion related to these tribes inhabiting the Islands and not any part of the main. It has since turned out very fortunate that I did not make an application to Shiraz on the subject, for yesterday evening His Excellency Mohummed Nibee Khan sent to me, wishing to speak with me. I of course went, and was not a little astonished after having received your advices of the 4th ultimo, when he read me a letter from Cheragh Alli Khan and a Firmaun from the Prince, mentioning that official accounts had been received from the southern ports and from Mulla Hussain Mainie, that Seyyud Budder with a fleet accompanied by you in a ship of war, had attacked Gombaroon and reduced the town and fort, and that Sayyed Budder had taken the latter, which he could have been able to effect without the assistance you afforded him; the letter and firmaun also mentioned that this was very strong conduct on our part, to act in such a hostile manner towards them, while such a good understanding existed between the two nations and to enquire of the Resident here how such a circumstance would take place and

for what reason, we should act in such a manner while they were exerting themselves to give us every satisfaction for the plunder and ill treatment of British subjects at Nackheloo. I answered the Khawn that the accounts sent to Shiraz must certainly be false, for that you would never cooperate with Seyyud Budder in hostile measures against any of the subjects belonging to His Majesty the king of Persia, that so far from it, you had made an application to me to know if some particular tribes were under the protection of the Persian Government or not, and purpose to avoid giving the least shadow of offence but that I should take the opportunity of advising you on the subject, and that I had no doubt but that the answers would prove the accounts forwarded to Shiraz to be false.

As the different tribes mentioned in your letter are under the protection of the Persian Govt. and as no regular complaint has as yet been made to them, for the restitution of British property and the redress of grievance on our part, which whenever done and denied us, I should then think it proper in us to act in such a manner as to enforce it, but not till then, unless we saw them in the very act of piracy.

I have to request your answer as soon as possible by the return of this boat, which I have taken up for the express purpose of giving you this information, and to acquaint you that I do not think it advisable in you to act in an offensive manner against any of the ports or islands on this side of the Gulph as it may interrupt the harmony now existing between the two nations, and even go so far as to stop the Embassy now on foot, from proceeding to Calcutta unless it is against Nackheloo and Busheab, and then unless it is at the particular request of Shaik Nasser, in which case should any blame arise it will fall on him and not on us.

I now enclose you a Persian letter to your address received here by the endeavour from Muscat.

Bushire	and I have the honor to be & ca.
30th June 1805	Signed/Wm. Bruce
pr. Boat	

True copy
Wm. Bruce

This letter was followed immediately by the comments of the Government of Bombay, which show how they viewed Seton's actions:[63]

Ordered that copies of the above papers be sent to the Resident at Muskat accompanied by an expression of our concern that he should have given the umbrage he appears to have done to the Persian Government in taking any part in the recovery of Gammbroon for the Muscat Government; considering that his instructions so fully cautioned him against every occasion of offence towards the Sovereigns of either Persia or Turkey.

Ordered that the acting Resident at Bushire be advised of the preceeding intimation to Captain Seton and instructed to represent thro' the ambassador (if still at Bushire) or otherwise to the Government at Shiraz in the event of any dissatisfaction still remaining in their minds on this account, that considering how clearly Captain Seton was in his instructions cautioned against any act that might prove in the least degree offensive the Persian Government (of which his application to Mr Bruce respecting particular classes of the piratical depredators in the Gulph is in proof) should he have been led to afford any assistance to Syed Bedar in the recovery of Grombroone it must have been in the idea and belief that instead of counter-acting he would thereby be promoting the views of the State of Persia, in restoring a place to the Muscat Government which it is understood to have long held in farm from that of Persia — and of which he must have been made to understand that the piratical powers in the Gulph had forcibly taken possession contrary to the intentions of His Majesty the King of Persia in the course of the confusion into which that quarter was involved immediately after the death of the late Syed Sultan of Muscat or otherwise, it could never have entered into Captn. Seton's mind to adopt any step in the most remote degree obnoxious or disagreeable to the Persian Government with whom he so well knows that it is so much the object of His Excellency the Most Noble the Governor General to cultivate the most perfect harmony.

Ordered that copy of the proceeding papers and of the intimation thereon be sent to Bengal.

Realising his blunder, Seton hastened to offer his apologies to Bruce.[64]

To
Mr William Bruce
Acting Resident at Bushire

Sir,
I have been favoured with yours of the 8th instant and duplicate of the 30th ultimo, the original is not yet arrived.

I am extremely sorry the court of Shiraz was allowed to receive the first accounts of my being employed against the Joasimee pirates from our enemies and you may assure the ambassador that the English ship did not fire a gun as Hadge Salmmon who was present will inform them, and how much I respected the subjects of the King of Persia, altho' they were harbouring notorious pirates who had plundered our vessel.

Bunder Abassee by a Firmaun was granted the Emaum of Muscat and they paid a tribute on the death of Seyud Sultan, it was given by the Vali in charge of Mulla Hussane Mainie to redeliver to the successor of Seyud Sultaun, and on Seyud Buder going to demand it they fired on him. Our vessel was present but did not fire. I lent some of our people to the Arab vessels and the Keladar making this a pretence for giving up his charge surrendered and told Mulla Hussane that should the English vessels open their fire on him he would not have a place to hide his wife in. Under this impression he wrote to Shiraz, but finding afterwards we would not fire he came on board ship to me, and told what he had done and warned me to prepare myself for complaint from court. I do not know whether he will write to rectify his mistake but your informing Mohummed Neby of the circumstance will be sufficient.

It is to be regretted you did not communicate my being in that quarter to the court of Persia. In every point of view they ought to have know it, I was serving and protecting their subjects; more than ten of their vessels were convoyed by the Arab fleet and by us in safety.

You appear ignorant of the connection between the Joasimee and Mainee and that Shaik Gaddif of Lingha and Shinas is the person who plundered the Shannon and also that the tribes on the island and the main are the same that this very Shaik was with forty boats and a thousand men at Kishmee where respect for His Majesty of Persia prevented our burning his fleet and simply shut him up till he promised to send back the Trimmer and refrain from piracy in future.

Muscat.   I am sir
1st August 1805   & ca. & ca. & ca.
                                                   Signed/David Seton
                                                              Resident

After receiving Seton's apology and explanation, Bruce wrote the following letter to the Court of Shīrāz:[65]

Translation of a letter from Mr William Bruce acting Resident at Bushire to Cheragh Alli Khawn, Minister to the Prince of Shīrāz dated 28th August 1805.

After Compliments,

I have the honor to acknowledge the receipt of your favour and which was delivered to me by the very respectable Aga Ali on the 23rd instant at a most propitious moment. At the very instant that I received it a packet was on the point of dispatch which afforded me an opportunity of sending the letter to Mr Manesty and I have every reason to suppose it will reach him safe and he will be highly gratified to receive an answer so soon.

I have the honor to acquaint you that on the 30th June His Excellency Mohummod Nebee Khawn informed me of Captain Seton the British Resident at Muscat having taken a very active part with Sayud Buder in the reduction of Bunder Abassee and enquired of me the reason for such strange conduct in use whilst such amicable terms existed between the two mighty powers and did not he, Captain Seton, know that Bunder Abassee was one of the principal sea ports of His Majesty the King of Persia. My reply your Excellency, has been informed of by the Khawn. I instantly dispatched an express boat to Captain Seton informing him of the circumstances and demanding his reasons for so doing. I was yesterday favoured with a reply from that gentleman and as I had before acquainted the Ambassador that I was confident a false account of the affair had been transmitted to Shiraz, it has now proved so for on Captain Seton and Seyud Buder arrival at Bunder Abassee the latter on going on shore was fired at by Mulla Hussun. The Keladar then sent to him telling him he had better come to some terms for if the English ship should fire on the place, he would not have a place to retreat to. Under this impression he wrote to Shiraz as observed before, but after finding that Captain Seton did not fire he went on board the English ship to pay him a visit and told of his having written and to prepare himself for a complaint from that quarter. This is the real part of the case. So far from Captain Seton's acting in any kind of hostile manner that he conveyed upwards of 10 sail of different kind in safety belonging to Persian ports, has respect for His Majesty the King of Persia, was so quiet that he refrained from burning a fleet of 40 sail of boats belonging to the Joasimee Arabs and commanded by Sultan Eben Ben Sugger the very person who took the Trimmer and Shannon British vessels and which were laying in the ports of Kishme where they might all have been destroyed without the least trouble on our part and you may rely on it that Captain Seton will not act in any manner contrary to the strict rules of friendship.

Shaik Gudeef the Governor of Lingua and Shinas was very active in the plunder of the Shannon British vessel and owing to his being under the protection of His Majesty the King of Persia, was the only reason of his not meeting with the punishment which he so richly merited.

I have now to inform your Excellency that the ships of war are ordered to cruise between this port and Muscat for the protection of British vessels and to act against the pirates and as it is impossible for the commanders of these vessels to distinguish the different tribes that inhabit the shores of the Gulf from each other, I have to request you will issue the necessary order to the different sea ports under the control of Persia for them not to go too near any ship or vessels they may see but merely to pursue their voyage for if they pretend to make towards any of the ships they will certainly be fired into. I have further to request (as it will in future prevent any misunderstanding taking place) that you will favour me with the names of the different ports on this side of the Gulf, as well as islands and the name of the various tribes which claim the protection of His Majesty the King of Persia, that I may communicate the same to the commander of the ships of war as also to Captain Seton at Muscat and have still further to request that orders may be issued to Mulla Hussan to afford us every assistance against the Joasmee if we should require it as also to the Emaum of Muscat as Vali of Bunder Abassee and Minab.

Should Shaik Nasser find his fire insufficient for reducing the refractory Shaik of Neckhiloo if he will only make it known to me I will direct one of the cruisers to assist him every way he should require.

I shall always be proved to be favoured with your commands and to have an account of your health and have to request an answer to this as soon as possible.

True Copy
Signed/Wm. Bruce

I have the honor to be,
& ca. & ca. & ca
Signed/Wm. Bruce

In this correspondence there are some contradictions that are relevant here with regard to who was responsible for the incident of the *Shannon* and the *Trimmer*. We may recall the uncertainty involved in the statements of the captains of the two brigs and the equivocation of Manesty. Now, it seems David Seton had a different point of view, since he wrote to Bruce as soon as he arrived at Muscat, 'the Bani Main and the Shaiks of Lingua and Chinas who were very active in plundering the Shannon and Trimmer'. Almost two months later he wrote to Bruce again, 'that Shaik Gaddif of Lingha and Shinas is the person who plundered the Shannon . . . this very Shaik was with forty boats and a thousand men at Kishmee where respect for his Majesty of Persia prevented our burning his fleet and simply shut him up till he promised to send back the Trimmer and refrain from piracy in future'. Subsequently Bruce wrote to the Court in Shirāz that Seton's respect for the King of Persia was such that he refrained from 'burning a fleet of 40 sail of boats belonging to the Joasimee Arabs and commanded by Sultan Eben Ben Sugger the very person who took the Trimmer and Shannon British vessels and which were laying in the ports of Kishme'. Bruce then added for good measure that 'Shaik Gudeef the Governor of Lingua and Shinas was very active in the plunder of the Shannon'. We shall return to the question of who was present at Qishm, but meanwhile it is now evident that although it is possible that Shaikh Qadīb of Linga could have been involved in the *Trimmer/Shannon* incident, Shaikh Sulṭān b. Ṣaqr and the Qawāsim of the Arab coast were in no way involved.

We must now turn once more to the military adventures of Sayyid Badr and David Seton in the summer of 1805. They had an easy victory, for in less than a week, and with practically no resistance, they captured Bander 'Abbās. On 15 June they sailed to Qishm hoping for another easy victory, but Mullā Ḥussain was there ready to do battle. As Sayyed Badr was unwilling to risk his soldiers on shore, the Omani and British gun-boats satisfied themsleves with blockading Qishm. We are told that on 5 July a Qawāsim fleet of 30 small ships with one thousand men on board reached Qishm. The Omani fleet, with the help of the *Mornington*, made a feeble attempt to block the fleet they supposed to have come to the rescue of Qishm. However, the Omanis soon lost heart, made a 60-day truce and returned to Muscat.[66] The *Mornington* naturally followed suit. But the question now is: were the Qawāsim involved at Qishm? Once more Shaikh Qadīb of Linga was the Qāsimī leader who was most likely to be involved, yet the attempt was again made to implicate Shaikh Sulṭān b. Ṣaqr almost in the same breath as the accusation in respect of the *Trimmer* incident. It is instructive to note that this certainty on the part of Bruce about the identity of the Qawāsim involved came at the same time that he was cautioning the Persians to instruct their boats to keep away from British ships in the Gulf which might fire on them because it was impossible for British commanders 'to distinguish the different tribes that inhabit the shores of the Gulf from each other'.

However, the fact remains that the Company's attempt to control the Gulf by using British gun-boats on their own or in alliance with the Omanis proved unsuccessful. Thirty small ships mustered by the Qawāsim were enough to force Sayyid Badr and David Seton to think again on how to proceed with their plans.

Sayyed Badr was preoccupied with his internal problems resulting from the struggle between the various members of his family and the pressure posed by the Saudis, and he therefore left David Seton to act on his behalf. The latter, now wary of getting involved in new adventures that might involve him in disputes with the Persians or the Saudis, sought the way of negotiation as the better part of valour. Although he did not particularly trust Mullā Ḥussain of Qishm 'on account of his connection with the Joasmee', this very connection could be used to provide a face-saving way to open up negotiations for a temporary *modus vivendi* with the Qawāsim. For his part, Mullā Ḥussain, whose sole interest was in peaceful trading, was only anxious to restore amicable relations between all the parties concerned. And he knew very well that the Qawāsim had no desire to prolong hostilities and every interest in restoring peaceful conditions that would allow them to trade, particularly with the Indian ports under British control. Apparently Seton asked Mullā Ḥussain to use his good offices to restore the *Trimmer* and the goods that were taken from it and from the *Shannon*. Mullā Ḥussain, knew perfectly well that these goods, if they could ever be traced, must by now have been in the hands of many different parties. As he had neither sufficient power nor prestige, he perceived that Shaikh Sulṭān b. Ṣaqr, the ostensible chief of all the Qawāsim, was the only person who could use his influence to attempt the almost impossible task of recovering these goods and the *Trimmer* itself. In the event, it was not possible to recover any of the goods but the *Trimmer* was somehow brought to Rās al-Khaimah. At this point a new incident occurred that complicated the situation further.

On 9 October 1805 Seton wrote to Thomas Skinner commanding all the Honourable Company's vessels in the Gulf of Persia informing him:[67]

> the Soree fleet now ready to sail for Bussorah being of the same tribe as the Joasmee will be ordered to accompany you and you will see them as far as the island of Kais, and prevent their going to Rasul Khimah or Lingua, or the boats of these places joining them and proceeding in company to Bussorah where in that case they will receive a supply of dates which would otherwise be refused them.
>
> As it is the intention of Sayud Beder to send here after a considerable fleet to Bunder Abbass I will most probably accompany it and it will be employed in blockading the Persian side whilst you are employed on the Arab coast. I will send you the earliest information of this event should it take place but affairs are so unsettled here it may not be in Seyud Beder's power to spare an armament.
>
> The Shaik of Kishem will first send the greatest friendship, but on account of his connection with the Joasmee it will not be safe to trust him and his being a subject of Persia will prevent your acting hostility (sic) towards him without his vessels are in company with the Joassmees.

In other words, Seton was ordering a blockade of the Qawāsim ports on both sides of the Gulf while Mullā Ḥussain was negotiating on his behalf and successfully so. The following correspondence speaks for itself:[68]

Bombay Castle: 1 November 1805
Recorded the following letter from the Resident at Muscat under date the 16th
October with four enclosures.

Honble Sir,

I have the honor to communicate the arrival of the Trimmer at this place
with an agent from Moolla Hussen who has been appointed by the Joassem
to negotiate a peace for them. Enclosed are translates of a letter from Moolla
Hussen to me and one from the Joassemee to him.

As I have already communicated the intention of the Joassim to send the
Trimmer in my letter by the Olive Branch Captain Shepherd, I am in hourly
expectation of the orders of Government on that head.

The Mornington and Timute sailed the 10th with the following instructions
No. 3 for Captain Skinner's guidance in case of his proceeding to hostilities,
No. 4 to suspend hostilities until further information.

My reason for refraining from hostilities is the impossibility of prosecuting
them with vigour or effect without offending the Persians or Wahabee.

Muscat   I have the honor to be & ca.
16 Oct. 1805.   Signed/David Seton
                                                          Resident

Translate of a letter from Moolla Hossane Shaikh of Kishm to Captain Seton
received the 11th October 1805.

When the Mornington returned from Abushire, the Trimmer had not been
brought from Julfar as I then wrote to you, but through God's blessings after
a world of trouble this has been at last accomplished, well knowing that the
Honorable Company would not value this, nor a hundred such vessels further
than it would show the submission of the Joasim to them and it will also show
my friendship towards the Honble Company by the trouble I have taken in
procuring her return.

I now send her in charge of Khadjee Aly the son of Mehomed Sherreef
and hope in God she will arrive in safety, I have also entrusted him with some
instructions which he will communicate in private and you will believe as from
myself.

Shaikh Sultan Ben Suggur Joassim has wrote me in Arabee, which I now
send for your perusal and know that whilst I live I shall never fail in any thing
I can perform for the service of the Honorable Company.

In regard to the sulphur promised I have sent two hundred candies on board
two botellas, which I hope will arrive safe and you will receive, and should
you have any further commands for me, don't stand on ceremony but write
me freely.

Memorandum: Enclosed in the above: although I am ashamed to send a
thing so unworthy of your acceptance, yet I hope you will accept as a mark
of my friendship of a candy of ammansar sulphur, now forwarded.

No. 3 by Captain Seton — the value of this, at Muscat is one hundred Dollars.

A true translate
Signed/David Seton

Translate of an Arabic letter from Sultan Bin Seggur Shaikh of the Joasmee, to Mulla Hussan Shaikh of Kishem — enclosed in No. 1.

From the servant of God (Mottazim Billa, Mutiwakkil Aaly) Sultan Ben Suggur Ben Rashed to his dear friend and beloved father Mulla Hussun Ben Mahomed al-Mansoor to whom be the peace, and mercy and blessing of God exaltation and a long life in this world and may he afford content in the next — — — at Rasul Khimeh where all arrived and happy and no news but good news as the bearer of this will have the honor to inform you.

I have understood your letter regarding the English ship, which I now send you and leave you, to act as you think best for both parties.

When you return the vessel procure an agreement that we may frequent India as before and study to remove all remembrance of what is past as it is my wish that matters should not only be as formerly but that they should be on a better footing and as I am sincere without the least reserve inwardly or outwardly, take care that no distrust in their part may remain after the settling of this business.

I am now setting out for Sharega to collect for Meer Sohood, but will return in a few days.

A true translate
Signed/David Seton
Resident

Thomas Skinner Esqre.
Commanding all the Honorable Co. vessels in the Gulph of Persia.

Sir,

The instructions you received in Bombay will have apprized you of the intentions of Government in employing the three vessels in the Gulf, viz. the protection of the trade from European privateers and Joassim pirates in regard to these last I am direct to point out to you, where you are to act.

Sir, the country of the Joassim begins eastward at Cussib opposite Anjam and extends westward to Charak including both places.

The harbours in this space are Cussib Rumz Rasul Khimah called by the Persian Gulphar, and to these bounds will your operations be confined.

The tribe eastward of the Joassim are named Shahee and will readily assist you with what their country affords, the tribe to the westward are the Bini Hiaza who are notorious pirates but as they have never offered any violence to our vessels you will refrain from hostilities towards them, without their vessels are aiding and assisting to the Joassims.

There are two ports on the Persian main called Lingu and Shinass laying behind the shoal of Bassedeo, belonging to the Joassims who furnish boats and men for their piratical enterprises the same as Rasul Khimah, yet as these places are within the dominions of the King of Persia no attack on their territories can be made until permission be obtained but this forbearance will by no means extend to their vessels which you will destroy wherever you meet them . . .

The shoal water on the entrance of the harbours of the Joassims preventing the vessels doing them much mischief there is a necessity for blockading them, and cutting off their supplies, in views to this.

The Sorie fleet now ready to sail for Bussorah being of the same tribe as the Joasmee will be ordered to accompany you and you will see them as far as the island of Kais, and prevent their going to Rasul Khimah or Lingua, or the boats of these places joining them and proceeding in company to Bussorah where in that case they will receive a supply of dates which would otherwise be refused them.

As it is the intention of Seyud Beder to send hereafter a considerable fleet to Bunder Abbas I will most probably accompany it and it will be employed in blockading the Persian side whilst you are employed on the Arab coast I will send you the earliest information of this event should it take place, but affairs are so unsettled here it may not be in Seyud Beder's power to spare an armament.

The Shaik of Kishem will first send the greatest friendship, but on account of his connection with the Joasmee it will not be safe to trust him and his being a subject of Persia will prevent your acting hostility (sic) towards him without his vessels are in company with the Joassmees.

Muscat	A true copy
9th Oct. 1805	Signed/David Seton
	Resident

Thomas Skinner Esqre.
Commanding the vessels & ca. & ca.
Persian Gulf.

Sir,

I have this moment received certain accounts of the Trimmer being on this coast with agents from the Joassim for a peace.

In this case you will proceed with the Sorie fleet agreeable to your first orders but refraining from all hostilities towards the Joassim but what you may judge necessary for the protection of your convoy, until you hear further from me.

If you proceed as high as Busheab with the fleet and afterwards return to the island of Tunb I shall know where to send an express to you with the result of our negotiations.

Muscat	Signed/David Seton
10th Oct. 1805	Resident

True copy

In acknowledging the receipt of the letter of the 16th of October the Secretary is to advise Captain Seton that altho we have not yet received the expected instruction from the Supreme Government for which he was informed that we had applied on the 4th of September last he is nevertheless now instructed in compliance with the expectation he has expressed of being speedily furnished with some rule for his guidance not to make peace with the Juwasim or any of the other piratical tribes in the Gulph until they shall as preliminary have made as ample restitution of or indemnification for the plunder committed respectively any or all of them on the vessels lawfully navigating under the British flag and Company's protection as he may be satisfied to be equal to their available means and accompanied likewise by adequate security against their recurrence to such practices in time to come, on which conditions he is authorized to restore any or all of them to a state of amity with the British power in India and to a consequent capacity of frequenting the British ports in India on their fair mercantile pursuits and until the parties in question can be brought to the reasonable and moderate terms thus required of them the war must needs be continued with them, Captain Seton being always careful to cause it to be conducted with an especial attention to avoid cause of umbrage or offence to the friendly powers in the same quarter, as has been originally enjoined to him in his first instructions and repeated in those above referred to under date the 4th of September last.

Ordered that the Supreme Government be advised of these instructions issued to Captain Seton in the interim of our being favoured with their own commands on a subject which as relating to the general polity of the British nation in the east falls we conceive more within their department than ours to decide upon, at the same time that from the urgency of the circumstances we have issued such intermediate directions as has appeared to us to be most expedient and applicable to the nature of the case.

The following letter is in consequence written to the Most Honorable the Governor General.

To
His Excellency
The Most Honble Charles Marquis Cornwallis KG.
Governor General & ca. & ca.

My Lord,

We have the honor to transmit copy of a letter from the Resident at Muscat dated the 16th ultimo respecting the pirates in the Gulph of Persia and to communicate the consequent instructions issued to Captain Seton under this date in the interim of our being favoured with the commands of the Supreme Govt. on a subject which as relating to the general polity of the British nation in the East Indies falls, we conceive, more within the Department of the Presidency of Fort William than that of Bombay to decide on at the same time that from the urgency of the circumstances we have issued such immediate instructions as has appeared to us to be most expedient and applicable to the nature of the case.

B.C.   We have the honor to be
1st November 1805   & ca. & ca. & ca.
                                                           Signed/J. Duncan

Meanwhile the Sūrī fleet, which was in fact an Omani fleet opposed to Sayyid Badr, took refuge in Rās al-Khaimah while on its way from Basra.[69] The matter was further complicated by the fact that Seton claimed that in the Sūrī fleet there were 'large sums of British property'.[70] While the Sūrī fleet was in Rās al-Khaimah 'the Bussorah merchants' property was detained till they saw how that govt. acted towards their (Qawāsim's) fleet then in the river at Bussorah and which report said was detained there'.[71]

The month of November 1805 was taken up by negotiations in which Mullā Hussain was the central figure making the contacts between all the parties concerned. Sultān b. Saqr was willing to make peace with the Company but rather reluctant to include Sayyid Badr. Seton was adamant on the necessity of peace between the Qawāsim and the Omanis, but he was surprisingly demanding of Mullā Hussain that he should ally himself completely with Sayyid Badr. His terms were recorded in a letter to Bombay written on 6 November 1805:[72]

Honble Sir,
    I had the honor to write on the arrival of an agent from Moolla Hussain.
    He returned to Kishem the 20th and by him I wrote as pr. enclosed translation.
    The paper mentioned in the translate as referring to Seyud Beder's peace with Mulla Hussain contained the following articles.
1. That Mulla Hussain should give monthly 2,500 maunds of Sulpher, free of charge.
2. Seyud Beder should give up all claim to the Bunder of Luft on Kishem for ever.
3. Allow Mulla Hussain's goods to pass at 4 pr cent at all his ports.
4. In case of war with the Joassim Mulla Hussain should not supply them with grain, dates or stores of any kinds.
5. The subjects of either sde who had withdrawn during the war, should be allowed to remain unmolested, where they chose, and withdraw whatever property they had left behind.
6. Mulla Hussain should not assist Seyud Ceiss.
    On these conditions Seyud Beder agreed to make peace with Mulla Hussain who in a verbal message, left me to settle what I pleased between them, so I have little doubt but it will be accepted.

Mullā Hussain was not slow to send the free sulphur demanded by Seton, along with the hulk of the *Trimmer* that he had persuaded Sultān b. Saqr to retrieve and send to him in order to proceed successfully with the negotiations.

The following is a translation of a letter from Mullā Ḥussain to Captain Seton received 15 November 1805 with three boats of sulphur:[73]

What you say regarding the brigg being empty of everything is true also of what passed when we were together.

I had much trouble to get this vessel empty as she was from the Joassim nor did I consider her intrinsic value but my object was to demonstrate the submission of these people to the English, you know them in regard to property whatever falls into their hands is spent immediately.

When I received the vessel I became bound for her value and hoped you would forward her to Government and settle with the Joassim a truce; writing them a friendly and kind letter to dissipate their doubts and fears and that ill minded persons might have no opportunity of stirring up discord, but if Government are not satisfied with this vessel I expect she will be returned by Hussain Ibrahim to prevent my meeting any loss being security for her to the Joassim, should she be returned, let Hadjee Hussain have a few clashes to bring her to Kishm, from that to Rasul Khimeh, I can manage.

You need not doubt my sending the sulphur for the Honoble Company, Hadjee Hussaine Ibrahim now carries fourteen thousand Muscat maunds in three batilles, the remainder will follow soon.

A true translate
Signed/David Seton

Seton answered Mullā Ḥussain with the following letter:[74]

Translate of a letter from Captain David Seton to Mulla Hussan of Kishem dated 20th October 1805.

I have received your letter by Mahomed Sherrief, and also his verbal message, purporting your arrival at Sohar and desire of effecting a peace with Seyud Beder.

The two botilles of sulphur arrived and Mahomed Sherrief will deliver you the account value of it.

The brig returned from the Joassim also arrived, you have had much trouble in this business.

I before informed you in Kishem that it was necessary the Joassim should send the vessel in 25 days, that no further expense might be incurred by the Honble Company, but they have allowed much time to elapse, and vessels at a considerable expense to arrive from Bombay, and despairing of the return of the vessel or of peace with them, I have entered into an agreement with Seyud Beder that our peace and war should be one, if they now wish war, we are ready, for peace we are also willing but how can I accept an empty vessel stripped of everything and Government submit to two losses, the value of the cargo 25,000 dollars and the expenses of the ships, I have therefore anchored the vessel as yours in Muscat till I have an answer, and you will have the goodness to inform the Joassim that if they will return the property and include Seyed Beder in the peace, it will be yet granted them and we do nothing till their answer comes.

I am also in want of five hundred candies of sulpher at the same price as the former, and will be answerable that what excess there may be, shall be taken care of, but what you send me must be picked and cleaned.

In a separate Arabic paper are the conditions Seyud Beder offers, for a peace. In addition it is expected you will return the goods freighted at Bussorah on your vessels by the inhabitants of Muscat last year.

A true translation
Signed/David Seton

Meanwhile a report was circulated that the Qawāsim had attacked some boats belonging to Bombay and also carrying some Omani goods off the coast of Makrān. Seton wrote to Mullā Ḥussain about this incident:[75]

Draft of a letter to Moolla Hussane Shaikh of Kishem, dated 1st November 1805.

I wrote by Mahomed Sherreef your agent respecting the brimestone and the peace with the Joassim. I then informed you that the peace must be equally with Muscat and the English, and on the strength of this our vessels refrained from hostilities.

I have the other day learned that the Joasmee have taken a number of vessels on the coast of Muckran loaded with the property of the Bombay merchants and also of Muscat and have sent this by the commodore of the vessels, supposing the Joasmee had sailed before they knew of the answer of Mahomed Sherreef and that they will return the vessels, the men and property in failure of which he must proceed to hostilities, you will therefore give him an answer as soon as possible that the Joasmee will refrain from all hostilities with Muscat and return the property they have taken.

A true copy
Signed/David Seton
Resident

At the same time Seton wrote to Captain Skinner the Commander of the Company gun-boats in the Gulf:[76]

To
Thomas Skinner Esqre
Commanding the Honble Company's Vessels & ca.
Persian Gulf.

Sir,

I have the pleasure to forward several letters to your address, on service.

A party of Joasmee, consisting of one bagla, two dows, four botellas and two bugaras have appeared on this coast and taken a nowree from Bombay and a dingey from Sind. The Honble Company's ketch the Queen, with the Cabrass ship and Abdulcuther dow, have gone from this to endeavour to retake them.

In consequence, the vessels with you had better proceed to Kishem and deliver the enclosed Persian letter to Moolla Hussane Shaikh of that place. Should he answer you the Joasmee will refrain from hostilities towards Muscat, you will also continue the truce, but if they do not comply with this I would recommend your proceeding and blockading the Joasmee agreeable to your first instructions.

A dow, with stores of every kind is daily expected here, immediately on its arrival, the Queen Captain Keys, will proceed to join you with her.

Muscat	I am
2nd November 1805	& ca. & ca.
	Signed/David Seton

A true copy
Signed/David Seton

Mullā Ḥussain wrote to Seton explaining that the Qawāsim were not involved in this attack on the Makrān coast:[77]

Translation of a letter from Mulla Hussain received by the Mornington 15th November 1805 to Captain David Seton.

I have been favoured with yours mentioning the Joassim having appeared on the coast of Muckran and carried off some of the property of the subjects of Muscat.

You are not ignorant that the Huzza, a tribe of the Beni Yas, in the time of the late Seyud Sultan were enemies of Muscat and plundered their property where they met it but the Joassim have no concern with these people, whatever they are independent and lawless you need not doubt what I write.

War exists between Seyud Badr and the Joassim and when they act contrary to agreement it is time to complain.

You have not yet settled with the Joassim, I before told you they had squandered the property and had nothing left to give except the brigg, which I have received and sent you empty, as complained of through Mahomed Shereef, the property is no object to the British Government and God knows if I had it to give I would give it myself. Everyone knows what is best for himself, but in my opinion Government ought to take the vessel as nothing more is to be got from these people and write that they may go and come as usual without dread. If this is not agreeable excuse me from being security and send back the vessel as I shall otherwise sustain a loss both in money and character.

Although the pace of the negotiation was gaining momentum, Mullā Ḥussain did not seem able to go to Muscat as he had promised Seton. The latter, anxious about the stability of the rule of Sayyid Badr, particularly in view of the constant Saudi pressure from the north, decided to go to Bander 'Abbās from where he hoped to be in closer touch with Mullā Ḥussain who could possibly bring him face to face with Sulṭān b. Ṣaqr. Seton wrote the following letter to Bombay explaining his intentions:[78]

The following letter from the Resident at Muscat with enclosures.

Honble Sir,
  I had the honor to write the 31st of December of my intention of proceeding to Bunder Abbas to endeavour to recover from the Joassim the property taken in the Shannon and Trimmer and to make peace with them.
  I have the honor to enclose an extract of my journal containing my proceedings there and also the draft of a treaty I have entered into with them.
  As I found the property could not be recovered without having recourse to hostilities and no prospect even then from their poverty of doing more than causing them a quarter comparative loss than they had caused us and they at the same time being subject either of Persia or of Wahabee, these powers would have been eventually in the dispute so that instead of settling the Gulf agreeable to the spirit of my instructions a commencement of hostilities would have caused a general warfare with the whole Wahabee coast and part of the Persian. I, therefore, judged it more advisable to make such an agreement as might be confirmed to a peace or not at the option of the Honble Board.
  On the agreement I have to observe that I have not given up the claim of this property, it being renewable in case of any future depredation nor have I implicated the Honble Company in the dispute of the Arabs, my insisting on peace with Seyud Beder being in other words adequate to their disarming and ceasing to cruise about the seas and to return to their former mercantile pursuits which is the wish of the bulk of the Joasmee tribe.
  The best proof of sincerity on their part is their behaviour since I have been in the Gulf they having in no instance attacked our vessels since their attempt on the Queen.
  From my own observation I agree in opinion with Mulla Hussun that they are a people from whom nothing is to be got.
  The Sorie fleet on their return from Bussorah in defiance of Seyud Beder's order went to Rasul Khimeh.

I should have prevented this had not Seyud Beder delayed the vessels at Sor and I reached Kishem a day too late. The Joasmee seized of this fleet 13 dows the property of the Jenebee and plundered them, but to what amount is not yet known, and to secure the return of this property a fleet of 32 sail of the Lingua Joassim has been stopped as the Shaikh of Resul Khimeh reports by the Mussulleem at Bussorah.

Muscat   I have the honor to be & ca.
4th March 1806   Signed/David Seton
                                                          Resident

Seton, newly converted to peace with the Qawāsim, was now pointing out their 'sincerity' and stating unequivocally that they had never attacked 'our vessels' since he had been in the Gulf. He started his journey on 31 December 1805 and entered all the details in his diaries:[79]

31st. Embarked on the Mornington bound to Kishem, touching at Burka.
1806
Jany. 1st. Sailed.
2. Arrived at Burka.
3. Landed and saw the Emam. Received from him letters for Sultan ben Suggur, Saleh ben Mahomed, Mullah Hussein and Mahomed ben Gaber, all to the same effect: that it was his intention to have sent Seyud ben Majit to treat with them, but Captain Seton going up the Gulph, he had left the whole to him, whose request Mahomed ben Gaber was to comply with as far as regarded peace and war. Sailed from Burka. Gave a certificate for a vessel to Madrass.
6th. At sea. In sight the swaddees. A storm wind. Light and contrary.
7th. Spoke the Wasp and received the following letter from Bushire.
8th. Arrived at Kishem. Came on board Moulla Hussein's son, Mulla Mahd.
9th. Went on shore. Sultan ben Suggur had left Kishem shortly before and gone to the island of Busheab but was supposed then as Ras al Khimeh. Sent a letter on express from Moulla Hussein to him and agreed to wait at Bunder Abas his arrival at Kishem. Sailed for and anchored at Bunder Abass.
10th. Landed at Bunder Abbas and put up at the Dutch house.
11th. Recd. information the Sorie fleet had gone to Ras al Khimeh with Sultan ben Suggur. Arrived a caravan of camels from Khorassan. The tribute arrived from Minab to Khan. The brother-in-law of Baba Khan, being at the Bunder waiting to receive it, he had sent his compliments overnight wishing I shd. visit him. Agreed to attend him. Mohamed ben Gabber recd. from Moulla Hussein 20 nds of wood in derision, the villagers keeping off an acct. of the Persian troops taking from those that come to market what they want. Received a visit from all the merchants, wishing the English to frequent their ports, as formerly, also a number of the upper country merchants, who were extremely anxious to have the peace on such a foundation as they might be sure of a market or means of sending their goods in safety to some other port. Noon. Waited on the Khan, named Ayub Mohamed Mehdi; after compliments,

and being seated, he expressed his pleasure at the arrival of the vessels, as he would now have it in his power to collect the revenue from Moulla Hussein, or shift the blame from himself to me. Laughing, he said the representations made to Shiraz and the real state of matters as they came under his observation were widely different, and that he found the place a nest of thieves and wondered that we had not destroyed them. Answered it would have been done long ago had the Govt. of Shiraz not wished to preserve them. He repeated now he wanted one of two things: the tribute or Mulla Hussein, and as the ships were here, he made sure of one. The rest of the conversation: immaterial accounts of the Sorie fleet going to Ras al Khimah.

12th. Recd. from the Khan a present of a horse, and according to the Persian custom paid his people his value: 135 Dollars. Wrote Moolla regards the Sorie fleet.

13th. Recd. a visit from the Khan. The conversation of little import.

14th. The Khan's people sent to exercise in front of the fort. Arrived an agent from Kishem with letters from Moolla Hussein by Mahomed Shiraif and the Sorie fleet being there prevented his leaving his country, and he had sent his uncle, Mutter ben Rehma, with full powers. Returned the Khan's present.

15th. Wrote Moolla Hussein that I expected the Sorie fleet would be satisfied and let go content and requested he would ascertain the full powers of Mutter before I saw him. Accompanied the Khan on board the ships, properly dressed for the occasion, with flags saluted from the ports, and vessels with all their guns going. Anchoring and presented him in the name of the Captain with a watch and rifle gun. He was highly satisfied with the sight of the vessel.

16th. The Khan's people removed the first horse and put another in his place; and expressed a desire to present the Captains of the vessels with swords, expecting them on shore.

18th. Recd. letters from Kishem by a batille on trifling matters, to pass dates, etc. In the evening Mahomed Sharif arrived with letters from Mutter announcing his arrival at Kishem and from Moolla Hussein to the same effect.

19th. Recd. a message from the Khan that he understood Moolla Hussein's man had come to treat regarding peace, and that he was here on the part of the King of Persia and wanted from Moolla Hussein 2,000 Toman tribute, which he hoped for my own sake, I would not forget. As it was in my power to procure it, the fault would be with me was it not procured. Waited on the Khan and said that Moolla Hussein from his connection with the Joasmee was both the King's enemy and mine, and had not the Govt. of Shiraz interfered and protected Moolla Hussein, both he and his friends the Wahabee would have been at the mercy of the King by this time. I would however use my good offices towards procuring the payment of the tribute. He said the real state of matters, was misunderstood at Shiraz where he would like to clear them up. Answered Mutter and Moolla Hussein as per translates, and added a note on the part of the Khan to Moolla Hussein, mentioning that he well knew the friendship between us existed from his being the subject of Persia, and if he knew of that allegiance he became nothing more than a sharer in the villanies of the Joasmee, who had not yet made good the damage they had done our trade. Communicated this to the Khan, who was satisfied.

NB: The Khan is little better than the wild Arabs, supposing every one in command may do as he likes. If I decline interfering, the Shiraz Govt. will be at Mohamed Nuby as before. If I say I have no orders, he can get them from Shiraz and engage the ships in a business that will last months. Not to interfere at all is to break abruptly. By offering my good offices should they succeed, it is to the credit of the British Government. If they do not, only let him know it the day I am off. I have no orders to go to greater lengths. Goodbye.

20th. Enquiries for water: plenty to be got at Nabone, and by stopping the river any quantity might be retained throughout the year for ships.

Translate of a letter for Shaikh Mutter 19th.

I have recd. your letter announcing your arrival at Kishem. In the first place, the two vessels you took have been returned, but not the property that was on board which must be returned before friendship can be reestablished between us; and also that Lingua Shaick and all the dependencies of the Joasmee join in this peace, when their vessels will be allowed to proceed to India as before. Enclosed is a letter from Seyud Beder, who must also be included in the peace, and that his friends and enemies shall be the same to you. He wishes nothing but peace; and you will forward his letter to Ras ul Khimih, and after the arrival of the answer, should be agreeable to visit. I will proceed to Kishem and finally adjust everything with you. Enclosed is also a letter from Seyud Beder to Saleh ben Mahd, which I hope will be forwarded.

21st. Arrived a boat from Kishem with letters; from Moolla Hussein, with an answer to the Khan, professing obedience to the King in every respect and that he was in expectation of a letter from Shiraz before he paid tribute. Sent it to the Khan. Also a letter from Mutter ben Rehma as follows:

I have recd. your letter, and my first wish is peace with the Honble Company; and will subscribe to whatever promise or oath you may require; and will remain firm in it whilst we live. With regard to peace with Seyud Beder in the way you have wrote, I hope you will not interfere in the peace between the Arabs, because we are many families and chance causes many disagreements amongst us. At present it is three generations we have been at war with Muscat, and having quarrels to settle with extent to boats, blood and property; and we shall be ashamed to mingle our quarrels with the English Govt. as it is impossible that those with Seyud Beder can be settled together with theirs.

With regard to the property on board the ships, you will know, or have heard from others, the whole fell into the hands of the rabble and was lost; and I swear by the unity of God that my son Shaikh Sultan has not the means of replacing it; and were there anything remaining, he would not hesitate to return it; so that if your inclination is towards peace with the English, let us meet together and finally settle it; but if you wish to include the Arabs, send me your answer that I may return to Ras ul Khimah quickly, as Sultan

ben Suggur will not consent to treat with both at once. Let me hear from you.
PS: With regard to a truce, it will be agreed to for two or three months,
entirely at your request; but keep in mind it may be broke, as the former
one, which will bring me to shame as I have full powers in everything,
and expect hourly an answer from my son Shaikh Sultan.
NB: The whole of this is a fabrication of Mulla Hussein's to endeavour to
make the peace with Muscat without giving a share in the mines or agreeing
to grant Beder the assistance of the Joasmee aganst Mulla Hussein's friend,
Seyud Ceiss; and the inclusion of the Arabs in a peace is the request of Sultan
Ben Suggur, who retains the Sorie fleet as a security for its being granted.

This appears in the postscript which is wrote by Mutter to prevent any bad
effects resulting from the letter.

22. Wrote Mulla Hussein and Mutter as follows; and the Khan and Mahomed
and Mehady. Wrote him also that obedience was not in words, but paying
the tribute; and he would now enforce his demand by arms. In the evening
arrived Seyud ben Majid in the Gunjave. Came on shore. Requested he would
write Mutter that, if he wishes, he might come to Gunjava to see him, or to
the Bunder, as he, by order of Seyud Beder in conformity to the request of
Mahomed Salih, was come to swear in the name of Seyud Beder to what should
be agreed on by Shaikh Sultan, and myself.
NB: The agreement of Mahomed Salih was peace with Muscat. This Moolla
Hussein knew not of, as one article was forcing to give a share of the mines.
Draught of a letter to Shaikh Mutter:

I had the pleasure of hearing of your health by your last letter. With regard
to the cargoes of the vessels, whether you sold or destroyed them, you know
best; but until the property is returned, and the peace general, I cannot consent to it; as oaths and promises you know have little hold on those who
are traversing the seas for plunder and see wealth within their reach. On
this account I wish the peace general with Seyud Beder as well as with the
Honble Company. You have wrote me you wish peace with me and not
with Seyyud Beder. But know our peace is one and the same; and our war
one and the same. And with regard to your going to Ras ul Khimah, you
are at full liberty to go where you please. Only let me know when you are
determined; and in what else I can serve you.

Draught to Moolla Hussein:

I have received yours with that of Shaikh Mutter; and have sent you the
answers. Until the property of the Sorie fleet and the English ships is returned, peace cannot take place. Therefore send someone to Muscat to take
charge of the vessel you sent back. With regard to the tribute, the Khan
himself writes you. And for the Joasmees, know that if their fleets assisted
as before by yours go to sea, they will take whatever they can master. But
once they disarm, everything will be at rest. But should they again go to
sea, it will be better if your vessels should not accompany them. Otherwise
I shall be under the necessity of taking them, but this is optional. Write
me in what I can serve you.

24th. Recd. the following letters from Moolla Hussein and Shaikh Mutter.
From Shaikh Mutter:
I have recd. your letter and fully understood its contents. In what you say
that your peace and Seyud Beder is one, it is at your option. But we do
not wish peace with Seyud Beder. But for yours I am ready to take any
oath or promise that may be required that the peace shall exist as long as
the world shall last without the least breach of good faith on our part, which
cannot be the case if peace with you and Seyud Beder is made at the same
time. This is my definite answer. And I know that Shaikh Sultan's wish
is exactly the same as mine. I shall not wait his answer. May God grant
all your wishes.

From Moolla Hussum:
You will herewith receive Shaikh Mutter's letter containing his sentiments
regarding peace. And what you wrote regarding my vessels not going to
sea I have never done you any harm; and when the Sorie or other enemies
are within my reach, I shall not fail to seize them; nor shall I ever fail in
anything that I can do to serve the Honble Company. But sending a man
to Muscat for the vessel is what I cannot do. And you may recollect our
first agreement was: in case peace was not concluded, you would send her
back, and trusting to this I have engaged in the business. The return of a
vessel depends on you.
The ships went in pursuit of a strange sail.
26th. Wrote Moola Nussein as follows:
    I have recd. yours and Shaikh Mutter's letters, but, supposing him gone,
I have not wrote him by this opportunity. But let me know of his going
by Abdulla Ben aly Khan who returns tomorrow. I am sorry your trouble
should have been in vain; but these Joasmees are a strange sect. They wrote
Seyud Beder for peace; and when they find me empowered to conclude
it, they do not wish it. It ought to be ascertained from Sultan Ben Suggur
himself if this is his real wish and intention and forward his answer to me.
Let me know in what I can serve you.
27th. The ships returned. Spoke the strange sail: the Cecilia from Calcutta,
last from Muscat.
Received the following letter from Mulla Hussein:
    I have recd. yours wishing to know when Shaikh Mutter went, finding
your wishes and his did not coincide, he is gone. In respect to my trouble
on this occasion, God and his Prophet are witnesses that not a hair [NB:
his head is shaven] of my head but what labored for the advantage of that
Honble Company through my friendship for you, and sorry am I that a
change of sentiments of friendship to me should have rendered all my pains
in vain. The first moment you arrived at Kishem, I told you the peace with
Seyud Beder and the English would not be agreeable to the Joasmee; and
in respect to what you write that the Joasmee requested peace of Seyud
Beder is true; but it was on his having before requested peace of the Joassim

without including you; and he concealed from you the request that the Joassim make of him as the price of this peace. And in regard to what you write of my ascertaining from Sultan Ben Suggur himself whether this was his real intentions, my good Sir, you are a man of understanding and knowledge: how would Shaikh Mutter leave matters in uncertainty and go away without he had full powers. I shall however write as it is your request to Sultan Ben Suggur; and whatever answer he gives I shall forward. Both the Joasmee and myself wish peace with the Honble Company; and we hold our ports and harbours from the Honble Company. And whether they or theirs shall have occasion to call at them; they will find every attention as formerly shewn them, and even more than formerly. And I hope to hear constantly from you until we meet.

Sent the ships to complete their water.

28th. Wrote Mulla Hussein:

I have received yours; and in regard to what you write that you all wish peace with the English, if you really did so you would return the property you have taken from them. And in respect to the great trouble you have had to bring about peace, had you not lent your Buglas to assist the Joasmee they would never have taken the Sorie fleet in which was large sums of British property. Moreover, you promised if I should come from Muscat to Kishem, Sultan Ben Suggur would meet me there, but this has not proved the case, the whole of this is false, and you have established your credit in Bussorah, India and Persia, and whoever tells you the contrary is your servant and speaks not the truth. And in regard to my writing whilst I stay here, know that the ships will be here three days; and, if in that time you bring Sultan Ben Suggur to Kishem and return the British property, and bring us face to face, so that we can know one another's intentions, I shall then be certain you speak the truth. But if you wish to serve Seyud Ceiss, by delays, know that it will be to your own loss as everything has its price.

A gale detained the boat two days.

Feby 5th. Arrived Abdulla Ben Cassim Ben Croosh from Ras ul Khimih with the following letters, having touched at Kishem.

From Mulla Hussein,

I have been favored with yours, and agreeable to your wishes have forwarded accounts of all that had passed to Ral ul Khimih; and, as Sultan Ben Suggur could not himself come, he has sent his confidential friend, Abdulla Ben Cassim Ben Croosh as his vakeel to settle with you; and there is no doubt but it will be so one way or other; and do not think that I am averse to peace, as it is my earnest wish it may take place.

Mutter Ben Rehmih to his friend Captain Seton:

When I reached home, and informed Sultan Ben Suggur Ben Rashid of what has happened, he desired me to write you that the property of the vessels was partly destroyed in battle, partly dispersed among the Baddns, and he had not the power to send it back. And respecting peace with Seyud Beder and with you, he, Sultan Ben Suggur, has empowered our friend and brother Abdulla Ben Khasim Ben Croosh to settle between us; and he has sworn by the most high to abide by what shall be determined on by you both; and he is also at full liberty in regards the peace with Seyud Beder. And as our friends and his and our enemies and his are one and Mulla Hussein and Mahomed Ben Gaber are included in the same peace, all join in wishes and promises before God to maintain it. Let me know in what I can serve you.

From Saleh Ben Mahomed Ben Saleh Ulcoasmee, to Captain Seton.

I have heard of your arrival at the Bunder, and what passed between you and Mutter, and his return without seeing you as he would not agree to peace with my brother Seyud Beder, between whom and I for many years there has subsisted a brotherly friendship. Our correspondence has been interrupted and may it ever subsist; and I have seen that you have remained firm in your endeavour to assist him and bring matters to a happy issue. Abdulla Ben Cashem is now sent by Sultan Ben Suggur with whole full powers to settle with you; and I have wrote circumstantially to Mahd. Ben Gaber regarding these things; and what else remains will be explained by Ben Goosh. I have recd. Seyud Beder's letter you sent; and whenever matters are adjusted with us, I am preparing with Sultan Ben Suggur to proceed to assist Seyud Beder against Seyud Ceiss.

Ben Goosh having delivered his letter and a message from Seyud Sultan that he would agree to any terms of peace we chose to offer but declared an utter inability to return the cargo of the two ships, as part of the Trimmer's cargo with her boats and gun had been blown up in a dow, in an action with Shaikh Burkat of Charek, and the remainder plundered by the different vessels that were in company, as well as that of the Shannon; and he had not the means of replacing it from his own funds.

6th. Seyud Ben Majit being present on the part of Seyud Beder, claimed the situation of the Sorie fleet their property. After much conversation, peace between the Joasmees and Muscat was agreed on and sworn to: Seyud Ben Majit for Seyud Beder; and Ben Croosh for Sultan Ben Suggur: their alliance offensive and defensive.

Sultan Ben Suggur had sent a clean sheet of paper sealed, and had sworn to Ben Croosh to adhere to whatever should be wrote over it, on the part of the Honble East India Company. In consequence, drew up the following terms and dispatched Ben Croosh to have it personally sealed and signed by Sultan Ben Suggur and sworn to by Saleh, Mutter, Gadeef and the whole of the Joasmee.

In his report to Bombay Seton added these remarks which do not appear in his diaries; the rest of the report is a fuller version of the diaries. Here we shall continue with the report:

The day passed in conversation on the subject, I on my part claiming the property and Ben Croosh in showing the impossibility of recovering it from people whose country afforded nothing but fish and a few dates and who existed by carrying freight for others and whose Shaikh was not more than the other heads of families who obeyed him or not, as they pleased, that if the war was continued we could certainly distress them much; but they would draw their boats on shore where we could not hunt them, and they would wait patiently whilst the expense of the vessels was more than the value of the cargoes and in regard to the stability of the peace, he hinted the plunder of the two vessels was brought by an accident, in which we were partly to blame, at a time that the whole of the Joasmee were in an uproar that everyone was now sorry for it and the Shaikhs would on the spot have remedied it had they had the power and he had made the heads of all the tribes swear separately to him to abide by what peace would now be concluded.

In addition, it occured to me that if these people were pushed on to desperation they would apply to Sohood, and this would become a general war attended with great expense and bloodshed and should it be ever so successful it would be attended with no advantage to us more than was now in our power as it was perfectly well known they had neither revenue nor produce and lived only on what they could pick up for the day — nor was there any instance in the memory of the oldest of their having returned any captured by the plunder of their Bussorah fleet which was then at Bussorah. I could have caused them a greater comparative loss than ours but this fleet was entirely composed of boats from Lingau, who had been received as friends in the Persian ports and I was restricted from touching them by my instructions. In this dilemma, I concluded on the following terms, subject to the approval of Govt. draught of Colnamih.

6th. Drew up the above in Arabic and delivered it to Ben Croosh to have it confirmed by Sultan Ben Suggur in duplicate.

Seyud Ben Majit being present on the part of Seyud Beder entered into an alliance, offensive and defensive, which was sworn to by him and Ben Croosh and for the Sorie fleet it was settled to send away the Jenebee satisfied and return what freight remained until Seyud Beder should be satisfied. The Sorie Joasmee had not been touched, Ben Croosh sailed for Rasul Khimeh, wrote as follows by him.

To Sultan Ben Suggur.

Your agent, Ben Croosh arrived and we have jointly drawn up a paper which he will show you. It contains the terms on which peace with you will be agreed to and of the peace with Seyud Beder, let me know how I can serve you.

To Saleh Ben Mahomed.

I have received yours by Abdulla Ben Casim Ben Croosh who will inform you of what has passed between us and as you are the friend of Seyud Beder, you will no doubt exert yourself to get the fleet set at liberty on which the peace now depends & ca.

9th. The ships returned from watering at Ormus. Reports prevailed at Lingau that their fleet was detained at Bussorah . . .

16th. Returned from Rasul Khimeh Ben Croosh with the treaty signed, he said Sultan Ben Suggur, by order of Sohood, had marched towards Dubba with 5,000 men to assist Seyud Beder till Geiss made peace and for the same purpose Saleh Ben Mahomed and Rasheed Ben Hummeed were to proceed by sea.

He was charged with the following message from Ben Sugger that he hoped English property would always be in ships so as to prevent mistakes. That the Sorie fleet had permission to leave Rasul Khimeh from whence they would soon set out, that the property of the Bussorah merchants had been secured till they ascertained how their fleet had been treated at Bussorah and the following letter from Sultan Ben Sugger.

Abdulla Ben Cassim Ben Croosh arrived here and informed me of what had passed between you and him. I have signed and sealed the paper you drew up and it is now confirmed and binding between us. I also have confirmed what was agreed on between Seyud Ben Majit and Abdulla Ben Croosh as the terms of peace with Seyud Beder to whom I write to this effect and thro' God's blessing all will now go well between us.

17th. Wrote Mulla Hussain.

I have the pleasure to inform you that peace has been established between the Honble Company and Joassim and also with Seyud Beder and I am now on my return to Muscat and would wish an answer to the letter from Seyud Beder delivered by me and to know whether he is to consider you as a friend or enemy, should the first be your choice, there is still time and I wait your answer . . .

Wrote Sultan Ben Suggur.

I have received yours by Abdulla Ben Cassim Ben Croosh and the treaty signed and also the verbal message and the confirmation of what had been agreed on regarding peace which I hope will continue long between us but the English subjects are many and of all descriptions and their trade is carried on in dows, ships and vessels of every kind which must go and come without molestation or hindrance that the peace may continue between us and what vessels of yours go to India will I hope be furnished with passes wrote by Abdulla Ben Cassim Ben Croosh and sealed by you that they may be known.

Answered Saleh to the same effect . . .

Embarked on board the Mornington accompanied by Mahomed Ben Gaber and received the following letter from Kishem towards evening . . .

20th. Sailed accompanied by a boat carrying baggage, found her too leaky to proceed, sent her to Kishem with a letter to Mulla Hussen to tranship the men and horses into a dow prepared for Muscat and to forward them.

Signed/David Seton
Resident

DRAUGHT

Colnameh or agreement between Shaikh Abdulla Ben Croosh, on the part of Shaikh ul Mashaikh Ameer, Sultan Ben Suggur Ben Rashid, Joasmee, and Captain David Seton, on the part of the Hon'ble East India Company.

In Bunder Abass this 6th day of February 1806, the following was agreed, promised and sworn to:

1. There shall be peace between the Honble East India Company and Sultan Ben Suggur, Joasmee, and the whole of his dependants and subjects on the shores of Arabia and Persia and they shall respect the flag and property of the Honble East India Company and their subjects, wherever and in whatever it may be and the same the Honble East India Company towards the Joasmee.

2. Should the Joasmees infringe the above they shall be liable in the sum of dollars 30,000 and on this condition Captain David Seton agrees to receive from Ameer Sultan Ben Suggur the brig now laying at Muscat and to drop the claims to the cargo, guns & ca. of the said vessel and the Shannon.

3. Whatever British property shall be found in the same fleet shall be restored.

4. Should any British vessel touch on the coasts of the Joasmee for wood or water or be forced on shore by stress of weather or any other cause, the Joasmee shall assist and protect the said vessel and permit it to be disposed of or carried away as their owners shall see fit without claim or demand.

5. Should Sohood compel the Joasmees to infringe this peace they shall give three months previous notice in all cases.

6. When the above is confirmed and ratified by both parties the Joasmee shall frequent the English ports from Surat to Bengal as before.

Signed/David Seton
Resident
Abdulla Ben Croosh — signed, sealed & confirmed
Signed/Sultan Ben Suggur

After having perused and duly considered the several circumstances under which the peace with Joasmees has been negotiated by Captain Seton, the Resident at Muscat, the Governor in Council approves thereof, subject to the final sanction of the Honble the Governor General in Council to whom the papers on the subject are accordingly to be immediately communicated as Captain Seton is to be advised.[80]

Perhaps the most unexpected article in this treaty is that concerned with pressure from the Saudis to 'infringe this peace'. Despite the widely held opinion that they encouraged and supported all so-called 'pirates' in the Gulf, there is not the slightest shred of evidence that they did so. Neither their boats nor their men were ever involved in acts of 'piracy'. In their correspondence with representatives of the Company they always disclaimed and denied any claims that they were involved in any way. The Company authorities must have realised this and accepted the fact that the Saudis were not involved, because in all their policy statements they asserted their wish not to be involved or to involve the Saudis in any hostile activities.

Such an article must have been included on the insistence of the Qawāsim, as a way out of the treaty when they needed it. Although they were anxious to reach a peaceful arrangement with the Company particularly to allow their ships to frequent Indian ports, they had had great doubts about combining peace with the Company with peace with Muscat and it was only under pressure that they agreed to go along with this stipulation on the part of Seton. Indeed, as we shall see, events proved that the Qawāsim were right in not trusting the Omanis.

On the other hand, events will also show that the British had no intention of maintaining the peace with the Qawāsim. The Company's policy of dominating trade in the Gulf had not changed. It was only delayed for a while. Malcolm's grandiose plans were waiting to be carried out. Manesty's greed and Seton's misguided moves were factors that caused a temporary lapse in executing these plans to the letter. But the main factor was the lack of military muscle to support the established British domination of the Gulf. A cruiser or two, the *Mornington* and the *Queen*, were not enough to overwhelm the naval power of the Qawāsim. The complete turn-around of Seton and his seniors was in recognition of this fact. Their decision must have been to play for time until they could muster enough power to carry out their plans.

Notes

1. J.B. Kelly, *Britain and the Persian Gulf 1795–1880*, (Oxford at the Clarendon Press, 1968), p. 67.

2. Bombay Archives (BA), Secret and Political Dept. Diary (S & PDD), no. 57/1797, pp. 1618–20.

3. *Selection from State Papers, Bombay (Sel. SP), regarding the East India Company's connection with the Persian Gulf, with a Summary of Events, 1600–1800*, ed. J.A. Saldanha, (Calcutta, 1908), pp. 336–7.

4. Kelly, *Britain and the Persian Gulf*, pp. 63, 65, 68.

5. *Sel. SP*, pp. 345–9, 374.

6. Collection of original documents in author's possession, Sultān Muhammad Al-Qāsimi, 'Arab "Piracy" and the East India Company Encroachment in the Gulf 1797–1820', Ph.D. thesis, University of Exeter, 1985, Appendix no. 8.

7. J.G. Lorimer, *Gazetteer of the Persian Gulf, Oman and Central Arabia*, (2 vols, Calcutta, 1908–15), p. 634.

8. India Office Library (IO), Extract of a letter from John Beaumont, Resident of Bushire, to the Board dated 10 March 1979, Political Residency (PR) Bushire, R/15/1/3.

9. Kelly, *Britain and the Persian Gulf*, p. 106.

10. IO, Letter from John Beaumont, Resident of Bushire, to the Board, dated 30 November 1778, PR Bushire, R/15/1/3.

11. IO, Extract of a letter from John Beaumont to the Board dated 8 January 1779, PR Bushire, R/15/1/3.

12. BA, *Summary of the Proceedings relative to the boats captured in the Persian Gulf*, vol. 77/1819–20, Minute by Mr Warden, pp. 9–10.

13. BA, S & PDD, no. 27, pp. 851–4.

14. *Selections from the Records of the Bombay Government*, New Series, no. XXIV; *Historical and other Information connected with the Province of Oman, Muscat, Bahrein and other places in the Persian Gulf*, compiled and edited by R. Hughes Thomas, (Bombay, 1856), p. 171.

15. BA, Minute by Mr Warden, pp. 132–6.

16. Kelly, *Britain and the Persian Gulf*, p. 106.

17. BA, S & PDD, no. 59/1798, pp. 133–6.

18. Ibid., pp. 137–8.

19. Ibid., p. 119.

20. ibid., pp. 88–92.

21. Ibid., p. 199.

22. Ibid., pp. 138–44.

23. Ibid., pp. 164–7.

24. Ibid., p. 79.
25. BA, Minute by Mr Warden, pp. 9–10.
26. Lorimer, *Gazetteer*, p. 179.
27. BA, Minute by Mr Warden, p. 137.
28. Ibid., pp. 136–7.
29. J.W. Kaye, *Life and Correspondence of Sir John Malcolm*, (2 vols, London, 1856), vol. I, p. 110.
30. Al-Qāsimī, Appendix no. 5.
31. Kaye, *Life and Correspondence*, vol. I, pp. 105–11.
32. BA, S & PDD, no. 87/1800, pp. 374–5.
33. Ibid., pp. 354–74; for the final text see Sel. from Records of Bombay Gov., pp. 249–50.
34. Lorimer, *Gazetteer*, p. 429.
35. Ibid., p. 273.
36. Al-Qāsimī, Appendix no. 5.
37. BA, S & PDD, no. 105/1801, p. 194.
38. Al-Qāsimī, Appendix no. 6.
39. BA, S & PDD, no. 116/1801, pp. 5900, 6009.
40. Ibid., p. 5967; no. 120/1802, p. 692.
41. J.S. Buckingham, Travels in *Assyria, Media and Persia*, 2nd edn, (2 vols, London, 1830), p. 210.
42. BA, Minute by Mr Warden, pp. 139–40.
43. BA, S & PDD, no. 164/1805, pp. 354–7.
44. Kelly, *Britain and the Persian Gulf*, pp. 105–6.
45. Ibid., p. 106.
46. Lorimer, *Gazetteer*, pp. 180–1.
47. BA, S & PDD, no. 164A/1805, pp. 611–14.
48. Ibid., no. 181/1806, pp. 2425–6. Mulla Hussein's real name was Hasan b. Muhammad b. Mansur.
49. Lorimer, *Gazetteer*, pp. 180–1.
50. BA, S & PDD, no. 164/1805, pp. 439–43.
51. Ibid., pp. 434–7.
52. Ibid., pp. 430–4.
53. *Sel. SP*, p. 8.
54. Kelly, *Britain and the Persian Gulf*, p. 55, cf. IO, *Persia and the Persian Gulf*, Vol. 18.
55. BA, Bussorah Diary, no. 209, pp. 123–5, 138–41, 241–2, 280.
56. BA, S & PDD, no. 164-A/1805, pp. 710–44.
57. Ibid., no. 151/1803, p. 7235.
58. Ibid., no. 165/1805, pp. 968–76.
59. Ibid., no. 165/1805, pp. 976–7.
60. Ibid., no. 165/1805, pp. 978–9.
61. Ibid., no. 170/1805, p. 4067.
62. Ibid., no. 170/1805, p. 4092.
63. Ibid., no. 170/1805, pp. 4092–9.
64. Ibid., no. 171/1805, pp. 4349–51.
65. Ibid., no. 173/1805, pp. 5441–3.
66. *Sel. SP*, pp. 37–8.
67. BA, S & PDD, no. 173/1805, pp. 5398–9.
68. Ibid., pp. 5391–5402.
69. Ibid., no. 181/1806, p. 2401.
70. Al-Qāsimī, Appendix no. 6.
71. Loc. cit.
72. BA, S & PDD, no. 173/1805, pp. 5684–5.
73. Ibid., no. 175/1805, pp. 6417–8.
74. Ibid., no. 173/1805, pp. 5688–90.
75. Ibid., pp. 5691–2.
76. Ibid., pp. 5690–1.
77. Ibid., no. 175/1805, pp. 6418–20.
78. Ibid., no. 181/1806, pp. 2399–402.
79. Al-Qāsimī, Appendix no. 6.
80. BA, S & PDD, no. 181/1806, pp. 2414–30.

3 The Attack on Rās al-Khaimah 1809

Subsequent events prove that the Qawāsim were wrong to have had any faith in the treaty of 1806 with the British, but their mistrust of the Omanis was more than justified. On 9 July 1806 Sayyid Badr was assassinated and was soon succeeded by Imām Saʿīd b. Sultān. The latter was the son of Sayyid Sultān who had concluded a treaty in 1798 with the British which was reconfirmed in 1800. Sayyid Saʿīd was determined to restore his father's policy of allying himself to the British in order to dominate the trade of the Gulf. In a letter to the Governor of Bombay, he wrote:[1]

> On the 21st of Rebbysessany (9th of July) by the direct of heaven and behest of the Almighty in consequence of the decease of the slain Syed Bedder Ben Saef Ben Imam, the Government of this state as descended by hereditry right from the late respected Syed Sultan, hath devolved upon me, and the just title hath now succeeded and am established on the seat of power of my ancestors and if it pleases God, I place my reliance that the treaties of friendship which were in force in the time of my parent, Syed Sultan, between this state and the Honble Company will continue to be observed as in the aforesaid time of my father and that both sides by the requisites of a thorough and permanent good understanding will not fail to operate without any difference or estrangement and that you will keep me truly acquainted with your objects and desires in this quarter with respect to which God willing there shall be no failure believing me to be firmly attached to the British Government, relying to experience a reciprocity on your part.

Having thus allied himself to the British, Sayyid Saʿīd believed he had a free hand and a good opportunity to bring the Qawāsim under his sway, if not to destroy their power altogether.

In less than two months after becoming the Imām of Muscat, he started what proved to be a long and protracted campaign against the Qawāsim. It began on 5 September 1806 when Sayyid Saʿīd sailed towards Rās al-Khaimah with a fleet consisting of six ships boarded by a detachment of his army. With such a surprisingly small force his avowed intention was no less than to punish the Qawāsim and their alleged allies the Banū Maʿīn of Qishm Island. The Qawāsim had just been persuaded, against their better judgement, to include the Omanis in their treaty with the British concluded a few months earlier, and they certainly had not committed any crime against the Omanis during the interval, for which they deserved any punishment. Similarly, the Banū Maʿīn were innocent of any possible crime or aggression against the Omanis. Any allegations that the Qawāsim took advantage of the assassination of Sayyid Badr and captured Khor Fakkān and Kalbā[2] were unquestionably false, because these two ports had always been in

84

the hands of the Qawāsim and it was the Omanis who had always aspired to conquer them and include them in their own domains. However, Sayyid Saʿīd did not attack Khor Fakkān or Kalbā; his inexperience, in addition to his over-confidence, led him to attempt to attack Rās al-Khaimah instead, and it turned out to be a complete failure. Indeed, no fighting occurred at all, for the Omani fleet could not enter the creek and all the inhabitants of Rās al-Khaimah had to do was to retire further inland. After a useless wait the Imām had to turn away with his fleet and proceed to Qishm. Mullā Hussain, the leader of the Banū Maʿīn, sued for peace and the Imām agreed to return to the same conditions that had been the basis for peace between his father and Mullā Hussain.³

In 1807, shortly after the conclusion of peace and the return of the Imām to Muscat, Mullā Hussain was seized in a surprise attack and taken to Muscat where he was confined. Collusion between the East India Company and the Imām was obvious from the fact that the Company's ship *Alert* was sent from Muscat to receive possession of Qishm and Hormuz from Mullā Hussain's family to whom Mullā Hussain was to be delivered in return. This act of piracy and blackmail on the part of the Omanis and the British would have constituted a perfect crime had it not been for the quick action of Shaikh Sultān b. Saqr al-Qāsimī who fortified the garrison of Qishm with his own men. As a result, the garrison felt strong enough to refuse to surrender the island although this, of course, meant the continuation of the confinement of their leader Mullā Hussain.⁴

Aware of the aggressive intentions of the Imām but probably encouraged by the dismal failure of his moves, Sultān b. Saqr decided to take the initiative himself and to strike at his opponent while he was still unprepared. In May 1807 twenty-two ships loaded with Qawāsim men sailed from Rās al-Khaimah and landed at the Omani port of Sūr where the Qawāsim had reason to expect support from the local Omanis. But when the battle with the Imām's forces was joined the Qawāsim were badly defeated, losing 250 men left dead on shore and many others wounded. When they boarded their boats and withdrew, they were chased by two armed ships from Muscat. Again the Omanis inflicted further defeat on the Qawāsim, sinking one ship and driving two others ashore. Many of their crews were killed.⁵

In spite of this victory over the Qawāsim, the Imām realised that his situation would continue to be precarious as long as differences with members of his family were not resolved. In May 1808 he took a major step towards this objective and established amicable relations with his chief rival, his uncle Qays b. Ahmad. As soon as his internal position had been strengthened, the Imām immediately began preparations for an expedition against Khor Fakkān. In this respect he managed to persuade Muhammad b. Matar, a Chief of Fujaira, to join him against the Qawāsim. With his two new allies the Imām attacked Khor Fakkān and at the start of the battle some 150–200 men of the Qawāsim were slain.⁶ But the battle soon turned in favour of the Qawāsim. Sayyid Qays lost his life while trying to escape; about 500 of the Imām's men were cut off, and the Imām himself found great difficulty in reaching his ships.⁷ He was eventually carried to a boat from whence he escaped to his ship. In the process he received a slight wound and was subjected to the indignity of losing almost all his clothes. He also left behind his treasure and upwards of 30 vessels.[8] On the other hand, Sultan b. Saqr, who led the Qawāsim in this battle, came out with flying colours and was credited with chasing the Omanis into their own territories up to Sohār.[9] Kelly puts events in 1807,[10] but this can only be a result of confusing the attack of the Imām on Rās al-Khaimah in 1807 with the later attack on Khor Fakkān.

We now turn to the development of affairs between the Qawāsim and the British after the conclusion of the treaty of 1806. British testimony makes it clear that the Qawāsim had every intention of maintaining their agreements. In June 1807 David Seton reported from Muscat to the Governor of Bombay that 'The Joasmi have remained true to their engagements made with me in every point that regards the Honorable Company'.[11] On 31 March 1808 Samuel Manesty reported from Basra to Bombay:[12]

> it does not appear that the Joasimee Arabs have attempted to commit any piratical acts against the English since the intercourse which took place between the principal Sheikhs of that tribe, Captain Seton and myself at Linga and Rās al-Khaima in May 1806 and it may, I think, be reasonably supposed that they will adhere to their promise on that subject in future.

Although it is not known what Mr Manesty was doing in Rās al-Khaimah in May 1806, it is clear that almost two years later he was still claiming credit for future good relations with the Qawāsim.

Perhaps the attitude of the Qawāsim, and particularly that of Sultan b. Saqr, is illustrated by an event that took place in December 1807. A vessel belonging to the Persian Ambassador and carrying goods which were the property of Bushire and Muscat, which was hoisting British colours and had an Englishman, John Haverson, as captain but did not have a British pass, was seized and plundered by Shaikh Rāshid b. Humaid al-Nuʻaimī. Sultan b. Saqr, in spite of these suspicious circumstances, forced Shaikh Rāshid to surrender the ship simply because the Captain was an Englishman. The captain of the vessel made the following statement to Seton:[13]

> David Seton Esquire.
> Resident of Muscat.
>   I take the liberty to write you these few lines and to inform you of the incident that has befallen us in the Persian Gulf, that on the 27th October we experienced very strong N.W. winds with heavy sea after returning to beat being then in posn. 27.40 and the next day . . . I was obliged to come to at Bushab Island where I thought to be in quite safety, till such time the wind abated, but then we being short of water, I and boat's crew went on shore to find water, but finding it very hard for us to water where there is no water to be had we came on board again, and on the 29th the wind and weather being the same I did not start from my anchoring place for I thought to be quite clear of the enemy's hands; but the same day at sunset three boats set off from Bushaib Island, standing close to the wind to the northward; we then began to weigh

but the wind and weather being very boisterous we thought it best to remain where we were. At ½6 p.m. they boarded us and killed nine of our men. When they were within musket shot we hailed them, that the vessel was an English vessel. Nor much more did we fire at them for we were very badly armed and manned at the same time as well knowing that they have taken their oaths in your presence to never take a vessel under English colours; therefore we did not fire at them nor much more sail make on account of the wind and weather, at the meantimes she being a bad sailor for their boats do outsail us with only their jibs set. On the 30th they cut the cable and made sail for Hormuz. On the 3rd November . . . they plundered the vessel out of all her stores, and turned all hands of us on shore in attention for to sell, but providence being so much in our favour that Sultan having arrived from Rasul Khaima and brought a small force against them, they were not able to do anything further and he took possession of us on the 15th November . . . The Sultan wanted to lay my heart to find out if I was the son of an Englishman and if the vessel was under English colours. I told him I surely was the son of an Englishman and she being under English colours, this was the answer I first gave him and the same I last made. On the 22nd November, he called us on shore and said that he perfectly knows that she belongs to the Persian Ambassador but he only gives her up to us on account of I being the son of an Englishman and the word of honour they gave you Sir. I have likewise informed your Honored Sir, that we are in the miserablest state that ever God has made in this world, without a single farthing nor a stick of clothes more than what we had on. When we were near Bunderabass two boats were constantly on the same tracks that we used to be in, till such time we anchored at Bushaib Island and the boats anchored between the island and main lands. The same day arrived a dow from Muscat which was boarded by them, and on board the said dow was four horse-keepers that came round with us from Bombay which was left back. They did belong to the Persian Ambassador, who, we understand by the pirates, that they gave them intelligence that the vessel and property belongs to His Excellency the Persian Ambassador, and being badly armed. The pirates they said if they have had (sic) not received that intelligence by them, they would never have had attempted to take us, for they was (sic) quite afraid. Honoured Sir, I beg you would take it into your consideration at this present situation to assist us with little remedy by so doing will highly oblige your most obedient and most humble servant.
Muscat
Brign. Shannon
the 8th December 1807   Signed/John Haverson

David Seton enclosed the Captain's note in his own letter to Duncan:[14]

Honble Jonathan Duncan Esquire
Governor & President in Council, Bombay.

Honble Sir,
     The 6th inst. the Shannon arrived from Ras al-Khaimah with an agent from
Sultan Ben Sugger who was charged with letters for the Honble the Governor
but lost them by accident.
     I have the honour to enclose the Captain's statement of what has happened
as delivered by him to me.
     The message from Sultan Ben Sugger was that Rashed bin Hamid Haimaon
has taken the vessel on the information of some Persians on board an Uttoobee
dow, they spoke at sea, that she was Abushire property but the Sultan Bin
Sugger believing she has an English commander and had painted English colours, he had taken her by force from Rashed and returned her but that the
cargo, being Abushire and Muscat property, the Wahabee has supported Rashed
in the retension of it, and it was not in his power to force him to return it.
In this Rashed had acted of his own moment, and if Government wished to
reclaim it by force, he would assist to the utmost of his power with everything
his country produced.
     As the vessel had no pass I did not receive her but ordered her to be delivered
to the Ambassador's agent . . . who will return to Ras al-Khaimah for other
letters and follow there also.

Khunadee	I have the honor to be & ca.
9th December 1807	Signed/David Seton
	Resident

The British who were involved in this incident would appear to have been lend-
ing their colours to cover what obviously amounted to smuggling. They knew
it and so did Sultān b. Saqr, but his behaviour was certainly more honourable
than theirs. Unlike them, he did not take advantage of the treaty of 1806 but stretched himself beyond the call of duty to protect anything that could possibly be
British in order to maintain and observe the letter and the spirit of the treaty.
Nevertheless, he was accused of being a pirate, and by the British of all people.
Lorimer, of course, would not credit the Qawāsim with strict adherence to the
treaty of 1806. Instead as always, he presents his warped reasoning. 'For about
two years the Qawāsim remained quiescent; but their better conduct was probably due, in part at least, to the stationing of a large British squadron in the
Gulf in 1807–8'.[15] The best answer to these false allegations inadvertently comes
from Kelly who stated that 'the Government of Bombay hardly had the means
to conduct an effective campaign against the Qawasim. The Bombay Marine
possessed no more than a dozen ships in 1808 to carry out its numerous duties
in the seas between Calcutta and Suez'.[16] Once again, the 'large British squadron
in the Gulf in 1807–8' was no more than a figment of Lorimer's imagination.

The Khāraq Expedition

We recall that in 1800 John Malcolm proposed the establishment of a base in the Gulf from which the Company could exercise control over the trade there. Now in 1808, eight years later, the Company attempted through negotiations between the same John Malcolm and Fath Alī Shāh, the King of Persia, to obtain from him the islands of Qishm, Hinjām and Khāraq.[17] When these negotiations failed Malcolm was able to convince the Government of India to mount an expedition to occupy Khāraq Island. He argued:[18]

> with an established footing in the Gulf of Persia, which must soon become the emporium of our commerce, the seat of our political negotiations, and a depot for our military stores, we should be able to establish a local influence and strength that would not only exclude other European nations from that quarter, but enable us to carry on negotiations and military operations with honour and security to any extent we desired.

Here Malcolm based his argument, in order to persuade his superiors, not only on the necessity of the base for trade purposes but also as a defensive measure to protect India against possible European, i.e. French, plans. Accordingly, the Governor General in Council, on 19 April 1808, gave instructions to Duncan, the Governor at Bombay, 'for the foundation of a detachment of 4 or 5,000 men at Bombay to be eventually embarked for the Persian Gulf'.[19]

This resolute approach was followed by a farcical situation resulting from the contradictory behaviour of the British actors involved. Lord Minto, the Governor General of India, seems not to have been able to take a decision and see it through. In particular, he was unable to control Malcolm and keep him in line with the Government's general policy. Indeed, there does not seem to have been a general policy to be imposed, perhaps because Minto himself did not fully comprehend the situation in the Gulf. On the other hand, Duncan, who seems to have had some grasp of the situation, was too constrained by Minto's vacillating stance to be able to control his subordinates even when he tried. Furthermore, all those involved appeared to be panic-stricken by their fear of their own imagined plans of French advances on India. Most important of all, however, British moves in the Gulf at this stage were exaggeratedly influenced by the grandiose plans of John Malcolm for his own glorification. As Kelly puts it, 'His biographer has described him as seeing himself as master of the Persian Gulf under his country's ensign . . . lord of a fortified island and arbiter of the destinies of Persia and Arabia'.[20] This was the view of a sympathetic biographer, it is probably closer to the truth to describe him as a glory-obsessed military man of the worst imperialist kind who always preferred to shoot first. Throughout this period Malcolm was busy planning and pushing for expeditions to the Gulf while his masters were even busier trying to control him or muster the forces he demanded which they did not always have. The situation was further complicated by the intervention of Sir Harford Jones, the London emissary who was able to achieve by sensible negotiations what Malcolm could not do by his pompous attitude and his military threats.

Anyway the expedition ordered by Minto on 19 April 1808 did not materialise, albeit we soon see Malcolm travelling to the Gulf with great pomp and exaggerated military escort. He stopped at Muscat for a very short time and achieved little, then he went to Persia where he achieved even less, returning to India in July. In his arrogance he decided to by-pass Bombay and go directly to Calcutta which he reached on 20 August.

'Within two days of his arrival at Calcutta orders were on their way to Bombay for the preparation of an expedition of which Malcolm was to take command'.[21] Kelly wonders how Malcolm was able to get Minto to take such a decision so quickly, but the real wonder is that Minto changed his mind even faster and 'seemed for a moment to recover his sense of proportion. The expedition, he told Malcolm, would have to be abandoned, and Malcolm would have to proceed to the Gulf in a purely diplomatic character . . . Malcolm was not prepared to accept such a drastic reduction of his functions, and he wrote to Minto to protest against his decision'.[22] On the 31 October Minto made another about-turn and authorised Malcolm to proceed with his proposed expedition to the Gulf.

> Malcolm arrived at Bombay on 30th November 1808 to find preparations for the expedition well advanced. A force of 2,000 men — European infantry, sepoys, cavalry, artillery and pioneers — had been assembled and a further 4,000 men could be supplied from the Presidency if he needed them. All that held him back was the final orders from Calcutta. While he awaited them he sent off one of his staff, Captain N.P. Grant, to survey the Makran coast from Gwadar to Bander Abbas.[23]

We agree with Kelly that Malcolm was keen that Minto, as was his habit, should not change his mind about proceeding with the expedition, especially since he knew that Duncan at Bombay had been against the project from the start. It did not take long for Minto to change his mind, however, and on 27 January 1809 he wrote to Malcolm:[24]

> to say that the expedition to the Gulf would have to be put off indefinitely. The plan to consolidate the Company's Residencies on Kharaq Island, he consoled Malcolm, need not necessarily be abandoned but any establishment there would have to be on a smaller scale than that envisaged by Malcolm, and the island would have to be obtained by negotiation, not by seizure.

Meanwhile, in the autumn of 1808 some peculiar incidents took place at sea in the Gulf, between ships purported to belong to the Company and ships reported to belong to Arabs. These incidents in themselves were not of great importance, indeed to an objective observer they could only be adjudged as minor incidents. Nevertheless for the British officials of the Company and their representatives in the Gulf and indeed for later British historians, they were given an importance out of all proportion and were represented as of great significance to the direction of British policy in the Gulf. They were cited by officials and historians alike as criminal acts of 'piracy'' that justified fully-fledged military expeditions against a people who, to say the least, could not be proved guilty of these acts. In most cases the incidents were the result of misapprehensions and misunderstandings that could easily occur in the Gulf at that time. We have to recognise that animosities were rampant on all sides and that instability and internal troubles were the state of affairs in all lands bordering the Gulf. We must also point out that piracy and privateering were very common there and in the vicinity. The pirates and privateers were not all Arabs and the Arabs were not all Qawāsim. There were Indian pirates and there were French privateers, who for some strange reason were never called pirates. There were Arab pirates operating from their base near Qatar under the leadership of the ferocious Raḥma b. Jābir, but their aggressive attacks against all ships were tolerated as less than a minor irritation. Only once did the British contemplate attacking these pirates, but even then, as we shall see, excuses were found not to carry out this attack.[25]

The Qawāsim, on the other hand, were singled out as the most notorious and dangerous of all, and accusation after accusation was hurled at them in order to incite and justify aggressive attacks on them with the overt objective of destroying them altogether. The autumn of 1808 witnessed a spate of these rumoured accusations that were utilised by two long-avowed opponents of the Qawāsim who, as we shall see, combined their efforts to launch yet another expedition to impose British supremacy and control of trade in the Gulf. In accordance with their rigid *ideés fixes*, Malcolm and Seton planned and executed their personal war against the Qawāsim.

The first of these incidents involved the cruiser *Fury* which belonged to the Company. Lorimer, for reasons known only to himself, reported that the Qawāsim attacked this ship in 1805.[26] Fortunately the incident was fully reported by none other than Charles Gowan who was in command of the *Fury* at the time, and we quote the report in full here:[27]

To
William Taylor Money Esqre.
Superintendent of Marine & ca. & ca.
Sir,

As the Honble Company's cruiser, under my command was proceeding from Muscat to the Presidency in the morning of the 2nd May, having a light breeze from the westward, I perceived two dows in chase of us.

At 3 p.m. the dows still continuing the chase and coming up very fast, I fire two shots across them, showing our colours, at the same time, which they took no notice of, I thought it was their intention to attack us; at half past three, the dows coming up fast, I fired another shot across them, which they returned by a discharge of as many guns as they could get to bear on us.

At ¼ after 4 p.m. the dows still continuing their fire on us, being within musket shot, I commenced a heavy fire on them, which did not prevent them from attempting to board us.

At half past 4 p.m. the dows shot up on our starboard quarter, heaving spears and large stones into us, immediately after which, their crews attempted to jump on over decks but were repulsed, with great loss, by the continued fire from our stern guns and musketry; on which, they backed their sails and dropped astern, in a very shattered condition, getting their sweeps out and pulling away, as fast as possible under a heavy fire from our stern guns.

At a quarter before 6 p.m. a breeze springing up from the south and having on board two packets for Government and one for the Commander in Chief, and knowing the great superiority of the dows sailing, I deemed it most prudent to make sail on our course for Bombay. The largest of the dows mounted ten guns, appearing to have at least 300 men and from the remarkable fairness of the person, which I took to be her commander, I conceived he was European.

The other one rather smaller appeared to mount 6 guns, with several swivels, having on board at least 200 men, neither of them hoisted any colours.

With the exception of the gunner, two seamen and one sepoy being severely wounded, the boatswain, one sepoy and one lascar slightly, the Fury received little or no other damage, but a few shots though her sails and some ropes aft cut by them. It gives me the greatest pleasure to mention that the whole of the crew behaved greatly to my satisfaction.

Honble Company's	I have the honour to be & ca.
Schooner Fury,	Signed/Chrl. Gowan
Bombay Harbour	Lt. Commg.
May 10th 1808.	

List of men wounded on board the Honourable Company's Gun Boat Fury. May 2nd. 1808.

Severely	*Slightly*
Mr Wm. Brown, Gunner,	Mr Paterson, Boatswain
ball in his left arm.	on his body and arm.
John Fleetnor, Seaman,	One Lascar — head.
ball in his lower jaw.	One Sepoy — head.
John Jones, ball in mouth and	
throat.	
Shaik Hussain Sepoy ball on the	
side of his head	
True copy	Signed/Charl. Gowan
Signed/Charl. Court	Lieut. Commg.
Assistant	

From this report it is clear that:

(i) The incident took place on 2 May 1808, and not some time in 1805.

(ii) The cruiser *Fury* was sailing showing no colours to begin with.

(iii) Gowan 'thought it was their intention to attack'; the *Fury* fired first at

3 o'clock, then again at half past three, and then 'commenced heavy fire' fifteen minutes later.

(iv) The commander of one of the dhows was European.

(v) Neither of the two dhows hoisted any colours.

(vi) The *Fury* received little or no damage.

(vii) It lost one man and five men were wounded.

Here we have a ship showing no colours but under the command of a European. It is ludicrous that Lorimer and Kelly want us to accept that this was a ship belonging to the Qawāsim engaged in an act of piracy. It is now clear who the attackers were and it is no wonder that:[28]

An order was issued by the President in Council directing all the commanders of the Bombay Marine, not on any consideration to attack or molest these innocent natives of the Gulf, and threatening to visit with the displeasure of the Government any among them who might be found in any way to interrupt them or to provoke their anger.

Kelly acknowledges this order but substitutes 'the innocent natives of the Gulf' by the 'Qawāsim'.

The Minerva Incident

The next episode was that involving the ship *Minerva* and, as always, anything that belonged to Manesty was bound to evoke controversy. Lorimer assigned this incident to September 1808, while Kelly states that it took place on 23 May 1808. Lorimer claimed that the *Minerva* was attacked by a number of Qāsimī boats, but Kelly specifies that it 'ran into a fleet of fifty-five Qasimi vessels'. After this slight variance both are in complete agreement on all details in their prosecution of a savage Qāsim attack. Perhaps Kelly has the advantage as his description is the more graphic and we shall quote him in full.[29]

On 23 May, the country ship Minerva, owned by Samuel Manesty, ran into a fleet of fifty-five Qasimi vessels off Ras Musandam. She fought them in a running fight for two days before being taken. Most of the crew and many of the passengers were put to death, but among those spared was Mrs Robert Taylor, wife of Lieutenant Taylor of the Residency at Bushire, and her infant son. Minerva was taken to Ras al-Khaima where she was stripped of her cargo and fittings and sent to cruise against other merchant shipping. Most of the captives were later released, among them Mrs Taylor, who was bought by an Arab of Bahrain from the Qasimi chief for Maria Theresa $670 and ransomed by the resident at Bushire in Oct. 1809 for the sum of M.T.$1000.

Lorimer satisfied himself with stating that those who were killed were 'put to a cruel death by methods indicative of religious fanaticism'. In case one wonders how this fanaticism exhibited itself, Kelly goes out of his way to quote:[30]

> an officer of the Bombay Marine, who knew the Qawasim well, later remarked: 'I must confess, with a people who are not naturally cruel, I am somewhat surprised they should have adopted the savage and revolting principle of sacrificing their captives. They did so with circumstances of horrid solemnity, which gave the deed the appearance of some hellish religious rite.' No injunction to such an effect exists, however, in the otherwise fanatical faith they avow. After a ship was taken, she was purified with water and with perfume, the crew were then led forward singly, their heads placed on the gunwale, and their throats cut, with the exclamation used in battle of 'Allah Akbar!' — God is Great.

Kelly copied this from another historian[31] who, adding more drama to the script, had the

> wretched captives bound and brought forward singly to the gangway, where one of the pirates cut their throat, with the exclamation Mohammedans used in slaying cattle, ''Allah Akbar'' (God is Great), regarding this terrible deed of blood as a propitiatory sacrifice to the Deity. The captain was said to have been cut up into fragments, which were thrown overboard.

This kind of emotive language can have nothing to do with serious research.

In spite of the prominence of the *Minerva* incident and the attempt to depict it as a harrowing episode, there is very meagre information about it and the few reports we have are quite contradictory. This unusual dearth of information and lack of detailed reports by Company representatives leads us to believe that there was an attempt either to cover up something unbeknown ot us, or to suppress part of the truth in order to exploit the episode to maximum effect in government circles in Bombay. The correspondence about the ransom and release of Mrs Taylor was far more detailed and lengthy than that about any other aspect of the incident. This is the more surprising since the authorities in Bombay refused to reimburse Bruce for the expenses he had to pay to obtain her release. It is laughable, though tragic, that the Company should have instructed Bruce to refer to Lieutenant Taylor 'for reimbursement of the amount he may have disbursed for procuring the release of Mrs Taylor'.[32] Although compassion could not be expected from the Company, it was shirking its responsibility in this case unless it could justify this harsh behaviour towards its functionaries, perhaps because of their own mistakes or erroneous reporting.

Bruce was unusually brief in reporting the loss of the *Minerva*:[33]

> she has been captured by the Joasimee pirates and every soul killed except the captain, one officer and two Armenians who they have forcibly circumcised and made Mohametans. The ship they have carried over to their port

of Rasul Khyma, she had on board cargo for this place and Bussora to about 3 lacks of Rupees.

This was all he had to say; his concern about the circumcision of at most four men was equal to his disquiet about the killing of everybody else on the ship.

The same event was reported, with some obvious exaggeration, by an Indian passenger, albeit in more detail. Here is his report to compare with that of Bruce:[34]

> Translate of a letter from Borah Alimanjee at Muscat to his friends at Surat. I and another Borah were passengers on board the ship Minerva Captain Hopewood; on the 23rd of May 1809. Joasmees captured us, they were altogether large and small 55 vessels and had about 5000 Joasmees on board, they fought during two days, then after they captured us, the Captain and 2nd officer on board were killed, 77 persons were altogether on board of the Minerva, of whom 45 been killed and 32 persons been saved by God's favour. After the capture of the ship, they carried us to Russal Khyma, and kept us 33 days. They told us (i.e. to the writer of this letter and to another Bohara named Baker Bye) to pay them about six or seven hundred Rupees, we replied to them what we had, you the Joasmees have taken from us, at present we have nothing only our persons remain; if you want them take instant release or detain us or do whatever you please, then after that they released us (viz. 2 Borahs and 8 Lascars). Then on the 17th of July we arrived at Muscat and Baker Bye remained 10 days at Muscat and then after he is gone to Bussora.

Of course, one can discard the exaggeration of the 55 vessels with 5,000 'Joassmees' on board fighting one ship for two days. But in contrast to the four reported by Bruce as having escaped death, the passenger reported 32 persons to have been saved. The captain and the 2nd officer, reported killed by the passenger, were only circumcised according to Bruce. Then 10 persons were released and allowed to go to Muscat, and of them eight were soldiers. Bruce with a little effort could have got to know a great deal more about the incident and would have reported it to Bombay. It is probable that these soldiers, on their return to Bombay, reported the truth to their superiors who took exception to the behaviour of Bruce and Taylor who was also at the Residency at Bushire. Under these circumstances, a good deal of doubt is shed upon the reporting of this episode and the truth will have to await the discovery of other documents. But it seems that it was to Bruce's and Taylor's interest to allow only the exaggerated reports to reach Bombay. Thus the *Bombay Gazette*, claiming to be quoting an eye witness, reported on 4 October 1809:[35]

> The Minerva, Captain Hopwood, which we stated sometime ago to have been captured by the pirates in the Gulph appears to have been safely conducted into one of the ports belonging to these desperate set of people.
> We are enabled upon the authority of a person who was on board at the time of the capture to state a few particulars relative to this unfortunate event.

The Minerva was on a voyage to Bushire and had taken her departure from Muscat only a few days when she was in sight of a great number of dows who were then under easy sail. Captain Hopwood, we presume, being aware that safety could only be hoped for from flight, immediately set every stitch of canvas and steered in a direction to avoid the enemy, which he would certainly have effected had the wind continued, but unfortunately a calm ensued which gave the pirates a decided advantage who lost no time in availing themselves of it, as they were perceived making the most strenuous exertions with their sweeps, and as they approached, which was very rapidly, occasionally fired a shot. The Minerva may be considered to have been at this time in a very perilous situation from the almost total calm which prevailed and which occasioned the ship with great difficulty to answer her helm. The dows now came within gunshot in great numbers and in every direction which could not fail to render the hopes of a successful strength; numbers and guns of the enemy did not however operate in damping the spirits of Captain Hopwood, his officers and crew. They on the contrary had prepared themselves for a most sanguinary conflict and fully determined as we may reasonably infer either to beat off these desperadoes or fall in the attempt. The lady passengers, amongst whom was Mrs Taylor, had rendered themselves extremely useful in making a quantity of cartridges in case the stock on hand should be found insufficient. The engagement commenced in forenoon of the 29th May between the hours of ten and eleven and after the first broadside from the Minerva, 4 dows appeared to be in a sinking condition; a general action now took place and the havoc that was occasioned was dreadful beyond example.

The crew of the Minerva kept up a galling and spirited fire and behaved in a most gallant manner, animated by the conduct of the Captain, who displayed uncommon intrepidity.

During the engagement, which is said to have been continued for 36 hours, no less than 16 dows went down. Such part of the crews of which, as had not been wounded, found a ready retreat on board their comrades by which means the number of the enemy closely opposed to the Minerva was never diminished, and to this circumstance may be attributed the final surrender of the ship.

The fire of the Minerva had now slackened, from the incessant and continual exertions that had been made, and particularly in consequence of the killed and wounded of a great part of her crew. On the side of the enemy, the fire was kept briskly up. They had now apparently determined to board, as their vessels were gradually closing all round the Minerva; and having laid them close to, head and astern, these desperadoes instantly jumped on board and cut to pieces every person who came in their way.

Captain Hopwood received three severe wounds, but notwithstanding, continued to defend himself. At one time he fell insensible on the deck from the wound of a pistol shot; he again recovered and again attacked his assailants, and killed several with his own hand, till fatigued and overpowered he was literally cut to pieces. Mr Bejaun, an American gentleman, together with the purser and the supracargo were massacred in one of the tops after all resistance had ceased. The Chief Officer, the ladies and the other survivors were permitted to live on condition of their renouncing their religion. Between 30 or 40 lascars were killed.

We have seldom heard of any vessel having made a more obstinate and determined resistance than the Minerva on this occasion; and when we consider the circumstances under which she sailed, and how slightly equipped as a fighting vessel, it would be doing injustice to the memory of Captain Hopwood and his brave companions not to record the admiration which has been excited in the minds of his countrymen by this glorious although unsuccessful contest.

Here we have another sensational report adding glory to the *Minerva* which had sunk no less than 16 dows before it was captured. The rest of the details are not too far from the report of the Borah merchant; rumours were still circulating until the news of the expedition was to overwhelm the scene. But it is instructive to note that after the dust had settled and the true picture emerged the *Minerva* incident was reported in the *Asiatic Annual Register* in its 1809 issue, as follows (p. 146):[36]

The report, which has been for some time current at this presidency, of the capture of the Minerva, captain Hopwood by the pirates who infest the Gulph of Persia, and the neighbouring seas, is at length confirmed.

On taking possession of the Minerva, it appears that the pirates mitigated something of their usual ferocity; and no lives were lost, except in the gallant defence which was made by the unfortunate captives.

They have been all, however, obliged to reounce their religion, and not an iota of the preparatory ceremony of introduction to the Mahommedan faith was abated. Much as the men must have suffered on this occasion, it is comparatively nothing to the distress of the three ladies who were on board; and who, consequently, fell into the hands of these lawless and unprincipled violators. The subject is too painful to enlarge on. The indignities they were compelled to undergo can be easily conceived; and must excite the strongest emotions of pity in every feeling and delicate mind.

Here, practically a year later, the truth was allowed to come out and it turned out that 'no lives were lost', although a few men were probably circumcised; a far cry from the rumours that had earlier been circulated, and on the basis of which decisions were made to mount the 1809 expedition.

The Sylph and Nautilus Incidents

Perhaps the most serious incident, at least in terms of casualties, was that involving the Company's cruiser *Sylph*, in which thirty men were reported killed and three wounded. The *Sylph* was an 8-gun schooner of the Bombay Marine, which was part of a squadron that had escorted the British emissary Sir Harford Jones from Bombay to Bushire, and was returning to Bombay in company of the bigger and slower frigate the *Nereide* (36 guns) from which it was temporarily separated. What happened was adequately told in the report of Lieutenant W.T. Graham who was in commend of the *Sylph* at the time:[37]

> To:
> W.T. Money, Esqre.
> Superintendent & ca. & ca.
> Sir,
>   It is with the most unexpressible grief I am called on to state the lamentable fate that has befallen the greater part of the crew of the H.C. schooner Sylph.
>   On the 20th of October at half past 10 a.m. saw a large ship under a crowd of sail standing to the south, and at 11 a.m. two boats in her wake steering in the same direction about three miles distant. At noon passed H.M. ship Nereide, Captain R. Corbett, the two boats not altering their course until they had neared us within a cable's length when one of them which appeared to have the advantage in sailing, kept away from our larboard bow, but still I was determined not to commence before they attacked us as I understood it would meet with the displeasure of Government when immediately bore up and while in the act of wearing, received a volley of small arms, which we returned with a broadside; however, from their great superiority in sailing, one boarded us on the starboard quarter, while his companion closed and sent all his men on board, and appeared desperately bent on carrying the Sylph before H.M. ship Nereide would come to our assistance, which every possible effort was made by H.M.S Nereide from the commencement.
>   As the enemy was lashed alongside we could not depress the guns sufficiently to strike her between wind and water or elevate them enough to destroy any part of her crew; I ordered all the crew to the small arms to prevent them from boarding which we succeeded in, until our decks were much thinned and the enemy having the whole range of the starboard sde. We were soon completely overpowered and shortly after taken in tow.
>   At 4 p.m. H.M.S. Nereide having neared us sufficiently to hull the vessel they slipped the tow rope, and left the Sylph with the intention of escaping, but in this instant they were completely disappointed, as H.M.S Nereide pursued them, sunk one while her companion bore up close to the frigate and saved her crew for a short time, as there is every reason to believe she met with a similar fate.
>   Acting Lieutenant Denton, from whom I received the greatest support was killed towards the close of the action and the whole crew behaved with the greatest resolution and fortitude.
>   In the evening the H.M. ship Service hailed the Sylph, and when Captain Corbett was informed of the circumstances, sent his boat for me and the distinguished attention I received from him, when it was intimated I was

wounded, call forth my warmest acknowledgements of gratitude having accommodated me in his cabin and every comfort generously proposed, that my
case required; which will be remembered to the latest hour of my life.

   Lieutenant Conyers has taken charge of the Sylph, with six Europeans from
H.M. ship Nereide, and Captain Corbett has desired him to proceed to Muscat
and remain there with Mahomed Hussen Cassin, until one of the cruisers from
Bussora touches there. I now beg leave to lay before you a list of the crew
that suffered in the action.

Nereide, Bombay   I have the honour to remain
28th October 1808   Signed/W.T. Graham
                                                    Lt. Commanding

Killed in the action   *Wounded in the action*
Lieut. Denton   Lieut. W.T. Graham,
Wm. Banham gn. mr.   dangerously.
One Syrang   One Sepoy, ditto.
Thirteen Lascars   J. Gall, ditto.
One Haveldaur
One Narque
Eleven Sepoys
One Artificer belong   Total killed thirty
to Sir Harford Jones.   Wounded: three

P.S. I omitted mentioning the Sepoy was removed also on board the Nereide
and recovering quite fast.

                                              Signed/W.T. Graham
                                                         Lieut.
                                                      True copy
                                              Signed/Charles Crerit
                                                Assistant to Supt.

   Although the commander of the *Sylph* stated that it was one large ship and
two boats that attacked his cruiser, Lorimer with his usual exaggeration made
these into 'a fleet of large Arab vessels'. Kelly was more moderate and spoke
only of 'two large dhows'. More important is the fact that both Lorimer and Kelly
were certain that these ships belonged to the Qawāsim, although the commander's
report never said the ships were Arab, let alone Qawāsim. Furthermore, Lorimer
and Kelly spoke of two ships involved in the incident, the *Sylph* and the *Nereide*.
Lieutenant Graham mentioned the *Service* being in the vicinity on the same evening, and nobody has volunteered to tell us what this ship was doing there. The
interesting point is that both Lorimer and Kelly emphasised that the *Sylph* was
'precluded by regulations from using her guns until it was too late'. Nevertheless,
Kelly pointed out that 'the Qawasim grappled and swarmed on board, overcom-
ing the crew by weight of numbers', and Lorimer spoke of the crowd of boarders
which the Arab ships hurled on her deck from their towering bows; and a wholesale
massacre of her crew, who perished fighting desperately, was the sequel. Lorimer

and Kelly had no doubt whatever that the attackers were men from the Qawāsim; on the other hand, they had no proof whatever that they were Qawāsim. The Arab pirates in the Gulf at that time were the Jalāhima of Raḥma b. Jābir, and the tactics of the attack indicate that it was more probable that it was they who were involved than any other party. The attack was in the style of well-trained pirates and such a style was never ascribed to the Qawāsim in any other incident, while it was typical of the attacks proved to be by the Jalāhima pirates. It should be noted that a few months earlier Raḥma b. Jābir had been blockading Bushire and threatening in writing N.S. Smith, the Resident there, with further action against British property and vessels.[38]

Lorimer informs us:[39]

> only three days after the Sylph incident the H.E.I. Company's brig Nautilus of 14 guns, Lieutenant Bennett, was threatened, while passing the island of Hanjām, by a squadron of two large and two small pirate vessels. In consequence of the order which prohibited British ships from taking the initiative in these affairs. Lieutenant Bennett considered himself obliged to hold his fire until the hostile squadron had advanced so near that the war dances and brandished spears of the Arab crews could be distinctly seen and their songs and shouts heard; he then hoisted the British colours and fired two shots across the bows. As they still continued to approach, the Nautilus immediately discharged a broadside at the two larger vessels; and a gunnery combat ensued which was maintained for nearly an hour, at length the Arab squadron took to flight, pursued by the Nautilus, who plied them with her shot as long as they were within range.

Taking this report at its face value, it seems that the British commanding officers sailing the Gulf, even close to straits and islands, considered that they and they alone had the right to be sailing there. Any other ship simply had to steer away from their path as quickly as possible. The sailors must also stop singing, otherwise they might offend British eyes and ears with what might seem like war dances. It should be noted that Arab sailors in the Gulf never engaged in war dances, or any dances at all, for that matter; they were usually too busy and too exhausted with their assigned tasks on board ship to have the time or energy to dance. Furthermore, Arab sailors were supposed to hide their spears when a British ship appeared, because they might be considered a threat to British personnel and thus might provoke them to fire on innocent passing Arab ships. The arrogance of these presumptions is beyond comprehension.

It is obvious in this case that Lieutenant Bennett was the first to fire and it is just as obvious that he had no reason to do so, whatever his imaginary fears might have been. Indeed, Bennett's report affirmed these conclusions, albeit he did not assert, as Lorimer did, that he had felt 'obliged to hold his fire' according to newly issued orders. The following is the only available extract from Bennett's report, dated 1 December 1808, Bombay Harbour:[40]

October 17th, entered the Persian Gulf, that morning passed a ship heading out of it, which I afterwards heard was the Diamond. At noon on the same day being off the Island of Angam, I saw three boats ahead apparently heading in for the land; at 2 p.m. I perceived them firing guns as signals to each other; at 2.50 another boat having joined them, the whole stood in towards the island of Kishm; at 3 when to windwards they wore round and stood towards, two of them, the largest, seemed dows and two large tranquays, the former keeping for our weather bow and the latter for the quarter. About half past four could discover that they were full of men, armed in spears and swords which they were striking at us, at the same time making great shouting. It was now apparent they intended attacking us, shortened sail and cleared for action about 4.40 finding them well within reach of our cannonades, hoisted Company's colours and fired two shots ahead of the largest dow, which did not appear to notice but kept pulling and sailing towards, having her boat ahead towing her. It being evident they intended boarding us, fired a broadside at them, which was returned and the action continued for about 25 to 30 minutes, when they stood from us close hauled on, the larboard tack; immediately wore and stood after them and kept occasionally firing at them, till 6.10 at which time perceiving the shot to fall short and it being nearly calm, resumed our course up the Gulf. At the beginning of the action Mr John Dennis, boatswain, was killed by a cannon shot that first penetrated the vessel's side and afterwards struck him on the breast; this is the only casualty we met with.

True Extract
signed/Charles Court
Assist. Supt.

There is one discrepancy here which is of some significance, Lorimer decided that the *Nautilus* incident occurred three days after that of the *Sylph*, which means that his date for it is 23 October 1808. Bennett put the date as 17 October 1808 and obviously he was the more truthful of the two. In other words it was the other way round; the *Nautilus* incident happened on 17 October and three days later, on 20 October 1808, the incident involving the *Sylph* took place. It transpires then that four big boats that could have been Qawāsim boats, and which were in a position to grapple with, attack and board the *Nautilus* did not choose to do so, in spite of the provocation of the latter by its firing first and its continuing to shoot at them long after they were out of range. We do not, of course, have the full report that might have enabled us to learn the whole truth about this incident.

Incidents off the Indian Coast

We shall now discuss an incident which we hope will prove beyond doubt that British Residents, army officers, naval commanders and even senior government officials simply did not know what they were doing and were mostly acting on the wrong information. Needless to say British historians were just as ignorant. Lorimer wrote:[41]

> In April 1808, off the coast of Gujarat, the schooner Lively, Lieutenant Macdonald, was hemmed in by 4 Arab vessels, each larger and carrying more men than herself, and an attempt was made by the enemy to board her; but it was repulsed by the determined fire of the Lively, which did great execution. Three of the pirate craft which took part in this affair were subsequently discovered at Surat and were taken to Bombay; but, though wounded men were found concealed on board and the identification in other respects appeared to be complete, the Government, 'in consideration of their long detention, set them free again to exercise their calling on some hapless coaster'. This they, or others resembling them, seem to have done with effect; for in the course of 1808, no less than 20 country vessels fell prey to Arab buccaneers off the Indian coast.

As we shall see, this was wrong enough, but Kelly's account was even worse. He wrote:[42]

> In November the Qasimi war squadron appeared for the first time in Indian waters. Forty dhows attacked the coastwise trade off Kutch, and on 26 November H.C.C. *Lively* fought a running fight with four dhows down the Gujerat coast.

He adds in a long footnote:

> Three days later the dhows . . . tried to conceal themselves in the usual crowd of trading vessels. The presence of wounded men aboard gave them away, and the vessels and crews were placed under guard by the commodore of Marine at Surat. Sent up to Bombay, they were detained for a time, then released, on the ground that they had been sufficiently punished by their detention. And concluded: Twenty merchant vessels fell prey to the Qawasim in November and at the beginning of December thirty prominent Parsi and Gujerati merchants of Bombay petitioned the Governor to take action against the pirates, declaring that they would be forced to abandon trading if they continued to be harassed by them.

There is a long history of piracy off the Indian coast. Here we shall give a brief account of some of the incidents that took place around that time, which should make it clear that the Qawāsim were definitely never involved in any acts of aggression in that area, and that it was Indian pirates who were the culprits.
    On 20 October 1805, when off Dew, a Portuguese ship and a ship under English colours belonging to Sheikh Mohamed Subedar, called *Saheb Sudder* of Bancoot, were attacked and taken to the Gulf of Kutch, where the cargo was landed and the crew and the passengers were sent to Porebander.[43]
    On 27 December 1805, the Captain of His Majesty's ship *Fox*, W.K. Dobbie,

attacked Dwarca, destroyed the town, and regained the British property on the vessels captured by the pirates of Dwarca.[44]

On 4 January 1806, the Superintendent dispatched orders to Lieutenant Blast, in the Company's schooner *Lively*, to take under his command the *Barbara* and the *Turrenow* of the first class of pattamars and two smaller vessels of the second class, and blockade the piratical ports of Bete, Gamtee and Kamrah for the restitution of the cargo that had been taken on the ketch *Salamat* of Surat.[45]

On 15 January 1806, a petition was sent to the Government of Bombay from Sudgoo Cooly that his ship *Darria Bahadoor* had been captured by the northern pirates of Bete.[46] Lieutenant Maxfield, commanding the *Lively* off the inner harbour of Bete, in a report dated 26 February 1806, stated that two or three English ships were detained at a place situated some distance up the Bete River, and that the Bete Rajah had promised to restore one British boat to him. The Rajah had assured Lieutenant Maxfield that he had delivered up to the Kutch Rajah five boats on the British Government's account. Maxfield reported that Sergeant Evans had joined him in the ship *Barbara* and brought with him a small pattamar restored by the Kutch Rajah, as being British property.[47]

We return now to the *Lively* incident. It must be said without hesitation that Lorimer and Kelly were completely wrong in their accounts. The Qawāsim were never involved. The whole episode was an object lesson in the misinformation that was put out against the Qawāsim, and a clear evidence of the bungling and mishandling of the Gulf situation on the part of both the highest and the lowest levels of officials of the British Government and the East India Company, if one can thus differentiate between them.

To clarify the incident of the *Lively*, we shall quote in full the report of a committee that was set up to consider the whole affair:[48]

Bombay Castle, 24th March 1809.
Letter from Messrs Money, Goodwin and Briscoe.
Hon'ble Sir,

In obedience to your commands, under date the 7th ultimo appointing us a committee to enquire into and report on the case of the dows, which had an engagement with the Lively schooner, and which have lately arrived from Surat, we have proceeded by an examination of all the parties, from whom we could derive information to make ourselves acquainted with the circumstances of this extraordinary case; and we have the honour of submitting the result of our deliberations on the subject.

2. It has appeared to us that there were two points in this case of superior importance, to which all others may be regarded as of subordinate consideration. First that of the real character of the Arab vessels. Secondly, that of aggression.

3. For the following reasons we are unanimously of the opinion that the character of the vessels was mercantile; when they fell in with the Lively they had not been longer from Soor, in the neighbourhood of Muscat, than was necessary for the accomplishment of an ordinary passage. They were, when

seen, steering a course which would have conducted them to Surat, and to that Port they ultimately proceeded.

4. Had there, therefore, been the slightest doubt as to the question of aggression, we should concur in opinion on the justice of releasing the dows, considering the Nakhoodas to have been sufficiently punished by the long detention which they have already experienced; but the fact of aggression having been established against the dows, our President and Mr Briscoe are of opinion for the reasons which will be hereafter stated, that their release would be an injudicious measure while, on the other hand, Mr Goodwin is of opinion that as their character was innocent in the outset, further allowances should be made for the error they committed, and that their dows should be restored to them with a serious warning to be more guarded in their further conduct.

5. The result of all the examinations has proved in the judgement of Messrs Money and Briscoe, that from the relative position of the Lively and dows, and the state of the wind, the latter, in compliance with those fears which the Nakhoodas say in their petition they entertained, had it in their power to have avoided the Company's cruiser. It also appeared that from the position in which they were placed with relation to the Lively with a perfect view of her mode of rigging, which it was not possible to have mistaken for that of a vessel from Moozafurabad, or of any country vessel whatever; more especially, such as these people have known to be employed in piratical pursuits; they proceed however on a course to meet a vessel with such fears as they have stated to have felt, and when within hail commence an unprovoked and wanton attack, and order her to lower her sails; immediately after which the Company's colours were seen, and known as such, yet no respect was paid to them but the act of unprovoked hostility was repeated and there can be no doubt that their object was, at that time, to capture the Lively.

6. Under these circumstances, the President and Mr Briscoe being decidedly of opinion that the safety of the Honble Company's cruisers, particularly those of a smaller class, is materially dependant on the protection which the Honble Company's colours ought to afford, and that the important public dispatches entrusted to their charge will hereafter be endangered by permitting such a flagrant breach of the amity subsisting between the British Government and the Arabian States to pass with the impunity they recommended; that the crews of the dows, being released, their vessels may be confiscated, as a memorable warning of the inevitable consequences that must ensue from any repetition of such aggressive conduct.

7. Mr Goodwin for himself, begs to observe that it appears to him most extraordinary and unaccountable that vessels of the acknowledged mercantile character of dows, bound from a friendly port, to one of our one should without any visible cause, attack several armed vessels of the Company's, when they allowed English trading craft, which the prospect of booty, might induce them to lay hands on, to pass perfectly unmolested, and that having made an assault on a Company's vessel which they must be aware would render them liable to be treated as pirates, they should continue, and complete their original voyage

to Surat, unless conscious of having after their first discharge of musquetry acted on the defensive alone, Mr Goodwin means not to say that the aggression was on part of our vessels; the Nakhoodas of the dows admit that they commenced the firing of small arms which, with the strange conduct observed by them, was sufficient to excite Lieutenant Macdonald's suspicions and to warrant his keeping them at a distance. But in support of the Nakhoodas' statement that they considered themselves chased, is the acknowledgement of Lieutenant Macdonald that he sent a pattamar ahead to reconnoitre the stranger and followed her himself, and that he did not alter his course until ten minutes before the action began. Hence then it is obvious to Mr Goodwin that the Company's vessels were for some time standing directly for the dows, a circumstance that might in his opinion have given rise to the apprenhension they describe, and have perhaps prevented their seeing the colours of the Lively, as well as distinguishing her rigging, which certainly did not seem to have attracted their attention, for even now they point her out as being a ketch.

8. Mr Goodwin has read Lieutenant Macdonald's logbook and affidavit, as well as the other papers before the committee, and in support of his opinion that the action in some measure sought, begs to quote Lieutenant Macdonald's report of 25th November being in 12 fathoms off Mangrole, on the 22nd instant at 11 a.m. I brought to close action four large piratical dows, mounting from four to six carriage guns each, and crowded with musquetry.

9. They were ably defended and repeatedly attempted to board us on both sides, till forty minutes past noon, when the sea breeze setting in light, enabled them in their shattered state to haul beyond the reach of our cannonades.

10. We pursued till they ran us hull down, and seeing no further prospect of again closing with them, our musquet ammunition, grape and canister shot being nearly exhausted with three feet water in the hold, I relinquished the chase and hauled to the S.E.

11. Neither is Mr Goodwin able to trace in Mr Macdonald's logbook, or his affidavit, or in any of the other depositions taken before the Superintendent of Police, those indications of determined hostility described or repeated attempts to board, and so far from being crowded with musquetry it is observable from the actual search of the dows at Surat, that there were no more than twenty-nine match locks, and eleven guns, (including swivels) on board the four whilst a reference to Mr Macdonald's log has satisfied Mr Goodwin's mind that these native commanders could not have tacked to avoid the Company's cruisers without deviating in some degree from their direct course to Surat.

12. Previously to the alienation of the dows, Mr Goodwin conceives a more minute examination of the crew on both sides is imperiously called for, in order to establish beyond the possibility of doubt, that the proceedings of our boats, while the vessels were approaching each other, and subsequently thereto, was entirely free from blame, and such as the obvious circumstances required, without an enquiry of this kind, Mr Goodwin does not conceive Government possess sufficient proof against the dows to justify, to an allied power, the extreme measure of confiscating the property of its subjects. On the contrary,

he considers the evidence defective and in a degree that the examinations before the Superintendent of Police cannot supply; and is therefore of opinion that the Nakhoodas of the dows have been sufficiently punished, for the first aggression, by the long detention they have experienced and that they should be released with an admonition to be more circumspect in future, when meeting with a vessel carrying British colours.

Bombay   We have the honour to be & ca. & ca.
                                           Signed/W.T. Money,
                                           R.T. Goodwin,
24 March 1809   C.J. Briscoe

It is important to note that this committee understood its terms of reference as 'first, that of the real character of the Arab vessels. Secondly, that of aggression'. The committee never questioned or even mentioned 'the real character of the Arab vessels', and we shall return to this point later. On the second question, 'that of aggression', the committee attempted a whitewash operation, trying to prove that the *Lively* was the innocent party that came under attack. But the obstinate honesty of Mr Goodwin made that impossible and must have embarrassed the other two members immensely.

The embarrassment of the committee must have risen to new heights when the members read the following letter from the Imām of Muscat to the chief of Surat:[49]

Translation of a letter from Imam of Muscat to the Chief of Surat, dated the 5th Mohurrum 1224 Hujree, or 21st February, as presented at the office of Country Correspondence by the Nakhoodas of the confiscated dows, on the 28th March with the envelope opened and supervised etc. received the 2nd of March 1809.

                                           Signed/N. Grant

A.C

Four dows, the Nakhoodas are Bakheet Ben Salim, Pishair Ben Sunan, Abdulla Ben Humeed, Saud Ben Salim, subjects of mine, having sailed from this quarter for India, have been by the divine decree seized by mistake by the officers of the Government and they are unable to prosecute their occupation and obtain livelihood in consequence of being detained by you. I therefore beg leave to trouble you with a request that you will, in consistence with the existing intimate and close connection, release the vessels in question and allow them to proceed to their destination; for whatever appertains to me concerns your Government, I am confident they will not experience longer detention, but that you will allow them to depart and thereby cherish and corroborate the relations of friendship, harmony and alliance so happily subsisting between the two States, continuing at the same time to advise me of the awareness of that quarter and to command my services in this question.

                                           A true translation.

Signed/R.T. Goodwin
Secy & Translt. in the office
of Country Correspondence

If we were surprised by the honesty of Mr Goodwin and his stand against the other members of the committee, we are equally surprised by the audacity of Jonathan Duncan, the governor of Bombay, who ignored all the facts which he knew very well and persisted against all reason in arguing a wrong case. His answer to the Imām is an outstanding example of warped argument, straight lies and intolerable arrogance:[50]

To
The Imam of Muscat, dated 30th March.

Within this day or two I have received from Crou at Surat the letter which you wrote to him under date the 5th Mohurrum 1224 Hejree, desiring the release of four dows therein adverted to as belonging to subjects of yours and having been as you observed seized by mistake by the officers of this Government.

This state of the case and the impressions your Excellency may in consequence have received must proceed altogether from the misrepresentations of the interested people who may be owners of the said dows, and who although fully conscious of the misconduct and atrocious acts of the people on board of them, in beginning to fire on and to seize and destroy the Honble Company's cruiser appointed for the protection of the fair trade, have nevertheless the audacity to assume the disguise of being honest men and innocent navigators, but the truth has been here clearly proved after the most minute enquiry, viz. that they unprovokedly attacked and endeavoured to carry our cruisers by seizing, in which intention they persevered till a protracted engagement, finding themselves unable to effect their criminal object, they betook themselves to flight and trusting not to be recognised, had the assurance to make their appearance afterwards at the Bar of Surat, which they were sent down to this place, where after the fullest and most impartial intention the aforesaid piratical attempt having been satisfactorily proved in them, the dows have been adjudged to be confiscated whilst were the rigour of the laws to be followed up in regard to the persons on board, the latter would be liable to be hanged. There being no crime held in such general detestation as that of piracy on the high seas, such as by the laws of all countries is punished capitally notwithstanding which these evil doers have, from an excess of limit on our part, been set at liberty and left to shift for themselves and will no doubt have already taken measures for returning to their country.

The plea of defence set up by these people of their having mistaken the Company's cruisers in country boats such as . . . about in plunder, is altogether nugatory and incredible for besides the Company's colours, the shape, masts and rigging of the Hon'ble Company's cruisers are in no respect similar or can be mistaken in country boats of any description as is well known by everyone.

Under the circumstances I persuade myself that you will concur with me in the indispensable expediency of making an example of these freebooters, more especially in times like the present, when as your Excellency knows, the Joasmee pirates infest the seas and were the principle one allowed of the Honble Company's cruisers being mistakable in country or piratical boats (which is in fact altogether impossible) these would be securedly in the navigation of any smaller vessels, whose present safety in the any voyages, they singly make depends in many cases not so much perhaps in their own separate though as from the general instructions of all the persons around that they can never be attacked with impunity (sic throughout).

I feel convinced that the several considerations I have from the real regard I have to you, taken occasion to submit to the candid consideration of your Excellency, will prove and suffice to satisfy your mind as to the justice and policy of the measures pursued with respect to the dows in question, at the same time that such is happily the connection between the two states and my consequent disposition to meet your wishes, that should your Excellency continue anxious to procure the release of these dows, they shall be given, upon my again hearing from you, whilst their immediate detention constitutes your Excellency will readily acknowledge the slightest desire of chastisement that under any view of the case its circumstances can possibly admit of.

Signed/J. Duncan
& ca. in Council

Duncan also wrote a letter to Seton:[51]

That he may deliver the same to the Imam and express upon his Excellency's mind the necessity there is for making the present example in times more particularly like the present, when piracy near the shores of Arabia has got to such a height in so much that it would be highly commendable in his Excellency that, instead of desiring the return of the dows in question, he will give consent to their being burnt in the harbour of Bombay as an example to other offenders, but still, if he really desire it, they shall be delivered up to his order; Government, however, depending that in such case, he will take official measures for preventing any of his subjects from venturing on such excesses in future.

Seton and Malcolm Once Again

We do not know the precise end of this episode, but we do now know that the Arab boats were Omani trading boats and that the Qawāsim were not at all involved. We also know that Seton was back in Muscat as of January 1809 on the explicit suggestion of Malcolm, who had just been entrusted by Minto with the superintendence of British interests in the Gulf. With Malcolm back in Bombay and Seton back in Muscat, their combined efforts were bound to create new complications for the whole area. Less than a month after his arrival in Muscat, Seton was filing one report after another to Malcolm, almost trying to create a crisis atmosphere. On 5 February, 1809, he wrote:[52]

To
Brigadier General Malcolm,
Sir,

I had the honor to write the 2nd instant on my arrival here and then mentioned the reports of pirates being at Khorfacan, a port on this side of Cape Mussendum.

Since that, they have been seen cruizing near Rasul Hud, and spoke a dow that arrived here yesterday they said they intended to line up the coast from Bombay up to Surat and Cutch, and then cross to Mocha; this last is a pretence to avoid pursuit. Eighteen other vessels are gone towards Sind.

The agents to Derraya to claim the restitution of Shinas and other forts taken from the vali of Sohar, were very ill received by Sohood, who informed them they would not be returned until the Emam sent his vessels against Bussora, or gave a proof of his attachment to the Mussulman cause by sending a predatory expedition to India; he added he was then going to Mucca and if on his return he found they were not prepared at Muscat to proceed to Bussora, he would visit Muscat in person.

The 4th I waited on the Seyud at his request. He enquired what cause of offence he could have given to Government that they had not answered three letters he had wrote them. I imputed the delay to a reference to the admiral being necessary in regard to the four ships bought last at Mauritius; he said he had something particular to communicate when we should be more private, and yesterday the 5th, I again waited on him. He stated his situation with the Wahabee, that owing to the disaffection of the chiefs of Oman he was unable to resist the Wahabee who insisted on his going with a fleet against Bussorah, and wished to know if he might answer the Wahabee, that the British Government would resist an attack on the Turks. He also mentioned his situation with the French, that he was determined to break with them altogether, and wished to know if the English would assist him in case of attack from the French, or if they would send a vessel as they had formerly offered to convoy the fleet from Muscat to Bengal. I could only promise to write and communicate what answer I should receive, but this is an object well worth the consideration of Government and requires a prompt decision, as on it depends whether the State of Muscat shall be reduced, like the Joasmee, to become pirates, or remain merchants.

Six Wahabee teachers are now at Muscat compelling the people by blows to pray in their manner, and they force the merchants out of their houses to go to the mosques.

They are building a large fort at Joh on the Western frontier of the Oman as a place of strength from which they may command it.

They exact from the Joasim a fifth of all prizes they make. In their last cruize the Joasim took twenty country boats of different sizes, which success has quite elevated them, and they are now sending upwards of forty boats towards Sind and Cutch; it must therefore be recollected in whatever orders are issued to act against the pirates, that they and the Wahabee are one.

From the news brought by the Minerva Junajine, your intended voyage to the Gulph will be delayed some time, but I hope I will be excused in bringing to your recollection that I have no orders on this head, and that there is an immediate necessity for something to be done, and also for suggesting that if a power was given me to collect the cruizers now in the Gulph and which will not be required at Bussorah from the peace with the Turks, and authority to act in concert with the Seyud, I have no doubt but these pirates would soon be reduced within their natural bound and prevented doing any essential injury to our trade until Government should take more effectual measures for their punishment.

The Seyud is very anxious for a decisive answer on the points I have stated above, and there is no doubt but that with our assistance he will resist the Wahabee to the last extremity and concur in every plan we may have in the Gulf.

Muscat Cove on board	I have the honor to be,
the Turnate	& ca. & ca. & ca.
5th Feburary 1809	Signed/D. Seton
	Resident

Three days later Seton wrote, this time to Duncan:[53]

Honble Sir,

I had the honor on the 2nd instant to notify my arrival at this place on the preceding day, and now enclose a copy of my letter of the 6th instant to Brigadier General Malcolm.

The Teynmouth Honble Company's cruiser arrived the 3rd from conveying the Minerva past Rusul Hud, the 7th she sailed again on a cruize in pursuit of the pirates reported to be in the Gulf.

Three vessels arrived yesterday, the 7th, from Bussorah and report that the vessel by Lieutenant Salter as coming within the time limited for the purchase of vessels from our enemies, by neutral powers, had been set at liberty at Abushire and had pursued her voyage to Bussorah.

The letters mention that peace had been concluded between the English and the Porte, and Russia.

The vessel that carries this has on board four hundred candies of sulphur, should that article be required for the Honble Company's use. I have desired the owner to give the refusal of it to Government.

The Wahabee have made a great progress in this quarter, during my absence, as detailed in the letter to General Malcolm, but if our vessels are allowed to co-operate with the Government here they will soon be repelled again, as the inhabitants both here and in Oman are well inclined to a vigorous resistance. At present the Seyud has agreed to go against Bussorah in the proper season, but will refuse if the British Government will give a decided negative to his going, which it will be their interest to do, to prevent the further progress of anarchy and confusion.

On board the Ternate   I have the honor to be,
8th February 1809   & ca. & ca. & ca.
                                                     Signed/D. Seton
                                                     Resident

Almost a week later Seton wrote again to Malcolm:[54]

To
Brigadier General Malcolm

Sir,

I have the honor to write the 6th instant detailing the requests of the Imaum of this place.

Seyud Mahomed Ben Kulfan came again to consult on the advisability of sending an agent to Bombay who might state matters more fully than could be done by letter. On the supposition that your coming might be delayed I recommend the measure to them, and an agent is now preparing to set off.

In the meantime I hope I will be excused for repeating the necessity of adopting some measures to put a stop to the ravages of the pirates, until Government can come to some definite determination regarding them.

Two men arrived from Izabara, stated that they and a number of others were taken and sold as slaves but these two being too old to work had been dismissed; that while they were at Rasul Khaimah an English brig and some boats had been brought in as prizes. They were part of a Surat convoy and this had caused great rejoicings all over the country.

Abdulla Ben Gabber, a noted pirate known by the name of Jillama, has taken a ship belonging to this port on her voyage from Bussorah, and murdered most of the crew.

There is now here a small ship, the property of Abdulla Aga, once Mussellum of Bussorah, now residing at Abushire, bound to Mauritius to claim the property of Persian merchants shipped at Bengal on English bottoms taken by the French. They say they have letters and lists of the goods from Mohamed Nuby, a letter from the French in Persia to the Governor of the Mauritius and a passport from Sir Harford Jones, but I have only seen the lists of these papers.

The goods have been long sold and the voyage in every respect a fruitless one, except the profit the owner may draw from the sale of his present cargo of salt and salt fish, an object too trifling for such an outfit, and I rather believe it is on the chance of recovering part of the property in ships, as in the instance of the Sherrif of Mecca to whom the French gave a ship in return for his money captured in 1806, in consequence of an order procured thro' the French Ambassador at Constantinople. Mohomed Nuby is said to have pointed out this method of getting ships to the King of Persia.

The pirates were reported to have captured a dingy near this port the 12th; in consequence the Ternate sailed in that direction but saw nothing, and returned on the 15th when I landed and took possession of the former house.

Muscat   I have the honor to be,
16th February 1809   & ca. & ca. &ca.
                                               Signed/D. Seton
                                                        Residt.

On 6 March Seton wrote another long report on the same subject, but with more details, to Malcolm.[55]

To
Brigadier General Malcolm
Sir,

I had the honor to write several times of late communicating the sentiments of this Government, and their wishes for forming a common cause with the Honble Company against those tribes that disturb the peace of the Gulf.

The 2nd instant Abdul Rehman Ben Rashed's brother son of Khulleefee Shaikh of the Uttoobee, waited on me and said that authorized by his relations the Shaikh of Izabara and the Shaikh of Graine, he had to consult me on the nature of the orders our cruisers had received from Government, as one of their boats had been pursued by a brig pulling with sweeps, and as he was aware the outrages on our trade were committed by the Wahabee and the Uttoobee were their subjects, he wished to know if Government had, or would include them, in the orders issued to the cruisers.

I assured him Government were as yet ignorant of the course that led to, or of the persons who committed the outrages he alluded to, and if they had been chased it could only have been with the intent of discovering if they were boats fitted for piracy, not with any intention of disturbing the Uttoobee in their lawful concerns.

He said the instigators to the attempts on our vessels were the Wahabee, who were daily pressing them to proceed on schemes of piracy to India, but they had heretofore avoided complying with their requests, and the Wahabee had received their excuses, as they had not the power of compelling them to join in their plans, for want of a naval force, and for fear of inducing them to retire to Behereen in the event of their being disturbed in their present residence of Iazbara; but now they had set aside the ruler of the Joassim and established their own officers in the country of Seer, they were provoking a war which must soon break out between them and the Joassim, without the Uttobee would join in their piratical schemes, and he wished from me a direct answer, whether in the event of their retiring the main and withdrawing themselves from the Wahabee allegiance, the British Government would lend them such support as would enable them to remain undisturbed in Behereen, and that the greatest assistance they could possibly ever require would be a vessel or two for a short time.

I answered such an assurance could only come from the Honble Company's Government in India, and I should write without delay and return them whatever answers I should receive.

In this he acquiesced, and requested that what has passed should only be divulged to those concerned.

It will be unnecessary for me to point out the advantages of such a connection in securing the future quiet of the Gulf, their situation on one side of the Joassim and that of Muscat on the other holds out every prospect of effectually checking this new and pernicious system arising from the avarice and fanaticism of a despicable tribe in the centre of the Nedjed who, by reducing their neighbours to misery and poverty, have made them the unwilling instruments of their robberies and piracies. It would be supposing the British Government had lost sight of those generous principles, that have heretofore actuated that policy to imply a doubt that they would not step forward to rescue from such an abominable slavery those who, by their trade, have so long encouraged their Indian manufacturers and cultivators, and it would be imagining them blind to their own interests to conceive they would allow those traders to be drawn into a state of actual robbery and piracy preying on their own subjects and allies without an effort to prevent it. It is therefore useless further to discuss the advantages or disadvantages of their connection, and our experience in the Gulf will render any further account of this tribe unnecessary, but the following particulars will show how they stand with this Government and enable you to form a distinct opinion on the nature of their requests.

The Uttobee were originally subjects of the Benecaled, settled in the Khadana and province of Burgutters, and resisted the Wahabee system to the utmost of their power, but unsuccessfully. Those of the Khadema collected in Graine where the Wahabee have never been able to make any impression on them, supported by the Shaikh of Zobier, and those of Bur Khutter driven from Izabara took refuge in the Island of Behereen in such numbers as to overpower the Persian Government there, and carrying a brisk trade to India direct without touching at Muscat, or paying the half duties paid by the other states in the Gulf to that power, induced Seyud Sultan to listen to the requests of the Wahabee and Persians to employ his ships against them, and Behereen was taken by him in 1801. The Uttobee thus subdued made their peace with the Wahabee and retiring from Behereen to their former residence with the assistance of the Wahabee, retook Behereen in 1802, but afraid of putting themselves in the power of Seyud Sultan, they remained subject to the Wahabee at Izabara and sent an agent to govern the Island for them; but they have suffered so much from the tyranny of the Wahabee, that of late they have endeavoured to conciliate this Government and have frequented the ports and paid duties as other states, and this Government have also in every occasion shown them a preference in remitting what duties might fall heavy on them, so that no obstacle now remains to a solid agreement between them and this Government, but the want of a guarantee, who could secure the due performance of it on both sides, and to this is their present request confined, that we will assist them against any naval power who might disturb them in Behereen. Whether the Persians would be equally to come into such a plan as the Muscat Government is, I am not sufficiently informed to say.

Muscat   I have the honor to be,
6th March 1809   & ca. & ca. & ca.
                                                          Signed/D. Seton
                                                                  Resident

Once more, three days later, Seton wrote another report to Malcolm, although the two reports of 6 and 9 March were dispatched together.[56]

To
Brigadier General Malcolm
Sir,
    I had the honor to write the 6th instant but the boat being detained by a strong northwester, it will accompany this.
    A boat arrived from Sind, with 180 sepoys part of three hundred coming for the service of the Seyud from that country, reports that 6 or 7 Joassmee vessels had appeared off Coratchee and been engaged by seven dingeys fitted out for that purpose from Coratchee and driven on towards Cutch; the same boat saw 6 or 7 others but did not speak them.
    A ship is to be sent from them to protect the trade from Mocha and Turguchar in consequence of another party of these dows having been seen on their way to Aden, and Burbora.
    A small boat sent to Figuira with agents from the Seyud to Sultan Ben Suggur, was detained by the Wahabee officer, but the garrison being in the pay of Ben Sugger, he set her at liberty and the Wahabee pursued her after she left port, but she outsailed them.
    The agents are, in consequence of the letters I mentioned as having been received from Ben Sugger, complaining of his situation and in wishing to make a common cause with the Government against the Wahabee, another express from Rasul Khimeh on that subject arrived the 7th; on the return of the Seyud the particulars will be known.
    A report prevails that Sohood, who went to meet the Tyrian caravan, was repulsed by it. There is time for such accounts to have reached Izabara, and the first boat from that will either confirm or refute this report.
    Seyud Said is now in Oman, in consequence of the flight of Mahomed Ben Nasser, whose seizure I mentioned in a former letter.
    The Seyud set him at liberty after taking possession of his forts Ismahe, and Bedbid, with permission to reside in paternal estates, but being afraid of his life he fled to a port belonging to the Gafrey.
    The Persian armies have seized Bustuck, and sent the leading men and their families to Sheraz in consequence of their not having paid their tribute for many years on pretence of their dependencies Charick and Shine being in

possession of the Wahabee; whether the troops will move on to clear these places, is not yet known.

Another party have gone against Banpore which would appear as if the Persian King has determined on re-establishing his power among the Balootchees, who have been independent since the time of Nader.

Reinforcements have been sent from this Bunder Abbas, the possession of which to Muscat has heretofore depended on the difficulty of subsisting a force equal to take it in its neighbourhood, which could not be done whilst the Bustuckee, Ahmedee and Balootchees who surround it, and Minab, were equally interested in maintaining their own, and its independence.

The Eliza sailed from the 26th ultimo and in consequence of the troubled state of the Gulf, I sent the Ternate to accompany her as high as the Quoins where two cruisers were reported to be, and if they engaged, to see her safe to Abushire; the Ternate should return, if not she should see her safe to her port.

His Majesty's ship Cornwallis, Captain Montague, arrived here last night and I received the enclosed letter from her Commander, to which I sent the enclosed answer.

Muscat,	I have the honor to be,
9th march 1809	& ca. & ca. & ca.
	Signed/D. Seton

On 21 March, Seton wrote another lengthy report to Malcolm:[57]

Brigadier General Malcolm.

Sir,

1. I had the honor to forward the intelligence of this place up to the 9th instant and now enclose a copy of a second letter to Captain Montague, who sailed with three Bengal ships the 14th instant for Abushire.

2. Accounts from Bunder Abbas confirm the taking of Bustuck; and that four of the chief men had been flayed alive for contumacy. Parties are employed against Lingua Charack & ca. whose inhabitants have taken to their boats, abandoning their habitations.

3. A small party on horse have also come to Khammeer to demand the tribute of that, and Bunder Abbas; the latter will be paid them.

4. The Khan who commands all these parties resides at Lar; for the present he has under him a thousand horse.

5. A ship will sail from this in five days, carrying back Wahabee teachers and a demand on Sohood for the return of the ship taken by Jillama.

6. The Seyud himself will go to Ormus in a week more; he is repairing and talks of removing the merchants from Bunder Abass to that fort, in case the Persians make any attempt on it. The report of Muscat's, having acknowledged the Wahabee has spread a great alarm in Persia, and it is supposed will induce them to resume the tributary places held by the Seyud.

7. The Seyud has expressed considerable anxiety for an answer to these points I wrote on in my first letter from this, which could not be expected as the accounts for the arrival of the vessels at Bombay had not yet been received

here; this I represented to him.

8. The pirates that have gone towards Mocha will find protections and aid at Hodaida and Lohaja. It would be advisable the Commander of the cruiser that may go to Mocha, or any resident who may proceed from Bombay, should be instructed how to act on this head.

9. The reports of the pirates on the coast of Sind are, that two boats had shown themselves off Coratchee and Allih Ruckih who was acting for Nur Khan at that place, had taken two dingeys belonging to merchants and two small vessels belonging to the Uttoobee, and put five hundred sepoys on board and sent them out to engage the two boats then in sight. These sailed away and drew the Coratchee boats within reach of nine others who were at anchor, who, getting under weigh, attacked the Coratchee boats and took one Uttoobee dow and one merchant dingey, killing 40 men of the Uttoobee and 18 of the crew of the dingey, and every sepoy they found in them; the other dingey and an Uttoobee bottilla got off.

10. Last night news arrived from Coratchee that the 2nd instant an English brig had engaged the Joassim fleet off Hengole near Sonmeany, sunk five of them and chased the other two small boats, a dingey and bottilla belonging to these pirates had been drifted ashore at Sonmeanay from whence an express, with accounts of the action, had been sent to Coratchee, where a boat being on the point of sailing brought the news here in five different letters received. There is no variation in the circumstances related.

A bottilla arrived this morning from Bunder Abbas; a Frenchman with two horses embarked on the boat the 12th instant, and off the Sevady Islands, seeing the Cornwallis and other ships, he ran in shore for B . . ., landed with his horses and is coming over land.

The Seyid this morning, the 19th, sent the Broker to say that reports had been received that Jullama had proceeded with the ship he took off Bussorah bar to plunder and in consequence, he was sending three other vessels, one to proceed to Bussorah bar direct, one to Khor Hassan where Jullama resides, and one to cruise in the Gulph, and as this would probably lead to a complete rupture with the Wahabee, would our Government also break with them. I answered that it was supposed in Bombay the piracy proceeded from the Joassim, I had wrote the true state of the matter and until I should receive an answer I could not say what were the sentiments of Government. The object of this is to prevent my making any demand for the detention of the Frenchman, or otherwise on the strength of his first propositions, till a definite answer is received.

The reports of the defeat of Sohood have been repeated from other quarters with the addition that he and many of his followers were killed in the engagement, but this report is by no means certain.

The Frenchman arrived here the night of the 19th is the same who was landed by the Sherreef of Mecca's vessel about 6 months ago, and found his way from this to Abushire and Tehran, the latter place he left the 23rd January and reached Bunder Abbas the 11th instant. He was accompanied by another

Plate 1

The Fleet under convoy of HMS Chiffone, Capt. Wainwright leaving Bombay Sept. 14th 1809. From the Apollo Gate (R. Temple HM 65th Regt)

Plate 2

Muscat Harbour/ from the Fisher-men's Rock (R. Temple HM 65th Regt)

Plate 3

Rus ul Khyma, with the attack of the H C-s Cruisers/ on the evening of the 11th Nov. 1809 (R. Temple HM 65th Regt)

Plate 4

The wall and beach near Rus ul Khyma, with the troops preparing to land/ on the morning of the 13th Nov. 1809 (R. Temple HM 65th Regt)

Plate 5

The troops landing at Rus ul Khyma/ at Sun-rise — 13th Nov. 1809 (R. Temple HM 65th Regt)

Plate 6

The storming of a large storehouse near Rus ul Khyma, where Capt. Dancey, of HM 65th Regt was killed / Nov. 13th 1809 (R. Temple HM 65th Regt)

Plate 7

Rus ul Khyma, from the S.W. and the situation of the troops/ at ½ past 2 pm Nov. 13th 1809 (R. Temple HM 65th Regt)

Plate 8

A view of Linga or Lung, from the sea/ during the destruction of the dows 6c Nov. 16th 1809 (R. Temple HM 65th Regt)

Plate 9

A view of Luft, 26th Nov. 1809 (R. Temple HM 65th Regt)

Plate 10

The attack on the Fort of Luft, Nov. 27th 1809 (R. Temple HM 65th Regt)

Plate 11

A view of Mutra from the East (R. Temple HM 65th Regt)

Plate 12

Schinaass from the sea (R. Temple HM 65th Regt)

Plate 13

The attack of the enemy's cavalry at Schinaass, Jan. 2nd 1810 (R. Temple HM 65th Regt)

Plate 14

Schinaass from the right of the encampment, on the morning of the 3rd Jan. 1810 (R. Temple HM 65th Regt)

Plate 15

The Storming of Schinaass, Jan. 3rd 1810 (R. Temple HM 65th Regt)

Plate 16

Ras ul Khyma, Persian Gulf — 1809 (J. Thirtle)

Plate 17

Khorfakkan

Plate 18

Bushire (Lieutenant-Colonel Charles Hamilton Smith)

Plate 19

Ras el Kyma, chief port of the Wahabee pirates (Lieutenant-Colonel Charles Hamilton Smith)

Plate 20

View within the harbour of Muscat (Lieutenant-Colonel Charles Hamilton Smith)

Frenchman who has remained at Bunder.

He had a letter and package of shauls from the Ambassador at Tehran to the Sayud; the letter was merely complimentary in answer to a letter wrote by the Sayud complaining of the French taking his vessels.

The season for Tungauber, Mauritius and Mocha is now past, and he must remain here for some time. I have not ascertained whether he has any packets with him or not. Khadje Cassim, the Agent of Mahomed Akil, who cut off the American ship in the Red Sea, has taken him under his care and prevents the access of those to him who could examine his saddlebags for papers.

The Frenchman knows nothing of Sir Harford Jones's movements, as he did not come by way of Sheraz — which place he supposes Sir Harford Jones has not yet left, and the king had not invited him to Tehran.

Lieutenant Hewart being unwell, and no medical assistance at this place, I have recommended his return to the Presidency by this opportunity.

Muscat   I have the honor to be & ca.
21st March 1809   Signed/D. Seton, Resident

Immediately the following day Seton wrote again:[58]

Brigadier General Malcolm
Sir,

The Joasmee fleet returned from the coast of Sind and anchored off Coratchee the 14th instant. The account they give of themselves is that after engaging the Sindians at Coratchee they went on to Cutch and off Jigat were engaged by an English brig in the evening and fought till night, when they separated and returned up the Gulf. They had taken no prize except the bottilla and dingey at Coratchee, which they had with them, and made in all eleven sail. They were very much shattered and full of wounded men they buried at Chehbar who died there. They delivered a paper signed by Hussan Ben Ghuss Joasimee, recommending Sohan to destroy all tombs in his country, or in the event of his not doing it, declaring war on him.

They were in great want of provisions and much disheartened from their said success.

I am in hopes the Cornwallis will fall in with them. She left this, the 14th, to stand up to the Gulf, and they left Chehbar the 15th to go the same way. As they sail fastest, there is every reason to think they would meet about the Quoins.

The person who gives their information was on board their boats as a messenger. He also brought from Chehbar accounts of Captain Grant having reached Gih and Cusser Hand in safety, and had a letter from Meer Sohan saying he had assisted him, Captain Grant, all in his power to get on, but expressing anxiety for his safety on account of the savageness of the people.

Muscat   I have the honor to be & ca.
22nd March 1809   Signed/D. Seton, Resident

A True Copy
Signed/D. Seton

There seems to be no end to Seton's reports to Malcolm. Although he was writing from Muscat, Seton took it upon himself to report on everything and to convey every rumour concerning the whole area, be it about Yemen, Oman, the Peninsula, Baṣra, Persia or the whole length of the Indian coast. Very little of his reports can be substantiated and most of it is incoherent ranting that cannot stand up to any measure of scrutiny. In light of the fact that he was never in good health and that he was to die a few months after writing these reports, it is not inconceivable that he wrote them while suffering from extreme fever or even worse illness. Nevertheless, it is obvious that he was working on a scheme whereby he could form an alliance between the British and the Omanis against the Saudis. The more allies he could get together, of course, the better. He conceived of the Saudis as a major threat not only to the Gulf, but to the British in India itself, which was absolute nonsense. To his sick mind the Saudi danger was most clearly represented in the imaginary piracies of the Qawāsim. Thus he believed, and probably encouraged, rumours that alleged a Qawāsim presence in practically every port in the Gulf or reported impossible attacks off every port on the Indian coast, and also off the Southern coast of the Arab peninsula. Of course, there was never any point in verifying such reports, they only had to be conveyed to Malcolm in Bombay as quickly as possible.

Malcolm himself must have recognised the invalidity and the fancifulness of these reports, because he does not seem to have taken any measures to meet the mounting crisis described by Seton. On the contrary, Malcolm seems to have lost his influence with Minto, at least momentarily. Minto, who put off the cherished expedition that Malcolm had always so badly wanted, now reached the decision that it should be abandoned altogether, making it clear that Seton's reports were sheer exaggeration and had no truth to them. Accordingly Malcolm wrote the following letter to Seton:[59]

Captain Seton.
Sir,
I have the pleasure to transmit a copy of a letter from the Right Honorable the Governor General, from which you will observe that the expedition under my order is abandoned and the troops under my command directed to return to their respective stations. You will of course no longer consider yourself under my orders but act agreeable to such instructions as you may receive from the Government of Bombay.

I have written very fully to the Right Honble the Governor General on the subject of the pirates and I hope some early measures will be taken to check an evil which threatens and can seriously interrupt our future intercourse with the Gulf. I feel it a duty to express the satisfaction I have derived from your successful endeavours to obtain information on those points on which I directed your attention when you went to Muscat.

Bombay   I am & ca. & ca.
31st March 1809   Signed/J. Malcolm

Revival of the Expedition

Malcolm must at that moment have been preparing to leave Bombay, but once more the unpredictable, undecided and perhaps unstable Minto changed his mind. Once again the expedition was on. The Supreme Government, in April 1809, furnished the following instructions to the Governor relating to the expedition:[60]

Honorable Sir,

    We conclude that you have had access to the documents of which copies were enclosed in Brigadier General Malcolm's dispatch to the chief secretary of the 9th ultimo relative to the expediency of undertaking in concert with the State of Muscat an expedition against Joasmee pirates.

2. Our chief secretary's letter to the chief secretary at Bombay of the 13th ultimo will have apprized you of the circumstances which induced us to suspend a final decision on the question. But the communications contained in General Malcolm's dispatch above mentioned, have superseded the grounds of our hesitation and induced us to resolve upon the adoption of the measure, provided the Commander in Chief of His Majesty's squadron in India shall be pleased to appoint a force adequate to the service. We have accordingly addressed a letter on the subject to Rear Admiral Drury, a duplicate of which is herewith transmitted to you under the supposition that he may have arrived at Bombay or be on his voyage to that Residency by the time you receive this dispatch; our letter to the Admiral is left open for your persusal.

3. You will observe that we have proposed to Admiral Drury the employment of two frigates on the intended service, on the grounds of Captain Seton's suggestion. Your local knowledge, however, will enable you to judge the necessity of augmenting that force, and in concerting with the Admiral or with the officer whom he may appoint to conduct the expedition, the detail of measures. You will of course communicate to him your sentiments on that point.

4. As a number of cruisers which you may have the means of employing on this occasion must depend upon this point, it must be left to the decision of your authority.

5. We beg leave to suggest the expediency of embarking on the frigates and cruisers, a detachment of European troops to serve as marines, the number to be determined by the apparent exigency of the service.

6. A proportion of gun boats or other armed small craft we conclude will also be necessary for the purpose of destroying the pirates' vessels and boats that may be in the shoal water of the bays and creeks or drawn on shore.

7. As soon as you shall be apprized of the Admiral's concurrence in the proposed expedition, we conclude you will judge it advisable to dispatch immediate communication of the intended undertaking to the Imaum of Muscat through the Resident, and also inform the vakeels of the Imaum, if agreeable to his intimation to Captain Seton he shall have dispatched any to Bombay, and you will of course suggest at the same time the nature of the cooperation which may be expected from him.

8. It occurs to us that the Government of Bussorah may also be induced to cooperate to the extent of its means; that Government being interested in the suppression of the pirates in a degree little inferior to the Imaum of Muscat, and we recommend you issuing such instructions on this subject as you may deem proper to the Resident at Bussorah.

9. If Brigadier General Malcolm should not have left Bombay at the period of your receipt of this dispatch, you will probably deem it advisable to take advantage of his local knowledge and experience in arranging the details of the projected expedition.

10. We are of opinion that the operations of the armament, excepting in cases of particular emergency, should be limited to the sea and to the destruction of the pirate vessels and that the crews of the ships and the troops embarked on them should not be employed on shore against the land forces in the service of the Wahabee ships. At the same time we are aware that their exertions may eventually be required to recover for the Imaum some of the seaports between Rasoolhud and Musseldum at present in the hands of the Joasmees, and we do not mean to restrict the employment of the force in such cases of exigency, but we consider it of some importance to manifest as much as possible both by declaration and by action, that the expedition is directed, not generally against the tribe of Wahabees, but exclusively against the piratical branch of that tribe which has so long infested the commerce of India and the Gulf.

Fort William	We have the honor to be & ca.
3rd April 1809	Signed/Minto
	J. Lumusdeen
	R. Colebrook.

The Supreme Government wrote to Drury, the Admiral of His Majesty's Naval Forces, to join the expedition with part of his forces:[61]

To:
Rear Admiral Drury.
Sir,

We have the honor to submit to your consideration the enclosed copy of a dispatch from Brigadier General Malcolm under date the 9th ultimo, representing the necessity of adopting vigorous measures for the suppression of the pirates who infest the Persian Gulf.

2. Although the indiscriminate depredation of these pirates, and the strength which they have now acquired, would alone perhaps require the adoption of active measures for the security of the commercial interests of India, as connected with the trade of the Gulf of Persia, yet it will be obvious to you from a perusal of the enclosed documents, that the interest of the British Government in the suppression of the pirates is not exclusively of a commercial nature, while at the same time our interference appears to be indispensibly necessary to avoid the great augmentation of the evil which would be occasioned by the addition of the ports, the shipping and population of Muscat to the resources

of these already powerful marauders. But in a political, as well as a commercial point of view, the independence of the state of Muscat is of material importance to our interests, and the preservation of that independence appears at this moment to turn upon the cooperation of the British power against the Joasmee pirates.

3. Under these circumstances we have no hesitation in suggesting to your consideration, the expediency of employing part of His Majesty's naval force in concert with the marine force of Bombay for the execution of this important service, and you will observe that the Resident at Muscat considers two frigates, with the assistance of cruisers and gun boats, and the cooperation of the Arab states which may be securely relied on, to be sufficient for this purpose.

4. If you should be pleased to concur in this suggestion, we request you will concert the details of the expedition with the Honorable the Governor in Council of Bombay, to whom we have issued instructions on the subject in the event of your absence from Bombay, that you will issue directions to that effect to the officer to whom you may think proper to entrust the conduct of it.

5. We beg leave also to recommend to your attention the application of the Imaum of Muscat for a ship of war to convoy the periodical trade of that port to India.

6. It is proper to take this opportunity of apprizing you that we have lately understood by a letter from Bombay, that the plans communicated to you in our despatch of the 27th Febry, for the conveyance of the 2nd Battalion 20th Regiment Native Infantry from Bombay to the Eastern Island, would be attended with a degree of expense which may be avoided by embarking the troops on the China ships which will sail under convoy from Bombay in the month of May or June, a season also more favorable for the voyage. We have therefore authorised the latter arrangement and the necessity of appointing a convoy for the transports originally proposed to be employed for the conveyance of the Battalion is consequently precluded under these circumstances. We trust you will be enabled to devote two frigates to the suggested service against the pirates without inconvenience.

7. Your characteristic zeal for the promotion of the public interest leaves us no room to doubt your readiness to employ the means at your command for the execution of a service so urgent and important as that which we have now the honor to propose to your consideration.

Fort William   We have the honor to be & ca.
3rd April 1809   Signed/Minto
                                                      E. Lumsden
                                                      H. Colebrooke

It is instructive to note that, while Malcolm was mainly interested in an expedition to establish a base in the Gulf in order to control it, Seton was primarily concerned with fighting what he considered to be an overwhelming Saudi menace. The Supreme government was most careful to avoid a fight with the Saudis, putting forward the explanation that 'the expedition is directed not generally against the tribe of Wahabees but exclusively against the piratical branch of that tribe'. General Malcolm was particularly instructed that his forces 'should not be employed on shore against any land forces in the service of the Wahabee chiefs'.

Malcom saw his task as an 'expedition against the Joassmee pirates in coopera- tion with the Imaum of Muscat'. What had been envisaged as an alliance bet- ween the British and the Omanis against the Saudis became a British-Omani alliance against the Qawāsim, with the specific proviso of avoiding any clashes with the Saudis. In his report to Duncan Malcolm wrote:[62]

Honble Sir,
  I have been favoured with the perusal of the dispatch under date the 3rd instant from the Governor General relating to the punishment of the pirates in the Gulf.
  From the advanced state of the season, it will . . . be impossible to under- take any expedition against the Joassmee pirates in cooperation with the Imaum of Muscat before the month of August or beginning of September, but the in- tervening period will afford an opportunity of obtaining the most correct in- telligence and of arranging all parts of the expedition with the Imaum whom it is surely of importance to carry along with us on this expedition.
  2. A detachment of as many European infantry as His Majesty's ships employed could convey and a detachment of sepoys on board the Honble Company's cruisers of nearly equal strength (amounting altogether to at least four hun- dred men) placed under the orders of all intelligent and experienced officers, would appear at present equal to the service, but this point will be more cor- rectly determined when our information regarding those places where pirates shelter their vessels is more full and particular. The object of the expedition must be destroying their vessels, . . . there is no other way as far as I can judge of putting an end to their depredations in the Gulf. The pirates are strong whose faith cannot be trusted, and who are too . . . to be deterred by any reverses from resuming their occupation of harbours and who, though they may be checked by the appearance of a Muscat force for one or two seasons, will, if their vessels are not destroyed, seize the first opportunity of commit- ting fresh excesses.
  3. As almost all the timber of which the Arab vessels are built is bought in Malabar, it would, I conceive, be a good auxiliary measure to the system in- troduced by the Governor General not to allow any wood to be exported from the province by the Arab timber vessels under a special permission from Government.
  4. It will not be easy to engage the Imaum or any other chief in the cause, without a prospect of advantage but as we want no conquests for ourselves, we would probably be able, in the course of operations, to gratify their ambi- tion without making that the object of the contest. The real and avowed aim of which should be the promotion of our commercial prosperity, which it was obvious we most effectually would do, by giving encouragement to all those Arab states who pursued trade and by destroying those who subsisted by piracy.

It will be of great importance to keep the period of sailing and actual destination of the expedition a profound secret as the greatest hopes of its being attended with complete success must depend upon the pirates being taken by surprise and the measure after its adoption being carried into effect with the utmost alacrity and vigour.

1st May 1809   I have the honor to be & ca.
                                                        Signed/John Malcolm
                                                                   B. General

The officials immediately concerned with the preparations for the expedition, General Jones and Mr Money, presented their report and their point of view to the Governor:[63]

Honble Sir,
     We have the honor to acknowledge the receipt of your chief secretary's communications of the 4th May, transmitting for our consideration a letter from the Right Honorable the Governor General in Council dated the 3rd of last month and its enclosures, with one from Brigadier General Malcolm on the same subject, and requiring our opinion on the best means and fittest reasons as may appear to us for carrying into execution the expedition which the Supreme Government has been pleased to order.
2. Having perused these papers with due attention and deliberated on the subject of your reference, we are of opinion that the force to be employed in the reduction of the Joassmee pirates in concert with the state of Muscat should consist of two of His Majesty's frigates, two of the Honble Company's, best cruisers and six gun boats. Each frigate should be reinforced with 100 Europeans and 300 sepoys with a proper proportion of commissioned officers should be distributed among the cruisers and gun boats, the whole to be commanded by a respectable intelligent field officer.
3. The following Company's cruisers to be employed on this service, viz.
Mornington
Ternate
Fury
Wasp
Vestal
     One building and two gun boats to be built which may be soon constructed and on the termination of the service they can be retained and two old vessels disposed of.
4. The weather, within a degree of the land, being fair through the monsoon above Cape Rosslgate, there can be no cause on account of the season for delaying the expedition and we are therefore of opinion that it should be undertaken without loss of time.

Bombay   We have the honor to be & ca.
13th May 1809   Signed/R. Jones
                                                                   W.T. Money

In May 1809, Captain Wainwright, a naval officer well acquainted with the Gulf, was appointed to lead the expedition. The following month he submitted the following progress report to the Governor in Council, which was also laid before the Board:[64]

Honble Sir,

I have the honor to acquaint you that His Excellency the Commander in Chief of His Majesty's ships in India, has instructed me to communicate directly with your Honor in Council, relative to the armaments and intended to crush the pirates in the Persian Gulf.

In pursuance of His Excellency's commands, I beg leave to recall to your Honor's recollection that in a conference I had with you soon after my arrival from the Persian Gulf, I submitted as my decided opinion that the best plan to ensure success against the pirates was to send the armament to sea as soon as the direct passage could be made, when all the advantages arising from season, expedition and economy could be best obtained, that you did me the Honor to accede to my opinion, but observed that as the territories of the Imaum of Muscat were threatened by the Wahabees, it became highly necessary to assist that chief and to secure the port of Muscat; under this persuasion the armament was immediately put in preparation. Now if I am rightly informed of the apprehension of the danger of Muscat subsided, and in that belief I beg to submit to the consideration of you Honble Sir in Council the propriety of delaying the departure of the armaments until the direct passage to the Persian Gulf can be made. In this case all the vessels of war, particularly the bomb and the gun vessels as necessary for the attack of the pirates and which are unequal to keep the sea during the continuance of the western monsoon, would sail at the same time. From this union of force and the quickness of the passage, the armaments would act immediately against the principal piratical port without touching at any place on the way to obtain water and refreshments, which would become necessary after a long voyage, and consequently without affording to the enemy any intimation of its approach. The intensely hot season which continues till October and which renders active operations almost impracticable being past, the troops and seamen would proceed in their work with the greatest vigor, neither would the service be materially delayed by the detention of the ships in the harbour, for if they sailed in the first spring tides of July, and before that time I do not think the transports will be ready, the passage to Muscat could not be made in less than fifty days and it would take seven more to complete the water there which brings the first week in September, whereas if the armaments depart in the beginning of September the voyage to Muscat will not exceed four weeks, and that period would be the utmost extent of the delay of its arrival. I have ordered the Captain of His Majesty's ship the Caroline which sailed on the 15th instant, to consult in the most secret and unreserved manner with the Honble Company's Resident at Muscat relative to the safety of that port and to act according to his discretion on the information he will receive from Captain Seton for its security. Now if the alarm of the Resident is unfounded, the Caroline and such of the Honble Company's cruisers as are at Muscat, and which can be spared from other services, may be most usefully employed until the approach of the armament in protecting the trade and in preventing piratical vessels from getting to the Persian Gulf which I think can be done by cruising in the entrance thereof; should your Honor in Council accede to my proposition of detaining the armament, it will be proper that a vessel should be despatched without delay to appraise Captain Seton thereof and to convey to the Captain of His Majesty's ship the Caroline the orders which it would become necessary for me to give on the occasion.

La Chiffone in   I have the honor to be & ca.
Bombay Harbour   Signed/I. Wainwright
20th June 1809   Captain

The Governor presented his own opinion in the following Minute and put it forward with Wainwright's report:[65]

President Minute.

In submitting for the notice and for the decision of Government a letter of the 20th of this month from Captain Wainwright I have annexed a connected summary of our proceedings hitherto on the intended expedition to the Gulf of Persia from which it will appear that this Government is acting therein ministerially by directions from the Supreme Government under date the 3rd April, wherein after adverting to the necessity for the early interference of the British Government to prevent the port of Muscat from being (according to the impressions conveyed by the information from General Malcolm and Captain Seton) altogether destroyed as a port of commerce and its inhabitants and shipping added to the force of the pirates, the Right Honble the Governor General in Council considers the destruction of these freebooters to be indispensable provided the Commander in Chief of the squadron would appoint a force adequate to the service inclusive of such operations by land as might prove eventually requisite to recover for the Imaum of Muscat some of the sea ports between Russul Had and Mussendum at present in the hands of the Joassimees, desiring however that it may be rendered as clearly understood as possible that the object of the equipment has no further or any direct relation to a war with any of the Wahabee chiefs.

2. The supreme Government having desired that General Malcolm should be consulted on the detailed arrangement for the expedition that officer gave it as his opinion by a communication received from him on the 10th May that from the advanced state of the season, it would be impossible to undertake any expedition against the Joassimee pirates in co-operation with the Imaum of Muscat before the end of August or beginning of September, observing that the greatest hopes of the expedition being attended with complete success must depend on the pirates being taken by surprise; and the measure after adoption being carried out into effect with the utmost celerity and vigour.

3. With this introductory information a reference was made on the 4th of May to the Commanding Officer of the Forces and Superintendent of Marines for their joint opinion as to the fittest season and best means of carrying the above mentioned order of the Supreme Government into effect, referring to them at the same time the remarks above alluded to from General Malcolm.

4. In the meantime a letter was on the 15th of May received from Captain Seton (by the Chiffonne Captain Wainwright) pointing out under date the 7th of that month, that any operations the British Government might intend against the Joassmee should not be delayed; the hot season being (according to that officer's opinion) the best to act against these people when they are near home or engaged in their pearl fishery or harvest of dates which need of the case was in substance concurred in by the first report from General Jones & Mr Money under date the 13th May and wherein they notice that the weather within a degree of the land being fair through the monsoon above Cape Rosulgate, there can be no cause on account of the season for delaying the expedition, and they were therefore of opinion (vide para 55th of the summary) that it should be undertaken without loss of time in pursuance of which it was signified on the same day to Captain Byng, the Senior Officer of His Majesty's Navy in port that Government would be ready to give effect to the Committee's suggestions in as far as they might have his concurrence and as soon as the frigates and other vessels might be ready to proceed on the service in question.

5. It was precisely when this progress had been made that two or three days after the arrival of the Chiffonne, I had the pleasure of a visit at Paulm from Captain Wainwright, when some conversation ensued to the effect adverted to in that very respectable officer's address this day recorded. With the distinction, perhaps, arising from my own previous impressions having been chiefly as to the expediency of repressing the Joassmees, who as being subjected by the Wahabees and now become dependent on the latter . . . might in conversation be understood, generally, under that appellation whilst the opinion of Captain Seton as brought over by the opportunity of Captain Wainwright's return from Muskat must have been what chiefly weighed with me in agreeing and desiring to proceed immediately with the expedition against them, the more especially as I had no sufficient reason to conclude that General Malcolm would not have been under similar circumstances of the same opinion, had Captain Seton's letter of the 7th May arrived in due time for him to have perused it.

6. The Committee composed of General Jones and Mr Money having afterwards had referred to them a notice from Captain Byng of his having heard or understood that the expedition could not take place before the end of August, observed in their letter of 20th May that they saw, in that respect, no reason to change their formerly expressed opinion that a considerable part of the equipment might certainly proceed from Bomcay in the course of the then ensuing month of June.

7. Soon afterwards, viz. on the 22nd of the same month, Captain Byng addressed the Board urging the immediate dispatch of the expedition.

8. In a further report on the subject from General Jones and Mr Money dated the 25th of May, they suggest that if the destruction of the pirates were the single object in view, it would be the most advisable to defer the departure of the force intended for it till after the monsoon which would, they observe, afford time to collect all the vessels of which the armament was intended to be composed, and thereby facilitate the effect of the proposed attack from port to port, wherever the pirates might be known to have taken refuge, besides that the passages would be much shortened in the months of October and November, and that season prove also more favourable to European constitution.

9. These considerations appeared however to the Committee more than counter-vailed by the strong expediency as urged by Captain Seton and fully adopted (as the same Committee notice) by the Gov. General of our attending to the protection of Muscat so as to prevent its falling into the hands of the Wahabee, an event which would in the opinion of the General and the Superintendent tend materially to frustrate the leading object of crushing the Joassmees.

10. The Committee having determined on these grounds to recommend the immediate outfit and sailing of the armaments, proposed that a detail of Euro-peans not less in numbers than 450 should proceed with it, of which the

Chiffone frigate to carry	. . .	50
The Caroline "	. . .	50
The Mornington cruiser	. . .	100
and Transport	. . .	250
		450

to which strength the Committee proposed to add 250 sepoys, of whom 200 to be embarked on the Eugenia private ship and fifty on the Mercury cruiser to be transferred to the Ternate at Muscat, making the whole force 700, rank and file, the increase of 300 men thus intended being proposed in view of the eventual necessity of their having to defend Muscat; which united force sail-ing hence in June would arrive at Muscat in time to commence their opera-tions in September in as far as may regard the defence of Muscat, whilst with reference to the destruction of the pirates, that object would, the Committee remark, be thereby greatly facilitated and in the commencement of October the whole of the marine vessels and gun boats allotted for the service will be collected at the place of rendezvous and the general attack on the pirates may, it is added, be made without interruption along the coasts of the Persian Gulf.

11. Upon the receipt of this letter, Captain Byng was furnished with a copy of it and written to on the 2nd of June for information whether if on certain of the grounds contained in it, we deferred the departure of the expedition, we might still rely on the assistance of the navy at the period when, according to General Malcolm's quoted letter, it might be the most seasonable that it should take place, in reply to which it was signified by Captain (now Com-modore) Byng, that although he could not decide on the admiral's intentions, yet it seemed to him more than probable that during the present reduced state of the squadron, it might be out of the Commander in Chief's power to

meet the wishes of Government in September.

12. Under the impressions conveyed by this answer, it was on the 6th of June unanimously determined by the Members of this Committee not to defer the outfit or sailing of armament, but to proceed therewith without delay, of which resolution it was on the same day determined to advise the Resident of Muscat (as the Supreme Government had desired) accompanied with instructions as forwarded to that officer on the 8th or 9th by the Vestal cruiser to lose no time in connecting with Syed Said the Imaum and with the Resident at Bussora on the most efficacious and speedy means towards the suppression of the Joassmee pirates, in co-operation with the British force which as on the occasion announced might be expected to arrive at Muscat about the middle of July; it being at the same time intimated that the armament might also become eventually applicable to the support of the Government of the Imaum within the extent authorized by the Governor General's instructions.

13. It remains under these circumstances for the Board to decide on the subject of Captain Wainwright's letter now to be recorded, as to which I request to be favoured with the opinions of my colleagues.

Signed/Jonathan Duncan

From this Minute it becomes clear that Seton and Malcolm had managed to convince their superiors that Muscat was about to fall. Yet it was never made clear to whom it would fall and what shape this danger was taking. The defence of Muscat against this imaginary threat should not involve any conflict with the Saudis. But the destruction of the 'freebooters . . . might prove eventually requisite to recover for the Imaum of Muscat some of the sea ports between Russul Had and Mussendum at present in the hands of the Joassimees'. Here we have the real purpose of the expedition; it was to capture the Qawāsim ports that were able to compete directly with Muscat and add them to the domains of the Imām, which would give him a bigger capacity for trade with India. The competition of the Qawāsim would be further reduced by the destruction of their ships, and the common interests of the Company and Muscat would thus be better served.

Seton and Duncan were in favour of the expedition proceeding immediately in order that the Qawāsim boats should be caught in their ports in the summer. Malcolm, with strong support from Wainwright, was for mounting the expedition in September in order to take advantage of favourable weather conditions. Duncan had finally to agree and ordered the expedition for the autumn. On 7 September Duncan issued his detailed instructions to Captain J. Wainwright, RN the Commander of the Expedition with Colonel Smith of the 65th Regiment:[66]

The following instructions are prepared to be issued to the commanders of the expedition with enclosures.
To
J. Wainwright Esq.,
Captain of HM Ship Chiffonne, and Commanding the sea force of the

expedition destined to the Gulf of Persia.
Lieut. Colonel Smith,
Commanding HM 65th Regt. and the land force of the expedition destined
to the Gulf of Persia.
Gentlemen,

The Governor General of India having determined as you are already apprised, to undertake an expedition in view to the destruction of the piratical
power in the Gulf of Persia, and procured for this purpose the cooperation
of part of His Majesty's Naval Force in India, and committed the equipment
of the land force to proceed with it to the Government of this presidency as
well as the general arrangement and dispatch of the armament in consideration of the vicinity of this port to the intended place of operations, it is in consequence intended to furnish you with the following general instructions for
your guidance, entrusting you to apply their spirit and purport wherever the
letter of them may not be found sufficiently apposite.
2. It may be useful briefly to premise who these pirates are, with whom they
are chiefly connected and by whom supported, as well as to designate who
are their principal opponents.
3. The province of Oman comprehends the south easterly region of Arabia,
extending from Cape Rassul Hud on the south, to the territory of Zobara on
the north eastern coast, and is divided into two principalities. The capital of
the first of which is Rostuck and of the other Sir or Julfar. Of the former,
the principal sea port is Muscat and of the latter, Ras al-Khaimah, but although
Rostuck be the ancient capital of that part of Oman, known to Europeans under
the denomination of the territory of Muscat, its inland situation rendering it
of less consequence than the last mentioned sea port, the Honorable Company's
communications have always been carried on with the chieftain of the latter,
as if he were the superior of the whole territory, whereas in strictness he may
rather be obedient to the real Imaum, whose ordinary residence is at Rostuck.
But as all the British treaties and engagements have been with that member
of the family in possession of the sea port of Muscat, and who also assumes
the title of Imaum and is moreover in possession of Zanzibar on the coast of
Africa and of Ormuz Gombroon, part or the whole of the Island of Kishem,
and other territories on the Persian coast, which he holds in farm or by suf-
ference from the Persian Government, all your intercourse must be with him.
The name of the present Imaum of Muscat is Syed Saeed, the younger son
of the late Sultan, who having been a prince of great activity and judicious
management, maintained not only his own dominions in good order, but
overawed the licentious spirit of his maritime rivals, the principality of Sir,
who under their known designation of Joasmee, have ever, more or less mixed the practice of piracy with some degree of addiction to commercial pursuits, and having of late years become willing or constrained, have come to
the reformed Mahommedan faith of the Wahabee who has overrun their country. They have more recently availed themselves of that want of coercive control, so beneficially exercised over them by the late Sultan, to have carried

their piratical depredations to a height scarcely ever before known, appearing to spare or respect no vessels whom they have the power of mastering, whether Arabian, Turkish or British; having of the latter description, captured within the last two years no less than three, viz. the Sylph cruiser, which was taken before they could carry her into port, and on the 3rd July 1809, the Deria Dowlut, Captain Fleming in June 1809, and the Minerva, Captain Hopwood, both of which may probably still be found lying in the harbour of Ras al-Khaimah, if one or both should not have been intermediately broken up.

4. The immediate or rather ostensible chieftain of Ras al-Khaimah is Sheik Sultan, the son of Shaikh Sugger, but there is reason to believe that his authority is not sufficient to restrain these unprincipled depredations (influenced and dominated over, as they are by the delegates of the Wahabee, who is said to receive a fifth of their plunder), could his own inclination be ever depended on, under some disgust arising probably out of these circumstances, this Sultan deserted Ras al-Khaimah in the course of last year, and retiring to a neutral territory, made overtures to Syed Saeed of Muscat, who is in a state of war with the Joasmees, to reconcile their differences; professing, on that occasion, a desire to conform to a treaty or convention which Captain Seton, the late Resident at Muscat, had entered into under the instructions of this Government, and the approbation of that of Bengal with his now deceased father Sugger, under date the 6th of February 1806, by which he engaged on the part of his tribe, as per copy enclosed, to respect British property, which having, however, failed to perform, and the present extension of this piratical annoyance having risen to a height which appeared to the Supreme Government to involve not only the safety and independence of Muscat, but the currency of the commercial intercourse between the Gulf and India, the object of your expedition is, according to the instructions from the same high authority, to be directed to the destruction of these pirate vessels, the operations of the force under your command being, excepting in cases of particular emergencies, limited to the sea, neither are the troops or crews of the ships meant to be employed on shore against any land forces in the service of the Wahabee chief, unless their being so should be found essentially requisite, either for the destruction of the piratical boats or to recover for the Imaum of Muscat some of the sea ports between Rassul Hud and Musseldun, at present in the hands of the piratical Joasmees, who are all more or less under the general protection, and even dominion, of the Wahabee power, which had also about ten months ago reduced Syed Saeed of Muscat and the other branches of the same family, particularly that sub-division thereof, the chieftain of which named Uzzan, holds his residence at Sohar, to much the same sort of subserviency, obliging them to acknowledge themselves subordinate to his power and engaging also, as is creditably reported to assist in the extension of the same innovating and oppressive influence, as well in the direction of Bussora as eventually towards India; giving admission also to the doctors of the reformed faith into Muscat and including of course, a cessation of hostility with the Joasmee, the same superior sovereign being thus understood to be at the head of both

states. It was, however, sufficiently obvious that these compulsatory acts on the part of Joasmee of Muscat, would be of no longer operation than the direction of the necessity that had led to them, nor had the latter ever made any formal avowal to this Government of his having been reduced to such a state of even temporary and only seeming subjection, from which it is understod that he has availed himself of the late extraordinary events in so many of the Wahabee family, including Sahood, its last chief, being not long ago cut off by the plague at Duria their capital, leaving only a minor son and heir to carry on their consequently feebled Government, to shake off the yoke and expel the Wahabee teachers from his capital, who are since said to have been murdered, through the indigation of the people, on their journey homewards.

5. However that may be, it may likely prove the most promotive of success to the Supreme Government object in your expedition, that you should, without stopping at Muscat, advance immediately with such native pilots as may be sent out to you from the latter place, to Ras al-Khaimah for the purpose of recovering as much as possible of the plundered property, concurrently with the liberation of the British subjects and natives of our settlements in India now held in bondage by these barbarians, but chiefly in the view of burning and destroying all the vessels and craft that may be found in that harbour, meddling no more with the town, and not employing the force by land any further than may be found indispensable for the attainment of the first mentioned object.

6. Besides the principal port of Ras al-Khaimah, there are several contiguous ones from Rums to Aboo Heyle (as laid down in a topographical sketch of that part of the coast procured from Syed Tuckey) the boats in which may, as appertaining to the same piratical power, be all destroyed if opportunity offers.

7. In addition to these ports on the Arabian coast, the piratical Joasmee possess on the opposite one of Persia the port of Linga with the three subordinate Road Steads, in the same Bay of Koonz, Hemeraum, and Bundi Mallum, and have also occupied the port of Luft on the Isle of Kishm, all the rest of which is still understood to be in possession of the Imaum of Muscat. With respect to the last mentioned of these places, i.e. port of Luft, Mr Bruce the present Resident at Muscat, will be instructed to procure and communicate to you the assent of the Imaum of Muscat to destroy the maritime equipment of the Joasmee at that station, and although this Government have not yet received an answer to a communication made by order of the Supreme Government in June last to the Persian Government through the acting Resident at Bushire, of the intended destination of the present armament accompanied by an invitation to the same Government, to join and cooperate in its objects, or can consequently be said to have hitherto procured the direct acquiescence of the Persian State to similar measures being carried on at the port of Linga and its dependencies, as well as such of the other ports and places on the Persian coast as you may find the pirates in occupancy. Still there can be but little doubt of the ready acquiescence of the Government being received by the earliest

opportunity as you will probably find to have been already communicated to the Residency at Muscat, or received perhaps direct intelligence of from Bushire, with which you should take the earliest opportunity of communicating for the purpose previously to the course of your operation extending necessarily to the Persian side of the coast, but in any case you need not hesitate to proceed to destroy the maritime equipment of the pirates on that side of the Gulf, wherever you may ascertain them to exist, taking care to proceed in all such cases with the utmost practicable respect towards the undisputed right of His Majesty the King of Persia the present ally of our Sovereign, and to cause to be well explained to such of his officers as the course of events may lead you in communication with, that the British Government have no other object than to free the commercial intercourse with the coast of Persia from the obstructions and heavy losses to which it is now, and has so long continued exposed, from the predatory attacks of the Joasmee, and other pirates, without the slightest intention to occupy any part of the territory or molest or annoy so much as one of His Majesty's loyal subjects whom in pursuance of the happily cemented friendship between the two states it is, on the contrary, the desire of the English nation to cherish and protect and promote the prosperity of, to the greatest practicable extent, on which subject you are moreover furnished with the triplicate of a letter from the Governor of Bombay to the Prince of Sheerauz, which it is left to you to forward or to make such use of as circumstances may point out the expediency of; as well as of its copies in English and Persian, which are likewise forwarded for such local communication or instruction as you may find conducive to the great object of precluding misconstruction to and insuring satisfaction with the course of your proceedings against the freebooters in question.

8. A similar application has been prepared for the cooperation of the Turkish Government in the object of the expedition, should you therefore receive any communication from the Resident at Bassora connected with that application you will not fail to attend to the same in as far as the nature of it may be found compatible with the general powers with which you are vested by those instructions, considering also that His Majesty's and the Signior's Government being now restored to a fortunate state of harmony and friendship, it will be the more desirable to cultivate the goodwill of the Turkish Government during the course of your operations.

9. The unfortunate loss by death of Captain Seton at a period so critical as the present when he might have been depended on for a variety of local information which must now remain defective, renders it necessary to caution you to consider the particulars adverted to in the preceding observations, as affording only some general views for your guidance, amounting to a line of indication for your own, more satisfactory, enquiries on the spot since, in several respects, local circumstances may have changed since the period of our latest advices from Arabia. But as enough has been said to intimate you the several points of primary attainment in the extirpation of the means of future annoyance by the pirates, the Governor in Council places the utmost reliance on your

approved zeal and ability to direct the application of the force in the most advantageous manner, towards the easiest and most effectual acquisition of its genuine object, as prescribed in the decision of the Supreme Government the devising of the best means of carrying which into execution, his Lordship having, as above observed, been pleased to devolve on this Government, under such suggestions as might be furnished by General Malcolm, the Governor in Council has, after consulting that officer, accordingly adopted the measures and appointed the force deemed in his, and other competent opinion, adequate to the service to be performed, the employment thereof of your professional skill and gallantry, which will not fail to surmount such intervening difficulties as may occur; and to conduct the undertaking to the most creditable termination for the general good and to the relief of the commercial world, against those irreclaimable pests to the general prosperity.

10. Your intercourse with the Imaum of Muscat will, of course, be carried on chiefly through the medium of Mr Bruce, the present Resident, in which channel you will ascertain the wishes of Syed Saeed, which you will attend to and even comply with, as far as may be found compatible with the general success of the service entrusted to your charge, and at the same time within the line of the preceding instructions, beyond which, as prescribed by superior authority, the Governor in Council is neither authorised nor disposed to proceed.

11. It might, no doubt, be desirable (more especially in view to their connection with and degree of dependence on the Wahabee power), that after the enjoined destruction of their vessels a conciliatory convention might take place between the British and their petty states, stipulating for their future quiet behaviour and forbearance from piracy, which if you can effect the terms thereof, may be concerted in conjunction with the Imaum of Muscat, and with a due regard to his permanent interest as our ally or, if the piratical powers prefer it, they might be allowed to send over authorised vessels by the opportunity of your return, to treat at this place for a permanent accommodation.

12. Whatever may occur in this respect you will be careful to disallow throughout the service on which you are about to proceed, any intention of hostility towards the Wahabee power, of whose present connection with the Joasmees it is not even necessary that you should acknowledge any affinity or acquaintance, or enter consequently at all into the consideration or discussion as to any share or interest that the chieftain in question may possess in their depredations but acting towards and treating with them altogether on the footing of an independent state, as they appeared to be on the occasion of the treaty concluded with Captain Seton, although no doubt they were even then in constrained subordination to the superior power of the Wahabee, who did not, however, think it necessary to obtrude himself ostensibly in those transactions.

13. The Governor in Council earnestly recommend that the opportunity of obtaining the most accurate topographical information of the countries inhabited by the Joasmees, should now be best (sic: lost?) and you will no doubt select

for this purpose proper officers, marine as well as military, to survey and make charts and sketches of the coasts, creeks, harbours and countries that are in the possession of the Joasmees.

14. The Governor in Council would also be happy to be favoured with your opinion in respect of the most eligible island in the vicinity of the Joasmee ports which it would be advisable for us to occupy as a maritime station or residency in preference to Muscat, with the view of more effectually commanding the entrance of the Gulf and checking the future depredations of the pirates, accompanied by your sentiments in respect of the force that may be necessary to maintain the possession, not only against the native powers in the Gulf, but with with reference to such European force as occasionally visits that quarter and which it is not to be supposed will ever exceed two French frigates at the utmost. So long as we maintain our maritime superiority, the removal of the Residency from Muscat is the more desirable from the lamentable casualties that have occurred at that insalubrious station, at which perhaps every object we have in view would be attainable through the agency of the native broker, controlled by the presence of the Resident at a vicinal port.

15. The cruisers and transports composing the armament are enumerated in the margin,* and I have the honor to enclose an embarkation return of the detachment and a copy of the instructions issued to the Resident at Muscat under this date. The discharge of the transports at the earliest practicable period after the performance of the service by a return of as many of the troops as you can dispense with, will not fail, the Governor in Council is persuaded, to engage your attention.

16. Mr Watson Henshaw, the agent for the supply of the cruisers in the Gulf, and to whom is also committed the supply of the Company's vessels attached to your force, will officiate as your interpreter and will with that view be placed entirely under your orders.

Bombay Castle   I have the honor to be & ca.
7th September 1809   Signed/F. Warden, Chief Secretary

The main point of attack was to be Ras al-Khaimah, but all other Qāsimī ports from Rams southwards were to be attacked and their ships destroyed. Orders were given, however, to avoid any clash with the Saudis. Instructions were also given to attack all Qāsimī ports on the Persian coast. Almost to appease Malcolm, the commanders were asked to investigate the site for a naval station on an island in the Gulf from which to watch over not only the native powers in the Gulf but also any possible European intruders.

It is strange that the organisers and the leaders of the expedition did not possess accurate information on the whole Arab coast. They did not even know the exact location of their main target, Rās al-Khaimah. According to Kelly, 'some time

*HMS Chiffone	Ariel
HMS Caroline	Fury
Cruisers:	Stromboli
Mornington	Transports:
Aurora	Minerva
Nautilus	Friendship
	Duncan and Mary

after the expedition had departed, Duncan made enquiries among Persian and Parsi merchants at Bombay, familiar with the Gulf, and from their replies drew up a report on the naval and military strength of the ports which he forwarded too late to be of any use, to Smith and Wainwright'.[67]

Finally on 14 September the expedition sailed from Bombay. The force consisted of:

Chiffonne frigate	35 guns
Caroline frigate	36 guns
The East India Company's cruisers:	
Mornington	20 guns
Aurora	16 guns
Ternate	16 guns
Nautilus	14 guns
Ariel	10 guns
Vestal	10 guns
Fury gunboat	6 guns
Stromboli Bomb	
Transport:	
Minerva	Carrying about 700
Friendship	European and 500
Duncan and Mary	native troops

829 European soldiers
529 sepoys
252 followers

On the night of 14 September for some unknown cause the bomb vessel foundered, and 16 persons were drowned. By this melancholy accident a very material weapon was removed from the armament.

Owing to contrary winds the squadron did not arrive at Muscat until 23 October, and in consequence of the length of the voyage and the defectiveness of the water casks on board the cruisers and transport it was obliged to remain ten days before the rewatering was completed.[68] It was also a bad omen that on their arrival the news reached them of the death of David Seton on 2 August 1809, at his country house at Bushire where he had been taken from Muscat in a very poor state of health and dangerously ill.[69]

At the end of October the Imām of Muscat sent a letter to Duncan, the Governor of Bombay, stating the following:[70]

> In the first place as connected with the sailing of the fleet, I am happy to say it has (Praised be God) arrived in safety, and as to the despatch of the troops for the purpose of destroying and extirpating the Joasmees, who are equally the enemies of both states, I am informed that they are under the

command of two officers . . . with whom I had a meeting the day after their arrival at Muscat when I made myself acquainted with all their sentiments on the subject, and in view to the firm attachment which I bear to the Hon'ble Company's Government, I communicated to the aforesaid officers, the nature of the engagement which I had contracted with Captain Seton. I also laid before them in the most friendly manner, my own ideas as to the most eligible mode of proceeding against the pirates, with reference to the advantage of both states, but they would not listen to me.

Wainwright reported differently, however:[71]

The Commanders had at this place an unexpected difficulty to struggle with: the Imaum, whom reports said was in the interest of the French, was alarmed at the magnitude of the force sent . . . and so far from a ready cooperation there was great trouble in obtaining from His Highness even the assistance of the country boats; the fast of the Ramazan was also in celebration, during which the Mohammedans cannot be prevailed upon to work. At length on the 3rd November, the armament put to sea accompanied by twenty trankees, seven of which parted company on the voyage to Rasul Khaimah.

This town situated on the Arabian coast is the principal place of the pirates, and so strong was it considered by the Imaum, that he deemed the attack intended against it to be rash in the extreme, not only from the number of armed men in the town, but because the Joasmees could readily call to their assistance the Bedouin Arabs to the number of 20,000 men.

On 11 November the whole force assembled in sight of Rās al-Khaimah, but they soon discovered that their frigates could not get within four miles of the town; the smaller ships like cruisers and transports could do better and advance to within two miles. In Wainwright's words:[72]

The squadron anchored within 4 miles of Rasul Khaimah on the 11th November about two o'clock in the afternoon. On its approach, four very large dows which were going on a predatory excursion to the Red Sea sought refuge in the harbour. The Minerva, armed ship, in the hands of the Joasmees, retired to the westward of the town under cover of a tower. She was immediately attacked by the boats of the squadron, supported by some of the cruisers, carried and burnt. On the next day the town was cannonaded by the small cruisers and gun boats with visible effect. So destitute of personal apprehension were the Arabs, that the moment a shot fell numbers came to pick it up.

The place having been reconnoitred and the plan of attack formed, the troops were put in the boats early in the morning of the 13th and rowed towards the shore. A feint was made upon the N.E. part of the town a little before daybreak with two gun boats and 130 sepoys. The Arabs, who were in the mosque at prayer at the instant the gun boats opened their fire, rushed to repel the apparent attack while the main force consisting of His Majesty's 65th regiment, the flank companies of the 47th, the marines from the frigates and the small party of artillery with a howitzer and field pieces, advanced towards the southern end. The instant they discerned their mistake the Arabs ran towards the point of debarkation with tumultous shouts; but the grape shot from the gun boats shook them a good deal, and the troops landing in great style soon overpowered them. Brave and skilful in single combat, they were unable to withstand the shock of adversaries acting in a body. By ten o'clock the Joasmees were driven out of the town, the shells and spherical case shot from two howitzers and five field pieces annoying them very much. The former setting fire to some cadjan huts soon spread the conflagration to the town, a great part of which with the whole of the dows and naval stores were burnt by 4 o'clock. Thus, in a few hours was this enterprising and powerful people reduced to poverty and weakness.

Upwards of 50 dows were destroyed, 30 of them of very large dimensions. The troops embarked on the next day, and the Commanders of the armament had the satisfaction to find that the service had been performed with the trifling loss of 4 men killed and 19 wounded.

In his final report Wainwright gave the full details of the destruction of Rās al-Khaimah:[73]

Sir,

I have the honor to acquaint your Excellency that by the actions of the troops and the squadron under the respective command of Lieutenant Colonel Smith and myself, Ras al-Khaimah, the principal town of the pirates who have so long infested the Persian Gulf, has been completely destroyed, together with all the vessels in the port, amounting to upwards of fifty (about thirty of them very large dows) and of every species of naval stores.

The ships arrived off this place in the afternoon of the 11th instant but, in consequence of the shallowness of the water, were not able to approach the town within four miles, with exception of the small cruisers and two of the transports. These anchored from it as near as two miles. On the same evening the Minerva, an English ship, prize to the pirates, was burnt within twice her length of the shore.

On the following day the town was cannonaded for three hours by the small cruisers and gunboats, with considerable effect, and a little before day-break on the 13th instant an attack was made on the northern end of the place with two gunboats under the command of Lieutenant Leslie of the Chiffonne and a detachment of native troops; the main attack commenced at the southern end about half an hour afterwards consistently with an arrangement by the Lieutenant Colonel. The troops were soon landed and gallantly executing the admirable plan of their Commander, had possession of Ras al-Khaimah by ten o'clock, driving out the enemy to the opposite shore. The gunboats kept up a fire of grape shot on the sea side as the soldiers advanced. Before four o'clock all the enemy vessels were in flame together with their naval stores and houses in the town.

I received the most effectual assistance from Captain Gordon of the Caroline, who was with me at the landing and of the officers and men of His Majesty's ships, also from the respective Commanders of the Honble Company's cruisers attached to the armament and their officers and men. The marines of the Chiffonne and Caroline were disembarked with the army.

By the accompanying return your Excellency will have pleasure in observing that the loss of men on our side is trifling, while that of the enemy has been very severe.

I have the satisfaction to say that the most perfect cordiality subsists between the army and navy; such as promises to ensure complete success in all the subsequent operations.

The troops began to embark at daylight this morning and notwithstanding the great want of boats were all on board the transports before noon.

I have the honor to be & ca.

A true copy   Signed/J. Wainwright
Signed/J. Wainwright

Company's cruisers:

Mornington	Capt. Jukes
Aurora	Lieut. Conyers
Nautilus	Lieut. Walker
Prince of Wales	Lieut. Allon
Fury	Lieut. Davidson
Ariel	Lieut. Saltier

The Vestal joined on the 12th.

A return of men killed and wounded on board of and in the boats of the ships employed in the attack of Ras al-Khaimah on the 11th, 12th and 13th November, 1809

Ships' Names	Mens' Names	Quality	Killed or Mortally wounded	Wounded		Remarks
				Severely	Slightly	
H.M. La Chiffonne	James Gady	A.B.			slightly	
	Alexander Hood	A.B.			ditto	
H.M. Caroline	James Bryant	Ord.		severely		
Hon. Co's Cruiser	Andrew Wilson	Seaman		severely		
Mornington	William Gridby	A.B.		ditto		
Aurora	Mohomed Jaba Khan	Laskar	mortally wounded			
Nautilus	Francis Carrario	Ord.		severely		
	Ferraro	Top aft			slightly	

Ships' Names	Mens' Names	Quality	Mortally Wounded	Killed or Wounded		Remarks
				Severely	Slightly	
Prince of	Bellaul	Laskar	Killed			When
Wales	Accoob	Laskar	Killed			on shore ...
	John Brown	Boats'n		severely		a tower
	Alexander	Seaman			slightly	where the
	Burt					Minerva lay.

	Total killed:	2
	Mortally:	1
Wounded	Severely:	5
	Slightly:	4

Signed/J. Wainwright,
Captain of HM Ship La Chiffonne

It remains to be said that British sources estimated that 'from seventy to eighty of these vagabonds (i.e. the Qawāsim Arabs) were killed and many must have fallen in the previous bombardment'.[74]

The return of the killed and wounded of His Majesty's 65th Regiment shows:

1 Captain killed

1 Captain wounded

1 Serjant ditto and 2 rank and file.

Of His Majesty's 84th Regiment attached to the 65th:

1 Lieutenant wounded

Marine Battalion:

2 sepoys wounded

Total killed 1 officer

Total wounded 2 officers, 1 serjant and 7 privates

Names of officers killed and wounded

    65th Regiment   Captain M.M. Dansey

                      Captain D. Digby

    84th Regiment   Lieutenant J.F. Imes

It was also noted that Captain Dansey was killed by a spear, which was an indication of the ferocity of the fighting.

Perhaps it was a good indication of the wealth of the Qawāsim of Rās al-Khaimah that we have reports of considerable plunder of the town by members of the British force:[75]

It is said, in private letters from the expedition under the command of Lieut.-Colonel Smith that several privates of the detachments, both native and Europeans, had been fortunate in securing considerable sums of money during the ransacking of the town of Rus ul Khima; one soldier, of His Majesty's 65th regiment, is said to have found 1,400 gold Mohurs.

Charles Pasley, the Political Agent at Bushire, confirmed such reports when he boasted in a letter to the Persian Court in Fars:[76]

our troops obtained considerable property by the plunder of the town after the destruction of Rasul Khima & all the vessels in its harbour the squadron proceeded towards the ports of His Persian Majesty which were in the possession of the Joasmees and in a little time they will be entirely annihilated.

On 15 November 1809 the squadron sailed to the Persian coast to attack the Qawāsim there. In Wainwright's words:[77]

On the 15th, squadron sailed to attack the pirates on the Persian coast. On the 17th it was off Linga, that town was abandoned on the approach of the ships, and all the piratical vessels, twenty in number, nine of them very large, were destroyed without loss of lives.

The following is the report by Captain Wainwright to Admiral Drury:[78]

His Excellency
Rear Admiral Drury
Commander in Chief & ca. & ca.
Madras.
Sir,
My letter of the 16th November, a duplicate of which is enclosed, will have given your Excellency account of the proceedings of the ships and vessels under my order to that date.
On the 17th the vessels in the piratical port of Linga, amounting to twenty, nine of them large dows, were burnt without any loss on our side; the inhabitants having abandoned the town on the approach of the ships.
The contemptible holds of the Joasmees called Congo Bunder Mallum and Hemeraun were next reconnoitred but no vessels were there.
I then dispatched the cruisers Ternate and Nautilus to the eastward of Kishem to prevent the escape of the remaining pirates, while I entered the channel between the island and the main at the western end, but having got the ship I command aground in endeavouring to work through it, as I had no pilot acquainted with the navigation, and as the channel was too intricate to pass without buoying the shoals, which would have taken up too much time, I determined to proceed to Luft by the eastern channel leaving the cruiser Vestal to guard the western end of Kishem.
His Majesty's ship the Caroline had been previously detached to Barka Road with the heavy transports.
On the 24th ultimo the Ternate and Nautilus joined, and having procured pilots at Kishem I proceeded up the channel in His Majesty's ship under my command with the ships and vessels named in the margin,* and arrived off the town of Luft on the 26th noon.

*H.C. Cruisers: Ternate, Nautilus, Fury, Mornington; Transport: Mary

Twenty-four hours having been expended in fruitless negotiation with the chief Moolla Hussein; the Ternate, Nautilus and Fury were anchored off the town and the troops, preceeded by the gun boats, approached to the attack which commenced at two o'clock in the afternoon of the 27th ultimo. The enemy made no resistance until the troops came close to the very strong fort and attempted to force the gate, but then commenced to fire, I am sorry to say, most destructively as your Excellency will see by the accompanying return added to that of Lieut. Colonel Smith to the Government. The piratical vessels, eleven in number, three of them very large dows, were in the meantime burnt by the seamen and the gun boats and the cruiser Fury which, being of light draught of water, had been towed within musquet shot of the fort, kept up a ruinous fire which very much shattered it by sunset. The Sheikh then consented to yield up the place on the following day to the English on the part of the Imaum of Muscat together with all the property in it belonging to His Highness's subjects. This was accordingly carried into effect, the Sheikh departing after Lieutenant Colonel Smith and myself had guaranteed his personal safety.

The fort having been delivered in trust for the Imaum to Sheikh Derish the head of the Benimain, a tribe of Arabs who have always been firmly attached to his Highness, I sailed the next morning in La Chiffonne leaving the Mornington to bring on the cruisers and the transport to Burka, off which place I anchored this day.

The several officers and men employed with me behaved so as to merit my warmest approbation. The marines under Lieutenant Drury were landed with the troops and Lieutenant Critchton of the Chiffonne assisted with a party of seamen in dragging the howitzer close to the fort.

The loss of the enemy has been very great, he acknowledged to upwards of fifty, independent of those who were killed in the tower adjacent to the fort and . . . precipices to the eastward thereof.

I have the honour to be, with great respect,
H.M.S La Chiffonne
Barka Road   Sir & ca. & ca.
7th December 1809   Signed: J. Wainwright
                                                             Captain

A return of men belonging to His Majesty's ship La Chiffonne, and to the Honble Company's cruisers, Mornington, Nautilus, Ternate and Fury, who were killed or wounded at the attack on piratical port of Luft on the 27th November 1809

Ship	Name	Quality	Killed	Wounded
La Chiffonne	John Shay	Private Marine	''	
	Ed. Fane	''	''	
	R. Bulford			dangerously
	M.McNaughton			slightly

Ship	Name	Quality	Killed	Wounded
	A. Johnson	A.B.		dangerously
	H.L. Hormitte	ord'y.		dangerously
	W. Gilbert	Corp. of Marine		dangerously
	W. Crevard	P.M.		dangerously
	J. Wilkinson	A.B.		severely
	Thomas Kearney	A.B.		severely
	Thomas Hall	ord'y.		severely
	J. Mitchell	Q.M's mate		slightly
	J. Varseance	A.B.		slightly
	W. Crinton	A.B.		slightly
	Thos. Ellis	S.M.		slightly
	W. Moredith	P.M.		slightly
	Saml. Wyn	do.		slightly
	John Curry	do.		slightly
Mornington	M. Hay	md		slightly
	M. Ferrars	a.b.		slightly
	A. Hassan	sepoy		slightly
	Sheikkary	do.		slightly
	Naique Motor	do.		slightly
Ternate	J.W. Gay	md		slightly
Nautilus	Thos. Smith	boats'n		slightly
Fury	Raturning . . .	sepoy		dangerously
	Counsel Rd . . .	do.		dangerously

The recapitulation of the attack of the fort of Luft:

Killed	:	2
Dangerously wounded	:	7
Severely wounded	:	3
Slightly wounded	:	15
Total	:	27

Lieutenant-Colonel Smith of His Majesty's 65th Regiment reported that of the men under his command 31 were killed and wounded during the attack on Luft on 27 November 1809, and he estimated the Arab loss at about 80 to 90 men killed and wounded.[79]

Having accomplished their designs against Linga and Luft the British sailed towards Muscat on 29 November, arriving there on 7 December. There they hoped to be joined by the forces of the Imām for the purpose of attacking Shinās, Kalbā and Khor Fakkān.[80] On 24 December the expedition sailed from Muscat while the Imām led his forces northwards along the coast towards Shinās, both he and the British hoping for an easy victory and not completely realising the difficulty of the task ahead of them. Colonel Smith sent the following detailed report to the Governor in Council:[81]

Hon'ble Sir,

I beg leave to acquaint you that the expedition sailed from Muscat on the 24th ultimo and arrived at Shinas on the evening of the 31st in company with the vessels and troops of His Highness the Imaum.

Captain Wainwright and myself having reasons to hope from our success against other places that the Sheikh of this fort might be induced to

surrender without bloodshed, it was accordingly summoned on the 1st instant, but as this had no effect it was immediately bombarded by the ships and
gunboats. The situation of the fort was too distant to be reduced by these means
it was determined to land the troops the following morning, at which time also
those of His Highness took their ground on the left of the British. In the course
of the day our camp equipage ordinance and a week's stores of all description
were landed from the fleet in case of its being driven off by bad weather; I
was enabled to take up a very strong position in which I entrenched myself.

We had great hope that a few shells from a 10½ inch mortar and 2 howitzers
would have driven the enemy out of the fort, but they appeared determined
to hold out to the last and it became immediately necessary to raise a battery.
Although I had no heavy guns, this deficiency was speedily made good by
the zeal of Captain Wainwright, who was good enough to have landed from
the fleet with two twenty-four and one twelve pounder carronades, and three
brass twelve pounders. The battery with their guns and three field pieces was
completed in the evening of the 2nd instant and opened a very heavy fire at
daybreak on the 3rd between 9 and 10 o'clock. A breach was made in the
curtain and shortly afterwards one of the towers of the fort fell in. The guns
were directed to the other towers, from which however it was impossible to
drive the enemy out. I had appointed 2 o'clock to storm, in which a body of
400 of His Majesty's troops were also to assist, and I am sorry to say that
whilst our different detachments were taking up their station of attack, the
Omaun troops from thinking we had gone forward, or misunderstanding the
orders, got before the British and entered the breach first but the moment we
could get up, they readily yielded the remaining labour and honour of the day.

By 5 o'clock the fort was entirely surrendered and shortly afterwards we
gave it up to the Omaun troops. It is impossible to contemplate a more obstinate
resistance than was made by the enemy in this position. His defences were
nearly battered to ruins and the greatest part of his garrison lay around in mangl-
ed heaps, still in this hopeless condition after the body of his fort was occupied
by the British and Omaunees did he persevere at the least cessation of our
musketry to fire upon us from two of his towers, which were not sufficiently
destroyed that we could immediately dislodge him. It was in vain that we attempted to scale; every access to these buildings was strongly barricaded and
defended by long spears with showers of large stones from their tops. Evening was fast approaching, humanity and every other consideration called for
termination to such a dreadful sum of carnage. The few survivors in the fort
were therefore called upon to surrender and save their lives. They replied that
they preferred death to submission. I had now brought up from the battery
two twelve pounders and three field pieces and opened a heavy fire with double shot close under the tower, in order to level them, but the enemy still kept
up his fire and seemed determined to be buried in their last ruins. We resorted
to hand grenades and fire balls. These he returned upon us before they could
burst with the most deliberate resolution as the towers were rapidly falling
in and every soul within them must have perished in a short time more. I again

ceased firing and made another effort to save their lives. Happily, one man acquainted with the English character, at length came forward and after reiterated assurances of protection from the Omaun troops, we were enabled by his means to save 110 other persons who now are our prisoners, but it was difficult to prevent their being destroyed by our allies.

I enclose a list of killed and wounded and rejoice it is so small which is to be entirely imparted to our artillery; the enclosed copy of orders will show the disposition of the attack, and express how much reason I have to be satisfied with the brave little force under my command.

Lieutenant Leslie and Sir Charles Chambers of His Majesty's ship La Chiffonne and the gunner of His Majesty's ship Caroline, with parties of seamen worked the ship guns in the battery, without which it would have been impossible to reduce the fort, and I cannot sufficiently express my obligation to Captain Wainwright and these gentlemen for their zealous and hearty exertions.

The Royal Marines of the two frigates under Lieutenant Drury did duty with the 65th ashore, during the whole affair and were of great assistance.

The Imaum's troops were between 3 and 4000 in number and suffered but little in the storm but they had frequent skirmishes with various success and loss. The loss of the enemy was at least four hundred killed.

I am sorry to say the fort was so greatly demolished by our fire that His Highness did not think it prudent to keep possession of it.

Head Quarter H.M.S.   I have the honor to be
8th January 1810   Signed/L. Smith
                                                                        Lieut. Col.

His Majesty's 65th Regiment and Hon'ble Company's Marine Battalion

	Killed	Wounded		Killed	Wounded
Europeans:			Sepoys:		
Lieutenants	—	2	Soobadars	—	—
Sergeants	—	1	Jamadars	—	—
Rank & file	1	6	Havildars	—	—
			Rank & file	—	2
Total	1	9	Total		2

After the capture of Shinās the plan called for a combined British-Omani attack on Kalbā and Khor Fakkān. It is not clear why this attack did not take place; what is clear is that the British expeditionary force spent the rest of January 1810 in an orgy of destruction. Lorimer testifies that:[82]

leaving Shinas, the expedition returned to the Persian Gulf and on the 15th January 1810 reached Rams where 10 large vessels were given up to be burned. At Jazirat-al-Hamra, the next place visited, the people at first made a show of resistance, but learning that the town of Rams had been spared, they eventually surrendered 8 large vessels for destruction. At Sharjah no large vessels in good condition were found. The war fleet of Ajman evidently was spared or escaped, for in 1811 we find it cruising in the Gulf in company of the pirate Rahmah-bin-Jabir. On the 21st of January the armament, having crossed the Gulf, anchored at Mughu on the Persian Coast, and four Sharjah boats found in the anchorage were destroyed. Nakhilu, Charak, Kung and Band Mu'allim were visited, but no large craft were found; a strict warning was addressed, however, to the Sheikhs of the first two named ports.

At the end of January Colonel Smith informs us that:[83]

The objects of the expedition having been thus far performed the transports were ordered to repair off Muscat preparatory to their return to the . . . Captain Wainwright and myself proceeding to inform ourselves of some eligible spot for the eventual formation of a Residency or military port as required by our instructions. While off the Island of Hangam on this duty we were joined on the 30th instant by His Majesty's ship Psyche having on board Brigadier General Malcolm.

Although there was no further mention of the investigation of an island suitable for a British military base in the Gulf, Malcolm gave Smith and Wainwright new food for thought since he brought with him fresh orders for the expedition to attack Khor Hassan, the base of the real Arab pirate of the area, Rahma b. Jābir of the Jalāhima. It is an established fact that Rahma was a 'Utūbi whose main adversaries were his cousins the 'Utūbis of Kuwait and Bahrain. However, he did not always confine his attacks to ships belonging to Kuwait and Bahrain; ships from 'Irāq, Persia, Oman and India were subjected to plunder by his hyperactive fleet. It is arguable that he did more damage to Arab-Indian trade in the Gulf than any other group accused of such activities in the area, but the British authorities in India seemed to want to ignore his activities and to pretend that they did not really affect their trade in the Gulf. When they were finally forced to think about taking some action against Rahma, it came almost as an afterthought in the form of a message which Malcolm was asked to deliver to Wainwright and Smith, who were about to lead their expedition back to base. What followed was an extraordinary four-cornered argument involving the leaders of the expedition, the Resident in Bushire and Muscat, Mr N.H. Smith, who was also the brother of Colonel Smith, Mr Bruce, the long-time acting Resident of Bushire, and Duncan, supported by his Chief Secretary, Francis Warden. The voluminous correspondence between these officers and officials is too long to quote here and is also not really worth discussing. They argued as to whether Rahma b. Jābir was really doing any harm to British interests, and when this argument was settled against him they argued as to whether to negotiate some agreement with him or to mount an attack on his base. This latter argument was interlocked with another one, as to whether Rahma was an ally or a subject of the Saudis. The net result was that no action was taken,[84] and the expedition returned to India in February 1810.

Kelly's evaluation of the results of this expedition is rather instructive:[85]

> judged in terms of its objectives the expedition of 1809–10 was not very successful. Several dozen Qasimi dows had been destroyed and their chief port battered, but most of the Qasimi fleet had escaped destruction. . . . No marked benefit accrued to the Sultan of Muscat from the attack on Shinas or the chastisement of the Qawasim. Khaur Fakkan and the other harbours on the Shamaliyah coast remained in their hands, and he continued to lose ground to the Wahhabis, abandoning all Oman north and west of the Batinah to them.

Kelly seems to have forgotten that the expedition was not intended for the benefit of Oman but was directed against the Qawāsim and was specifically ordered not to have any confrontation with the Saudis.

One other measure of success which the British failed to achieve was to obtain the help they had solicited from the Persians and the Ottomans in their attack on the Qawāsim. They had asked the Persians for a force of as many as 10,000 men to attack the Qawāsim ports on the Persian coast and then to cross the Gulf to Rās al-Khaimah and join the British forces in the attack.[86] Although the Persians promised help against the Qawāsim, at least on the Persian coast, this help never materialised.[87] The Ottomans in 'Irāq did not respond at all to the British request for help against the Qawāsim.[88]

If the expedition was not very successful from a military point of view, it was even less so from a political point of view because by the end of the campaign no treaty had been concluded with the Qawāsim in accordance with the orders to Captain Wainwright and Colonel Smith. The latter wrote to the Governor in Bombay explaining that:[89]

> We consequently proceeded off Rasul Khaimah but have been unable to fulfill the instructions of Government to form any treaty, Ben Sugger the former chief of that place having been seized by the Wahabee and his Government completely overthrown in consequence of the loss he sustained from the English, independent of which we have now well ascertained that no treaty could ever be binding without the direct authority and participation of Sohood, or his sons (to whom he has resigned his power), the Joassmees being entirely dependent in all things on that tribe.

Here Smith tries to imply that Sulṭān b. Ṣaqr was not in the area at all at that time. Yet we have proof to the contrary. Sulṭān b. Ṣaqr might have been away outside Rās al-Khaimah itself but he was certainly in the vicinity, as he explained in his letter to the leader of the expedition:[90]

> Translation of a letter written in the Arabic character by Sultan Bin Sugger Joasmee, to the commanders of the armament and brought by Abdulla Eben Kassim Eben Croosh, as given by Mr Hanshaw, interpreter.
> In the name of the most merciful and beneficial God.

Seal

I who am Sultan Eben Suggur Ben Rashid Ben Mootur have called God to forgive me, and I present my respect to the great English Sirdars whose prosperity God grant may increase.

You have come to my capital and whatever you wished you accomplished, but such was the will of the Almighty, and between you and I a treaty did exist as well as friendship for some time past through the agency of Mr Seton. When you came I was not at Ras Al-Khaimah, I went to collect troops in the country for the purpose of fighting against those who have been the cause of creating dissention between you and me. When your property was seized and captured I was not present, I was at Deriah; and when you arrived at Ras al-Khaimah you did not give me time to negotiate with you as we were before friends. I sometimes since wrote to you* and now my man Abdulla Eben Kassim Eban Croosh is sent to you and whatsoever matter exists between you and me he will advise you of, and whatsoever information you require he is qualified on my account to afford and whatsoever misfortune has befallen me he will impart to you, so that you be not ignorant thereof. My respects to you and whatsoever God wills must be.

Dated Shaval in the year of the Hejira 1224.

A true copy
Signed/J. Wainwright Capt.
L. Smith
L. Coll

*If this means writing to us, we have never received that letter.

J. Wainwright.

Smith and Wainwright may not have received the other letter referred to by Sulṭān b. Ṣaqr but they certainly must have received this one and must have met the messenger of the Qāsimī leader.

To clarify this point we must explain the situation of Sulṭān b. Ṣaqr in his own country. We know that he was still in Rās al-Khaimah in March 1809 when he went to Darʻiyya 'with gazies to dispute with Saood on the legality of his proceeding to Seer, the Qawasim country'.[91] It is not clear, nor could it be proved, whether he was ordered to go or whether he was arrested in Darʻiyya. However, it was reported that he returned via Mokhā and Muscat. Most important is the fact that while he was in Muscat he met with the Imām who tried to persuade the Qāsimī leader to co-operate with him against the increasing encroachment of the Saudis. But Sulṭān b. Ṣaqr refused the Imām's approaches. At that point he probably wanted to wait until he returned to his capital, when he would be in a better position to judge the whole situation.

The undeniable fact is that he returned. The disputed points are: when did he return, and to where? Lorimer implies that he was away for five years and was then reinstated in 1814 with the help of the Imām of Oman, and even then was reduced to only Shārjah.[92] We shall return to this last point later on but there is no doubt that Sulṭān b. Ṣaqr returned to Rās al-Khaimah before the death of

Seton in August 1809, for Seton wrote to Malcolm:[93]

> Sultan Bin Sugger Joassim rendered a cypher in his own country by the appointment of Wahabee officers Qazy has applied to Seyud Said to lay aside their quarrels, join together against the common enemy. Sugger is now at Luft, and has wrote me on the state of matters in his country, professing his readiness to maintain the treaty he made but regretting his inability; I have not yet received the letter but have heard of it.
>
>   Hussun Ben Aly and four other officers have been appointed in the different countries dependent on Ras al-Khaimah and have superceded all the former authorities.

The authority of Sultān b. Ṣaqr might have been diminished by the appearance of Hasan b. ʿAlī, the long troublesome chief of Rams, in concert with four other local leaders as Saudi representatives, but Sultān b. Ṣaqr was there, and he was trying his best to reach a peaceful settlement with the British even when their forces were battering his capital. As is clear from his letter to Bruce dated 20 January 1817:[94]

> The past offences occurred without my authority and sanction for as Saood had then established his supremacy over my subjects, I lost the power of restraint, and punishment. I still feel myself bound by the treaty established between us, and the sincerity of my friendship remains unchanged, for the almighty hath declared in his sacred volume 'who ever breaketh a treaty, injureth himself', and there is also no power of the full extent of which I am not informed.

Indeed, the inconclusive results of the British action seemed to have encouraged his hopes for a peaceful settlement as the basis for his future policy.

Notes

1. Bombay Archives (BA), Secret and Political Department Diary (S & PDD), no. 188/1806, pp. 7389–90.
2. J.B. Kelly, *Britain and the Persian Gulf, 1795–1880*, (Oxford at the Clarendon Press, 1968), p. 110.
3. BA, S & PDD, no. 194/1806, pp. 10, 009–11.
4. Ibid., no. 208/1807, p. 4947.
5. Ibid., no. 205/1807, pp. 3835–7.
6. Ibid., no. 236/1808, p. 7526.
7. Ibid., no. 238/1808, pp. 8299–300.
8. Ibid., pp. 8265–6.
9. Ibid., no. 327/1809, pp. 3557–67.
10. Kelly, *Britain and the Persian Gulf*, p, 110.
11. BA, S & PDD no. 207/1807, p. 4368.
12. Ibid., no. 232/1808, p. 5886.
13. Ibid., no. 220/1808, pp. 139–41.
14. Ibid., p. 139.

15. J.G. Lorimer, *Gazetteer of the Persian Gulf, Oman and Central Arabia*, (2 vols, Calcutta, 1908–15), p. 182.
16. Kelly, *Britain and the Persian Gulf*, pp. 113–14.
17. Lorimer, *Gazetteer*, p. 176.
18. *Selection from State Papers, Bombay (Sel. SP), regarding the East India Company's connection with the Persian Gulf, with a Summary of Events, 1600–1800*, ed. J.A. Saldanha, (Calcutta, 1908), p. 116.
19. BA, S & PDD, no. 231/1808, p. 5390.
20. Kelly, *Britain and the Persian Gulf*, p. 98.
21. Ibid., p. 91.
22. Loc. cit.
23. Ibid., p. 93.
24. Loc. cit.
25. Lorimer, *Gazetteer*, pp. 641–2.
26. Ibid., p. 638.
27. BA, S & PDD, no. 232/1808, pp. 5669–71.
28. J.S. Buckingham, *Travels in Assyria, India and Persia*, 2nd edn. (2 vols, London, 1830), p. 226.
29. Kelly, *Britain and the Persian Gulf*, p. 111.
30. Loc. cit.
31. C.R. Low, *History of the Indian Navy*, (2 vols, London, 1877), Vol. I, p. 320.
32. BA, Political Department Diary (PDD), no. 347/1809 (not indexed), pp. 11145–8.
33. Ibid., no. 336/1809, pp. 7342–6.
34. Ibid., no. 339/1809, pp. 8444–5.
35. BA, *Bombay Gazette*, Wednesday 4 October 1809.
36. BA, *Asiatic Annual Register*, 1809, p. 146.
37. BA, S & PDD, no. 251/1808, pp. 12991–6.
38. Ibid., no. 232/1808, pp. 5835–9.
39. Lorimer, *Gazetteer*, pp. 602–3.
40. BA, S & PDD, no. 255/1808, pp. 14147–50.
41. Lorimer, *Gazetteer*, p. 641.
42. Kelly, *Britain and the Persian Gulf*, p. 114.
43. BA, S & PDD, no. 175/1805, pp. 6525–7 and no. 177/1806, pp. 337–8.
44. Ibid., no. 177/1806, pp. 331–4.
45. Ibid., pp. 150–2.
46. Ibid., no. 178/1806, pp. 486–8.
47. Ibid., no. 181/1806, pp. 2309–13.
48. Ibid., no. 325/1809, pp. 2780–93.
49. Ibid., no. 326/1809, pp. 3145–7.
50. Ibid., pp. 3147–54.
51. Ibid., pp. 3154–6.
52. Ibid., no. 325/1809, pp. 2622–8.
53. Ibid., pp. 2619–22.
54. Ibid., pp. 2629–33.
55. Ibid., pp. 2692–5.
56. Ibid., p. 2702.
57. Ibid., no. 326/1809, pp. 3243–50.
58. Ibid., pp. 3210–11.
59. Ibid., pp. 3213–4.
60. Ibid., no. 329/1809, pp. 4382–5.
61. Ibid., pp. 4386–8.
62. Ibid., pp. 4392–4.
63. Ibid., pp. 4621–3.
64. Ibid., no. 334/1809, pp. 6276–81.
65. ibid., pp. 6281–94.
66. Ibid., no. 339/1809, pp. 8428–44.
67. Kelly, *Britain and the Persian Gulf*, p. 117.
68. Al-Qāsimī, Appendix 1.
69. BA, PDD, no. 339/1809, p. 8079.
70. Ibid., no. 346/1809, pp. 10932–4.

71. Ibid., pp. 10936-7.
72. Ibid., pp. 10945-6.
73. Ibid., no. 347/1809, pp. 11165-9.
74. Ibid., p. 11174.
75. BA, SDD, no. 261/1809, pp. 230-1.
76. BA, *Asiatic Annual Register*, 1809, p. 164.
77. Al-Qāsimi, Appendix 7A.
78. BA, PDD, no. 350/1810, pp. 13-21.
79. Ibid., pp. 22-36.
80. Ibid., no. 347/1809, pp. 11176-8.
81. Ibid., no. 351/1810, pp. 828-34.
82. Lorimer, *Gazetteer*, pp. 648-9.
83. BA, PDD, no. 352/1810, p. 1169.
84. Ibid., pp. 1169-71; no. 353/1810, pp. 1458-60.
85. Kelly, *Britain and the Persian Gulf*, p. 123.
86. BA, PDD, no. 338/1809, pp. 7998-9.
87. Ibid., no. 347/1809, pp. 11189-90.
88. Ibid., no. 338/1809, pp. 7996-7.
89. Ibid., no. 352/1810, pp. 1116-17.
90. Ibid., no. 350/1810, pp. 48-50.
91. Ibid., no. 327/1809, p. 3748.
92. Lorimer, *Gazetteer*, pp. 649-51.
93. BA, PDD, no. 325/1809, pp. 2644-5.
94. BA, Secret Department Diaries, no. 312/1819, pp. 1058-62.

4 Negotiations and Treaty 1814

Up to this point it has been seen that British policy-makers in India were determined to destroy the naval power of the Qawāsim in the Gulf. Although the war was obviously a trade war, the British had managed to convince themselves that it was a war waged to rid the Gulf of piracy. They were in no doubt, with or without reason, that the pirates were the Qawāsim, whom they accused of every possible evil deed in the seas around them. As we have seen, many of these accusations were proved to be false; nevertheless such lies continued to be circulated in the reports of British agents and Indian brokers alike. They continued to turn a blind eye towards their favourite pirate Raḥma b. Jābir. As Kelly argued:[1]

> If the extirpation of piracy in the Gulf was the Bombay Government's aim, then the destruction of Raḥma's power was plainly called for. He had committed piracy against most of the Gulf states, in circumstances of almost unbelievable atrocity, and his name was reviled from Basra to Muscat. In the last days of 1809 he brought off the greatest coup of his career, when he captured twenty Kuwait vessels bound up the Gulf from Muscat and massacred their crews to a man.

But this did not represent a threat to the Company's trade and thus could be ignored.

Proverbial British hypocrisy also extended in another direction. Although the Qawāsim were emphatically accused of acting on behalf of and under the complete influence of the Saudis, these were to be left alone and unchallenged. It became a cornerstone of British policy, which was communicated to every official in the Gulf, not to get involved in hostile activities with the Saudis and to refrain as much as possible from any acts of provocation towards them. The Omanis were fighting the Saudis and the Qawāsim. The British were willing to ally themselves to the Imām in any attack on the Qawāsim, but they were not prepared under any circumstances to stand by him against the Saudis. Indeed, they urged the Imām to establish peace with the Saudi leaders. As early as 1807 N.H. Smith, the then Resident at Bushire, corresponded and exchanged gifts with the Saudi leader Sa'ūd b. 'Abdil'azīz, while Manesty kept in touch with the Saudi Agent in Kuwait.[2] The Company's point of view was made very clear in a letter dated 18 September 1810, to the Chief Secretary of the Supreme Government:[3]

To Francis Warden Esqr.
Chief Secretary to Government.
Sir,
   I am directed to acknowledge the receipt of Mr Secretary Osborne's dispatch under date the 17th ultimo enclosing copies of a letter from the Imaum of Muscat

and of the Hon'ble the Governor's reply and desiring by direction of the Hon'ble the Governor in Council the communication of the sentiments of the Supreme Government regarding the advice to be offered to the Imaum with reference to the observation contained in his letter that he had refrained from taking advantage of the peaceable overtures of the Wahabee in consequence of his connection with the British Government.

2. The Right Hon'ble the Governor General in Council observes that this declaration on the part of the Imaum proceeds no doubt from a wish to consider the British Government to be united with him in his present action with the Wahabees, and to give general currency to the belief. The Imaum may expect to derive advantage from the reputation of having the support of such a powerful ally and may hope that a general belief of our being in a state of war with the Wahabee by exciting the hostility of that Chief may actually kindle a war with him, and thereby secure to himself the aid which he has solicited.

3. It is of some consequence therefore to discountenance this supposition, and as far as regards the understanding of the Wahabee himself upon this point, such an impression will probable be removed from his mind by the tenor of the reply to the letter of Saood and Rehma Ben Jauber to the address of Mr Smith suggested in my dispatch of the 7th ultimo.

4. It is proper however that the Imaum should be undeceived upon this subject or rather, that he should have no room to propagate the belief of our being a party in the war in which he is engaged with the Wahabees, against whom various considerations render it at present inexpedient and indeed, unpracticable, to afford him effectual assistance however desirable it might be, on abstract grounds of policy to support the independence of Muscat.

5. The Governor General in Council therefore recommends that the first opportunity be taken of adverting in a communication to the Imaum, to that part of his letter to which the Honorable the Governor has suspended a reply, by intimating to the Imaum that it is unnecessary to regulate his reply to any overture on the part of his enemy by a reference to his connection with the British Government, that Government having always considered itself to be at peace with the tribe of Wahabees, and having lately cooperated with him not in the prosecution of war against that tribe generally, but merely for the extirpation of the pirates whose augmented power and audacity had endangered the security of his dominion as well as interrupted the commerce and navigation of the Gulph. That therefore the British Government is no further interested in the existing contest between him and the Wahabees, than as it is soliciting for the welfare and property of the Imaum. That under the influence of this solicitude and of a just sense of the benefits and blessings of a state of peace, it is recommended to the Imaum, to grant the term of pacification solicited by the Wahabee, if consistent with the honor and security of the state of Muscat.

On the same day Duncan, the Governor of Bombay, wrote a letter to the Imām conveying to him almost *verbatim* the recommendation of his superiors.[4]

Disappointed in the British, the Imām turned to Persia for help against the

Saudis. Although the Persians were quick to help, their mercenary army of 1,500 men, including, strangely enough, 42 Russian prisoners of war, was of no noticeable effect. They spent the months from December 1810 until March 1811 trying to dislodge the Saudis from the fortresses they had occupied in the mountains of Oman but were badly defeated.[5] On 5 March the Imām with his army attacked the Qawāsim at Kalbā. There they killed a number of people and burnt their town and their boats. Having achieved very little on the Arab coast, the Imām and his troops made a passing attack on Linga before returning home.[6]

The Imām must have felt the pressure of the Saudis and was desperate for support, because in June 1811 his emissary Mājid al-Sūrī arrived at Bombay seeking help. On 7 June 1811, Goodwin, the Secretary and Translator in the office of Country Correspondence, wrote the following letter:[7]

> To
> Francis Warden Esqre
> Chief Secretary to Government.
> Sir,
>   Having, in pursuance of instructions conveyed in Mr Deputy Secretary Babington's letter, under date the 3rd instant, communicated with Shaikh Majod Sooree, relative to the object of his mission to this Presidency, I beg to acquaint you, for the information of the Honble the Governor in Council, that the agent in question is commissioned, by his master, to solicit, under the present happy union of the two States, such an auxiliary force as this Government may be able to allot to the service, to be stationed during the ensuing season, in Oman, for the general protection of that territory, against the attempts of the hostile associations of armed Arabs situated in the vicinity of his frontier, but more particularly to overawe the Wahabee by the presence of a British detachment, to the extent, as the Imaum would wish, of about two thousand men, and thereby divert that chieftain from his projected measures against the existing Government of Muskat, which has been most powerfully assaulted during the expired season, by the combined forces of the Wahabee, and of the different independent petty tribes in the vicinity of the Imaum's possessions.

Bombay, Country	I have the honor to be,
Correspondence Office	& ca. & ca. & ca.
the 7th June 1811	Signed/R.T. Goodwin
	Secy. & Transl. in the Office of
	Country Correspondence.

But once more the Bombay Government refused to ally itself against the Saudis, and the Board resolved as follows:[8]

> Board's Resolutions.
> Minutes
> 7th June. The Agent of the Imaum to be addressed by Mr Goodwin, that if

ever the powers of this Government were equal to a compliance with his agent's request without the sanction, previously to be obtained, of the Right Honble the Governor General, the season of the year is absolutely adverse to the detaching for some time to come of any force in his master the Imaum's assistance, but that the Governor in Council will avail himself of the impending departure of a ship proceeding to Malabar, where the Governor General now is, to obtain as soon as practicable his Lordship's sentiments such as may accordingly be expected to reach by the opening of the fair season, October or November, next sooner than which it would not, under existing circumstances, be advisable to pursue any active steps towards detaching a force from India to Arabia, as the ships could only reach by the circuitous course of the southern passage after a harassing and probably sickly voyage, such as it must during the next five or six months, be deemed quite unadvisable to attempt.

Independently of these considerations, it is further to be noticed to the present agent of the Imaum by Mr Goodwin, that considering the announced desire of the British Government in India to avoid hostilities with the Wahabees, it seems at least doubtful how far his Lordship the Governor General may be induced to enter on a war with them, notwithstanding the strong and sincere regard which his Lordship has always expressed towards the security of the state of Muscat, which must, even in the event of the Supreme Government's acquiescence in the object of the present overture expect to be called on to defray the whole of the expense of the armament, such as it will accordingly be for his Highness to consider in due season whether his means be equal to; since in all equity the utmost that can be looked for from the goodwill of the most friendly auxiliary, is to lend its force for the support of its ally without thereby incurring in like manner a heavy pecuniary charge, in a case not otherwise interesting to it, than as relating to the interests of a state in amity, and the preservation thereof perhaps from subjection by an upstart and encroaching Government, such as that of the Wahabee has hitherto proved, but with which the Honble Company have never yet had any open and direct breach.

Mr Goodwin is to take this opportunity of stating to the Imaum's agent the contents of the recently received report from Captain . . . of the most unfriendly conduct of his master's agent at Zanzibar, to the Honble Company's trading subjects from Surat; such as but ill conforms with all the friendly expressions with which the Imaum's letters to the Governor are so frequently filled.

This last statement accurately reflects the diverging interests of the trading Company and the merchant Imām.

Approaches to the Saudis

While the British were distancing themselves from the Imām, they were trying to bring themselves closer to the Saudi leader Saʻūd b. ʻAbdilʻazīz, using Raḥma

b. Jābir as a go-between. In his report to Bombay, William Bruce wrote from Bushire that on 4 March 1810 he had sent a letter to Raḥma in which he also enclosed a letter to Saʿūd. In his letter to Raḥma, Bruce tried to persuade him to stop his acts of piracy and to keep the peace. In his letter to Saʿūd, Bruce entreated him to use his influence with Raḥma in particular and all his subjects in general, to desist from piracy and committing acts of cruelty or injustice on the high seas.[9]

Raḥma b. Jābir answered Bruce with the following letter:[10]

Translation of a letter from Rahma Ben Jauber to the British Resident without date. A.C.

I have received your communication and comprehend the matter therein stated; I have also forwarded your letter to Sauood Ibn Abduool Azeez, who is the high priest (Imam) of the Mohumeddens and the followers of the faith of the Chief of antiquity and posterity (meaning Mohammed) may the almighty afford him assistance and God willing you will receive a letter from him, the contents of which are sufficient.

With respect to the keeping aloof from your quarter, as desired in that letter, no new act has taken place on my part with regard to your territories, nor have I attempted to injure you, nor have you acted with me contrary to agreement, and it does not befit you to unite with my enemies. I am not acting in opposition to the professors of the faith. I am only carrying on hostilities against those Mohumedens who have departed from the institutions of our prophet and introduced innovations in our faith; such as neither Arab, Persian or Turk has attempted.

If therefore your view be directed to the maintenance of peace between us, and of an intercourse between our respective ports, God willing, we shall not offer molestation to your coasts, wherever there may be anybody established and in like manner, you must neither molest our shores nor extend aid to our enemies. I will further furnish you with a letter to the Arab tribes in general, professing the Mohumeden faith which, God willing, will prevent any excess on their part. I will also obtain a letter from my High Priest Saood to the end that you may be apprized that the faith is powerful and victorious. The authorities of my Imam extend from Syria (Sham) to Imadu (name unknown) and his commands are in force in the Mohumeden army. If you be disposed to cultivate a salutary and cordial intercourse, you must keep back from the shores of the High Priest of the faith and afford his enemies no assistance.

For the rest I submit this sincere advice to your notice, requesting you will expeditiously favour me with a reply.

A true translation
Signed/R.T. Goodwin
Secy & Translator in the
office of Country Correspondence.

At the same time Saʿūd also answered Bruce:[11]

Translation of a letter from Saood Ibn Abdool Azzeez, the Chief of the Wahabees to the British Envoy (Elchee) without date.
A.C.

Your letter has been received and the purport thereof comprehended; what has happened commenced on your part, and the Imam's son has only desired your disgrace. I had no suspicion that you entertained hostile views against me, nor had I determined to attack you for you did not intentionally enter into a war with me and the Almighty has not in his mercy and goodness involved me in disgrace and ignominy in the war with the Europeans and Asiatics; on the contrary, the eyes of all my enemies have become cast down. The cause of the hostilities carrying on between me and the members of the faith is their having turned away from the book of their creator and refused to submit to their own prophet Moohumeed. It is not therefore those of another sect against whom I urge war, nor do I interfere in their hostile operations or assist them against any one, whilst under the aid and power of the Almighty; I have risen superior to all my enemies, but as you have solicited peace I conclude what has happened on your part has proceeded from inadvertency, and you have been brought into ridicule by one who possessed no power of himself, nor did you foresee the result. Under these circumstances I have deemed it necessary to advise you that I shall not approach your shores, and have interdicted the followers of the Moohumeddan faith and their vessels from offering any molestation to your vessels. Any of your merchants therefore, who may appear to wish to come to my ports will be in security and any person on my part who may repair to yours, ought in like manner to be in safety. You will therefore extend your protection to any person in that situation and avoid doing that in my coasts which will disapprove; upon these terms peace is entirely restored, and the state of maritime affairs maintained uninterrupted. Do not interefere between me and any one of the Moohumedan religion, for they possess my regards and affection and know the religion which God has imposed upon them and I only engage in hostilities with him who has deviated therefrom. Be not therefore elated with the conflagration of a few vessels, for they are of no estimation in my opinion or in that of their owners, or of their country. In truth then war is bitter and a fool only engages in it, as a poet has said.

War in the first place may be assimilated to a young woman who, by her philtres, stimulates the exertions of the unexperienced youth until she kindles a blaze, and having succeeded in inflaming the ardour of his passions, she retires like an old woman without a husband. I request you will send me an answer for my information that I may thereon cause all vessels belonging to Moohumudans to desist from offering molestation to you. For the rest my salutations attend.

A True Translation
Signed/R.T. Goodwin
Secy & Translator in the office
of Country Correspondence.

Encouraged by Sa'ūd's reaction to Bruce's initiative, Francis Warden proposed that the answer to Sa'ūd's letter should come from Duncan the Governor of Bombay himself, and that he should explicitly express his desire to maintain and improve the new relationship with the Saudis.[12] Duncan therefore wrote the following letter:[13]

Copy of a letter from the Hon'ble Jonathan Duncan, Governor of Bombay to Saood Ibn Abdoolazzeez, the Chief of the Wahabee dated the 9th August, 1810.

Sir,

The Hon'ble Company's representative at the port of Bushire having submitted to my perusal a correspondence which has lately passed between himself and you, bearing reference to the measures that were so successfully adopted by the British Government for the chastisement of the misguided pirates who had so long infested the fair traders in the Gulph of Persia, I have observed with much pleasure that you state in your reply to the same very respectable officer that you had interdicted the followers of the Moohumadan faith and their vessels from offering any molestation to our shipping and that any of our merchants who may resort to your ports will be in security.

The British Government also receives with satisfaction the expression of your desire to maintain with it relations of amity and concord, a desire in which it cordially participates and has uniformly manifested. It is therefore proper that I should assure you that the late expedition to the Persian Gulph did not originate in hostility towards you, but was as above noticed, directed solely to the destruction of the pirates who had, in direct breach of their own positive engagements and with an entire forgetfulness of the former instances of condescending manifested towards them, long infested the seas in that quarter plundering vessels and murdering subjects of all nations indiscriminately for the British Government does not concern itself with the hostilities carried on by you against the members of the Mussulman faith, on account of their alleged deviation from the ordinances of the Koran, and its power will alone be directed against those who exercising the detestable profession of piracy are the accursed of all nations.

The channel of communication between us being now open, I request you will continue to afford me the pleasure of hearing of your prosperity and success.

A true copy
Signed/R.T. Goodwin
Secy. & Translr. in the office
of Country Correspondence.

While the Company officials, the Saudis and Raḥma b. Jābir were cementing their relationships and sometimes even acting in concert, the Qawāsim were trying to recover from the destruction caused them by the British attack of 1809–10 and to restore their former naval strength. Among the Company officials there were those who advocated an extreme point of view in dealing with the Qawāsim. Thus we see the zealous Mr Manesty writing to Bombay as early as 10 March 1810:[14]

> The brilliant success which has attended the late expedition to the Gulph has made a most evident local impression the effect of which will be long benefici- ally felt but such is the revengeful and vindictive spirit of the Wahabee tribe, and of the inhabitants of Arabia of the Gulph under the jurisdiction and authority of Shaik Sood Ibn Abdulazeez, that I am not without apprehension of their yet attempting even under the self condition of this, thereby exposing themselves to most imminent future danger to wreak their vengeance on any defenceless British vessels with which their fleets of dows and buggalows may earlier meet. At all events, such people are not to be trusted and I venture very strongly to recommend to Government the adoption of precautionary measures and the prohibition of the exportation of teak timber from the ports of India, either to those of the Red Sea or the Persian Gulph, even including Muscat, from which place if collected there, the pirates will by some means or other con- trive to procure it.

However, attempts to deprive the Qawāsim of the necessary timber for rebuilding their ships proved impractical, for they were able to get the timber from territories outside British control. We have to remember that the Qawāsim had suffered only a limited defeat and they were not to be expected to cease all their activities at sea, their main source of livelihood. Lorimer prefers to think that 'during the remainder of 1810 and throughout the year 1811, the H.E.I. Com- pany's cruisers "Benares" and "Prince of Wales" being for part of that time employed in the Gulf, there was a complete cessation of piracy; but in 1812 the Qawāsim showed signs of returning to their nefarious practices'.[15]

Kelly would have us believe that the Qawāsim 'made good their shipping losses by building new dhows with timber from Travancore and other places outside British control, and in the latter months of 1812 they were again out in strength along the Gulf shipping lanes'. Yet, with a rather strange logic, he continues:[16]

> H.M. frigate *Hesper*, at the request of the Bombay authorities spent from November 1812 until February 1813 cruising in search of the Qawāsim, but although she swept the Gulf from the Straits of Hormuz to the bar of Shatt al-Arab and back again to Muscat she did not encounter a single piratical vessel.

In other words, both Lorimer and Kelly are trying to say, in not too straightfor- ward a way, that the Qawāsim were subdued for 1810 and 1811, but that in 1812 there were rumours that they were back at sea, and as a result the British authorities mobilised two cruisers and a frigate that swept the Gulf and found nothing to support those rumours. Perhaps it is instructive to point out at this stage that the Egyptian campaign against the Saudis started in August 1811 and that the Egyp- tians captured Madīna in November 1812 and Makka in January 1813. Such momentous events in the Peninsula would certainly have had repercussions in the Gulf. The Saudis themselves would have been expected to attempt to keep things quiet on their eastern flank. The Qawāsim seem to have decided that in the circumstances their best course was to wait and see. The Saudi officers were still in control of Rās al-Kaimah and Sulṭān b. Ṣaqr was anxiously waiting for a chance to regain his lost position.

The Imām of Muscat, Sayyid Saʿīd, thinking that the Saudis were busy elsewhere, felt that the time had come for him to resume his plans to control the Gulf with the help of British support if it were available. Early in 1813 he sought the approval of the Bombay authorities to allow Bruce to accompany him with one or more of the Company's cruisers in an expedition against Rās al-Khaimah with the specific purpose of restoring Sulṭān b. Ṣaqr to his legitimate position there. He also suggested to Bombay that it would then be possible to conclude an agreement with Sulṭān b. Ṣaqr to make peace with Oman and the British and prevent any future fighting between the three parties. Kelly claims that with Bombay's approval, Bruce accompanied the Imām with one cruiser, but the expedition was a complete failure and nothing was achieved.[17] This failure seems to have given Lorimer and Kelly the chance to fan new rumours about acts of piracy by the Qawāsim. Both writers were undoubtedly wrong and even woefully negligent in their presentation of the events of this period, particularly where the Qawāsim were concerned. Both seem to have pre-judged the case, pronounced the Qawāsim guilty and tried to prove this guilt even against recorded facts. They even went to the extent of rearranging the sequence of events in order to justify their suppositions, regardless of the truth or the confusion they caused in the process. Lorimer claimed that 'In 1813 several large craft belonging to Kangun and Basrah fell into their hands, while some Indian trading vessels under the British flag were plundered by them, and others lay in enforced idleness at Porbandar, not venturing to put to sea'.[18] Kelly echoed these rumours: 'In the autumn of 1813 Qasimi dhows began to appear off the northern coasts of India, and early in 1814 they took several craft off the Kathiwar coast'.[19] While accuracy was not one of Lorimer's virtues, and indeed his recording of events compels the researcher to use the utmost scrutiny, Kelly might be expected to provide some evidence to support such serious statements that involve accusing innocent parties. Unfortunately we are left in the dark as to where this evidence is to be found. Indeed, research in the relevant documents produces a completely different set of events.

The records tells us about an incident that occurred early in 1810 involving two small native boats off the north Indian coast, and the report speaks for itself:[20]

Translation of a letter from Meer Gholaum Alee Khan Jalpoor Hakim of Scind, to the Hon'ble Jonathan Duncan, Esqr., Governor of Bombay, without date and received the 7th March 1810.
A.C.
   Having lately received a report that two dingeys, with a full loading were attacked on their voyage from Bombay to Bhownagar and other ports by the

salt water pirates who have plundered and carried them off, together with their cargoes, and there being no salt water within the dependencies of the Sind territories, unless indeed the inhabitants of Okha which is situated on the frontiers; in view, therefore, to the interests of the two states being identified, I lost not a moment in the circumstances being reported to me in nominating and dispatching an old and confidential servant of my own, with instructions to proceed to the confines of Scind, and to employ the utmost exertions in endeavouring to secure the pirates who plundered the dingeys in question, and having apprehended and placed irons about their necks and feet to cause them to restore the said dingeys with the property that was on board, relinquishing not even a twine or needle, and then to dispatch the dingeys to Bombay, inflicting at the same time severe punishment on the depredators. Should it so happen that the pirates belong to any other country, or ports, you will of course adopt such measures as may be proper on the occasion. For the rest, everything is tranquil in this quarter, and as your correspondence affords general pleasure, I feel persuaded you will avail yourself of every opportunity that presents itself of conveying to me that gratification which I cannot fail to desire from receiving, thro' your friendly and agreeable communications, the account of your welfare and your commands in this quarter.

A true translation
Signed/R.T. Goodwin, Secy & Transl.

The ruler of Sind did not attempt to implicate the Qawāsim in any way, but Governor Duncan in his reply sought with conspicuous failure to do so when he wrote, 'I have since learnt that the pirates in question hold their principal haunts at Seer which is, I understand, a spot or islet off the coast of Scind and that is probably within the limit of your Highness's Government'. The confusion and ignorance of Duncan at this point can only be described as deliberate and laughable. It is incredible that the Governor of Bombay should put Seer, the Qāsimī coast on the mainland of the Arabian Peninsula, within the land governed by the ruler of Sind, and he compounds this ludicrous mistake by describing it as 'spot or islet off the coast of Scind'. We include the whole letter for the record:[21]

The following answer is written by the Hon'ble the Governor to Meer Gholaum Ali Khan, the Governor of Bombay to Meer Gholam Ali Khan Jalpoory.

I have had the pleasure to receive your letter announcing the measures which your Highness had ordered to be pursued for destruction and apprehension of the pirates who, having taken up their abode within the limits of the maritime parts of Scind, do thence annoy the trade of the Honble Company's subjects.

The attention thus shown by your Highness proved the more agreeable from my receipt of the intelligence which you have been so good as to convey having followed so closely on the application. I had found myself obliged to transmit thro' your Highness's vessel (then at this place but since embarked on his destination to the presence of the Right Hon'ble the Governor General) of the depredations of that reprobate race of evil doers.

I have since learnt that the pirates in question hold their principal haunts at Seer which is, I understand, a spot or islet off the Coast of Scind and that is probably situated within the limit of your Highness's Government in which case I feel confident that your Highness will not fail to root them out, not only from thence but from every part of your Highness's dominions.

For further particulars, I refer to the respectable Monshee whom Mr Smith left in your Durbar and to whom I doubt not of your Highness continuing to extend the cheering influence of your Highness's countenance and protection. What more can I write but to express my solicitude to be favoured frequently with accounts of your Highness's welfare.

Dated 15th March 1810

The Macaulay Incident

The following incident involving the country ship *Macaulay* was reported in the records as having taken place in February 1811. Lorimer described as unsuccessful an attack by the Qawāsim on the *Macaulay* in 1816.[22] Kelly, obviously copying confidently from Lorimer, though without evidence, states that the *Macaulay* was 'chased and fired upon by the Qawasim early in 1816'.[23] The records say otherwise:[24]

The following letter from the Secretary in the Marine Department.
To
Francis Warden Esq.
Chief Secretary to Government
Sir,

In obedience to the directions of the Honble the Governor, I called upon the commander of the Macauley, to account for his not having made an official report at the Marine Office of the circumstances of an attack made by the pirates, in the Gulph of Persia, on his ship in her passage down the Gulph from Bushire.

2. Mr Waddington can afford no good substantial reason for his omission in not communicating intelligence at the proper office, than that in the hurry of business on the ship's arrival it had been forgotten, and from ignorance to whom the communication ought to have been made, but that he considered his account since published would afford sufficient notice to guard other vessels against the pirates, which by some mistake was delayed being printed until Wednesday Gazette.

3. The commander stated that off Polior, the Macaulay was attacked by four large and seventeen small boats, who, after repeated attempts to board during a period of near eight hours, they quitted him and pursued to the west side of . . . the Macaulay had English colours flying.

Waddington reports that he hailed the pirate frequently and told him he was an English vessel without producing any good effect or at all inducing them to relax their hostile attempts on the Macaulay. On Mr Waddington's arrival at Muscat, he understood that this fleet of pirates has captured some vessels of that port, also two dows belonging to Bussora, and that they were a part of those who had fled from Rasulkhyma and now belonged to an island situated in the south western part of the Gulph called Bombassa, or as I apprehended Bomosa, Mr McCluer, placing an island of that name, and in the same situation. 4. I particularly enquired of Mr Waddington if he had any suspicion of that pirate nation by whom he was attacked being that of or at all connected with Rama Ben Jaubers, which are reported to be at sea, and Mr Waddington thinks from what he heard at Bushire, that they cannot be Rama Ben Jaubers, who was in one of the southern ports, but undoubtedly the Bomasa, or rather former- ly the Rasulkyma people as before stated.

Marine Office	I have the honor to be
Bombay	& ca. & ca. & ca.
23rd February 1811	Signed/N.J. Hamilton
	Secy. Marine Dept.

It is important to note here that Mr Waddington, the commander of the *Macaulay*, claimed to have been attacked by no less than 21 ships but he did not report any damage or casualty, though apparently an eight-hour battle had taken place. In Muscat Mr Waddington must have known he was among the enemies of the Qawāsim; he was assured that those ships belonged to pirates originally from Rās al-Khaimah, though temporarily based on the Island of Abū Musā. In Bushire, where Bruce was making friendly gestures to Raḥma b. Jābir, Mr Wad- dington was given to understand that this pirate had nothing to do with the attack on the *Macaulay*. Apart from being negligent, Mr Waddington was obviously very gullible about what he heard anywhere in the Gulf, and he probably added some lies of his own in order to give his superiors what they wanted to hear. And indeed they were quick to act not against Raḥma b. Jābir, but against the Qawāsim. On 1 March 1811 the Governor of Bombay resolved as follows:[25]

In consequence of this intelligence in today's newspaper of the attack made on the Macaulay by certain piratical boats in the Gulph of Persia, which Cap- tain Waddington might, on his arrival, have been reasonably expected to have made a regular report of, I propose that the Mercury and Prince of Wales be equipped in the service of that Gulph, against those who are really pirates, and direct their annoyance against the British commerce refraining at the same time from hostilities with such of the Arab tribes (as those for instance of Khor Hassan) until their enmity shall be ascertained, to the end that the fair object and laudable intentions of our Government may be rendered manifest as not seeking to oppress the interior commerce of the Gulph, but merely to protect our own interests therein, and to repress and disperse the armed vessels of those who among it, such as the Joasimees, all of whom still deserve to be considered as our enemies, since no reconciliation, or terms of peace, have yet been concerted with them, and we cannot suppose but they will gladly avail themselves of any opportunity of revenging themselves the losses they have sustained, by the expedition under Captain Wainwright and Lieutenant Colonel Smith.

There may be combined with this expedition the completion of the survey of the coasts of the Gulph, in such parts thereof more especially as are pointed out to require it, by the remarks of Captain Wainwright accompanying his letter of the 10th January 1811 of which copies, accompanied by transcripts of the several charts therein referred to, should be furnished to whoever may proceed in charge of that part of this proposed duty, such person being selected from the body of Marine Officers, if there be any found qualified for such a service, or otherwise taken from the military.

The Emaum of Muscat should be informed of the general purpose of the destination, and requested as well as the broker Vesshendass to afford all requisite and reasonable assistance and information to the officer in command who will in due course be named and introduced to him.

The range of the cruise of the Prince of Wales and Mercury must depend on the intelligence they will receive at Muscat, and other places within the Gulph, of the scope of the piratical depredations, but in general it will be expected that they maintain the security of the British navigation throughout the Gulph, and particularly from Muscat to Bushire, and beyond that as far as the mouth of the Bussorah river, on the . . . of the intelligence such as the acting Commissioner Resident at Bushire and will be directed to be diligent and attentive in furnishing therewith may appear from time to time to require matters should they to return until in case of urgent necessity until they shall have cleared the Gulph of every notoriously piratical vessel and particularly every Joasimmee, the vessels from Khor Hassan always excepted, until as already provided their Commander Rahma Benjaber should have departed by some evil act, from his present pacific profession, in which were there will remain no reason for his not experiencing the same treatment as the other delinquents.

Ordered that a copy of the preceding resolution with the exception of the 3rd paragraph, be transferred to the Marine Department and the order issued.

It is evident that the Bombay Government, not having succeeded in completely destroying the Qawāsim by the 1809–10 expedition, was anxious to take advantage of their apparent weakness at that stage to deal them a blow from which they could never recover. From Bushire Bruce was forming an alliance with a real pirate, and from Bombay they were sending expeditions against imaginary ones. These contradictory moves by the Government of Bombay inspired opposition from within the Council when it resumed consideration of its resolution respecting the measures to be pursued against the pirates in the Gulf. Mr Richards, a member of the Council, delivered the following minute:[26]

When this minute of Council was first circulated I had not seen the letter in the Gazette on which it was founded. I have since read it and observe it does not state who the pirates were that attacked the Macaulay. By a later arrival from the Gulph a letter has been received from the Acting Resident at Bushire stating that Rahma ben Jauber is again committing piracies, that he has put to sea with five large boats; whence, as well from the place the Macaulay was attacked there is reason to believe it was this freebooter or his adherents who committed the act. I think therefore no delicacy whatever should be observed towards him or his boats if, as I have now no doubt, our cruizers shall find that they either are or have been at sea, on piratical pursuits whilst this conduct of Rahma Ben Jauber (and it is positively asserted of him on other letters received by the Prince of Wales) is the best justification that can be adduced of the advice given by Mr Smith in respect to this man in February 1810, and which I then thought as per my minutes of the 17, 18, 22 and 28 of that month there was every reason to approve.

Signed/R. Richards

The Governor's recorded remarks reveal his determination to proceed with his plans against the Qawāsim although it was obvious that he had no proof of his case against them:[27]

Governor's remarks.
We have against this . . . the opinion of Captain Waddington, the Commander of the vessel that was attacked, and the discordance of the circumstance as related by him and reported by Mr Bruce; the latter mentioning only five boats as composing the force of Jauber, whereas the Macaulay was attempted by fifteen; for the reasons already assigned, I consider it of importance to preserve the distinction on which we have hitherto proceeded in regard to Rahma bin Jauber, which involves no impunity to him, if he become our enemy.

Signed/J. Duncan

The Governor did not waste much time in writing to the Imām in Muscat to inform him of the impending plans and to urge him to join the British expedition against the Qawāsim. He assured the Imām that they, and not Raḥma b. Jābir, were responsible for the attack on the *Macaulay*:[28]

Copy of a letter from the Honble Jonathan Duncan Esqr. Governor of Bombay to the Imam of Muscat, dated 5th March 1811.
A.C.
The amicable relations subsisting between the two states require that I should now acquaint your Excellency that in consequence of intelligence having reached this of an attack having been recently made on an English maritime vessel, called the Macauley, by certain piratical boats in the Gulph of Persia, I have caused two of the Honble Company's armed vessels, the Mercury and Prince of Wales attended by the Chaser armed boat, to be equipped for service in that Gulph, to act against those who are really pirates, and direct also their

annoyance against the British commerce, but to refrain at the same time from hostilities with such of the Arab tribes (as those for instance of Khor Hassan) until their enmity shall be ascertained, to the end that the fair object and laudable intentions of this Government may be rendered manifest, as not seeking to oppress or disturb the interior commerce of the Gulph, but merely to protect its interests therein and to repress and disperse the corsairs and deprecatory craft that annoy it, such as is still said to be the case with a remnant of the Jowassimees who are reported to have escaped from Rasul Khyma and fixed themselves on the desert island of Bumosa, whence they are now surmized by the commander of the Macauley lately arrived here, to have launched forth again into their former excesses as being by him understood to be those by whom he was attacked.

In view to which it might be well for your Highness to take measures for driving them out of that retreat, in which case Captain Conyers, the commander of our present three vessels would, I am sure, be disposed to afford you any assistance and co-operation in his power; and I would accordingly recommend it to your Highness's consideration to consult and concert with him, the means of bringing these bandits to an effectual sense of their misconduct, so as to lead to permanent conditions of peace with the Jowassimee tribe, on advantageous and honble terms for yourself as well as the Company.

A true copy
Signed/S. Babington

The intentions of the Bombay Government were made very clear in the instructions issued to Captain Sealy of the Marine Service in command of the Hon. Company's cruiser *Benares* on the occasion of his proceeding with his expedition to the Gulf. These instructions also reveal that the Government of Bombay ordered this act of war against the Qawāsim, not only without any proof that they had committed any offence against the British, but also on the dubious grounds of rumours reported in the Bombay newspapers, the *Gazette* and the *Courier*. We have seen how unreliable and sensational the *Gazette* was in the case of the *Minerva*, and now a little over a year later the reports of these discredited newspapers were treated as gospel by the Government. These amazing instructions are as follows:[29]

To
Captain Charles Sealy
Commander of the H.C. Cruizer Benares
Sir,

I convey the directions of the Honble the Governor in Council that winds and weather permitting you proceed to sea on the company's cruizer under your immediate command and make the best of your way to the Gulph of Persia taking under your orders the vessels named in the margin,* which have

* Prince of Wales, Chaser.

been equipped for the present service in the Gulph, its object being the repression of the pirates that are said (as per accompanying extracts from the Gazette and Courier of the 20th and 23rd February, and my report of the last mentioned date) to have again appeared in the Gulph to the annoyance of the British commerce, particularly by the projected attack on the Wahabee which it is to be apprehended that they may have carried in their attempts against others of our ships.

2. You are at the same time to be careful to abstain from hostility with respect to such of Arab tribes (as those for instance of Khor Hassan) until their enmity shall be ascertained, to the end that the fair object and laudable attention of the British Government may be rendered manifest in its endeavour to avoid by their requisite destination all under constraint or detriment towards the interior commerce of the Gulph, confining for this purpose your proceedings within the single object of extending due protection to our own commerce, by attacking and destroying or dispersing the armed vessels of those who annoy it, such as the Joasmees, all of whom deserves to be considered as enemies, since their conciliation or terms of peace have not yet been effected with them, since they broke their former treaty with the late Captain Seton, of which a copy is herewith enclosed; nor can it be supposed that they will fail to avail themselves of every opportunity of evincing their resentment for the chastisement they have already experienced by the necessary and well conducted expedition under Captain Wainwright and Colonel Smith.

3. The range of cruize of the H.C. vessels under your command must accordingly be left to depend on the intelligence you will receive at Muscat and other places within the Gulph of the scope of the piratical depredations but in general it is required and expected that you lose no time or opportunity in proceeding against the pirates wherever the state of your information may render probable your falling in with them, particularly between Muscat and Bushire and beyond that, as far as the Mokha and the Bussora river, according to any intelligence which you yourself may procure or receive from the Imaum or Broker at Muscat; with the letters severally addressed to whom you are herewith furnished, accompanied with translations for your own information and guidance as which may be supplied to you by the Acting Resident at Bushire or Assistant at Bussora, both of whom have likewise been written to, to the like effect, as to the Broker aforesaid.

4. In the event of your seeing cause to take part in a joint expedition with the Imaum of Muscat for the more effectual destruction of the piratical power in the Gulph, as indicated in the Governor's letter to that chief, it is trusted that the utmost caution will be used in the adopting of any such measure and that in its execution, every admissable means and spirited exertion will be pursued to ensure its success.

5. Should the Chieftain of Rasulkhyma or if the headman on the part of any other body of these pirates be induced to make conciliatory tenders of pacification, you will receive and transmit them to Government by the earliest opportunity, granting them a truce in the meantime if the terms you may thus bring

them to should be such as in your appreciation to offer a fair and due foundation for a permanent peace but until they may be reduced to an acquiescence in such terms you are not to cease to exert against them all the annoyance to which the force under your command may be deemed competent.

6. It is known that the Jowasmees are under the general protection of the Wahabee power which is supposed to keep them in a state of unwilling subjection; however that may be, you are to cause it to be understood that the British Government have no quarrel with Saood, the present Chieftain of the Wahabees, but desire on the contrary to cultivate with him the relations of amity in the manner already communicated in a letter written to him by the Honble the Governor under date the 9th of August last, of which you are herewith furnished with a transcript.

7. The vessels under your orders having manned and equipped in the most efficient manner in the service they are intended to perform, it is expected that you continue your cruize as long as possible for the more complete destruction of the pirates with the exception already inferred with reference to Rahma ben Jauber, the Chieftain of Khor Hussan, unless he should be found to have in the meantime departed by some evil act from his hitherto pacific professions, in which event there will remain no reason for his not experiencing the same treatment as the other delinquents.

8. Government desiring to avail itself of the opportunity of your cruize to revise some part of the existing surveys of the Persian Gulph and having made choice of Captain Sealy of the Corps of Artillery for this duty, he will embark, and is to be accommodated in a suitable manner on board of the Benares and you will be careful to afford to that officer all available opportunity and facility towards accomplishing the object of his instructions, of which, for your fuller information, you are herewith furnished with copies.

9. The Rd. Mr Martyn proceeds a passenger on board of your own vessel for Bushire, as does Captain Lockett on the Prince of Wales, but you are not to deviate from the chief object of your voyage by making any direct passage on their account to the port of their destination, it being sufficient that you land them whenever the purposes of the expedition may admit, since it is on that condition and under such knowledge they are allowed to embark.

Bombay	I am & ca.
25th March 1811	Signed/N.J. Hamilton
	Secy to Government
	Marine Department

To go back to Lorimer's statement that 'during the remainder of 1810 and throughout the year 1811, the H.E.I. Company's cruisers "Benares" and "Prince of Wales" being for part of that time employed in the Gulf, there was a complete cessation of piracy'. While it is true that the two cruisers were 'employed' in the Gulf, they did not play any part in the cessation of piracy there. They were particularly instructed not to interfere with Raḥma b. Jābir, and we have no reports of either of them getting involved with the Qawāsim in any offensive or defensive operations. Perhaps the only conceivable outcome of this expedition was the revision of some part of the existing surveys of the Gulf.

As mentioned before, the Imām of Muscat tried unsuccessfully to restore Sultān b. Saqr to his former position as ruler of Rās al-Khaimah. However, soon afterwards we find Hasan b. Rahma, a nephew of Sultān b. Saqr, in charge of Rās al-Khaimah, while Sultān b. Saqr himself remained in charge of the rest of the Qawāsim territories. Francis Warden was of the opinion that Hasan b. Rahma was 'devoted to the interests of the Wahabees', and that it was under his government of Rās al-Khaimah 'that piracy has been carried on'.[30] On the other hand, the Imām and William Bruce were certain that Sultān b. Saqr would be well disposed towards Muscat and the British Government.[31]

Kelly claims, albeit without evidence, that:[32]

In the autumn of 1813 Qasimi dhows began to appear off the northern coasts of India, and early in 1814 they took several craft off the Kathiawar coast. Three cruisers were ordered north from Bombay to search for them and to warn them of the consequences of remaining in Indian waters.

Presumably these were the same native ships which Lorimer refers to: 'in August 1814 some native craft under the British flag were taken by Arab pirates at sea off Porbandar'.

We have a copy of a letter from Francis Warden, the Chief Secretary in Bombay, to William Bruce the Resident in Bushire, informing him of this incident and asking him to look into the matter:[33]

To: Lieutenance Bruce
Resident at Bushire
Sir,
I am directed by the Right Honourable the Governor in Council to transmit for your information the accompanying copy of a letter from the Agent at Porebunder dated 22nd instant, containing intelligence of six Joasmee piratical boats full of men having appeared off Caratchee on the 14th inst. and captured two Bombay boats loaded with grain, and to desire that you will use every exertion in tracing the port from which the boats may have come and report to the Government the result of your enquiries, in order that such measures may be taken as may be effectual for preventing further depredations on British commerce.
Bombay Castle   I have the honour to be, etc.
31st January 1814   Francis Warden
                                                          Chief Secretary

One cannot help but wonder how anyone in far away Bushire could know any more than people in Bombay about an event that took place off the Indian coast. It is not surprising that it took Bruce more than three months to give the following answer:[34]

To Mr Chief Secretary Warden.
Sir,

I have the honor to acknowledge the receipt of the Government commands under date the 31st January 9th and 29th of March, transmitting copy of a letter from the Agent at Pore Bunder, copy of instructions to Captain Galwill of the Benares, and copy and translation of a letter from the Broker at Muscat, and I have now the honor to transmit for the information of the Honorable Board copies and translations of my letters written in consequence of the receipt of the above Government commands to the Wahabee chief, Shaik Hassan the Jowasmies Shaik and to Shaik Rama Bin Jauber, the tenor of which communication I hope will meet the approbation of the Honorable Board. These addresses I have dispatched by a boat taken up for the occasion to proceed to Katife and Rasul Khyma and to wait until answers arrive, with which he will return to this place, and for which service I have agreed to pay the boat 400 piasters (as she will be absent about 2 months and hope the Honorable Board will sanction this amount), and have little doubt in my own mind but these letters will have the desired effect and that the boats which have been captured, if they should really belong to colours, will be British Government and have had passes and colours will be restored, for I have not the smallest idea that the Joassmee have any intention to infringe these engagements to us or to insult or molest our trade in any way, for they cannot have forgot the severe punishment they received at our hands only a very few years back, as they are perfectly aware that we still have the means to do the same whenever necessity requires it. The report of the death of Saud the Wahabee Chief, is without the least foundation. I have purposely addressed a letter to him in consequence of the profession made to me by his envoy as also those made by Mohamed ben Salama to the broker at Muscat, as otherwise if we should find it necessary to adopt any decisive measures against the Joasmees, he would have cause to complain of our doing so without first having appealed to him at their conduct which, if he did not take measures to prevent a recurrence of them we, of course, might adopt such steps as we thought proper. This address will also have its due weight with the Joassmee who, whether subject or not to the Wahabee Chiefs, are notwithstanding much in awe of him as they are aware that Soud has appeared of late anxious to cultivate an alliance. I shall await answers to these communications before I proceed myself to Rasulkhyma, by which time some respectable cruizer will most probably offer to enable me to go down the Gulph and have a personal conference with Shaik Hassan, the Chief of the Joassmee. From the best accounts I have been able to procure at this place I understand that the boats which have visited the coast of Cutch, Scind and Caratchie were Joassmees from the port of Rasul Khyma.

Bushire	I have the honor to be
7th May 1814	Signed/Wm. Bruce
	Resident

Meanwhile, Bruce wrote the following letter to Sa'ūd b. 'Abdil'azīz on this same subject:[35]

Translation of a letter to Ameer Soud, Chief of the Wahabees, dated 1st May 1814.

After Compliments. A few months previous to this Abrahim iben Abdel Karim, your envoy to Shiraz, paid me a visit and acquainted me of your friendly disposition towards the British Government, which gave me great satisfaction, and of your having issued orders to all your subjects to respect and pay attention to the British flag and to all persons navigating under it. Abrahim no doubt made you acquainted of the conversation which he had with me since which, no great time elapsed, when accounts have reached me from Bombay and Muscat that a fleet of Joassmee boats, which are subject to your authority, have been cruising off the coast of Kutch and since have molested our trade and captured 6 or 8 boats with British passes and colours. This conduct is very different from what I was led to expect from the professions made by Abrahim. I have therefore, as I am not perfectly acquainted with the particulars of the capture of these vessels, written to you to beg you will let me know if the Joasmees are subject to your authority and if so, why they have behaved so contrary to what Abrahim, in your name, led me to expect. If they are not subject to your authority I beg to be made acquainted as you must be well aware that the British Government, by the favour of God, have it fully within their power to chastise them or any others that offer insults or molestation to its trade, and we have in this instance only refrained from taking measures to do so until we hear from you, for which purpose I have dispatched this boat to Katif with this address and hope to be favoured with your early reply. I have also written to Sheikh Hassan, Chief of the Joassmees, to a similar effect requesting he will have the vessels which have been captured belonging to British subjects ready for delivery, as we can never allow such conduct to pass unnoticed, and have therefore to request if the Joassmees are your subjects and you want to remain on friendly terms with us, that you will write by return of boat to Sheikh Hassan to the same effect and issue strict orders that in future no insult or molestation be offered to British subjects or vessels.

On the same day, Bruce also wrote the following to Ḥasan b. Raḥma, chief of Rās al-Khaimah:[36]

Translation of a letter to Shaikh Hassan iben Shaikh Rama iben Shaik Matur Shaik of the Joasmees dated 1st May 1814.
After Compliments.

I deem it necessary to acquaint you that accounts have reached me from Bombay and Scind that a fleet of Joasmee boats had been cruizing off Carachee and Scind and had captured 6 or 8 boats belonging to people subjects and under the protection of the British Government. This information has surprised me much as the treaty between you and the British government was that no molestation was again to be offered to our trade or to vessels navigating with British passes and colours, whereas in the present case your boats have infringed the treaty and captured our vessels without ever considering the consequences likely to result from such conduct, which cannot pass by without being noticed. Were you to leave off this predatory way of life and take to that of trading as you formerly used to do like the other tribes in the Gulph, I am convinced it would be much better in the end for you, but if you reply and say you cannot exist without following this occupation it is requisite you should issue strict orders to all your subjects not to cruize in the Indian Seas or to come near or molest vessels sailing under the British flag and pass; that is, if you intend to stand to the engagements entered into with the British Government; if not, I request you will let me know, as have it specifically in our power to protect our trade and chastise those who behave improperly, nor is it attended with much trouble for us to do so as you must be well aware of, I have now received instructions from Government to demand all the boats which you have captured navigating with British papers and colours with all their property in like orders as they were when taken, and expect therefore you will deliver them as we can never admit of such conduct passing, understand for this reason I have dispatched this boat to you purposely to acquaint you of these circumstances that you may prepare the vessels which have been captured for delivery and let me know thereof, that I may take an early opportunity of paying you a visit to receive the boats and cement the ties of friendship entered into more firmly with our Government. If on the contrary, you should not feel inclined to listen to . . . just and friendly overture I beg you will let me know that we may adopt such measures as are requisite on the occasion. I deem it however proper to acquaint you, that vessels have been sent to cruize off the coast of Cutch and Scind for the protection of our trade and to chastise those who persevere to offer any insult or molestation to it.

I have also written these particulars to Amer Soud and wait replies thereto.

True Translation
Signed/Wm. Bruce, Resident

It should be noted here that in this letter Bruce demanded that Ḥasan b. Raḥma should issue strict orders to all his subjects 'not to cruize the Indian Seas'. The arrogance of this demand is the clearest indication of British policy in the Gulf. They wanted the Qawāsim to stop trading at Indian ports. But, for themselves, the British wanted not only the full freedom trade in the Gulf but also the right to issue passports to others to do so.

As we know, Sa'ūd b. 'Abdil'azīz died in May 1814. Bruce's letter must have been received by his successor and son 'Abdullah who answered Bruce with the following letter:[37]

Translation of a letter from Abdolla Iben Soud, the Wahabee Chief to Wm. Bruce Esqr. Resident at Bushire received 2nd October, 1814.
After Compliments,

Your communication has been received regarding the proceedings of the Joasmees towards your people. You are well acquainted that I have never authorised either the Joasmees or any other tribes to molest or interrupt any of your people. Your letter reached me at the time that Hassan ben Rehma, the Ameer of the Joasmees was in attendance, the purport of which was made known to him. He replied that to his knowledge, no property of the English had been taken by him. I have now directed him to write to you that whatever property can be proved against him, he is to deliver up to you and I am better than those who merely fulfill treaties as is said by God, 'O true believer perform your contracts you are allowed to eat the brute cattle other than what ye are commanded to abstain from ' passage of the Koran.

Hassan ben Rehma now deputes a man to you; you will hear what he says that they have not taken any English property. I will make strict enquiry and if they have taken any property, insist on its being restored. Their enemies charge them with things that they have never committed. Let me know who are your subjects and their distinguishing mark as the vessels of true Mahomedans are constantly cruizing at sea.

True Translation
Signed/Wm. Bruce
Resident

The last sentence of this letter is quite clear and it ended a very conciliatory letter. 'Let me know who are your subjects and their distinguishing mark as the vessels of true Mahomedans are constantly cruizing at sea'. However, Kelly's understanding of this sentence is 'that the Qawasim attacks on non-British shipping would continue'.[38]

Ḥasan b. Raḥma sent an even more conciliatory answer to Bruce:[39]

Translation of a letter from Hassan Ben Rehma Ameer of the Joasmee to Wm. Bruce Esqre, Resident at Bushire received 2nd October 1814.
After Compliments,

I have had the pleasure to receive your letter by your messenger and understood its contents and wish to have returned an answer by him accompanied by a man from myself, but on my arrival at Guttar in a taliaa I was driven back by a strong breeze to Oman, after which I went to meet Abdolla ben Soud and there saw your letter to him regarding me. You are well acquainted that anything that may be proved against us, we will restore, without your applying to Abdolla ben Soud or anyone else. You mention that our vessels go towards Scind which is very right, but we have scarce brought anything from that quarter, merely a little coarse rice, small quantity of wheat, a little cotton and some iron. But other tribes also visit this quarter; the Joasmees, who are subject to Sayd Saeed of Muscat, and others who take property and then charge us with having done it. You know very well that we have a great many enemies who strive to foment matters between us, that we may be on bad terms, and this because they are old enemies of ours, but it must be well known to you that we have no wish for you and your subjects being losers. The Treaty between us is very full and firm which we wish to cement still stronger; anything that you can prove against us, by the Grace of God shall be fulfilled and returned to you, but do not give ear to bad people such as those of Muscat regarding us. Your messenger came to our country: ask him if he saw any property belonging to your people, boats or anything else. I have now deputed Hassan ben Gaith to you; whatever he says consider as from me, and if you wish to renew engagements between us, he is fully authorised by me to do so. And I hope that you will not be too severe in scrutinizing the past and request you will point out the extent of your possessions towards Scind and those who are your subjects to me. I have always understood that your people go about in ships and not in dingees, etc; these belong to Scind, Dewelle and Caratchee, nor do we wish to molest your people or break our engagements. You will now be honored by a letter from Abdollah ben Soud, my wish is that we should be on the best of terms and not that you should be displeased with us. What is in our hearts is the best towards you and our wishes are to be able to visit India and carry on mercantile concerns and have to request you will favor me with pass so as to enable our vessels to go there; when your messenger reached me I intended to have paid you a visit in a botille, but God directed otherwise, and I now write this letter on my way back to Rasul Khyma and shall wait your answer with my man at Oman. Let me know your wishes which shall be attended to.

Dated 9th Ramazan or 16th August
A True Translation
Signed/Wm. Bruce
Resident

The tone of this letter is not in the least aggressive; it does not threaten anything nor does it try to ignore the issue. It faces the accusation with a straight answer and asks only for friendship and to be allowed to visit India. In his report to the Board Bruce himself accepted the word of Ḥasan b. Raḥma that the Qawāsim had not captured any boats off the Indian coast:[40]

To F. Warden Esq., Chief Sec. to Gov't, Bombay.
Sir,
I have the honour to transmit for the information of the Hon'ble Board copy and translation of a letter from Sheikh Hassan ben Rahma the Joassmee Chief dispatched by my man from Deria whom he had carried on from Rasul Khyma for that purpose. The hon'ble Board will observe by this document that Hassan ben Rahma denies having captured any boats with British passes and colours, and I am much inclined to think they have no wish to do so.
It is with deference I suggest to the Hon'ble Board that all vessels which may receive British passes from Government have it wrote in Arabic in addition to the languages in which the pass is wrote, which will prevent their pleading ignorance of no pass being on board. And that those vessels who

are furnished with passes be compelled to hoist British colours, as it is I am told by no means an uncommon thing for the boats to hoist a plain red flag such as the Arabs use, notwithstanding they may have a British pass. I only wait the opportunity of a cruiser's arrival at this place, at a time that other vessels may be in the Gulf to carry such packets as may arrive at Bussorah, when she can be spared without stopping the Europe intelligence, to proceed at Rasul Khyma where I have little doubt of being able to renew the treaty with them on the terms Government have directed, but also to recover such property as I may be able to prove against them as being English.

I have honour etc.   W. Bruce, Resident, Bushire,
9th September, 1814

Enclosure:

Translation of a letter from Hassan Ben Rahma, Shaikh of Rasul Khyma, dispatched from Deria the Wahabee Court, to W. Bruce Esq., Resident at Bushire. Rec'd 8th September, 1814.

After Compliments.

I have had the pleasure to receive your acceptable letter acquainting me that some of our vessels have been cruising off Kitch and Carrachee; what you say is very true. Our boats have been there, but boats belonging to other tribes have also been there. The Muscat vessels with Rahma ben Jauber. Those who have acquainted you of this circumstance have forgot to inform you that other vessels besides ours cruise there, in fact everybody as well as us visit this quarter. You must be well acquainted with my people and that it is the farthest thing from our wishes to molest or injure in the slightest any of your subjects, therefore don't give credit to anything but the best intentions on our part, or that we will in the slightest way molest or injure your vessels or property. And I have now to acquaint you that I have repeated strict injunctions to all my people to respect all vessels that may bear English colours and anyone that fails in this will be considered by me as an enemy; in fact it is incumbent on us to respect you in every way, and if it is your wish to renew the treaty existing between us, very well, but there is no necessity, as the one formerly entered into is in extistence and perfectly binding and respected by us, nor shall you ever have cause to say we have infringed it but on the contrary, we shall study to be more intimate than ever, and hope you will therefore let us know what people are your subjects and have all vessels provided with passes and colours that we may be able to distinguish them. The boats mentioned by you we never saw. Those we met had neither passes nor colours and when they were boarded, had no people on board but were abandoned. Our boats therefore left them in the same state, but you know the Indians and Scindians in this quarter are our enemies, so also are they yours; you do not however think them worth notice. I beg you will let me know your wishes on every respect and rest assured they shall be attended to; also acquainting me whether it is your intention to visit this place via Katif or Hassa. I beg you will not pay attention to the reports you receive from Muscat or others as we have many enemies who strive to injure us.

The boats which we fell in with belonging to Caratchee and the River had nothing on board but hydes and few other articles . . . and were left without being touched. You may rely that all vessels that are subject to you will be respected by us, as we are very well acquainted with English ships and vessels with their crews, and it has always been our custom when we have seen them to show our colours and proceed on our voyage. I have again to request you will not give ear to what our enemies say, indeed you are better acquainted with these things than I am.

True translation
W. Bruce, Resident

Moves Towards Agreement

Before his death in May 1814, Sa'ūd b. 'Abdil'azīz had started would could best be described as a diplomatic campaign and had sent emissaries to Persia, Bushire and even Muscat. Of course this was an attempt to secure his eastern flank while the pressure was increasing from the Egyptians in the west. An envoy by the name of Ibrāhim b. 'Abdilkarīm was sent to Shīrāz; on his way he stopped to see Bruce at Bushire where he assured him of the Saudi 'friendly disposition towards the British Government'.[41] Sa'ūd also sent Muḥammad b. Sulaymān as his goodwill ambassador to the Imām of Muscat to try to mediate between him and the Qāsimī leaders Ḥasan b. Raḥma and Sulṭān b. Ṣaqr. The Broker at Muscat reported to the Governor of Bombay:[42]

With regard to local occurrences I have to answer to you that a person named Mohamed Bin Sulamee who is one of the principal officers of Bin Sawood Wahabee arrived at a city called Dubaye with several dispatches from Bin Sawood and that he has written from that place that he intends to repair to Muscat as a mediator for the purpose of restoring peace between Bin Sawood, Syed Saeed and the inhabitants of Rasoolkhyma.

His Highness Syed Saeed wrote a letter in reply to Mahomed Bin Sulamee and forwarded it to Dubaye. In that communication he stated that he would dispatch a botella to Dubaye and desired him to proceed with confidence to Muscat to communicate his views to him. A vessel of that description has accordingly been this day being the 11th of the month of Suffer or 2nd February, prepared that she might start today or tomorrow for Dubaye to bring Mahomed Bin Sulamee to Muscat to arrange the preliminary conditions and engagements at this place and to restore peace between His Highness, the Wahabee and the inhabitants of Rasoolkhyma which shall maintain the inhabitants of Rasoolkhyma in their own position and Sooltain Bin Sukur in his footing at Sharchee and restore the means of communication between every other tribe.

The same Broker later reported:[43]

With regard to Mahomed Bin Sulamee who has come here with Bin Saood, Wahabee, some negotiation has taken place between His Highness Syed Saeed and that person. The latter expressed a desire to restore the relations of amity and His Highness declared his willingness but observed that if that wish were really entertained the peace must embrace every state from the confines of Muscat to the port of Bussorah, all of whom were connected with him. In reply Mahomed Bin Sulamee proposed that the peace should extend to every tribe with the exception of the Ootoobees who could not, he said, be included in it, but His Highness declined to accede to those terms, at all events as the negotiation between them had proceeded thus far. I hope matters will assume a new appearance in two or three days and change whether in favour of peace or war shall be duly communicated to you.

Muhammad b. Sulaymān had another commission besides his mediation between the Imām and the Qawāsim. He made contacts with the British in Bombay who sent the following letter to him to Muscat:[44]

Copy of a letter from the Right Honorable Sir Evan Nepean Governor of Bombay, to Mohomed Suleman the Agent from the Wahabee Chieftains to the state of Muscat, dated 18th April, 1814.
A.C.

I have had the honor of receiving your Excellency's letter, announcing your arrival at Muscat, in the capacity of envoy, from His Highness Imaum Saood to the Government of Oman, for the purpose of endeavouring to restore the relations of amity between these powers.

The distinguished mark of favor and confidence which your sovereign has conferred upon you by this appointment has afforded me sincere satisfaction; and in offering to your Excellency my cordial congratulations on the occasion, I beg to express a hope that your Excellency's exertions to bring to a termination the differences which unhappily exist between their Highnesses Imaum Saood and Syud Saeed, may be crowned with complete success; and that your sovereign will hereafter have an opportunity of honouring you with the just rewards of so important a service.

Entertaining, as I have always done, the most friendly disposition towards your master, I conceived it my duty, even previously to the receipt of your letter, to instruct Mr Bruce, the Resident at Bushire, to communicate with his Highness Saood bin Abdool Azeez, and to establish such an amicable intercourse with him as cannot fail to be equally advantageous to both countries, as well as for the general benefit of their respective neighbours, and it is with feeling of particular satisfaction I have observed your Excellency has stated that a corresponding desire is sincerely entertained by His Highness Saood bin Abdool Azeez, and I shall therefore look forward with confidence to the speedy attainment of our reciprocal wishes.

Your Excellency's recent visit to Muscat has no doubt afforded you the means of knowing that ships and vessels belonging to the subjects of the British nation, are always to be distinguished by the colours they wear, and that all such as may be employed on the commerce of the merchants and other persons of this Presidency, are furnished with regular passports under the signature and seal of the Governor of this Presidency, which ought to be respected by all friendly states. I am concerned however to be compelled to state that the contrary has been the case, and that the proceedings of the Joasmee and Uttoobee tribes in attacking and seizing the vessels belonging to our subjects, navigating under our colours and passports, have reduced me to the necessity in vindication of our national character, to order our armed cruizers in case of their meeting with any vessels belonging to those tribes, which may have committed depredations on our trade, to take or destroy them. Your Excellency may be assured that no British vessel whatsoever has been in league with, or has assisted, either of these tribes in their recent depredations.

For the rest I beg to acquaint your Excellency that Mr Bruce is in full possession of the intention of this Government with regard to the chieftains in the Persian Gulph, and to recommend to your Excellency to have recourse to him on all occasions, which have relation to the interests of the two countries.

A true copy
Signed/J. Babington
Assistant Secretary and Translator in the
Office of Country Correspondence

While these peaceful contacts were taking place an incident occurred and, as usual, the Qawāsim were accused of being involved. Lorimer says:[45]

In 1814 'Ahmad Shah' a native vessel under British colours was plundered while aground near Qais Island by the Shaikh of Chārak, and part of the booty was carried to Rās al-Khaimah by Qawāsim who were probably concerned in the crime.

There is a great deal of correspondence about this incident, mainly because the Shaikh of Chārak was a subject of the Government of Persia with whom the British Government had a treaty. The British also did not have a strong argument to put forward against him, let alone using their usual methods of intimidation. The Shaikh of Chārak did not attack the *Ahmad Shāh*. The ship was wrecked and he actually helped to rescue the crew and passengers and to take them to safety. It was after this rescue that he started what was arguably a salvage operation. There seems to have been a disagreement about his reward, or what he believed to be his right, because the Bushire and native Indian merchants on board were rather reluctant to part with any percentage of the cargo. There were also horses and mares on board which belonged to the Company; some of these were rescued and taken ashore with great risk and difficulty, the rest being left on board because of the high winds. It was some of these horses that a passing ship was accused of taking before the *Ahmad Shāh* was burnt down to the water level. This passing ship was rumoured to belong to the Qawāsim and that was the extent of their involvement in the plunder of the *Ahmad Shāh*.[46]

The insignificance of this incident was underlined by the fact that negotiations continued to take place between the British, the Saudis and the Qawāsim. The following is a report from Bruce to Chief Secretary Warden dated 9 October 1814:[47]

Despatch from the Resident at Bushire to
Mr Chief Secretary, Warden, dated the 9th October.

Right Hon'ble Sir,

I have the honor to acquaint you that on the 2nd instant a vakeel on the part of Ameer Hassan Ben Rahman the Joasmee chief arrived here in a dispatch boat from Katif with letters from the Wahabee Chief, Abdoola Ben Saoud and Hassan ben Rehmah, copy and translation of which I have now the honor to enclose and from which the Hon'ble Board will observe that the Wahabee chief by no means approves of the conduct of Hassan Ben Rehmah and his tribe, and has in a manner bound himself to compel the latter to deliver up such property as we can prove them to have captured. At the same time Hassan Ben Rehmah continues to deny having captured any British property and hopes that we will not be too severe in scrutinising the past. The Hon'ble Board has also observed that he had authorised Hassan Ben Mohumed ben Gaith, the bearer of these letters to enter into engagements with me, which after a great deal of conversation with him on their late predatory conduct and insisting on their leaving off this mode of life if they wish to enter into engagements of friendship with the British government; Hassan bin Gaith replied they were anxious to be on the best of terms with the British Gvoernment, whose good-will they should study hereafter to deserve and that we might rest assured any engagement that might be entered into with us would never be infringed, that if they respected our flag and subjects and did all they could to promote our wishes, what more could we desire of them, and that therefore he hoped we would not insist on their leaving off cruising against those states who were at enmity with them as according to the law of nations amongst the Gulph blood could only be repaired by blood, that if they were not to follow this kind of warfare they would lose their rank amongst the Arab states, and not only that, but that those tribes who were at enmity with them would come to their very houses to attack them. Besides this they were compelled by the Wahabee Chief to wage war against the Mahomeden States of the Gulph to bring them under the yoke and religion of the Wahabee and only to respect the British flag and subjects to whom they were directed to be attentive and afford every assistance in their power and cultivate their alliance; that if we would guarantee on their leaving off this mode of proceeding that none of the Arab states would molest them or their vessels and that if they did so, we would chastise them for it and restore their property back as also guarantee their safety from the vengeance of the Wahabee chief for not obeying his commands, they could then leave off this way of life, but otherwise their natural situation in the Gulph was such that they were compelled to be enemies to the greatest proportion of it, as there was a great deal of truth in what Hassan ben Gaith said regarding the peculiar situation and the system amongst the Arabs; as also their peculiar religion is different from the other Mahomeden sects which of itself makes them the enemy of all other Islam sects, as also all other Islam sects to be their enemies and as Hassan Ben Gaith says, his chief and relation Hassan Ben Rehmah intends deputing this season to the Presidency a vakeel fully authorised to ratify and enter into more full and firm engagements with the British Government. I have therefore after mature deliberation, entered into a few preliminary articles with Hassan ben Gaith, agreeing to drop all claims and forget what has past upon certain conditions; I have been induced to this from the circumstances of our not having proof that the boats taken by them last year off Scind had either passes or colours; at the same time I have stipulated that all such property as may have been taken from the Island of Khen belonging to the Ahmed Shah shall be restored and that the port of the Joasmees shall be open to all British subjects. They are also in future to hoist colours different from the other Arab states which are simple red. The articles entered into have been duly signed and sealed to three copies by Hassan ben Gaith and myself, one of which I have delivered to him to be kept by Hassan ben Rehmah, another I have now the honor to enclose for the consideration of the Right Hon'ble the Governor in Council, and third I have retained here and only hope it will meet with approbation and ratification of the Hon'ble Board.

Hassan ben Gaith and his attendants I have considered as the guests of the Hon'ble Company during their stay here and consequently accommodated them in the factory; their expenses with a few presents made to Hassan ben Gaith and some European articles sent along with him for Hassan ben Rehmah, the Joasmee chief on the conclusion of the engagements, I trust will be authorised by the Hon'ble Board as the whole amount does not exceed 1200 Rupees.

I have the honor to enclose duplicate of my address to Government under date 8th instant the original of which will be delivered by the vakeel which Hassan ben Rehmah intends deputing to the Residency.

Bushire   and I have the honor to be & ca. & ca.
11th October 1814   Signed/Wm. Bruce
                                       Resident

Translation of a letter from Abdolla Iben Soud, the Wahabee Chief to Wm. Bruce Esqre. Resident at Bushire received 2nd October 1814.
After Compliments,

Your communication has been received regarding the proceedings of the Joasmees towards your people. You are well acquainted that I have never authorised either the Joasmees or any other tribes to molest or interrupt any of your people. Your letter reached me at the time that Hassan ben Rehma the Ameer of the Joasmees was in attendance, the purport of which was made known to him. He replied that to his knowledge no property of the English had been taken by him. I have now directed him to write to you that whatever property can be proved against him, he is to deliver up to you and I am better than those who merely fulfill treaties as is said by God, 'O True believer perform your contracts' you are allowed to eat the Gate cattle other than what ye are commanded to abstain from' passage of the Koran.

Hassan ben Rehma now deputes a man to you; you will hear what he says that they have not taken any English property. I will make strict enquiry and if they have taken any property insist on its being restored. Their enemies charge them with things that they have never committed. Let me know who are your subjects and their distinguishing mark as the vessels of true Mahomedans are constantly cruizing at sea.

True Translation
Signed/Wm. Bruce
Resident

Translation of a letter from Hassan Ben Rehma Ameer of the Joasmee, to Wm. Bruce Esqre, Resident at Bushire received 2nd October 1814.
After Compliments,

I have had the pleasure to receive your letter by your messenger and understood its contents and wish to have to returned and answer by him accompanied by a man from myself, but on my arrival at Guttar in a taliaa I was driven back by a strong breeze to Oman after which I went to meet Abdolla Ben Soud and there saw your letter to him regarding me. You are well acquainted that anything that may be proved against us, we will restore without your applying to Abdolla be Soud or anyone else. You mention that our vessels go towards Scind which is very right, but we have scarce brought anything from that quarter, merely a little coarse rice, small quantity of wheat, a little cotton and some iron. But other tribes also visit this quarter, the Joasmees who are subject to Sayd Saeed of Muscat, and others who take property and then charge us with having done it; you know very well that we have a great many enemies who strive to foment matters between us, that we may be on bad terms and this because they are old enemies of ours, but it must be well known to you that we have a wish for you or your subjects being losers. The Treaty between us is very full and firm which we wish to cement still stronger, anything that you can prove against us, by the Grace of God shall be fulfilled and returned to you, but do not give ear to bad people such as those of Muscat regarding us. Your messenger came to our country; ask him if he saw any property belonging to your people, boats or anything else. I have now deputed Hassan ben Gaith to you; whatever he says consider as from me and if you wish to renew the engagements between us, he is fully authorised by me to do so. And I hope that you will not be too severe in scrutinising the past and request you will point out the extent of your possessions towards Scind and those who are your subjects to me. I have always understood that your people go about in ships and not in dingees, etc; these belong to Scind, Dewelle and Caratchee, nor do we wish to molest your people or break our engagements. You will now be honored by a letter from Abollah ben Soud. My wish is that we should be on the best of terms and not that you should be displeased with us. What is in our hearts is the best towards you and our wishes are to be able to visit India and carry on mercantile concerns and have to request you will favor me with pass so as to enable our vessels to go there. When your messenger reached me I intended to have paid you a visit in a botille, but God directed otherwise, and I now write this letter on my way back to Rasel Khima and shall wait your answer with my man at Oman. Let me know your wishes which shall be attended to.

Dated 9th Ramazan or 16th August.

A True Translation
Signed/Wm. Bruce
Resident

Colnamah or agreement between Wm. Bruce Esqre, Resident at Bushire on the part of the British Government and Hassan Iben Mahomed Iben Gaise Joasmee on the part of Ameer Hassan Iben Rehma, the chief of the Joasmee at Rasel Khima entered into this day at Bushire. That strict friendship from henceforth shall exist between the British Government and the Joasmees of Rasel Khima and all transactions that have heretofore passed be buried in oblivion on the following conditions.

Article 1. That the Joasmees shall respect the British Flag and offer no molestation or interruption to vessels of whatever description they may be either ships, dows, boats, etc. navigating under British pass and colours but on the contrary aid and assist them in the prosecution of their voyage.

Article 2. That the Port of Rasel Khima and all others under the Government of the Joasmees shall be open to British subjects who shall have free permission to visit them and carry on their mercantile transactions the same as in other ports of the Gulph, and that in like manner the British ports in India shall be open to the Joasmees on the same terms as the other Arab states and chiefs.

Article 3. That in case of shipwreck or vessels meeting with other accidents on the shores or islands in the Gulph every aid and assistance shall be afforded to such vessels and crew and every precaution taken to prevent the property & ca. from being destroyed or embezzled.

Article 4. That the Joasmee vessels from henceforth to prevent their being mistaken for other Arab states agree to hoist as a distinguishing mark from other Arabs a Red Flag with an Arabic inscription of − − − − − −. There is but one God and Mohumed is his prophet in the middle, and that this is to be considered as the Colours of the subjects of Hassan iben Rehma and the Joasmees of Rasel Khima in future.

Article 5. That all property which may be on board of any boat or vessels of whatever description belonging to tribes at enmity with the Joasmees of Rasel Khima and can be proved to be the property of subjects under the British protection shall be immediately restored on application should such vessel be captured by the Joasmees.

Article 6. Hassan iben Gaise the Vakeel of Hassen iben Rehma with whom this agreement is written into does hereby solemnly promise immediately on his return to Rasel Khima to restore such of the H.C. mares and property as is reported to have been carried over by a Joasmee boat from the Island of Khan and belonging to the Ahmed Shah and to forward such property to Cojia Golab, the Hon'ble Company's Broker at Muscat.

Article 7. It is further agreed that if it should be found necessary to annul this engagement, previous notice is to be given by the party who finds it necessary to annul it. He that breaketh his vow, breaketh with the Lord — Arabic verse.

Article 8. That as Hassan iben Rehma intends deputing to Bombay at an early period a Vakeel fully authorised by him to discuss and enter into more full and firm engagements with the British Government, these preliminary articles are entered into for the time being subject however to the approval of the Right Honble the Governor in Council of Bombay, to whom they are to be forwarded by the earliest opportunity for consideration.

Executed in Bushire this 6th day of October 1814, or 21st of Shaval 1229 Hijree.

Witness our hands and Seals.   Signed/Wm. Bruce
                                                                           Resident

Duplicate.

Right Honble Sir,

I have the honor to acquaint you that I concluded on the 6th instant articles of engagements with the deputed Agent of Hassan Iben Rehma, the Ameer of the Joasmee which I shall have the honor of more fully explaining to the Honble Board in a day or two, this is merely written at the request of Hassan ben Mohummed ben Gaith the Vakeel of the Joasmee Chief as an introduction for the authorised Vakeel which the latter intends deputing to the Presidency at an early period, that the Honble Board may be aware who the person is, on his arrival at Bombay.

Bushire   and I have the honor to be
8th October 1814   & ca. & ca. & ca.
                                                                 Signed/Wm. Bruce
                                                                           Resident

Lorimer, commenting on this agreement, says:[48]

Towards the end of 1814, in connection with demands made by the British Resident for reparation in a particular case, an emissary bearing letters from the Wahhabi Amir and the Shaikh of the Qawasim appeared at Bushehr; and a preliminary agreement for the discontinuance by the Qawasim of their attacks upon vessels under the British flag, for the restitution by them of certain specific property, and for their adoption of a distinguishing flag was executed; but it remained a dead letter.

At ths point Lorimer prefers not to explain why the agreement remained a dead letter, although his comment is a clear attempt to belittle it. Kelly does not even acknowledge the existence of the agreement, he merely remarks that Bruce was told that, 'Hassan ibn Rahmah was willing to give a written undertaking not to attack British shipping. Although the Resident, Bruce, privately doubted the value of such a pledge, he thought it advisable not to decline the offer. His decision was afterwards approved at Bombay'.[49]

The fact remains that the Qawāsim and the Saudis were eager to reach peace with the Company, and it was the latter who did not want to go through with the final stages to establish peace. There is an early indication of this attitude on the part of the British Government in India. This was clearly understood by Bruce who wrote the following letter to the Governor in Bombay:[50]

Sir,

I have the honor to acknowledge the receipt of the Government commands in this Department under date 31st March transmitting for my guidance copy of a letter from the Secretary to the Supreme Government dated the 18th February superceding the authority given under date the 10th January to negotiate a treaty with Saood bin Abdul Azeez Chief of the Wahabee directing however that I carefully observe the directions of the Right Honble the Governor General in Council to maintain a friendly intercourse with that Chieftain and to endeavour to confirm the amicable disposition which he appears to entertain toward the British Government and in particular that he should restrain his subjects from committing depredation in the trades of India.

In reply I beg you will acquaint the Honorable Board that my conduct shall be guided by the instructions alluded to and hope that the Honorable Board will approve of the tenor of my address to Saood the Wahabee Chief enclosed in my letter of yesterday's date.

Bushire
8th May 1814

I have the honor to be,
Signed/Wm. Bruce
Resident

Notes

1. J.B. Kelly, *Britain and the Persian Gulf, 1795–1880*, (Oxford at the Clarendon Press, 1968), p. 122.

2. Bombay Archives (BA), Secret and Political Department Diary (S & PDD), no. 222/1808, pp. 1083–91.

3. Bombay Archives (BA), *Political Department Diary* (PDD), no. 361/1810, pp. 4743–6.

4. Ibid., pp. 4770–1.

5. Ibid., no. 372/1811, pp. 1741–5.

6. Ibid., pp. 1742–3.

7. Ibid., no. 375/1811, pp. 3121–3.

8. Ibid., pp. 3124–8.

9. Ibid., no. 355/1810, pp. 1996–2004.

10. Ibid., no. 358/1810, pp. 3063–5.

11. Iid., pp. 3066–9.

12. Ibid., no. 360/1810, pp. 3912–4.

13. Ibid., pp. 4163–5.

14. Ibid., no. 355/1810, pp. 2048–9.

15. J.G. Lorimer, *Gazetteer of the Persian Gulf, Oman and Central Arabia*, (2 vols, Calcutta, 1908–15), p. 650.
16. Kelly, *Britain and the Persian Gulf*, pp. 129–30.
17. Ibid., p. 130.
18. Lorimer, *Gazetteer*, p. 650.
19. Kelly, *Britain and the Persian Gulf*, p. 130.
20. BA, PDD, no. 353/1810, pp. 1540–2.
21. Ibid., pp. 1542–4.
22. Lorimer, *Gazetteer*, p. 195.
23. Kelly, *Britain and the Persian Gulf*, p. 132.
24. BA, PDD, no. 370/1811, pp. 919–22.
25. Ibid., pp. 914–18.
26. Ibid., pp. 1182–4.
27. Ibid., p. 1184.
28. Ibid., no. 371/1811, pp. 1358–60.
29. Ibid., pp. 1494–1501.
30. BA, Selections on Pirates in the Persian Gulf (not indexed), Vol. 73/1819, Sel. 73.
31. BA, PDD, no. 398/1813, pp. 2265–8.
32. Kelly, *Britain and the Persian Gulf*, p. 130.
33. India Office Library (IO), Political Residency Bushire, Ser. R/15/1/15, p. 93.
34. BA, PDD, no. 412/1814, pp. 2695–7.
35. IO, Pol. Res. Bushire Ser. R/15/1/14, pp. 152–3.
36. BA, PDD, no. 412/1814, pp. 2700–2.
37. Ibid., no. 419/1815, pp. 125–6.
38. Kelly, *Britain and the Persian Gulf*, p. 131.
39. BA, PDD, no. 419/1815, pp. 126–8.
40. IO, Pol. Res. Bushire Ser. R/15/1/14, pp. 188–9, and pp. 19–20.
41. Ibid., pp. 152–3.
42. BA, PDD, no. 408/1814, pp. 1266–6.
43. Ibid., pp. 1263–4.
44. Ibid., no. 410/1814, pp. 2164–8.
45. Lorimer, *Gazetteer*, p. 194.
46. IO, Pol. Res. Bushire Ser. R/15/1/15, pp. 128–38; R/15/1/14, pp. 168–70; R/15/1/15, pp. 138–41; R/15/1/14, pp. 171–75; R/15/1/14, pp. 177–9; R/15/1/14, pp. 179–80; R/15/1/14, pp. 180–2; R/15/1/14, p. 182; R/15/1/14, pp. 192–4.
47. BA, PDD, no. 419/1815, pp. 122–8.
48. Lorimer, *Gazetteer*, pp. 193–4.
49. Kelly, *Britain and the Persian Gulf*, p. 131.
50. BA, PDD, no. 412/1814, pp. 2704–5.

5 The Destruction of the Qawāsim 1819

The 1814 agreement between Ḥasan b. Raḥma and William Bruce envisaged a state of peaceful co-existence of the Company and the Qawāsim in their respective territorial waters, in which each side would respect the other's vessels and allow them to trade freely in the other's ports. The Qawāsim conceded these rights to all 'ships, dows, boats &ca. navigating under British pass and colours', which meant that the Company could extend its protection to Indian subjects. The Qawāsim won back the privilege that 'the British ports in India shall be open to Joasmees on the same terms as to the other Arab states and chiefs'. But in fact, although the Company desperately wanted Indian vessels to trade at Gulf ports, it also desperately needed to prevent the competition resulting from Arab vessels trading at Indian ports. It was this crucial point that caused the 1814 agreement to be shelved by the Company, although Bruce himself might have wanted to carry it through. Company instructions were as strict as military orders, however, and he had to comply.

The Company's attitude towards the agreement must have been quickly realised by the Qawāsim and tension subsequently mounted between the two sides. Lorimer comments that 'the hollowness of the agreement was, however, very shortly demonstrated by the seizure, in Rās al-Khaimah harbour, of a boat in which Lieutenant Bruce, under the orders of the Government, had sent friendly letters to the chief'.[1] Lorimer considered this to be 'virtually a declaration of war'.[2] Bruce was no less exercised about the incident and on 17 January 1815 he wrote to Francis Warden in Bombay recommending 'dispatching a small force of five or six cruisers — to burn all their boats' on both coasts of the Gulf, although he reported that Rās al-Khaimah alone had about 300 vessels of all descriptions. Furthermore, he also revived the notion of prohibiting the Arabs from exporting timber from Bombay and the Malabar coast.[3] Here Bruce seems to have been telling his superiors in Bombay what they wanted to hear. Indeed, with the change of governors in Bombay, the Government there adopted a new attitude towards the Arabs of the Gulf. The new Governor, Sir Evan Napean, was willing, as events were to prove, to pursue a far more aggressive policy than his predecessor Jonathan Duncan, and Bruce was only too willing to be his compliant instrument.

Once more rumours of piratical acts attributed to the Qawāsim began to be circulated. Lorimer reported that in August 1814 'some native craft under the British flag were taken by Arab pirates at sea at Porbandar'.[4] Kelly explained, albeit without proof, that:[5]

> Soon after the start the fair season in October 1814 Qasimi dhows again appeared in force off the northern coasts of India. An appeal from the Amirs of Sind for naval protection against the Qawāsim was rejected at Bombay on the grounds that piratical attacks on non-British shipping were no concern of the Company.

This is an absurd explanation of the Company's policy at a time when its most urgent and compelling need was to afford protection to Indian ships carrying British passes and navigating under British colours. It is the more absurd since at this same time the Bombay Government was instructing its naval force to afford protection to vessels sailing off the Sind coast 'under British colours or not'.

These instructions were given in a letter from S. Babington, Secretary to the Government, to J. Prior, Captain of His Majesty's ship *Acorn* on 22 October 1814:[6]

Sir,

The letter and papers transmitted to Captain McKay of His Majesty's ship Mallard previously to his leaving the port, which it is understood have been left with you, will place you in possession of all the information which had at that time been received of the proceedings of the Joassmee and Uttobee pirates on the coast of Scind and Mackran, and of the interruptions which the trade had experienced from the acts of these free-booters.

The success which attended their operations previously to the monsoon and their avowed determination of returning to their cruising ground after its termination, induced the Right Honourable the Governor in Council to apply to the Naval Commander in Chief for His Excellency to assist in checking those depredations, and by a letter received from Captain McKay, the Governor in Council has been informed that the Commander in Chief has directed that the ship you command shall be appropriated for the express purpose of co-operating with this Government in the execution of whatever service might in its and in your own opinion be considered most beneficial to the public.

I have now the honour of enclosing to you a copy of a letter received from Mr Bruce the Honourable Company's commercial resident at Bushire, by which it would appear that the return of the pirates to the coasts of Scind and Mackran at least those of the Joassmee tribe is improbable, but as no information has reached this Government of the intention of the Uttobees, beyond the accounts adverted to in the first paragraph of this letter, the Governor in Council is of the opinion that it would be advisable that you should proceed to the coast above mentioned for the protection of the trade against any of the piratical vessels above described, or any others that may attempt to interrupt it.

The declarations recently made to Mr Bruce by the chief of Ras Al Khaimah would lead to their belief that the cruisers under his authority have been distinctly forbidden to offer any interruption to vessels or craft of any description navigating under British colours and passes, whether any hostility may have been intended or not, there is the greatest reason to believe that vessels falling under that description have suffered in a material degree by the interruptions of the piratical cruisers, and such is the dread manifested by the crews of trading vessels, when falling in with them, that instances have frequently occurred of their quitting their vessels and leaving them to their fate, to the great injury of their owners.

You will perceive by the letter of Mr Bruce before adverted to, a suggestion with a view to the further security of British trade, namely that an Arabic translation should be inserted on the back of the passport of any vessel navigating under the British flag, and that suggestion will be adopted as soon as it can conveniently be done, but as many trading vessels are navigating under papers already granted, this precaution cannot perhaps be taken during the present season. In the interval however, it can be by no means admitted in justification of hostile proceedings against any vessel so circumstanced, that no Arabic translation has been affixed to her pass.

The season has now arrived wherein the piratical vessels, if they should carry their original design into execution, may be expected on the coast; I have in consequence been directed by the Governor in Council to request you will be pleased to take the first favourable opportunity of proceeding to the nor-thward, ranging along the coast of Guzerat from the neighbourhood of Din, until you shall reach the eastern entrance of the Gulf of Persia, and in the event of you receiving information, which according to your judgement ought to be relied upon, that any of the piratical cruisers have taken or destroyed any vessels or craft navigating under British colours and passes recommend to you to retaliate by taking or destroying any of the piratical vessels which may be found upon those coasts.

In order the better to enable you to execute this service the Governor in Council has ordered the Commanders of the Honourable Company's cruisers named in the margin* to place themselves under your orders, and you are ac-cordingly at liberty to furnish them with any instructions which you may deem necessary for their guidance, in the execution of the service confided to you.

On your reaching the coast of Guzerat the Governor in Council would ad-vise you to call at Porebunder, for the purpose of communicating with Cap-tain Elwood, and availing yourself of such information as he may be able to afford you, in respect to any recent proceedings of the piratical cruisers and you will of course be guided in some measure under the intelligence with which you may be furnished.

If on your meeting with the Joassmee or other piratical vessels you should be satisfied that they have not been offering any interruption to any vessel navigating under the British pass and colours, you are to advise them to return to the Gulf, letting them understand that it will be impossible for the British Government to permit any armed force of this description to remain cruising upon our coasts to the eastward of the Gulf, for the interruption of the vessels and craft which may be passing to and returning from the ports of this coun-try, in execution of their commercial pursuits, whether they may be navigating under the British colours or not, and that if after such warning be given to them they do not quit their cruising ground and shall continue to interrupt the trade of our coasts they will be considered as enemies, and shall be treated as such accordingly.

If after proceeding along the coast in the manner pointed out to you it should

* Mercury, Sylph

appear that none of the piratical vessels above described should be cruising there, you will in such case be pleased to order the Mercury and Sylph to return to this place, and having so done follow any orders you may have received but should no particular service be pointed out to you, it would be desirable that you should return here by the middle of December, and in the interval the Governor in Council is of the opinion that your appearance in the Gulf might be advantageous to the public service, but he would not advise you proceeding thither if it should be likely to render your return to the port at the time above mentioned in any degree doubtful.

By the correspondence of this Government with the Agent of Porebunder, and the Resident at Baroda, you will perceive that several acts of piracy are supposed to have been committed during the early part of the present year by vessels belonging to the port of Urmurrah on the coast of Mackran, and particularly one on a dhingee, loaded with cotton, and bound to Karachi in Scind, when navigating under a British pass and colours. If it should not be likely to be attended with inconvenience, in the execution of the more important service entrusted to you, the Governor in Council is desirous that you should communicate with the chieftain of that place, and call on him to cause immediate compensation to be made to the owners of the pattamar for that portion of their property which may be still unrecovered, to which they are entitled on every principle of equity and justice.

The state of the country and the poverty of the inhabitants of the coast would probably render it impossible for you to enforce the payment of compensation should your claim, as will probably be the case, be evaded and failing to obtain satisfaction, it will be proper to appraise the chieftain that measures will probably be resorted to for obtaining satisfaction for the injuries sustained, should the unwarrantable acts of which we complained remain unredressed, and that we cannot allow the employment of the vessels carried on with our ports, whether navigated vessels under British colours or not. The Governor in Council is desirous of learning the result of this communication, before he proceeds to the consideration of the further measures to be adopted on the occasion.

The little knowledge obtained of the coast of Mackran has left the Governor in Council under doubt of the practicability of your communicating with the chieftain of Bela who, it appears by Captain Elwood's letter of 12th August last, is disposed to discountenance piratical acts and is to have the head man (as he is called) of Urmarrah in custody, but on what account is not distinctly ascertained; should it be convenient to you it would be desirable that you should communicate with the first mentioned person for the purpose of gaining information of the proceedings of the pirates, and endeavour to establish such a friendly intercourse with him as may enable this Government from time to time to take advantage of his ports, or of his authority, for the purpose of checking the depredation of his neighbours, apprising him that any unfriendly acts on his part will not remain unrequited.

I have the honour etc.
Signed/S. Babington

Secretary to the Government,
Bombay Castle
22nd October 1814

It is clear from this letter that the authorities in Bombay were not certain of any details of the alleged incidents off the Indian coast: what was done to which ships by which pirates at which place? Certainly the Qawāsim were mentioned as possible attackers, but so were other Arabs and, indeed, Indians.

The instructions issued to Henry Meriton the Superintendent of Marine by Francis Warden the Chief Secretary perhaps reveal more of the intentions of the Bombay Government:[7]

1. I have received and communicated to the Right Honble the Governor in Council your letter of the 4th instant and I have been directed to inform you that he is pleased to approve of the arrangement you have proposed for the employment of the Sylph and Bowany pattamar for the protection of the trade to the northward with the Turrarow now at Surat, but as the Vestal which has returned from the Gulph will now be available for the conveyance of the despatches to Bussora it is judged advisable that the vessels before mentioned should be placed under the order of the commander of the Prince of Wales.

2. The commander of the Prince of Wales, after being joined by the Turrarow off Surat, should be directed to proceed to Porebunder for the purpose of communicating with Captain Elwood and availing himself of such information as he may be able to afford in respect of the recent proceedings of the piratical cruizers by which he will of course in some degree be guided in his proceedings against the pirates.

3. If on his meeting with Joasmee or other piratical vessels he should be satisfied that they have not been offering any interruption to vessels navigating under the British pass and colours he is to advise them to return to the Gulph letting them understand that it will be impossible for the British Government to permit any armed force belonging to the native powers inhabiting the Gulph to cruize on the coast without it for the interception of trade which may be passing to or returning from the ports of this country in execution of commercial pursuits, whether they may be navigating under the British colours or not, that if after such warning be given to them they do not quit their cruizing ground but continue to interrupt the trade they will be considered as enemies and be treated as such and in case the force of enemy should be such as to leave no doubt of his being enabled his orders he should use his best endeavours to take or destroy them.

4. But if from the number and description of the piratical vessels above mentioned they should appear to be more than equal to the force under his command . . . not to run the risk of any hostile operation, until he shall have reported the circumstances and have been furnished with further instructions for his guidance.

He is to be directed to continue to cruize in the coasts to the . . . of Porbunder and between that place and Cape Gaudel 13 long as his provisions and may last sending occasionally to the first mentioned port and to Carrachee for intelligence and when he shall find it necessary to replenish he is to return to this place.

Bombay Castle   I have the honor to be & ca.
28th February   Signed/F. Warden
                                                              Chief Secy

Without any doubt these instructions meant that all Qawāsim or other vessels involved in trade off the Indian coast were to be ordered to return to the Gulf and that was the cardinal point of the Company's policy. When William Bruce was informed about these instructions he commented that though 'many instances have recently occurred . . . it has been difficult to establish to what particular tribe these depredations are to be attributed'.[8] However, Bruce was soon reporting to Bombay about the 'piratical' acts off the Indian coast. On 22 March 1815 he wrote to the Chief Secretary, F. Warden:[9]

Sir,
    A few days since a boat arrived here from Lingua bringing accounts that a fleet of boats belonging to Rasel Khima which had been out on a cruize of the coast of Carratchee and Scind had returned after having captured six boats, three belonging to Muscat bound to Mocha, 1 bugalah from Malabar with her planks and timbers, 1 pattamar from Muscat bound to Bombay and 1 dingey from Carratchee, the crews of these vessels it is said were most all unhumanly murdered. The same . . . states that the company's horses which were on board the bugulah Darabee, the capture of which I had the honor to report to Government under date 29th January, had been sent under charge of the horsekeepers by land to Muscat and that they were contemplating of sending the bugalah, which I had despatched to them in December and which they captured at the entrance of Raselkhima to Muscat, to the broker, finding her, I suppose, but of little value and fearing the consequence of retaining her and the horses they conceive by delivering them up, we shall be satisfied. I trust however the Hon'ble Board will now perceive the almost absolute necessity of adopting some decisive measures towards giving an effectual check to the depredations of these inhuman barbarians, such indeed is the dread of these bandits at this place that no boat or native is to be prevailed upon on any consideration to convey a letter over to the other coast.

Bushire   And I have the honor to be & ca.
                                                        Signed/Wm. Bruce
                                                              Resident

These were the six native vessels that Lorimer claimed the Qawāsim had taken.[10] Obviously they were all boats belonging to Muscat and its trade. At that time the Qawāsim were at war with the Imām who was doing his best to destroy them, their ports and their trade. Had it really been they who had taken these boats off the Indian coast, their action would have been justifiable as an act of war against an inveterate enemy, or at least as an act of self-defence. But the truth of the matter is that it was not the Qawāsim who were involved; Indian pirates had taken these ships. This fact was reported by J. Prior, the captain of His Majesty's ship *Acron*, who had been charged to take his ship along with the Company ships *Mercury* and *Sylph* to cruise along the Indian coast to investigate the incident and to protect the trade on the coasts of Sind and Makrān. In his report Captain Prior wrote, 'From every information I have been able to acquire, I am persuaded no Joassmee vessel has been to the eastward of Cape Gaudel, and that if piracies have taken place they have been committed by the people of the coast of Mackran, Scind and Guzerat'.[11]

Of course this exoneration of the Qawāsim was ignored by the Bombay Government under Nepean; they had their own plans for action against the Qawāsim in the Gulf and were determined to carry them through. The case against the Qawāsim was being built up on the basis of rumours and falsehoods, and no amount of truth was going to change the mind of Governor Nepean and his subordinates. The reports of the Company's agents continued to try to implicate the Qawāsim in every incident, and the government authorities in Bombay were happy to accept any rumours as established facts. Lorimer and Kelly, convinced as they were that the Qawāsim were involved in every act of piracy in the Gulf, appear not to have bothered to check the records and verify the facts. Indeed, their accusations against the Qawāsim are sometimes more vehement than those that reached the Company at the time.

Lorimer tells us that 'In 1815 a British Indian vessel was captured by the Qawāsim near Masqat, the majority of the crew being put to death and the remainder held to ransom'.[12] The records report two incidents involving attacks on ships near Muscat in or near enough to 1815. The first was an attack late in 1814 on a ship owned by a certain important personage in Baṣra, Ibn Rizq, who was highly esteemed by the British. The second was an attack in 1815 on the ship *Sultana* that was carrying Lieutenant J. Macdonald, a British functionary, from Baṣra to Bombay. Both attacks were committed by the famous favourite pirate of the British, Raḥma b. Jābir.

Mr Gideon Colquhoun, the Assistant in charge of the residency at Baṣra, reported to Chief Secretary Warden in Bombay on 29 December:[13]

Sir,

I beg leave to enclose for the information of the Right Hon'ble the President in Council a copy of my letter to Mr Bruce dated the 4th instant and of his reply.

2. Upon these papers I beg leave to remark that Rama in his correspondence brings forward no excuse for his unprovoked attack on the buggullah and his murder of the crew (of which only 6 out of nearly 60 escaped) except his irreconcilable enmity to the Turks and those under their government. He does not even deny that he knew she was under British protection.

I have taken some pains to collect from the men who escaped the true statement of the circumstances which attended the attack and capture of the buggullah. They said that when they arrived off Angar it was nearly a calm and two small bottillas approached and hailed them; they replied that the buggullahs belonged to Ben Risk and that she was laden with English horses that the bottillahs then fired and the action commenced.

....

4. I have explained in my letter to Mr Bruce the circumstances which . . . to my engagement with Ben Risk upon that occasion. I not only gave him protection for his boats similar to what had proved sufficient on former occasions but I promised that I would detail the disinterested and valuable and I may add, hitherto unrewarded, services rendered to us by his family to the Right Hon'ble the Governor in Council and request that his buggullah might, on her return voyage from Bombay, be allowed to accompany and have the advantage of the protection of the . . . cruizer leaving Bombay for Bussora. To this promise he probably owed his present misfortune as his confidence induced him to dispatch his vessel with a reduced establishment, whereas on former occasions stated in my letter to Mr Bruce when Ben Risk dispatched his boat singly with our packets, her crew consisted of about 80 picked men which would have been the crew, had she sailed without a cruizer; of these circumstances Rahma was perfectly aware as he has regular spies here.

5.   ....

6. Had the buggalah been taken by the Joasmees I should not so much have wondered, because I have never expected that any treaty could be permanently binding on a body so loosely connected and so little under control. But I must confess I never entertained the smallest suspicion of Rama, who owes his very existence to the forbearance of our expedition and who has been expressly protected from our cruizers in the Gulph for the last four years, any two of which could at any time, had they been authorised to attack him, have destroyed every boat belonging to him.

7. But at the present time there was little to be feared, even from the Joasmees.

....

the experience of the last four years has convinced them that this commerce takes place, while the sword of the English hangs over their heads suspended by a hair and while they are shut out from Malabar a treaty therefore solicited should relieve them from their inseparable obstacles even for a short time was an object of vital necessity for their existence. To gain this point I know they would have agreed to any terms and for a time the chiefs would have exerted themselves . . .

8. But whatever may be the opinion of government upon this subject I humbly hope they will not allow Rahma Ben Jaber to profit by his ingratitude nor suffer a family which for so long a series of years had presented an example of active and disinterested attachment to our interests to sustain so serious a loss, where it was meant to bestow an honorable reward. It is but a word from the Right Hon'ble the President in Council, and Rahma must not only restore the vessel and property but be happy to make compensation for the lives of those who fell victim to his barbarity. I have undoubted information that Rahma depends greatly upon the influence and protection of the Imaum of Muscat

to whom the capture of a Bussorah boat was a sort of triumph and who has received the pirate into his service in consequence. Indeed, without some such reliance Ben Jaber would never have dared to have made the experiment.

His conduct since that time has been extremely hostile and he went so far at Muscat as to threaten to take the Prince of Wales. The Imaum's conduct in supplying him with ammunition and allowing such language in his port, shows how much he depends upon Rahma's aid in carrying his intentions against Bussora into execution.

Bussora	I have the honour to be & ca. & ca.
29th December 1814	Signed/Gideon Colquhoun
	Assistant in Charge

This unequivocal report lays the blame squarely on Raḥma b. Jābir. In addition, it clears the Qawāsim from any accusation that might be raised against them during almost all of this period. It also confirms their desire to reach an agreement with the Company on 'any terms'.

In the case of the other ship, the *Sultana*, we shall let the report of Lieutenant Macdonald speak for itself:[14]

To
The Chief Secretary to Government
Fort William.
Sir,

On my return to India from my journey in Asia Minor and Persia in the month of October last, I embarked on board the Sultana (an Arab vessel taken up by Mr Colquhoun the Acting Resident at Bussora) the whole of my baggage, mathematical instruments, books amounting to upward of (10,000) ten thousand rupees besides ten Arab horses, a number of valuable manuscripts, medals and antiques which I had collected at much trouble and expense during the time I was employed in those countries. In her passage down the Persian Gulph this vessel was captured by Rahma Ben Jauber a Joasmee pirate, (who has on more occasions than the present insulted the English flag with impunity) and the greater part of her crew including one of my own servants were inhumanly butchered.

The whole of my baggage was seized and publicly exposed for sale in the bazaar of Muscat, the port of a prince who states himself an ally of the British Government whilst those horses left after the action were sent down by the pirate to Bombay under condition of being renumerated with the same freight for each, that the owner of the Sultana was to have received for transporting them from Bussora nearly double the distance. Five of my horses died of their wounds whilst three of the others have been lamed and rendered unserviceable for life and it is worthy of remark that the pirate had no merit in sending the horses to Bombay on such conditions, because the freight which he received alone amounted to a larger sum than he could have sold the horses for in the Gulph had he kept them.

Placed by the Hon'ble the Court of Directors under the Supreme Government during my survey I have hitherto delayed appealing to the Right Hon'ble the Governor General in Council in the anxious expectation that the pirate of Imaum of Muscat might have been induced to restore my private baggage but as I now understand from Mr Colquhoun that they absolutely refuse to do so, I take the liberty of humbly soliciting that they may be either publicly called upon to deliver up my property consisting of articles of trifling value to them but great to me, or that I may receive some indemnification for the loss which I cannot afford to sustain.

Fort St George
4th May 1815

I have & ca. & ca. & ca.
Signed/J. Macdonald
Late Surveyor in Turkey and Persia

Here it was made clear that Raḥma b. Jābir was the culprit responsible for the attack on the *Sultana* with at least the acquiescence of the Imām of Muscat, and the Qawāsim were in no way implicated.

The War with Muscat

The Qawāsim were certainly pursuing their fight against the Imām of Muscat, however. Towards the end of 1814 they attacked the boat *Darabie* belonging to the Imām. William Bruce was quick to report this legitimate act of war as a further depredation committed by the Qawāsim pirates. He wrote:[15]

To: F. Warden Esq., Chief Secretary to
Government of Bombay.
Sir,
    In reference to my address under date 23rd instant regarding the proceedings of the Joassmees pirates, I am now under the necessity of reporting for the information of the Hon. Board their further depredations, yesterday a boat from Asseloo arrived bringing accounts of the bugalah Darabie belonging to His Highness the Imam of Muscat being captured by two Joassmee boats while laying at anchor in the Roads of Mogoo on this coast, and the only persons who escaped were those who jumped overboard and swam on shore, and those who had gone on shore previously, the remainder of the crew of which the greatest portion remained on board and defended the vessel were all massacred. This boat further informs that the people of Mogoo were privy to the intentions of the Joassmees and had in fact transmitted the intelligence to them of the bugulah being there.
    The Hon. Board will observe by the duplicates of my addresses now transmitted/originals per Darabie/that I had shipped on board this vessel on account of Government twenty-one horses for the remount of H.M. 17th Reg. received here from Capt. Lindesay as also a quantity of native sulphur for the gun powder department. I was induced to prefer this vessel to some others

which sailed near about the same time particularly as no cruizer was then in this quarter to afford convoy, from the circumstance of her belonging to the Imam of Muscat who was then on terms with the different predatory Arab chiefs, and in consequence this vessel was looked upon as perfectly safe from molestation owing to which she got a very full cargo from this port for Bombay. The Nawab Abbas Koly Khan with his attendants as stated in my address under date 26th ultimo also embarked on this vessel under this conviction. The report however is that he was on board but had not been killed.

The Hon. Board will now therefore see that any further hopes of binding these lawless bandits down to a peaceable mode of life is futile in the extreme as nothing but the effect of our last expedition has kept them quiet so long and that perhaps principally from not before having sufficient vessels to commence their depredations openly, nothing had taken place between the Imam and the Joassmees to lead to the act of capturing any of his vessels, but that horrid want of every kind of faith which such lawless vagabonds always possess. The accounts from the southward also say that a fleet of twenty-five larger Joassmee vessels were out cruizing at the entrance of the Gulf. I am therefore under great apprehensions for the safety of any vessel that may be on its passage up from India and not without alarm for the Vestal cruizer which sailed from this on the 18th instant.

I have the honour to be, Sir,
Sm. Bruce, Resident
Bushire
29th January, 1815

At the beginning of June 1815 the Imām of Muscat attacked the Qawāsim fleet; the Imām was wounded and his fleet was defeated. Bruce reported this to Warden in Bombay, but of course not as an act of piracy. It was simply a report about a battle that His Highness the Imām had lost:[16]

On the 2nd instant I had the honour to report of a fleet of Joassmees consisting of a ship and 25 bugalahs and battils being out on a cruize at the entrance of the Gulf, yesterday by a boat arrived from Asseloo letters have been received that His Highness the Imam of Muscat, with his fleet consisting of his new ship lately built at Bombay and 2 others with a number of bugalahs and battils, fell in with the Joassmee fleet off Cape Koriat, that a smart action ensued, in which the Joassmees attempted to board the Imam's ship and had actually got possession of the forecastle when they were dislodged by the guns from the poop being fired pointed forward loaded with grape. The Imam's other vessels having fallen astern, he was obliged to bear up and run into Muscat. Two dingeys were sunk by the Imam's ship which had been captured by the Joassmees a few days previous. His Highness who commanded in person on board the new ship, has been slightly wounded by a musket ball, but he has lost a great many men as also have the Joassmees. After refitting for two days and taking on board a supply of ammunition His Highness again put to sea with his vessels after the Joassmees, and fell in with them off Sohar, from which he chased them to Rasul Khyma, keeping up a constant fire at them from his chase guns. His Highness has since returned to Muscat.

I have the honour to be Sir,

Your obedient servant,

W. Bruce, Resident.

Bushire.

9th June, 1815

A few months later the Imām tried to redress the situation; he attacked Rās al-Khaimah from the sea and blockaded its port for nearly four months until early in 1816. In the words of William Bruce, however:[17]

His Highness the Imaum of Muscat has been obliged to return to port having effected nothing against these pirates notwithstanding he blockaded the port near four months nor will His Highness be able to effect anything without our support, which he is extremely anxious to get, and would I have little doubt from the information I possess from an intelligent native at Muscat who is in his confidence, be glad to cede to us any of the ports or islands in the Gulph, which are subject to him to obtain our assistance.

Naturally the tension increased in the Gulf in 1816 as a result of this persistent war between the Imām and the Qawāsim, and, as was to be expected, many allegations of piracy were made against the Qawāsim. Indian merchants and Company representatives amongst other interested parties added rumours to allegations, and facts became difficult to find in the confusion. Even modern historians, in their anxiety to prove the case against the Qawāsim, have got their facts mixed up. Thus Kelly tells us:[18]

Early in 1816 the Qawasim began attacking European vessels in the Gulf. The country brig *Macaulay* and the American ship Persia were chased and fired upon, and a French schooner from the Mauritius was boarded and looted. Her captain was told that if he and his crew had been British they would have had their throats cut.

The last statement about cutting throats was borrowed from *The History of the Indian Navy*, doubtless for dramatic effect.[19] But the other details were just as baseless. The incident of the *Macaulay*, as has been already mentioned, happened in 1811 and not in 1816.[20] The incidents involving the American and French ships should not have exercised the British over much since they were not exactly at peace with either country. Indeed the British had left the White House smouldering in 1814 and had done more damage to American property than the Qawāsim could ever have done.

Continuing his allegations, Bruce wrote to the Governor in Bombay:[21]

Right Honble Sir,

By the arrival of Euphrates country ship on the 18th ultimo accounts reached here that the Hon. Company's cruizer Aurora had been attacked by a fleet of twelve sail of Joasmee pirates about the Tombs and that after a few guns from the cruizer being fired at them, they hauled their wind and stood away. The Euphrates herself was chased by seven boats nearly in the same place and by letters from the southward I am informed that twenty five sail of these lawless vagabonds are out cruising. It would appear that they have now determined to attempt every vessel they fall in with as a fleet of five sail chased and fired at the American ship Persia and schooner Cintra near Cape Masseldom and did not desist until one of the boats received a shot from the Persia between wind and water which obliged her to lower her sail instantly, a breeze springing up at the same time enabled the Americans to outsail them on which they gave up the chase. These two vessels arrived here on the 5th and Captain Austin informed me that he thinks the boat which he fired into was sinking as she laid over a great deal.

Your Honorable Board will therefore be in the necessity of adopting some measures to check the depredations of these inhuman pirates who equally disregard the laws of God and man. I am therefore in a considerable apprehension for the safety of two or three ships now daily expected from Calcutta, with very valuable cargoes.

His Highness the Imaum of Muscat has been obliged to return to port having not effected anything against these pirates notwithstanding he blockaded the port near four months, nor will His Highness be able to effect anything without our support which he is extremely anxious to get, and would I have little doubt from the information I possess from an intelligent native at Muscat who is in his confidence, be glad to cede to us any of the ports or islands in the Gulph, which are subject to him to obtain our assistance.

I have the honor to be & ca.

Bushire   Signed/William Bruce
8th February 1816   Resident

Evidently Bruce did not think much of the reported attack on the *Aurora*, although he piled up a list of allegations which amount to nothing more than passing ships firing random shots at each other and no harm being done. It is more important to note at this point the significant parts of Bruce's report where he seems to be building up a case for demanding military action against the Qawāsim. Notwithstanding the recent failure of the Imām against the Qawāsim, Bruce was suggesting supporting the Imām in return for ceding 'to us any of the ports or islands in the Gulph which are subject to him'. Here a new approach was introduced which reveals a typical colonial mentality not too different from that of John Malcolm.

There is no end to the list of accusations against the Qawāsim. Lorimer even quotes a rather laughable report 'a ship under the British flag, of which the name was never ascertained; this vessel was taken by fire pirate boats and her crew and passengers were put to the sword'.[22] This report about a nameless ship whose crew and passengers were massacred must have been communicated to Lorimer by the pirates themselves: who else?

In a more serious vein and still in 1816, the field of the alleged attacks by the Qawāsim was stretched to cover not only the Gulf, the Arabian Sea and practically the whole of the Indian Ocean but also, strangely enough, the Red Sea. In Lorimer's opinion[23]

> Matters were at length brought to a head by the capture in the Red Sea, in 1816, of three Indian merchant vessels from Surat, which were making the passage to Mokha under the British flag; of the crews only a few survivors remained to tell the tale, and the pecuniary loss was estimated at Rs. 1,200,000. The pirates were commanded on this occasion by Amir Ibrahim, a kinsman of Hasan-bin-Rahma, the *de facto* Shaikh of Ras-al-Khaimah. In this new and remote quarter the offences by the Qawasim had their beginning in 1815; and it was probably about this time that, as tradition relates, they made cruel raids at various points along the southern coast of Arabia including the Kuria Muria Islands and Hasik on the mainland, both of which they left virtually depopulated.

Unfortunately Lorimer does not tell us to which 'tradition' he refers, nor what he means by this term. Is it a rumour or just exaggerated gossip of Indian sailors? However, he admits that 'the circumstances of the outrage upon the Surat vessels took some time to investigate'. Indeed, almost all of the survivors were questioned and we do have copies of their sworn statements which are too long to quote here. There is, however, such a striking similarity in their wording that they give the impression of being from one source. Furthermore, the only evidence that the attackers were the Qawāsim was the report that they were led by Amīr Ibrāhīm; it was therefore concluded without any corroborating evidence that he must have been Ibrāhīm b. Raḥma, the brother of Ḥasan b. Raḥma, the leader of Rās al-Khaimah.[24] The fact that he was referred to as 'Amīr' is a strong indication that he was not a Qāsimī, because the Qawāsim leaders have never been referred to at any time as anything but shaikhs. Indeed, after lengthy correspondence Governor Nepean concluded that none

> of the documents . . . contain any precise information of the names of or the Commander of the piratical vessels nor is it clear whether they are Joasmees or to what other tribe they belong. In this state of uncertainty and apprized as the Governor in Council is that other tribes besides that to which piracy is attributed, not only within the Gulph of Persia, but also on the coast without it to the eastward up to the Gulph of Arabia, have been engaged in similar piratical proceedings . . .[25]

In spite of the obvious strong doubt that the Qawāsim were involved, Governor Nepean instructed Captain P.H. Bridges of HM sloop *Challenger* to take his ship, along with two Company cruisers, the *Mercury* and the *Vestal*, and proceed to 'assist the Resident at Bushire in recovering the cargoes and securing the punishment of those responsible for the massacre of the crews'. If Ḥasan b. Raḥma refused to heed these demands he was to be told 'that he must expect the displeasure of the British Government to be visited upon him'. On no account, Bridges was warned, was he to attempt naval action against the Qawāsim.[26]

From Bushire Bruce accompanied Bridges and his little expedition to Rās al-Khaimah in November 1816. There some meaningless though protracted negotiations and correspondence took place, ultimately leading to a sort of a dialogue of the deaf, neither side addressing exactly the same subject as the other. Although Bruce put forward excessive demands which he could not possibly have expected to be accepted, such as the surrender to him of Ibrāhīm b. Raḥma, Ḥasan b. Raḥma, in spite of his superior power, showed great patience and appeared willing to reach an accommodation with the Company. Finally when it was obvious that there was no meeting of minds, Bruce and Bridges decided to leave, but not before a few futile shots that fell short of the target.[27]

From Rās al-Khaimah Bruce sailed to Shārjah, Linga and Chārak in a wild-goose chase, making preposterous demands of the leaders of these places for the return of property that had been lost years before. This was mere provocation that yielded nothing and, as Kelly mildly put it, 'on all accounts the demonstration at Ras al-Khaima had been a failure'.[28] Indeed, the whole expedition was not even necessary.

Further Approaches to the Saudis

Finding himself powerless against the Qawāsim and realising that he had neither the right argument or evidence, nor the force to coerce the Qawāsim, Bruce turned to the Saudi chief, 'Abdullah b. Sa'ūd, in an attempt to further the designs of the Company. His report to Bombay on this matter and the accompanying letters of the Saudi leader throw a great deal of light on the Company's attempts to monopolise all trade in the area through the exclusive use of Indian ships to transfer all goods:[29]

Sir,

I have now the honor to transmit for the notice of the Honorable Board copy and translation of a letter from the Wahabee chief referred to in my address of the 28th ultimo which the sudden departure of H.M. Brig Challenger prevented me from submitting to their judgement by that opportunity.

The importance of this document relatively with the reports I have lately had the honor to forward respecting the Jawasim induce me to offer my opinion of its contents rather more at large than I should in any other case have done.

The style and general tenor of this communication of the Wahabee chieftain are neither courteous or friendly; he confesses that the whole of the correspondence which I carried on with his subjects of Rasoolkhymah under the instructions of Government had been forwarded for his examination and that a calm exercise of judgement on these papers has led him to a conviction that we have declared ourselves inimical to his interest without adequate cause. He clearly asserts as did the chiefs of Rasool Khymah that the provisions and benefit of the late treaty were in his conception meant to extend only to Englishmen and that we are now intensively desirous of admitting to a participation in the benefit of the treaty those who are not our subjects. He declares also that if it can satisfactorily be proved to him that the Jawasim have plundered British property, he will cause it to be restored. The benefit of this declaration however is immediately afterwards destroyed by his assertion that he has ascertained that almost the whole village of which we complained belonged to individuals in the Red Sea who were his enemies.

He next placing his cause in the hands of God declares himself equally ready for peace or war. In the event of our being anxious to avert his wrath he states the terms upon which, and which alone, this may be effected, distinctly enumerates those who are his enemies and affirms that he is induced equally by inclination and the inevitable and pure fiat of the Almighty to slay the infidels and seize and appropriate their property wherever he may find them. The close of his communication too conveys an intimation that an occasional abstinence from the discussion of irritating claims is both wise and politick.

This document plainly and closely expressed as it is decidedly asserts and justifies the propriety of the conduct of his subjects and of its consistency with all those principles of religion and justice which his sectaries hold sacred and which form their civil and political demeanour. It proves that their views have been and ever will be piratical and that he will permit no part of the produce of India belonging by purchase to far the greater body of inhabitants on the shores of the Red Sea and the Gulph of Persia or the returns of this produce of whatever kind to be conveyed in British bottoms. The amount of public loss from such a decision if abided by will be clearly apparent from the accompanying statements lately framed by the particular instructions of Government. This last proof of the injurious maxims of the Jawasims and of the Supreme Chieftain who abets and upholds their measures, conjointly with the reflections I have already had the honor to forward to the notice of Government, will I trust have clearly displayed their dangerous and ambitious character, together with the necessity that there exists of adopting measures of firm and permanent coercives to prevent its further noxious operations.

The Shaikh of Bahrain, as I have ascertained from sure and confidential communication, is continuing to afford the fullest and most effective aid, in his power in grain and stores of all kinds to the Jawasin, who hourly frequent the ports of his islands.

Bushire
6th March 1817

I have the honor & ca.
Signed/Wm. Bruce
Resident

Translation of a letter to William Bruce Esquire Resident at Bushire from Abdoollah ben Abdoolazeez, Chief of the Wahabees.

In the name of God the most
Merciful the benevolent.

From Abdoollah bin Saood to Master Bruce Beg whom God lead to the truth.

We have acquainted ourselves with the purport of the letters which you addressed to Hussain ben Rahmah and his colleagues of Rasoolkhymeh. I have completely altered my opinion of you. Men of such wisdom as you generally are usually labour to secure and confirm the reciprocal interests of two friendly parties, nor do they ever hasten to kindle the flame of mutual enmity and opposition.

The treaty which had been established between the Moslims and the English, specified that both should abstain from hostility, and that to us two the paths of continued intercourse should remain open; you however are now desirous of admitting to a participation in the benefit of that treaty those who are not your subjects, and our present enemies among the people of Turkey, Yemen, Muscat and other places are doubtless highly pleased at the occurrence of hostilities between us . . .

How can you suppose that we will restore booty taken from our enemies? We have clearly ascertained that the greater part of the plundered property belonged to the people of Egypt, and what did not belong to them, belonged to the people of Jedda, and the ports of the Shereef Humood.

If you prefer war to peace, God's will be done! God is our aid! A powerful and all sufficient abettor! Should you on the contrary be more eager to remain at peace with us, I declare myself responsible for the demeanour of all Moslims towards English subjects. The people, however, of Egypt, Jedda, of Yemen, of Sheher, and Makella, of Muscat, of Bussora and Irak, and the Persian subjects of Saeed ben Sooltan, all these are our enemies, and by the Almighty aid where ever we may find them or their property, he will assuredly slay the one, and seize the other; in pursuance to the commands of that God whose praise is great and ineffable; whose name is pure and unpolluted, 'Slay the infidels wherever you may find them'.

If you approve of these conditions, and are anxious to treat with us on such a basis, address to us a treaty including the whole of my subjects and dependants, stipulating that you will neither commit hostilities against them yourself, nor, to their detriment, afford assistance to their enemies.

Whatever may have preceeded this letter, if in their acts you can clearly and satisfactorily prove the plunder of British property I will as I have already declared cause it to be restored; should you however forego such a discussion and overlook what has passed it will be pleasing to us, (for there are periods at which the abstinence from irritating arguments is gratifying). Transmit to us your intentions.

Our friendship is of more real value to you than that of others, our enemies are in truth the same, for were we not engaged in war with the Governor of Egypt, you would witness from him his subjects and other maritime powers far different conduct from that of which you now entertain the slightest supposition. To the prudent and the wise, even a glance is sufficient.

You cannot be ignorant that the last treaty was entered into by myself and the English. The people of Rasoolkhymah are merely subjects and dependants, and as such have neither the power to frame or to destroy a treaty of alliance without my intervention and authority. How then did you commence hostilities against them without previously informing me of your intentions? May the peace and mercy of God be upon Moohummud, his disciples and descendants.

A True Translation
Signed/R. Taylor

The following month Bruce wrote again to the Governor in Bombay:[30]

Sir,

In reference to my address under date 6th ultimo, I have now the honor to transmit copy and translation of a letter from the Wahabee Chief to me, received via Bussora on the 10th instant. The Honorable Board will observe by this document that the tenor and tone of this letter is rather more mild than the last, this I conceive to arise from the circumstance of his being much harrassed and straitened by the Turkish troops under Ibrahim Pacha the son of Mahommed Ally Pasha, the Viceroy of Egypt, who is within five short marches of his capital.

Bushire   I have the honor to be & ca. & ca.
12th April 1817   Signed/Wm. Bruce

In the name of God the merciful and beneficient.

From Abdoollah been Saood to Master Bruce Beg whom may the High God lead to such acts as may be most acceptable in his sight.

Your letter reached me by Abdool Uzzeez bin Direes and its answer has already been forwarded to you by a servant of ours Moohummed ul Farisee. The particulars too of what passed between you and our subjects of Rasoolkhymeh have come to our knowledge; our expectations with regards to you were far different! How could you venture to injure individuals subject to our authority without previously conveying to us information of your intentions? All obligations of a pacifick nature can exist only between yourself and us, and the treaty entered into by the Chiefs of Rasool-khymeh was accomplished without our participation or authority, if then your late proceedings were effected with a view of rousing us to war and of destroying the bonds of alliance, God's will be done. Your dependence however on us and the policy of preserving unbroken the relations of amity are on your side more imperiously necessary than on ours, and this will please God, be fully accomplished in the result of our proceedings. If on the contrary you remain firm to your ties and obligations, I pledge myself as a sufficient security on our part provided you abstain from aiding any of our enemies, to the prejudice of those subject to our sway. Persons situated as you are rather endeavour to bind more securely the cords of alliance, than wholly cut them asunder. What now remains to be replied to on my part will be personally communicated to you by Abdoollah ben Direes. Prayers then for the prophet Moohoomaud for this descendants and disciples, with all whom be Peace.

True Translation
Signed/R. Taylor

In the name of the merciful and benevolent God
From Abdoollah ben Saood to Master Bruce Beg whom God lead to good acts and preserve from all unrighteousness.

Your letter has reached me, with what you mention regarding the demeanour of the people of Rasool Khymeh, and that they have broken the treaty and have acted thus and thus. You are not ignorant that we are members of a religious sect acting according to the words of God, and the precepts and example of his prophet (to whom be peace and benediction) one of the tenets of which inculcates a strict observance of all compacts, as hath said that being high in exaltation 'Oye! who are of the true faith, accomplish ye your engagements'. If then we are responsible for this property which has been taken, or it should appear that either I, or my father, had any knowledge of this, or that protection had been conceded to any other, than Englishmen, produce your proofs to me, and we shall be found the truest of these who adhere to their engagements.

If you urge that a treaty existed between you and the people of Rasoolkhymah, I ask: how can this plea be admitted by any sound understanding, that a subject can enter into any compact without the sanction or participation of the ruling authority?

Nevertheless, appoint an agent on your part and we will direct the people of Rasool Khymeh to assemble together with him in presence of the adjudication of the laws of the sect of Mahomet, and whatever may be the nature of this officer's sentence regarding them, we will, by the might and power of God, oblige them to act according to this decision.

If however your views are other than these, and you prefer war to peace, let the will of God be done, we are his servants, who strive in the path of his commandments and to whom he has promised by the mouth of his Prophet (on whom be blessings and benediction) that he will aid us against those who seek to injure us according to his holy words, 'He it is who hath sent his Prophet as a guide and in the true faith he might give him victory over all religions, Yea even should the unrighteous murmur'.

As to your threat that you will destroy Rasool Khymeh, as if it had never been, we say 'Fate is with the high and Great God, who is powerful and above his servants, and is mighty and full of wisdom and this God will prevent and the armies of Islam will hasten to aid their brethren'.

The value of our friendship to the English and the necessary policy of preserving our union, are not unknown to you. If then they determine upon war and favour the wishes of the vile Cur of Muscat God's will be done. If however they desire peace all past events must be consigned to oblivion, and as to the future, depute to us a person on whom you repose confidence, and instruct him in all your views, that we may, by the power of God, reciprocally renew friendly ties and engagements, and reestablish fixed and sure determination, such as shall prevent all future contention.

The blessings of God on Mohomet, his descendants, and disciples, and peace be with them all.

A True Translation
Signed/Wm. Bruce
Resident

From this correspondence it becomes absolutely clear that what the British wanted was to allow Indian ships, whether belonging to their subjects or not, to transport all trade in the area at the expense of Arab ships. The British also wanted to grant their protection to goods and ships belonging to other nations, irrespective of their animosity to the Arabs of the Gulf. It also becomes clear that the Arabs were willing to allow British goods and ships to pass unmolested even to unfriendly ports. The desire of the Arabs to reach an agreement with the British was as great as their determination to fight when necessary, but the British appear to have been planning all along to use force, when it became available, to impose their domination on the Gulf.

Lorimer, followed by Kelly, continued to report, though without any evidence, many piratical attacks off the Indian coast and attributed them to the Qawāsim. Such reports are simply a repetition of exaggerated rumours which were not even credible at the time they were supposed to have taken place. Thus we find the following comments by Company representatives about these rumours. Captain Elwood, Government Agent at Porebunder, wrote 'I cannot implicitly rely on native intelligence as to extent of force which is frequently exaggerated'.[31] Mr J. MacMurdo, the Resident at Cutch, testified that 'Accounts vary as to the numbers of vessels which compose the pirate fleet'.[32] Another report asserts that the information received 'is not sufficiently authenticated for me to give credit to it'.[33]

It was on the pretext of such unconfirmed reports that instructions were issued to all commanding officers of the Company's cruisers to destroy all 'vessels and crafts belonging to the Joasmees and other piratical tribes'. The following letter is an example of these instructions:[34]

To
William Hill Esqre,
Captain of His Majesty's Ship Towey.
Sir,
1. I am directed by the Right Honble the Governor in Council to acknowledge the receipt of your letter of the 26th instant and to acquaint you that instructions have been transmitted to the Commanders of the Honble Company's

Cruizers in the Gulph, the names of which are noted in the margin,* to put themselves under your orders, or the orders of the Senior Officer of His Majesty's ships for the time being in the Gulph.

I am, at the same time, instructed to acquaint you, that it is the intention of the Governor in Council, whenever an adequate force can be spared, from other more pressing service, to send an expedition to the Gulph for the purpose of destroying the vessels and crafts belonging to the Joasmees and other piratical tribes, in that quarter, which can only be effected by the presence of military force.

It is probable that this measure may not be practicable for several months; and in the meanwhile the great object to which your attention is requested is to protect the trade passing and repassing, up and down the Gulph, against their depredations, and to take or destroy any of their vessels where they can be met with.

The Imaum of Muscat has manifested the strongest wish to preserve the most friendly relations with the British Government; and it is desirable that in all cases the ships or vessels of His Highness may receive from us every sort of protection which can be afforded to them, whenever they may require it and to distinguish the vessels belonging to Muscat, I have to inform you that a sort of signal has been established of which I enclose a copy.

But however disposed the British Government may feel to afford protection to His Highness and his subjects, it would be unadvisable to undertake any expedition in conjunction with His Highness against any of the territories of the piratical tribes, at the present moment, which it is by no means improbable, may be proposed to you by His Highness.

Bombay Castle   I have the honor to be, Sir,
28th November 1817   Your most obedient
                                                        humble servant

Here we have at least six Company cruisers, the *Psyche*, the *Ariel*, the *Benares*, the *Thetis*, the *Teignmouth* and the *Aurora*, joined by at least His Majesty's ship the *Towey*, with others to follow when possible, all sent to the Gulf with the specific instructions of 'destroying the vessels and crafts belonging to the Joasmees', and 'to take or destroy any of their vessels wherever they can be met with'. Although these instructions were issued in November 1817 we know for a fact that one of these Company cruisers, the *Psyche*, had already been involved in aggressive operations against the Qawāsim in March of that year. The following report describes these operations:[35]

To
The Right Honble Sir Evan Nepean
President and Governor in Council.
Right Honble Sir,
1. I beg to state for the information of the Right Honble the Governor in Council

---

* Psyche, Ariel, Benares, Thetis, Teignmouth, Aurora.

that I have received a communication from Lieut. Tanner, commanding the Honble Company's cruizer Pscyhe dated Bushire Roads 22nd March, wherein he reports that he left Muscat on the 8th of that month with despatches for Captain of His Majesty's ship Towey who had proceeded on towards Bushire, on the 12th being off Bombarack Rock fell in with a small squadron of Joassmee pirates consisting of two large trankeys crowded with men and two of a smaller size who showed but few hands, they were working up along the Persian coast, apparently returning towards their port after a cruize. Lieut. Tanner having perfectly satisfied himself (from their manoeuvres) that they were pirates, cleared ship for action and gave them chase, but they immediately separated and ran away, as soon as the guns would bear. Lieut. Tanner opened a small fire upon the nearest who had hauled in towards Bombarack Rock in the shoal water. Every exertion exercised on the part of Lieut. Tanner for several hours to destroy or capture those marauders which he regrets to state proved unsuccessful owing to their superiority in sailing, and their light draft of water, enabling them to keep in such shoal water near the shore that the Psyche's shot did not take proper effect, she had sounding along the shore in chasing round Cape Jack from 4 to 8 fms. and some of the cannon shot struck the boat and covered her completely with grape and cannister four or five, several times.
2. I have also received two more communications from Lieut. Tanner dated 3rd and 19th April last wherein he reports that on the 27th March he left Bushire with despatch from Captain Hill which he delivered to the Honble Company's Broker at Muscat, for the purpose of being forwarded on the Bombay and that he (Lieut. Tanner) was then warping out in Company with the Honorable Company's cruizer Ariel and three country ships and had received information of a fleet of the Joassmee pirates consisting of 25 sail being at sea cruizing off the Quoins to intercept the trade, altho' it sound probable those reports might have some foundation yet he thought the Muscat people in general exaggerated those matters a little.

Supdt. Office	I have the honor to be,
Bombay	Right Honble Sir,
5th May 1817	Your most obedient humble servant,
	Signed/Henry Meriton, Supdt.

It is instructive to note that this report speaks of the fact that 'the Muscat people in general exaggerated those matters a little', and these were matters concerning information and Qawāsimī boats, numbers and movements. Lieutenant Tanner commanding the *Pscyhe* was not innocent of exaggeration himself in reporting his action. The 'squadron of Joasmee pirates' he attacked were no more than four rather small ships returning to port hugging the coast. And that coast was the Persian and not the Arab coast. Yet the trigger-happy Lieutenant judged them to be pirates, and Qawāsim at that, and immediately starting firing on them. The so-called 'Joasmee pirates' did not even return his fire and simply managed to escape with their lives.

This incident was reported in a completely different and honest manner by Captain Hill, the commander of H.M.S *Towey*, Lieutenant Tanner's senior officer at the time. Hill wrote:[36]

Lieut. Tanner of the Pscyhe fired on three boats passing Bombarrack rock but I cannot learn that they were pirates, his only reason for supposing them such was that they endeavoured to avoid him. What their future intentions are is difficult to determine, they however now seem to be quiet, as no molestation whatever has been offered any of the ships passing up or down.

It must be noted that Captain Hill was in His Majesty's service and not in the Company's; he had no axe to grind and no reason to exaggerate. Indeed, his extraordinary honesty led him to comment that, 'neither have the cruisers or myself since I have been in the Gulph, met with any of the Joasmee vessels'.

The Vestal Incident

The ludicrousness of the situation becomes clear when we realise that some of the ships the British attacked at this time, at the height of their campaign in 1817, were ships that eventually proved to be not those of 'Joasmee pirates' but belonging to the Imām of Muscat, their close ally. In May 1817 Lieutenant F. Faithful, commanding the Company cruiser *Vestal*, committed such a blunder and it took six months of correspondence, explanations, prevarication and retraction to clear up the matter. Here we shall cite all the reports concerned, which clearly prove the ignorance and ineptitude of the Company's commanding officers. The first report was as follows:[37]

To
The Right Honble Sir Evan Nepean
President and Governor in Council.
Right Honble Sir,
    I beg to state for the information of the Right Honble the Governor in Council that I have received a communication from Lieut. F. Faithful, Commanding the Honble Company's cruizer Vestal, dated Muscat Cove 14th May, wherein he stated that on the afternoon of the 7th instant being close to the Quoins he saw a large bugglow with two trankies, and a ketch in tow. The ketch a grab, painted with a broad yellow streak and square stern, he had strong suspicion that the ketch was a prize to the boats, but having no orders and a ship under convoy, did not stand after her. He shortly after saw five small boats close in with Cape Mussledom the Vestal being at that time to the southward of the Quoins, and in about one hour after Lieut. Faithful saw nine boats and a ship, the boats apparently chasing her. He immediately made every exertion to join the ship but the wind falling very light the Vestal was not able to close with her until 9 p.m. The ship also upon seeing the Vestal used her endeavours

to join, when Lieut. Faithful hailed the Alexander (for so she proved) and directed her to keep her station close the Vestal's larboard quarter, when her commander informed Lieut. Faithful that he had been chased since one p.m. by fifteen boats and that there were at that time five more lying to ahead to intercept him. Lieut. Faithful directed him to prepare for battle and knowing that the Alexander had the late Bagdad guard on board expected much assistance from her. They continued to stand on their course with a very light air from the N.N.W. and at 10 pm. finding themselves close to the boats began to fire on them. The Alexander opened her fire with very considerable effect. The boats were drawn up in a crescent and Lieut. Faitfhul did not think it prudent to pass thro' them, but continued, altering his course until he had passed the whole of them. The boats did not make any resistance but kept continually calling themselves Muscat boats to induce the Vestal and Alexander to desist from firing, and Lieut. Faithful frequently directed the fire to cease, not liking to keep up fire on those who made no defence. On that occasion the Vestal broke one of the larboard carronade carriages which Lieut. Faithful hoped to get repaired at Muscat. As the Vestal fired principally grape and cannister, she is now short of both.

It is Lieut. Faithful's wish that the vessel should be supplied with four two pound, swivels two to be placed forward and two aft loaded with 50 or 100 musquet balls as they would be an effectual check to the enemy's boarding, the only point in which he has anything to apprehend from them.

On the ensuing morning the Vestal was followed by twenty boats, two of them very large, but they were at a considerable distance and Lieut. Faithful since his arrival at Muscat found no doubt of the boats having been Joassmee, and that the ketch was a vessel belonging to Bownaghar bound to Muscat taken near that port and part of her crew then there.

Lieut. Faithful also states that he fears such an opportunity for destroying part of the Joassmee boats will not occur again but he confesses he could not, consistent with his feelings, continue to destroy men who opposed no resistance though he cannot but regret that his feelings and the uncertainty under which he laboured, should have operated so much in their favour.

Supdt. Office   I have the honor to be,
Bombay   Right Honble Sir,
23rd May 1817   Your most obedient servant
                                        Signed/Henry Meriton, Supdt.

On the face of it the gallant Lieutenant Faithful was discharging his duty attacking pirates who 'kept continually calling themselves Muscat boats'. Although after what must have appeared to be foolish action, he 'directed the fire to cease not liking to keep up fire on those who made no defence'.

A few weeks later the retraction started, and lies were offered to justify the blunder when it was realised that the *Vestal* had actually attacked Muscat boats. This is clear in this second report:[38]

To
The Right Honorable Sir Evan Nepean Bart.,
President and Governor in Council.
Right Honble Sir,

As connected with my letter, under date the 23rd ultimo I beg to state for the information of the Right Honble the Governor in Council, that I have received another communication from Lieut. Faithful, dated Muscat Cove 24th May, wherein he reports that the boats on which he fired were Muscat boats and that 12 or 14 boats sailed from Bunder Abass for Muscat and fell in with several Joassmees, from whom they were endeavouring to escape, but seeing the Honble Company's cruizer Vestal they lowered down their sail, and continued to lay too until the Vestal should come up. The Alexander being chased by the same boats that had been in pursuit of the Bunder Abass boats, unfortunately mistook the latter for a part of the fleet that were in chase of her, and it was under that impression Lieut. Faithful fired on the Muscat boats, the night preventing him from distinguishing one from the other. The vessels received some damage but few lives were lost, the people lying down in the bottom of the boats, two men and one woman killed and one woman wounded.

Supdt. Office	I have the honor to be,
Bombay	Right Honble Sir,
10th June 1817	Your most obedt. hum. servant
	Signed/Henry Meriton. Supdt.

Some five months later Lieutenant Faithful was still mixing lies with apologies to justify his blunder which, he had to admit, had resulted in the killing of two men and two women:[39]

To Henry Meriton Esqr.
Superintendent of Marine
Sir,

I have to acknowledge the receipt of your letter of the 1st instant requiring an explanation of the circumstances detailed in mine of the 14th and 24th of May last.

In reply thereto I shall in the first place detail all the events of the day previous to the attack and thereby show how strongly I was impressed with the necessity of firing on the boats for the safety of my convoy and of the vessel under my command.

At 3 o'clock on the 7th of May three boats were seen having a ketch in tow; the latter being a description of a vessel seldom or ever seen in the Gulph, I could entertain but one opinion on the subject, that of her being a captured vessel; shortly after five more boats were seen standing in the same direction as the former. I should certainly in this instance have endeavoured to examine the ketch but was deterred by the very defenceless state of the William Petrie then under convoy, but before the Petrie closed with me sufficiently near to take any steps, nine other boats were seen as also a ship. It appearing to me that the boats were in chase of the ship, had only one object left, that of closing with and protecting her as quickly as possible tho the strange ship was not more than 6 or 7 miles from us and making every exertion to close, yet it was not effected before 9 o'clock at night when Captain Studd of the Alexander informed me he had been chased since 1 pm of that day by fifteen boats and that there were more lying to ahead to intercept her. Upon my further questioning Captain Studd as to his belief whether the boats would have attacked him he replied 'most certainly'. It will be here necessary to remark that the boats which Captain Studd reported to be lying to were not seen from the Vestal.

After the Alexander joined a direct course was steered for Muscat, with a light wind from the northward, and at 10 pm boats were seen close on board of us in the larboard bow, the helm was immediately put aport to avoid them, when others were seen on the starboard bow. In this situation I had no resource, the boats were so close that a few minutes would have brought them alongside and as the Vestal from her very weak crew was ill able to oppose a resistance should the boats once board us, I judged it most advisable to use the only means I had of defending myself and a valuable convoy, that of commencing a fire on the boats.

Tho' it is true that the boats declared themselves to be friends, yet I considered this to arise from the circumstance of their finding themselves opposed by a larger force than they expected, the boats not having been seen from the Vestal, I concluded they had not seen us until too close to avoid our shot indeed after our fire commenced I observed three boats close to the Alexander, one very large immediately under her fore-chains and I was for some time apprehensive that that ship was actually boarded more particularly so, as her fire had entirely ceased. I think it necessary to be observed that in consequence of the boats hailing us, our fire was occasionally withheld, and only renewed upon finding ourselves approached by fresh boats, and that I did not seek the boats, but on seeing them did all in my power to avoid them and immediately the vessel was clear of the boats our fire ceased without attempting to pursue them.

When the preceding occurrences of the day are considered I trust I shall not be judged to have acted rashly, more particularly so as the darkness of the night rendered it impossible to discover whether they were war or merchant boats independent of the difficulty there is at all times of knowing the one from the other, and I was the more strongly impressed with the belief of the boats being Joassmee being the season of the year when their boats would be returning from the Gulph of Arabia and the coast of India.

I cannot precisely state the casualties that occurred on this unfortunate occasion, a man belonging to one of the boats on his arrival at Muscat came on board the Vestal and mentioned that two men and two women were killed and one woman wounded.

Bombay   I have the honor to be, Sir,
5th November 1817   Your most obedt. servant

Signed/F. Faithful,
Lieut. Commr.

True Copy
Signed/Henry Meriton
Supdt.

Needless to say, there was no attempt made to put Lieutenant Faithful on trial or to court-martial him. Obviously his 'error' was the kind that was an everyday occurrence in the Gulf, particularly against 'Joasmee pirates'. William Bruce reported to Francis Warden in May 1817 that the Company's cruiser *Mercury* saw some piratical small boats off the Bar near Baṣra, 'which did not however offer to molest' the *Mercury*. Six other 'Joasmee boats' chased the cruiser, but then simply 'hauled off'.[40]

While Company officers and representatives were always reporting sightings and encounters with 'Joasmee pirates' and their boats, the officers in command of His Majesty's ships consistently reported that they neither heard of nor saw any piratical ships in the Gulf. The following is a report to this effect:[41]

To
The Right Hon'ble
The Governor in Council
Bombay
Sir,

There being no present occasion for the service of the Hon'ble Company cruizer Psyche up the Gulph, and a considerable time having elapsed since she was at Bombay, I have ordered her to proceed to your Residency to be refitted.

The force now in the Gulph consist of His Majesty's sloop under my command and the H.C. cruizers Benares and Thetis.

I have neither seen or heard of any piratical cruizer since my arrival in the Gulph.

I have the honour to be, Sir,
Your obedient servant,
Sd. P.H. Bridges
Commander

H.M. Sloop Challenger
Bushire Regt.
Dec. 9th 1817

Lorimer and Kelly tried to give the impression that 1818 witnessed an increase of incidents on the high seas that added considerably to the apprehensions of the British authorities in India, but the undeniable fact is that until at least October almost the whole year passed without any reports of alleged piracies or encounters with pirates.

It is therefore all the more surprising to realise that during this peaceful period the British were actually engaged in the planning of an expedition in 1819 to destroy the Qawāsim. Apparently Nepean was able, some time during the first half of 1818, to persuade the Marquis of Hastings (previously the Earl of Moira), the Governor-General of India, to approve the execution of such an expedition. In September 1818 Nepean reported to Hastings 'the measures to be adopted for carrying your Lordship's commands into execution'.

And all this in spite of the fact that Nepean had to admit that 'the only vessel belonging to the Hon'ble Company hitherto captured by the pirates was a small pattamar commanded by a native syrang which they destroyed after putting to death a great part of her crew. I have not heard that any ships or vessels navigated by Europeans or owned by British merchants has yet been taken'. One must again point out that this was Nepean's testimony in September 1818. His line of reasoning is almost unbelievable. He asked for help in order to meet the combined forces of the Qawāsim, which he estimated to be 10,300 men, 89 large vessels and 250 small vessels. He suggested seeking the help of the notorious Raḥma b. Jābir, who was at the time 'in hostility with the Joasmees attacking them in some dowes he still possesses on all occasions that present themselves'. On matters of policy, after the destruction of the Qawāsim Nepean recommended that their lands should be given to the Imām of Muscat. Bahrain should also be conceded to the Imām.[42]

Hasting's reply to Nepean was his decision to postpone the expedition for a year in order to invite the co-operation of Ibrāhīm Pasha of Egypt who, at the time, was victoriously advancing on Dar'iyya. Nepean had informed Hastings that:[43]

a communication has been made to me by Mahomed Ali of overtures having recently been received from the piratical chieftains by the Imaum for the cessation of hostilities, and of a desire to be at peace with His Highness. How far the piratical chieftains would be content to admit of His Highness's continuance in a state of neutrality must be doubtful, but if under the pressure of necessity he should while giving shelter to the enemy be compelled to prohibit our access to his ports, the consequences would be severely felt by our trade to the Gulph.

Here Nepean succinctly pointed out the major threat to British trade in the Gulf as represented by a possible alliance between the Imām and the Qawāsim, that would close Muscat and its ports to the British while they would remain open for the Qawāsim. The British were astute enough to recognise this danger, and thus it was to their advantage that the fight between the Imām and the Qawāsim should continue. Of course, they also tried not to alienate the Imām. The latter, in his blind desire to dominate the Arab traders of the Gulf, did not realise the benefits of an alliance with the Qawāsim which would have made them the major trading partners of the area at the expense of even the Company. For their part, the Qawāsim were willing and often tried to reach an accommodation with the Imām but to no avail. Perhaps among the leaders of the Qawāsim Sulṭān b. Ṣaqr was the one who most recognised the advantages of such an alliance with the

Imām. The other leaders, Hasan b. Rahma for example, thought an alliance with the Saudis against the Imām would prevent him from dominating them and at the same time assure them of help against British attacks.

At this stage one must admit that the pressure of the Egyptians from the west on the Saudis must have persuaded the latter to improve their relationship with the British in order to secure their eastern flank. Naturally the Qawāsim would act accordingly and try to reach a *modus vivendi* not only with the Imām but with the Company as well. Thus we find 'Abdullah b. Sa'ūd and Hasan b. Rahma corresponding with William Bruce and asking for terms of accommodation between them. Hasan b. Rahma's terms were clear: the British should stop attacking the ships of the Qawāsim and in return the latter would not attack ships belonging to the Christian British, meaning the Europeans, which of course excluded ships belonging to Indians. In other words, the Qawāsim were willing to allow British ships belonging to the Company to trade in the Gulf. But they were not ready to allow cheap Indian transportation of goods to compete with them in the trade between India and the Gulf under the protection of the British cruisers. The Saudis' terms were more difficult: in addition to the terms for which the Qawāsim asked, 'Abdullah b. Sa'ūd demanded that the British should not afford their protection to his enemies the Ottomans in Basra, or the Egyptians and the Yemenis in the Red Sea.[44]

Bruce, who must have been made aware of Nepean's plans, demurred and simply repeated his demands for restitution of goods and ships alleged to have been plundered by the Qawāsim.[45] It was time to revive the scare-mongering campaign against the pirates in order to persuade those in the Company who might have had some hesitation in supporting an expedition to destroy the Qawāsim. Bruce had an ardent ally in the person of Captain F. Loch of HMS *Eden* who arrived in the Gulf in December 1818 and who, unlike other officers commanding His Majesty's ships, was willing and eager to do the Company's dirty work, which its cruisers alone could not do.

According to Lorimer:[46]

In December 1818 the H.E.I. Company's brigs 'Thetis' and 'Psyche' assisted by H.M.S. 'Eden' succeeded in cornering 14 piratical Qawasim vessels in Gwatar Bay, but time having been allowed them until the morning, in opposition to the advice of the Company's officers they made their escape during the night . . . On Christmas morning 1818 H.M.S. 'Eden' and the Company's brig-of-war 'Pscyhe' rescued a captured boat from two pirate Trankis, which managed to escape . . . and on the 10th and 11th of January 1819 H.M.S. 'Eden' sunk 2 piratical Baghlahs off Qishm and Hanjam.

Captain Loch was very pleased with himself and with the commander of the *Psyche*, Lieutenant J.W. Guy, as he reported to his seniors in Bombay:[47]

His Majesty's Ship Eden
At Anchor in the Bay of
Gutter, 27th December, 1819
Sir,

I beg to inform you of His Majesty's ship under my command, having on the 25th instant in company with the H.C. cruizer Psyche fallen in with off Gaudell, two Joasmee Trankees having a prize in tow, the latter was captured and destroyed, the former after a chase of 13 hours escaped owing to the light winds the sweeps giving them so great an advantage enabling them after dark to gain such a distance, as to permit their altering their course without being perceived.

I cannot help bringing to your notice the exertions of the commander of the Psyche (with whom I have every reason to be pleased). The force of the vessels chased is but trifling but their coolness, courage and manoeuvring required every exertion to gain the smallest advantage and that only while the breeze was too fresh for their sweeps.

To: I have the Honor to be
Sir, The Honorable   Your obedient servant.
Governor of Bombay   Sd/Francis E. Loch
                                                 Captain

However, in his excitement Captain Loch neglected to report that the 'prize in tow . . . captured and destroyed' was nothing more than 'a small boat laden with cotton . . . of no comparative value', as reported by Lieutenant Guy himself.[48] Captain Loch also neglected to report that the cruiser Thetis 'chased a few fishing boats'.[49] On 28 December 1818 Loch attacked and destroyed more vessels in the Gulf, as detailed in the following letter:[50]

Letter from Captain Loch, dated 2nd January 1819.

I have to inform you of His Majesty's ship under my command having on the 28th of last month fallen in with two bugallas and two trankeys, belonging to the Joasmees having 3 prizes in tow. Two of the latter were captured in one of which was found 16 Joasmee people who could not escape to their own vessel having them in tow, owing to their being close under the ship's guns. One of the vessels the prisoners inform me, was sunk but which I am disinclined to believe (it being so dark as to prevent our distinguishing) and that the number of people that perished through swimming were those who jumped overboard preferring that mode of death to the chance of being sunk by the ship's guns.

The lightness of the winds and the vessels − − − − also the superiority their sweeps give, baffled very exertion (during a chase of 16 hours) of the officers and ship's company, I have the honour to command, to capture and destroy more of them. The vessels had overboard 550 men and eight guns, each bugalo having 140 men and four guns, one trankey 120 and the other 100, the two latter had swivels and small arms only.

Since I wrote the above I have procured a list of the names, force of the different vessels chased by us are mentioned:

Shima Bugalo — Said Eben Hasun — 4 guns — 150 men.
Tomasha Bugalo — Sebit Eben Yema — 4 guns — 130 men.
Awad Trankee — Hamett — 2 guns — 110 men.
Swaybien Trankee — Salem — 1 gun — 160 men.

Reports about sighting pirates continued to be circulated. As usual Lorimer assumed them to be true and he was in no doubt that these so-called pirates were Qawāsim:[51]

> Between October 1818 and January 1819 the Company's cruisers 'Thetis' and 'Psyche' encountered the Qawasim sailing in flotillas of 2 to 10 vessels no less than 17 times, and continued to drive them from place to place; but, on account of the superior sailing qualities of the Arab boats, the British vessels seldom or never succeeded in bringing them to action.

In other words, the British commanders of the Company cruisers considered any two ships sailing together in the Gulf to be pirates and deemed them as targets for destruction whenever possible; and that was at a time when men like Captain Loch were engaged in indiscriminate attacks on any ships in the Gulf. Captain D. Conyers commanding the HC cruiser *Mercury*, who was very active in the Gulf at that time, reported in February 1819, that his ship 'pulled in shore towards some boats said to belong to Rasil Khyma'. Although it was not proved that they were Qawāsim or in any way engaged in piracy, Conyers attacked and took possession of two of the boats which he destroyed.[52]

There were a number of reports of Company cruisers attacking trading boats which proved to belong to friendly powers on the pretext of baseless suspicions. There was the case of the *Ahmady*, a boat belonging to Bahrain, which took four months and a great deal of correspondence to clear up. As it turned out, Captain J. Arthur commanding the cruiser *Antelope*, in co-operation with a Muscat boat, attacked, seized and plundered the *Ahmady*. The question of this co-operation came to light when they disagreed on the division of booty and, indeed, Captain Arthur seems to have appropriated some jewellery for himself. To cut a long story short, the *Ahmady* was finally returned to Bahrain but of course without the plundered property and Captain Arthur was reprimanded.[53]

In February 1819 two boats belonging to Muscat were seized and, as the Imām himself explained in his letter of thanks to Bombay:[54]

> the commanders of the company cruizers had in the first instance suspected (the two boats) to be Joasmee vessels, and had accordingly detained them, but that it had been afterwards proved they belonged to my subjects, and that you have been so good as to liberate them, I duly appreciate your Excellency's kind offices on the occasion.

In May 1819 Captain Loch came close to committing just such a blunder in attacking Muscat boats. Chasing what he thought to be four 'Joasmee' boats, he realised his mistake when he captured the smallest of the boats on which there were six men, one from Malabar, two from Muscat and three 'Joasmees'.[55]

In July 1819 Captain Walpole, commanding HMS *Curlew*, captured a boat belonging to Muhammad b. Qadīb, the Qāsimī chief of Linga, and towed it to Bushire where it was detained. It was released on the orders of the Persian Prince of Shīrāz.[56] This same Captain Walpole, captured a boat belonging to Shārjah in September 1819,[57] but the Prince of Shīrāz could not, of course, order its release.

There are endless reports of attacks by British warships on vessels alleged and assumed to belong to 'Joasmee pirates'. In September 1819 Lieutenant Guy, commanding the Company cruiser *Psyche*, reported burning a 'Joasmee battile' and capturing three of its crew. He also captured a small boat which was in tow.[58] The following month Captain Hale of the Company cruiser *Teignmouth* captured and destroyed a boat, and it is worth noting that he did not even bother to claim it was a 'Joasmee' or looked like a pirate ship.[59]

The indiscriminate attacks on all Arab ships continued audaciously and relentlessly, even when it was more than obvious that the attacked ships were nothing but trading vessels. It became abundantly clear that the British objective was to disrupt and destroy the trade of the Qawāsim even between Gulf ports. Indeed, the attempt was being made to starve the Qawāsim. In November 1819 Captain Loch submitted the following report:[60]

> To
> The Right Honorable
> The Governor of Bombay
>
>
>
> His Majesty's ship Eden
> Bushire Roads
> 11th November 1819
>
>
> Sir,
>   I have to inform you of the boats of His Majesty's ship under my command having this day captured a pirate batille of considerable size having 29 men on board with two six pound guns and a proportion of other arms for that number of men.
>   The batille originally sailed from Debay and Bothebee on the south coast of the Gulph proceeding for Nacaloo with a pass from the Sheikh Mohamed Ben Heza (the proprietor) requesting the Sheik of Nacaloo to provide the batille with a pass for this part of the coast with which she proceeded to Assaloo where she procured a second pass and a person to protect her, with letters to the Sheik of Bushire.
>   On his first being boarded by the boats of the Eden the people called themselves from Assaloo, consequently was permitted to pass into the harbour, but was soon proved to be a pirate, therefore was captured by the boats.
>   The batille has been driven to this scheme owing to the great scarcity of dates throughout the pirate coast.
>   I shall send the prisoners to Bombay by the first opportunity for the disposal

of your Hon'ble Board.

I beg to acquaint you that it has been entirely owing to the excellent information of Mr Bruce, Resident, that I have been able to detect this fraud and capture the vessel which I could only do by taking her out of the harbour when the naquadah was on the point of entering into terms for a cargo with the Shaik of this place.

> I have the honor to be, Sir
> Your most obedient servant
> Francis E. Loch, Captain

Here was an Arab boat sailing from Dubai to Abu Dhabi and then trying to find some protection to cross to the Persian coast in search of dates. It had no more than 29 men on board. The boat was seized and the men captured and sent to Bombay before they were able to arrange for a cargo of dates. Captain Loch and Resident Bruce accused these men of being pirates; but what was worse was the fact that they reported this operation, as part of their duty, to their superiors in Bombay.

There are two other striking reports filed by Captain D. Conyers of the Company cruiser *Mercury*, also in November 1819, that leave no doubt of the Company's intentions to destroy the trade of the Qawāsim. The first report was about an attack on two Arab boats sailing near Abu Dhabi, with 14 men aboard armed with spears and matchlocks, three of them passengers. There were also 200 dollars on board:[61]

To
The Right Honorable
The Governor of Bombay
Sir,

I have the honor to acquaint you that the H.C. cruizer under my command on the 1st of November at 2.30 pm bore up and gave chase to two suspicious boats, at 3.30 the sternmost boat showed white colours, at 4 boarded her (bugara) now under the red colours, three days from Bothebee said to be bound to Asaloo. No cargo on board 14 men belonging to above tribe a place between Bachune and Bothebee on the main by their accounts, armed with spears, matchlocks, &ca. wore round and took her in tow, finding there was no chance of coming up with the next boat, made all sail to join the convoy the next day sent an officer on board and examined her found (two hundred dollars) got her mast and yard down.

It appears that her consort was from the same place and bound also to Asaloo, that one of the crew of the detained bugara got on board the other boat taking with him the papers belonging to the boat he left.

Out of the 14 men who compose the crew of the bugara, three belong to Asaloo, and are passengers, they are all of the Wahabee or Joassmee tribe.

H.C. Cruizer Mercury   I have the honor to be
Bushire Roads   Sir

9th November 1819   Your most obedient servt
                                                    D.D. Conyers

The second report was even more laughable than the first. Captain Conyers spotted five Arab ships trying to cross to the Persian coast. Having captured one of them, it turned out to belong to Linga and had a cargo of salt fish, cloth and dye stuff. And this was a pirate boat![62]

Sir,
    I have the pleasure to inform you that at 5 am on the 13th inst. gave chase to a boat standing to the eastward, shortly after saw six more at anchor in Cove Musa, the strangers steering for them.
    At 6 am it getting dark anchored in 5 fathoms. The pilot refused to take the ship further in, at daylight sent the cutter to sound Dieu Island but about one mile the one with the high land of India 26 NI/2 N. weighed and made all sail in chase of the boats (five) at noon one of the strangers near us, the other four out of sight from the deck.
    At 1 pm fired a shot at the stranger who finding she could not escape bore up sent and took possession of her, she proved to be the Linga batille with nineteen men, a boy, also two women and a boy which had been captured by the pirates in a boat belonging to Grane bound to Dilam and put on board the batille by them.
    It appears that the pirates had captured four boats belonging to Grane two of them they sent to Omel-Gawain, the port the pirates belonged to, the other two boats run ashore having shown their cargoes (dates) on board and made their escape to the shores.
    When the pirates put the women and boy on board the batille they did not molest the crew or cargo except in taking out the Bushire pilot.
    The batille had been in company with the pirates five days, was armed and their arms ready for use. The cargo consists of salt fish, cloth and dye stuff, she did not bear up till she found it impossible to escape and made every effort to effect it.
    From Cove Musa proceeded off the Bar, and having examined the coast returned to Karrack to complete our water which we left yesterday and am now proceeding to cruize to Cape Bang.
To   I have the honor to be, Sir
Francis E. Loch   Your most obedient servt.
                Captain of H.M. Ship Eden/Sd. D.D. Conyers, Captain

    In the midst of all these bombastic reports, Captain Loch imparted one interesting item, though it has not been possible to confirm it from any other source. According to Loch, 'the Sheikh of Sharga (i.e. Sultān b. Ṣaqr) has declared war against Ras-al-Khyma and entered into a treaty of peace with His Highness the Imam of Muscat'.[63] It is rather difficult to believe that Sultān b. Ṣaqr would go so far as to declare war against Rās al-Khaimah, and his friendship with the

Imām would not require the conclusion of a peace treaty. But Loch could have been reporting political attitudes rather than formal moves.

On another political front, things were moving on a more formal level. The Government of Bombay, having agreed on the expedition against the Qawāsim, decided in April 1819 to send Captain G. Forster Sadlier of HM 47th Regiment on a mission to the Imām of Muscat and then to Ibrāhīm Pasha in central Arabia, both to synchronise moves against the Qawāsim and to collect as much intelligence as possible about internal conditions in the peninsula. The progress and the results of Captain Sadlier's journey are too well known to be repeated here, although it should be pointed out that he was a man capable of writing very long and detailed reports containing a wealth of information.

Suing for Peace

While the aggressive intentions of the Government of Bombay were escalating almost daily, the approaches of the Qawāsim to British representatives were taking on an increasing urgency that could only underline the Qawāsim's desire to reach an agreement. It comes almost as a surprise, and certainly as proof of the mendacity of the accusations of the British, that Hasan b. Rahma, the Qāsimī leader most accused of promoting piracy, was the same person who was most anxious to establish peace with the British. As early as March 1819 he pleaded with 'Abdullah b. Ahmad the Shaikh of Bahrain to mediate between him and the British. The Shaikh of Bahrain had, the previous month, mediated between the British and Hasan b. Rahma in a question of exchange of prisoners. The Qawāsim showed their goodwill by releasing and delivering to Captain Conyers 17 British women subjects who had been detained in Rās al-Khaimah and Shārjah in return for setting free an apparently small number of Qawāsim prisoners in Bombay.[64] When 'Abdullah b. Ahmad wrote to Bruce, the latter answered asking for terms which he would forward to Bombay. Hardly a month later in April 1819 Hasan b. Rahma wrote also to Captain Loch, protesting that 'a treaty existed that we were not to molest each other and which we both abided by as our conduct has shown, after which it pleases God that Bruce should arrive here with some ships and make certain demands which he had no grounds for, and this broke the treaty and commenced hostilities'.[65]

Of course, Loch was even less inclined towards peace than Bruce. Consequently he wrote to Bombay enclosing the letter of Hasan b. Rahma 'where he states he has sent terms of peace to Bombay and such terms I feel convinced no British Government can for a moment listen to. Had the terms been at first transmitted to me I should have without hesitation turned them down'.[66] The terms Loch referred to were that the Qawāsim of Rās al-Khaimah should not molest British people and vessels and that the British should reciprocate. The extent of British territories was to be 'from Kutch to the extremes to the southwards'. British vessels should have, besides English colours, a separate distinguishing mark, and vessels from Rās al-Khaimah should have a white flag with a distinguishing mark on it. Each side should respect each other's property.[67]

Loch recommended that these terms should be rejected out of hand and so of course did Bruce:[68]

Letter to the Right Honourable Sir Evan Nepean President and Governor in Council, Bombay. Right Honourable Sir, In reference to

By the letter from Hassan Ben Rahmah your Honourable Board will notice their anxiety to enter into terms with the British Government. This I can see arises more from the fear they entertain of the hostile intentions of Ibrahim Pasha, than from any immediate ones from us although they are aware that ultimately we shall amply chastise them for all the depredations that they have committed on our trade and subjects. They are therefore anxious to secure themselves from the annoyances of our vessels of war in the event of their being attacked by land from the Turks.

I have the honour etc. Signed William Bruce, Resident.

30th March, 1819

Accordingly, Governor Nepean wrote a most hypocritical and arrogant letter to Hasan b. Rahma:[69]

Copy of a letter from the Right Honourable Sir Evan Nepean, Governor of Bombay, to Ameer Hassan Bin Rahmah, the Chieftain of Rasul Khaymah, dated 24th April 1819.

I have received your letter which it was impossible to peruse without feelings of astonishment and indignation aware as you were, when it was written, that the amicable relations to which you allude had hardly been arranged with your Imam, and submitted to this Government for its consideration, when the vessels and craft of the subjects of the Honourable Company, who though natives of India, are as much their subjects as if they had been born in England, and were navigating under the British flag, were attacked and captured by the cruisers belonging to Rasul Khymah, acting under your own immediate authority. And it was in consequence of these very acts that Mr Bruce proceeded off that place, in order to obtain redress, which was not afforded.

The propositions you have now transmitted are completely inadmissible, and however the subjects of the Honourable Company and its allies may be affected by a continuance of hostilities, it is impossible for the Government to listen for a moment to any propositions on the principle you have suggested.

In spite of this rebuff from Nepean, Hasan b. Rahma, still hopeful of peace, wrote to Bruce in September 1819 offering to send three deputies 'to enter into discussions with you and make terms of peace, whatever they engage we bind ourselves to bind by'.[70] When these representatives arrived at Bushire, Bruce dismissed them with the utmost contempt and wrote to Bombay on 25 October, 'I trust the Right Hon'ble the Governor in Council will approve of the line of conduct we have adopted towards these Joasmee Vakeels as they call themselves, that have arrived, as treating with such low dignity of the British nation'.[71] This was the attitude of the British hardly a month before the arrival of the expedition at Rās al-Khaimah on 25 November 1819.

While these negotiations were going on between Hasan b. Rahma and the British, an impressive show of unity was staged in the Gulf, as reported by Bruce to Bombay on 19 August 1818:[72]

The Right Honble Sir Evan Nepean Bt
President and Governor in Council
Bombay.
Right Honble Sir,

I have the honor to acquaint you that I have learnt thro' a private correspondent at Raselkhyma and which is confirmed thro' another from Bahrein that the chiefs of the Hiza Arabs, Beni Yas, Soodauns, Sultan Sugger himself; the Beni Uttoobees of Bahrein with the chiefs of Lingua, Moogoo and Charak have all met at Raselkhyma and have entered into engagements to support each other, in the event of an expedition coming up the Gulph on the part of the British Government and that Raselkhyma is to be considered the headquarters; and where they are all to assemble with their forces at the shortest notice. Rasklkhyma has been much strengthened by an additional wall and several towers and my correspondent writes me they feel confident of success from the accession of strength which this league has given them. If unfortunately from inconsistances an expedition on the part of the British Government should not come up this year I fear the greatest portion of the Gulph will be compelled to submit to these pirates even His Highness the Imaum as he cannot withstand the united force of these confederate chiefs.

This most unusual gathering of all the leaders of the Qawāsim on both sides of the Gulf, including Sultān b. Saqr, supported by their allies from the hinterland and the 'Utūbis of Bahrain, had important implications. Clearly these leaders, in their determination to defend Rās al-Khaimah, realised that if it was conquered by the British their first line of defence against British encroachment would collapse. The issue was not piracy; the only proven pirate in the Gulf, Rahma b. Jābir, did not take part in this meeting and the 'Utūbis of Bahrain did take part although they were never labelled as pirates and they certainly maintained good relations with the British. The participation of the 'Utūbis emphasised the impression that the issue was the wider one of the protection of Arab trade in the Gulf against the threat of its destruction by British military force. The presence and support of the leaders of the Qawāsim of the Persian coast signified their fears for their own future if Rās al-Khaimah were to fall. The fact that Sultān b. Saqr took part in this meeting must have alarmed the British because of the possibility of their being confronted by a united Qāsimī front.

The Government of Bombay was quick to take measures to weaken this impending unity to resist its plans in the Gulf. Mr Bruce was instructed to proceed to Bahrain where he was to assure the 'Utūbis of British support in maintaining their independence.[73] This marked a high point in British hypocrisy, because they had already promised the Imām of Muscat their support in his claims over Bahrain,[74] which was also claimed by Persia. On the other hand, the Imām himself, probably feeling isolated, decided to take the initiative and once more attacked Rās al-Khaimah and blockaded it for three months before going back empty-handed. He then corresponded with Ḥasan b. Raḥma, offering to mediate himself between the Qawāsim and the British, but, as mentioned earlier, Ḥasan b. Raḥma was at the time proposing to Bruce that he should send three representatives to negotiate.[75] In their anxiety the British also solicited the help of the Persian Government, whom they requested to attack all ports in Arab hands, Qawāsim or not, in concert with the planned expedition.[76] It goes without saying that they requested and indeed were assured of all the help they required from the Imām of Muscat.[77]

The details of the expedition are best described by its leader Major General Sir William G. Keir in a letter to the Adjutant General of the Army dated 9 December 1819 from his camp at Rās al-Khaimah:[78]

Sir,

I have the satisfaction to report that the town of Ras Al Khaimah, after a resistance of six days, was taken possession of this morning by the force under my command.

Previous to making you acquainted with the circumstances which led to this fortunate result, I shall do myself the honor, briefly, to detail the events which occurred between the period of my last communication and the commencement of the operations before Ras Al Khaimah.

On the 18th Ultimo, after completing my arrangements at Muscat, the Liverpool sailed for rendezvous at Kishme. On the 23st we fell in with the Fleet off the Persian Coast and anchored off the Island of Larrack on the 24th, November.

As it appeared probable that a considerable period would elapse before the junction of the ships which were detained in Bombay, I conceived it would be highly advantageous to avail myself in that interval in acquiring accurate knowledge of the strength of the defences of Ras Al Khaimah as personal observation could supply and I gladly embraced the proposal of Captain Collier that the Liverpool should proceed for that purpose. The Senior Engineer was accordingly taken on Board and, having sailed from Larrack on the morning of the 25th, we anchored off Ras Al Khaimah the same evening. From this date till the 27th the place was closely and repeatedly reconnoitred and, the weather continuing favourable for our operations, I determined to order down the Troops and to commence the attack without waiting for the rear Transports as the season of the N.W. winds was rapidly approaching and Captain Collier appeared apprehensive that a further delay might prove detrimental to the enterprise. A vessel was therefore despatched with instructions to Captain Walpole, who was left in charge of the Fleet, and on the 2nd Instant the Transports arrived under convoy of the Curlew.

No time was lost in making the necessary preparations for landing which was effected the following morning without opposition at a spot which had previously been selected for that purpose about two miles to the Southside of the Town. The Troops were formed across the Isthmus connecting the peninsula on which the Town is situated with the neighbouring countryside and the whole day was occupied in getting tents on shore to shelter the men from the rain, landing Engineers' tools, etc and making arrangements preparatory to commencing our approaches the next day. On the morning of the 4th the Light Troops were ordered in advance, supported by the Pickets, to dislodge the Enemy from a bank within 900 yards of the Outer Fort, which was expected to afford good cover for the men and to serve as a depot for stores previous to erecting the Batteries. The whole of the Light Companies of the force, under the command of Captain Buckhouse of H.M. 47th Regiment, accordingly moved forwards and drove the Arabs with zeal and gallantry from the date groves and over the Bank, above described, close under the walls of the Fort, followed by the Pickets under Major Molesworth who took post at the sand Bank whilst the European Light Troops were skirmishing in front. The Enemy kept up a sharp fire of musketry and, commanding these movements, etc, I regret to add that Major Molesworth, a gallant and zealous officer, was killed by a cannon and that, at the head of the Pickets, Lieut. Suprey of the 65th was wounded on this occasion. The Troops however maintained their position during the day and in the night effected a lodgement within 300 yards of the Southernmost Town and erected a Battery for 4 guns and another Battery on the right and a trench of communication for the covering party.

The weather became rather unfavourable for the disembarkation of stores required for the siege. It was with considerable difficulty that this primary object was effected but every obstacle was surmounted by the zeal and indefatigable exertions of the Navy and, on the morning of the 6th, we were enabled to open three 10 pounders on the Fort, a couple of howitzers, and 6 pounders were also placed in the Battery on the right, which played upon the defences of the Towers and nearly silenced the Enemy fire. The Liverpool, during these operations, worked in as close to the shore as her draught of water would permit and opened her guns on the Town, which must have created some considerable alarm in the garrison, but unfortunately she was at too great a distance to produce any decided effect. The Enemy, who, during the whole of our progress, exhibited a considerable degree of resolution, withstanding and ingenuity in counteracting our attacks sallied forth at 6 o'clock this morning along the whole front of our entrenchments and crept up close to the mortar battery without being perceived and entered it over the parapet after spearing the advance sentries. The (British) Party which occupied it was obliged to retire, but being immediately reinforced, charged the assailants who were driven out of the battery with considerable loss. The attack on the left was repelled instantaneously by the spirited resistance of the covering party under Major Warren, who distinguished himself much on this occasion by his coolness and gallantry. The Enemy repeated his attacks towards morning but was vigorously repulsed. During the 7th every exertion was made to land and bring up the remaining guns and mortars which was accomplished during the night after incessant labours by the sailors assisted by working parties from the Troops and those of His Highness the Imaum who cheerfully volunteered their services. These were immediately placed in Battery together with two 24 pounders which were landed from the Liverpool and in the morning the whole of our Ordnance opened on the Fort and fired with scarcely any intermission till sunset when the breach in the Curtain was reported nearly practicable and the Towers almost untenable. Immediate arrangements were made for the Assault and the Troops ordered to move down to the trenches at daybreak on the next morning. The bombardment continued during the night and the Batteries having recommenced their fire before daylight completed their breaches by 8 o'clock.

The accompanying Orders will explain to His Excellency the dispositions of the attack as well as the measures taken to guard against the possibility of failure in the event of the Enemy defending himself as desperately as might have been expected from his previous defence. These precautions however were unnecessary, the party moved forward about 8 o'clock and entered the Fort through the breaches without firing a shot and it soon became apparent that the Enemy had evacuated the place. The Town was taken possession of and was almost entirely deserted, only 10 or 20 men and a few women remaining in their House.

Upon the whole it appears evident, considering the spirited behaviour of the Enemy at the commencement of the siege, that their sudden resolution to evacuate the place was occasioned by the overwhelming fire of the Artillery, of which they could have formed no previous idea, and which the ample means placed at my disposal enabled me to bring against the Town.

Our loss I am happy to say is much less than could have been expected from the length of the siege and the obstinacy with which the Enemy disputed our approaches. I have no means of ascertaining theirs but it must have been severe.

I beg that you will assure His Excellency that I feel entirely satisfied with the conduct of the Troops, their gallantry has been exceeded only by their patience and cheerfulness under every species of privation and fatigue and the peculiarity of this service has called forth a full display of their qualities which are equally creditable to the Soldiery as the most intrepid acts of bravery. By the Orders which I do myself the honor to enclose His Excellency will be enabled to estimate the services performed by Captain Collier of the Naval part of the expedition and I can only add that the acknowledgements therein expressed are scarcely adequate to the assistance I have received from them.[78]

It will be noted that General Keir was gallant enough to pay tribute to the 'considerable degree of resolution, withstanding and ingenuity' of the Qawāsim. Nevertheless, Rās al-Khaimah was razed to the ground; its ships that were not destroyed were shared between the British and the Imam.[79] Fortified houses and towers at the ports of Rams, Jāzirat al-Ḥamra, Umm al-Qawain, 'Ajmān, Fusht, Abū

Hail and Shārjah were demolished. Their ships were also destroyed, and according to British estimates the number there was 184 ships.[80]

But perhaps the most offensive fact was that Bruce, without orders, accompanied Loch in an orgy of destruction of Arab ships on both sides of the Gulf. Loch was detailed to lead a squadron composed of his own HMS *Eden*, HMS *Curlew* and Company cruiser *Nautilus* to inspect the Gulf ports for any ships of the Qawāsim that had escaped destruction. As Kelly mildly put it,[81]

On his way up the Gulf Loch heard that several pirate vessels were sheltering at the port of Asalu, on the Persian side, and he decided to invstigate. Three vessels were found anchored in Asalu harbour, two of them from the port of Charak further down the coast, and one from Dubai. From their armament Loch suspected them to be pirates, so he had the two Charak vessels burned and the Dubai vessel taken in tow. Further up the coast at Kangun, he found two more armed vessels from Lingah, and suspecting them to be pirate craft he burned them also . . . Keir suspected that Loch had not adequately established the piratical character of the vessels concerned before destroying them.

Nevertheless, General Keir, the leader of the expedition did nothing to censure such reckless acts of piracy which were committed with great rancour. However, one should perhaps remember that these five ships were a minor addition to the 184 ships already destroyed by Keir's forces. One should also remember that the Qawāsim were only accused of attacking two British ships and even these were not proven.

On the political side, the British victory resulted in the deposition of Hasan b. Rahma as ruler of Rās al-Khaimah and the re-institution of Sultān b. Saqr in his place. The British also imposed on the hapless leaders of the Qawāsim, their allies and the 'Utūb of Bahrain, the dubious terms of the 1820 treaty.

Translation of the general TREATY with the Arab Tribes of the Persian Gulf.
In the name of God, the merciful, the compassionate!
Praise be to God, who hath ordained peace to be a blessing to his creatures. There is established a lasting peace between the British Government and the Arab tribes, who are parties to this contract, on the following conditions:—

ARTICLE 1
There shall be a cessation of plunder and piracy by land and sea on the part of the Arabs, who are parties to this contract, for ever.

ARTICLE 2
If any individual of the people of the Arabs contracting shall attack any that pass by land or sea of any nation whatsoever, in the way of plunder and piracy and not of acknowledged war, he shall be accounted an enemy of all mankind and shall be held to have forfeited both life and goods. And acknowledged war is that which is proclaimed, avowed, and ordered by government against

government; and the killing of men and taking of goods without proclamation, avowal, and the order of a government, is plunder and piracy.

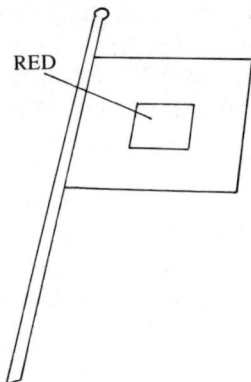

RED

ARTICLE 3

The friendly (literally the pacificated) Arabs shall carry by land and sea a red flag, with or without letters in it, at their option, and this shall be in a border of white, the breadth of the white in the border being equal to the breadth of the red, as represented in the margin, (the whole forming the flag known in the British Navy by the title of white pierced red), and this shall be the flag of the friendly Arabs, and they shall use it and no other.

ARTICLE 4

The pacificated tribes shall all of them continue in their former relations, with the exception that they shall be at peace with the British Government, and shall not fight with each other, and the flag shall be a symbol of this only and of nothing further.

ARTICLE 5

The vessels of the friendly Arabs shall all of them have in their possession a paper (Register) signed with the signature of their Chief, in which shall be the name of the vessel, its length, its breadth, and how many Karahs it holds. And they shall also have in their possession another writing (Port Clearance) signed with the signature of their Chief, in which shall be the name of the owner, the name of the Nacodah, the number of men, the number of arms, from whence sailed, at what time, and to what port bound. And if a British or other vessel meets them, they shall produce the Register and the Clearance.

ARTICLE 6

The friendly Arabs, if they choose, shall send an envoy to the British Residency in the Persian Gulf with the necessary accompaniments, and he shall remain there for the transaction of their business with the Residency; and the British Government, if it chooses, shall send an envoy also to them in like manner; and the envoy shall add his signature to the signature of the Chief in the paper (Register) of their vessels, which contains the length of the vessel, its breadth, and tonnage; the signature of the envoy to be renewed every year. Also all such envoys shall be at the expense of their own party.

ARTICLE 7

If any tribe, or others, shall not desist from plunder and piracy, the friendly Arabs shall act against them according to their ability and circumstances, and an arrangement for this purpose shall take place between the friendly Arabs and the British at the time when such plunder and piracy shall occur.

ARTICLE 8

The putting men to death after they have given up their arms, is an act of piracy and not of acknowledged war; and if any tribe shall put to death any persons, either Mahomedans or others, after they have given up their arms, such tribe shall be held to have broken the peace; and the friendly Arabs shall act against them in conjunction with the British, and, God willing, the war against them shall not cease until the surrender of those who performed the act and of those who ordered it.

ARTICLE 9

The carrying off of slaves, men, women, or children from the coasts of Africa or elsewhere, and the transporting them in vessels, is plunder and piracy, and the friendly Arabs shall do nothing of this nature.

ARTICLE 10

The vessels of the friendly Arabs, bearing their flag above described, shall enter into all the British ports and into the ports of the allies of the British so far as they shall be able to effect it; and they shall buy and sell therein, and if any shall attack them, the British Government shall take notice of it.

ARTICLE 11

These conditions aforesaid shall be common to all tribes and persons, who shall hereafter adhere thereto in the same manner as to those who adhere to them at the time present. End of the Articles.

Issued at Ras-ool-khyma, in triplicate, at mid-day, on Saturday, the twenty-second of the month of Rabe-ul-Awul, in the year of the Hegira one thousand two hundred and thirtyfive, corresponding to the eighth of January one thousand eight hundred and twenty, and signed by the contracting parties at the places and times under written.

Signed at Ras-ool-khyma at the time of issue by

(Signed)W. GRANT KEIR,
Major General.

(Signed) HASSUN BIN RAHMAH,
Sheikh of Hatt and Faleia, formerly
of Ras-ool-Khyma.

(Signed) RAZIB BIN AHMED,
Sheikh of Jourat al Kamra.

(An exact Translation)
(Signed) T.P. THOMPSON, Captain,
17th Light Dragoons & Interpreter

Signed at Ras-ool-khyma, on Tuesday, the twenty-fifth of the month of Rabe-ul-Awul, in the year of the Hegira one thousand two hundred and thirty-five, corresponding to the eleventh of January 1820.

(Signed) SHAKBOUT
Sheikh of Abooshabee.

Signed at Ras-ool-Khyma, at mid-day, on Saturday, the twenty-ninth of the month Rabe-ul-Awul, in the year of the Hegira one thousand two hundred and thirty-five, corresponding to the fifteenth of January 1820.

(Signed) HASSUN BIN ALI,
Sheikh of Zyah.

The seal is Captain Thompson's, as Sheikh Hassun bin Ali had not a seal at the time of signature.

Copy of the general Treaty with the friendly (literally the "pacificated") Arabs. With the signatures attached to it, up to the fifteenth day of January 1820 inclusive. Given under my hand and seal.

(Signed) W. GRANT KEIR,
Major General.

(Signed) T.P. THOMPSON, Captain,
17th Light Dragoons, and Interpreter.

Ratified by the Governor General in Council on 2nd April 1820.

Signed for Mahomed bin Haza bin Zaal, Sheikh of Debaye, a minor, at Shargah, on Friday, the twelfth of the month of Rubee-oos-Sanee, in the year of the Hegira one thousand two hundred and thirty-five, corresponding to the twenty-eighth of January 1820.

(Signed) SAEED BIN SYF,
Uncle of Sheikh Mahomed.

Signed at Shargah, at mid-day, on Friday, the nineteenth of the month of Rubee-oos-Sanee, in the year of the Hegira one thousand two hundred and thirty-five, corresponding to the fourth of February 1820.

(Signed) SULTAN BIN SUGGUR,
Chief of Shargah.

Signed, at Shargah, by the Vakeel on the part of the Sheikhs Suleman bin Ahmed and Abdoolla bin Ahmed, in his quality of Vakeel to the Sheikhs aforesaid, on Saturday, the twentieth of the month of Rubee-oos-Sanee, in the year of the Hegira one thousand two hundred and thirty-five, corresponding to the 5th of February 1820.

(Signed) SYUD ABDOOL JALEL BIN SYUD YAS,
Vakeel of Sheikh Suleman bin Ahmed and
Sheikh Abdoolla bin Ahmed, of the
family of Khalifa, Sheikh of Bahrein.

Signed and accepted by Suleman bin Ahmed, of the house of Khalifa, at Bahrein, on the nineth of Jemmadee-ool-Awul, in the year of the Hegira one thousand two hundred and thirty-five, corresponding to the twenty-third of February 1820.

Signed and accepted by Abdoolla bin Ahmed, of the house of Khalifa, at Bahrein, on the ninth of Jemmadee-ool-Awul, in the year of the Hegira one thousand two hundred and thirty-five, corresponding to the twenty-third of February 1820.

Signed at Faleia, at noon, on Wednesday, the twenty-ninth of the month of Jemadee-ool-Awul, in the year of the Hegira one thousand two hundred and thirty-five, corresponding to the fifteenth of March 1820.

(Signed) RASHED BIN HAMID,
Chief of Ejman.

Signed at Faleia, at noon, on Wednesday, the twenty-ninth of the month of Jemmadee-ool-Awul, in the year of the Hegira one thousand two hundred and thirty-five, corresponding to the fifteenth of March 1820.

(Signed) ABDOOLLA BIN RASHID,
Chief of Amalgavine.

(Signed) W. GRANT KEIR,
Major General.

The terms of this treaty did not reflect the actual intentions of the British so much as the order from the Government of Bombay to the Naval Commander in Chief to send HMS *Eden* and HMS *Curlew* to co-operate in blockading 'the port of Mocha and all other ports and places belonging to the Imam of Senna'.[82] There is no indication anywhere of the reason for this act of hostility towards

Yemen. There is not a single report or rumour that Yemenis ever took part in any piratical activities anywhere. The Yemenis at the time were under pressure from the Egyptians. But most important, they were no friends of the Saudis and as such would have been on the right side of the British.

The only explanation of this British move against Yemen is that, since they had just established their domination of the Gulf, they thought they might as well dominate the southern coast of the Arabian Peninsula, which, in turn, would allow them the greater share of the Indian Ocean trade. Furthermore, Bruce was ordered to proceed to Yemen 'to co-operate with Captain Loch as the Agent of Government on any negotiations that may be carried on'.[83] This could not have been a reward to Bruce and Loch for their orgy of destruction in the Gulf. It could only have been an invitation to these blustering men to repeat what they had just done to promote the Company's trade, which Bruce in particular could 'negotiate' to their best interest.

Perhaps the best way to conclude this study is to include two tables that show how the alleged piracy in the Gulf during the period 1801–21 helped to increase the volume of the Company's trade with the Gulf. Imports to Bombay more than doubled and exports from Bombay almost trebled. The Company was getting richer and the 'pirates' ' means of livelihood were systematically destroyed.

Statement of the Value of Imports to Bombay from Persian and Arabian Gulfs

Year	Persian Gulf Value in Rupees (Lakhs)	Arabian Gulf Value in Rupees (Lakhs)
1801/2	16,84,028	7,05,042
1802/3	17,74,469	12,70,147
1803/4	22,88,315	15,84,031
1804/5	20,47,017	32,37,272
1805/6	28,71,000	13,00,376
1806/7	33,74,821	14,60,878
1807/8	19,00,754	7,45,282
1808/9	30,28,784	6,27,632
1809/10	30,64,687	7,19,549
1810/11	22,38,814	6,56,863
1811/12	21,40,740	9,44,292
1812/13	13,86,192	11,17,543
1813/14	13,58,836	7,37,492
1814/15	24,86,801	12,44,047
1815/16	36,41,611	14,32,431
1816/17	28,17,308	20,78,072
1817/18	36,99,059	25,43,655
1818/19	52,12,544	16,94,753
1819/20	29,80,639	17,06,560
1820/21	34,87,754	18,63,817
1821/22	33,85,197	14,33,313

Source: India Office Library, Bombay Commerce, Internal and External Reports, Range 419, vols 39–57, 1801–21.

Statement of the Value of Exports from Bombay to Persian and Arabian Gulfs

Year	Persian Gulf Value in Rupees (Lakhs)	Arabian Gulf Value in Rupees (Lakhs)
1801/2	12,15,579	3,04,259
1802/3	12,36,207	4,62,609
1803/4	9,17,190	3,71,630
1804/5	10,41,586	4,49,928
1805/6	13,49,095	6,54,891
1806/7	17,64,852	3,10,556
1807/8	14,69,210	3,02,128
1808/9	17,94,113	5,54,060
1809/10	17,71,470	4,80,759
1810/11	10,21,953	4,32,313
1811/12	19,48,205	3,64,831
1812/13	18,13,119	4,43,127
1813/14	14,80,539	5,77,382
1814/15	15,18,243	9,33,133
1815/16	18,26,294	5,75,206
1816/17	15,06,779	13,74,623
1817/18	19,24,928	12,79,580
1818/19	23,18,072	9,98,025
1819/20	20,32,064	10,73,089
1820/21	28,39,193	8,66,840
1821/22	33,59,384	12,03,820

Source: Ibid.

Notes

1. J.G. Lorimer, *Gazetteer of the Persian Gulf, Oman and Central Arabia*, (2 vols, Calcutta, 1980-15), p. 653.
2. Ibid., p. 194.
3. India Office Library (IO), Political Residency Bushire, Ser. R/15/1/16, pp. 22-7.
4. Lorimer, *Gazetteer*, p. 194.
5. J.B. Kelly, *Britain and the Persian Gulf, 1795-1880*, (Oxford University Press, 1968), p. 131.
6. National Archives of India (NAI), Political, Letter No. 45, 20 March 1810.
7. Bombay Archives (BA), Political Department Diary (PDD), no. 420/1815, pp. 429-30.
8. Ibid., no. 421/1815, pp. 1020-2.
9. Ibid., pp. 1059-60.
10. Lorimer, *Gazetteer*, p. 653.
11. NAI, Political, Letter no. 47, March 20, 1810.
12. Lorimer, *Gazetteer*, p. 653.
13. BA, PDD, no. 419/1815, pp. 295-9.
14. Ibid., no. 424/1815, pp. 2076-7.
15. IO, Pol. Res. Bushire, Ser. R/15/1/16, pp. 31-3.
16. Ibid., pp. 92-4.
17. BA, PDD, no. 429/1816, pp. 819-20.
18. Kelly, *Britain and the Persian Gulf*, p. 132.
19. C.R. Low, *History of the Indian Navy*, (2 vols, London, 1877), p. 320.
20. See above, p. 161.
21. BA, PDD, no. 429/1816, pp. 819-20.

22. Lorimer, *Gazetteer*, p. 654.

23. Loc. cit.

24. Kelly, *Britain and the Persian Gulf*, p. 132. BA, Selection 124, Proceedings for the year 1816, vol. 72, pp. 1–2, 4–9, 11–18, 20, 21–7, 29–34, 36–43.

25. BA, Sel, 124, vol. 72, pp. 46–54.

26. Kelly, *Britain and the Persian Gulf*, p. 132.

27. BA, Sel. 124, vol. 72, pp. 56–8, 60, 63, 75–81, 83–91, 95–8, 99–104, 112–15, 118–19, 120–7, 128.

28. Ibid., pp. 177–82; Kelly, *Britain and the Persian Gulf*, p. 134.

29. BA, Secret Department Diary (SDD), no. 312/1819, pp. 1074–8 and pp. 1078–81.

30. Ibid., pp. 1084–6 and pp. 1091–4.

31. BA, Sel. 124, vol. 72, pp. 432–4.

32. Ibid., pp. 437–8.

33. Ibid., pp. 441–2.

34. Ibid., pp. 498–9.

35. Ibid., pp. 367–9.

36. Ibid., pp. 362–5.

37. Ibid., pp. 384–7.

38. Ibid., pp. 396–7.

39. Ibid., pp. 470–4.

40. Ibid., pp. 412–13.

41. BA Selection (Man.) on Pirates in the Persian Gulf, vol. 72/1816, p. 519.

42. Ibid., vol. 74/1819, pp. 1–16.

43. BA, SDD, no. 310/1819, pp. 301–9.

44. See Sultān Muhammad Al-Qāsimī, 'Arab ''Piracy'' and the East India Company Encroachment in the Gulf 1797–1820', Ph.D. thesis, University of Exeter, 1985, Appendix no. I/6.

45. Ibid., Appendix no. I/1.

46. Lorimer, *Gazetteer*, pp. 656–7.

47. BA, Sel. on Pirates in the Persian Gulf, no. 73/1819, p. 315.

48. Ibid., pp. 306–8.

49. Ibid., pp. 310–12.

50. India Office Library (IO), Bombay Political Proceedings, Range 384, vol. 39, Consultation 27 January 1819, p. 436.

51. Lorimer, *Gazetteer*, p. 657.

52. BA, Secret and Political Department Diaries (S & PDD), no. 465/1819, pp. 2510–11.

53. Ibid., no. 455/1818, pp. 5861–72.

54. Ibid., no. 465/1819, pp. 2536–8.

55. Ibid., no. 466/1819, pp. 3161–2.

56. Ibid., no. 469/1819, pp. 4314–21.

57. Ibid., no. 469/1819, p. 4322.

58. BA, Sel. on Pirates in the Persian Gulf, vol. 73/1819, pp. 127–8.

59. Ibid., p. 226.

60. Ibid., pp. 226–8.

61. Ibid., pp. 231–2.

62. Ibid., pp. 239–41.

63. BA, S & PDD, no. 466/1819, p. 3153.

64. Ibid., no. 466/1819, pp. 2381–2 and 3159–50; no. 465/1819, pp. 2623–4.

65. NAI, Political, Letter no. 13.

66. Ibid., Letter no. 4.

67. Ibid., Letter no. 16.

68. Ibid., Letter no. 18.

69. Ibid., Letter no. 14.

70. BA (Man.), on Pirates in the Persian Gulf, vol. 76/1819, pp. 97–8.

71. Ibid., pp. 91–6.

72. Ibid., vol. 74/1819, pp. 113–14.

73. Ibid., pp. 187–95.

74. Ibid., pp. 350–64.

75. Ibid., vol. 76/1819, p. 100.

76. Ibid., vol. 75/1819, pp. 434–9.

77. Ibid., pp. 441–4.
78. IO, Board's Collections, 17855, F/4/651, pp. 874–80.
79. BA, S & PDD, no. 485/1820, p. 3564.
80. Ibid., no. 479/1820, pp. 1258–78; no 484/1820, pp. 3432–4.
81. Kelly, *Britain and the Persian Gulf*, p. 161.
82. BA, S & PDD, no. 490/1820, p. 5696; no. 491/1820, p. 5977.
83. Ibid., no. 491/1820, pp. 5979–80.

Bibliography

Manuscript Sources

I   Algemeen Rijks Archief (General State Archives) in the Hague:
- (a)   Adnwinste le Afdeling, 1889, 23B.
- (b)   Family Archive, Geleynseen Jongh-nr. 260e, Travel to Basara 1645–6.
- (c)   Koloniaa Archief.
- (d)   Van de Oostindische Compagnie, (United East-India Company)

II   Bombay Archives:
- (a)   Bussorah Diary, 19 volumes (nos. 193–212).
- (b)   Secret and Political Department.
    - (i)   Secret and Political Department Diaries: (1755–1808) 268 volumes (nos. 1 to 260) and nos. 14, 17, 19, 33, 41, 66, 164 and 165.
    - (ii)   Secret Department Diaries: (1809–1820) — 180 volumes (nos. 318 to 497).
    - (iii)   Political Department Diaries: (1809–1820) 180 volumes (nos. 318 to 497).
- (c)   Selections on Pirates in the Persian Gulf (not indexed), 5 volumes (nos. 71, 73, 74, 75, 76).
- (d)   Selection — 124 vol. 72 (not indexed) Proceedings for the year 1816.
- (e)   Summary of the proceedings relative to the boats captured in the Persian Gulf, Vol. 77/1819–20, Minute by Mr F. Warden.

III   India Office Library.
- (a)   Bombay Secret Proceedings 1819, vol. 40 Consultation no. 17 of 14 April 1819; and vol. 41 Consultation no. 37 of 20th September 1819, Minutes by Francis Warden.
- (b)   Gumbroon Diary, 8 vols. (nos. 7–14)
- (c)   Political Residency Bushire, R/15/1/3.

IV   National Archives of India, Foreign Department, 1810, Microfilm Reel no. 3.

V   Revue d'Histoire Diplomatique la France et Muscate, Auzouk, A. Muscate; Documentation and Research Centre, Abu Dhabi.

VI   A Private Collection of Original Documents
Comprising:

(1) A sketch of the proceedings of the British Armament which sailed from Bombay in September 1809 for the purpose of destroying the vessels of the Joasmee pirates in the Gulf of Persia — undated.

(2) Return of a Detachment under Orders for Foreign Service commanded by Lieutenant Colonel Lionel Smith, His Majesty's 65th Regiment, Bombay, 7 September 1807.

(3) Letter from Mr Goble, at Spithead, dated 21 April 1808, clarifying the law of prize and ransom.

(4) Bill of Lading signed by Captain J. Wainwright, at Muscat, dated 7 May 1809.

(5) Extract from a letter from Captain Malcolm to the Earl of Mornington, dated 26 February 1800, considering possible sites in the Arabian Gulf for the establishment of a British settlement.

(6) Journal of a trip to Behereen and to Beder on the coasts of Arabia, by Captain David Seton, the Honourable Company's Resident at Oman, dated 1 November 1801.

(7) Directions for part of the coasts of Persia and Arabia, comprising Captain Key's Observations.

(8) A sketch map illustrating the State of the Ports and Tribes on the Arabian coasts between Ras al Zaad and Zobareh distinguishing in particular the eight ports of the plundering and piratical Jowasim.

(9) Extract from the *Mornington*'s Log Book of 8 March 1808.

(10) Sketch map illustrating the Bātinah coast from Dibbā to South of Shinās, with detailed description of Khor Fakkān, and a table of bearings and co-ordinates.

(11) View of Khor Fakkān.

(12) Names of different places in the Persian Gulf.

(13) Arabic sketch map of the Sūr Coast in the Arabian Gulf, noting contemporaneous translations.

(14) Sketch map of the coast of Southern Persia.

(15) Transcript of notes for sailing directions, at Ras ul Khyma dated 11 November 1809.

(16) Transcript of notes for sailing directions, with sketch.

(17) Transcript of notes for sailing directions — undated.

(18– Five letters in Arabic received from Moolla Hussun, Chief of the Fort
22) of Luft, previous to its attack and surrender.

(23) Transcript of notes in pencil — author and purpose unknown.

(24) Translation of the General Treaty of 1820.

Letters, orders, etc. passing to HMS Chiffonne

(25) Letter from W.O.B. Drury in Madras to Captain Wainwright, HMS *Chiffonne*, Bombay, dated 26 May 1809.

(26) Letter from W.O.B. Drury on board HMS *Russel*, Madras. Dated 9 June 1809.

(27) Letter from W.O.B. Drury on board HMS *Fox*, Madras to Captain Wainwright on board HMS *Chiffonne*. Dated 12 June 1809.

(28) Letter from W.O.B. Drury, Madras to Captain Wainwright on board
      HMS *Chiffonne*, Bombay. Dated 6 July 1809.
(29) Extract from a letter from Captain Robert Budden of the Honourable
      Company's Marine to W.C. Bunce. Dated 31 August 1809.
(30) Brigade Orders by Leiutenant Colonel Smith from Head Quarters on
      board HMS *Chiffonne*, Ras ul Khyma. Signed by N. Warren, Brig.
      Major to Captain J. Wainwright. Dated 14 November 1809.
(31) Brigade Orders by Lieutenant Colonel Smith from Head Quarters on
      board HMS *Chiffonne*, Luft. Signed by N. Warren, Brig. Major.
      Dated 27 November 1809.
(32) Letter from W.O.B. Drury, Bombay. Dated 1 December 1809.
(33) Letter from W.O.B. Drury on board HMS *Russel* of Ceylon to Cap-
      tain Wainwright, HMS *Chiffonne*. Dated 17 December 1809.
(34) Letter from Lord Minto, certified by G.C. Osborne, Secretary to
      Govt. to the Honourable Jonathan Duncan, Governor in Council,
      Bombay. Dated 28 December 1809.
(35) Letter from G.C. Osborne to Captain J. Wainwright and Lieutenant
      Colonel Smith. Dated 11 January 1810.
(36) Letter dated 27 January 1810.
(37) Letter from W.O.B. Drury on board HMS *Russel*, Madras Roads,
      to Captain Wainwright, HMS *Chiffonne*. Dated 28 January 1810.
(38) Letter from W.O.B. Drury on board HMS *Russel*, Madras. Dated
      30 January 1810.
(39) Letter from W.O.B. Drury on board HMS *Russel*, Madras Roads to
      Captain Wainwright, HMS *Chiffonne*. Dated 7 February 1810.
(40) Letter from Mr Charles Palfry, Political Agent to Captain Wainwright
      and Lieutenant Colonel Smith in the Gulph. Dated 7 February 1810.
(41) Letter from G.C. Osborne, Bombay Castle to Captain Wainwright
      and Lieutenant Colonel Smith in the Gulph. Dated 17 February 1810.
(42) Letter from N. Warren, Bombay Castle to Captain Wainwright and
      Lieutenant Colonel Smith, with accompanying General Order. Dated
      26 February 1810.
(43) Letter from W.O.B. Drury in Madras. Dated 5 March 1810.
(44) Letter from W.O.B. Drury in Madras. Dated 7 March 1810.
(45) Letter from W.O.B. Drury in Madras. Dated 8 March 1810.
(46) Undated letter from W.O.B. Drury to Captain Wainwright, received
      on 8 March 1810.
(47) Letter, plus enclosures, from N. Warren, Captain of H.M. 65th Regi-
      ment to N.H. Smith, Political Resident, Bushire. Dated 17 March
      1810.
(48) Letter from W.O.B. Drury, Madras to Captain Wainwright, HMS
      Chiffonne. Dated 20 March 1810.
(49) Letter to Captain Wainwright and Lieutenant Colonel Smith. Dated
      23 March 1810.
(50) Letter from W.O.B. Drury, Madras. Dated 23 March 1810.

(51) Letter from G.C. Osborne to William Taylor Money, Superintendent of Marine. Dated 23 March 1810.

(52) Letter, plus enclosure, from N. Warren on board H.M. Cruizer *Mornington*, Bushire Roads to Lieutenant Colonel Smith commanding the 63rd Regiment. Dated 27 March 1810.

(53) Letter to Captain Wainwright. Dated 31 March 1810.

(54) Letter to Captain Wainwright. Dated 1 April 1810.

(55) Letter to Captain Wainwright, Bombay. Dated 4 April 1810.

(56) Letter from W.O.B. Drury. Dated 12 April 1810.

(57) Copy letter to Jonathan Duncan from John Malcolm received 1 May.

(58) Letter from W.O.B. Drury, Madras to Captain Wainwright on board HMS *Chiffonne*, Penang. Dated 5 August 1810.

(59) Letter from W.O.B. Drury, Madras. Dated 2 September 1810.

Published Documentary Sources

1. Aitchison, C.U., *A Collection of Treaties, Engagements and Sanads relating to India and Neighbouring Countries*, 3rd edn., (II vols., Calcutta, 1892).

2. *The Asiatic Annual Register*, Vol. XI, for the year 1809, by E. Samuel (London, 1811).

3. Badger, Revd G.P., *History of the Imams and Seyyids of Oman* (London, Hakluyt Society, 1871).

4. *Bombay Gazette*, October number, 1809.

5. Buckingham, J.S., *Travels in Assyria, Media and Persia*, 2nd edn. (2 vols., London, 1830).

6. Captain T. Thompson's papers, Hull University Library.

7. Dighe, V.G., *Descriptive Catalogue of the Secret and Political Department Series, 1755–1820*, (Bombay, 1854).

8. Captain F. Loch's Memoirs, Edinburgh University Library.

9. *Al-Fath al-Mubīn*, by Humayd b. Ruzayq (Muscat, 1977).

10. *The Handbook of the Bombay Archives*, compiled by Sanyiv P. Dasai (Department of Archives, Govt. of Maharashtra, Bombay, 1978).

11. Jackson, J. *Journey from India towards England in 1797* (London, 1799). *

12. Kaye, Sir J.W., *Life and Correspondence of Sir John Malcolm*, (2 vols. London, 1856).

13. Kempthorne, G.B., 'Notes made on a survey along the Eastern Shores of the Persian Gulf in 1828', *Journal of the Royal Geographical Society*, v (1835).

14. Klerk du Reus, G.C., *Geschichtlicher Ueberblick der administrativen, rechtlichen und finanziellen Entwicklung der Niederlandisch-Ostindischen Compagnie* (Batavia — 's-Nage, 1894), Appendix IX.

15. Lorimer, J.G., *Gazetteer of the Persian Gulf, 'Oman and Central Arabia*, (2 vols., Calcutta, 1908–15). The Gazetteer was compiled in the Foreign Department of the Government of India on the orders of Lord Curzon, after his tour of the Gulf during his first Viceroyalty. Vol. II (geographical) was issued first,

in 1908, and Vol. I (Historical and Genealogical) in 1915.

16. Maurizi, V. ('Shaik Mansur'), *History of Seyd Said, Sultan of Muscat*, (London, 1819).

17. Milburn, W. and Thornton, J. *Oriental Commerce* (London, 1825).

18. Minto, Countess of (ed.), *Lord Minto in India: Life and Letters of Gilbert Elliot, First Earl of Minto, from 1807 to 1814, while Governor-General of India*, (London, 1880).

19. Niebuhr, Carsten, *Description de l'Arabie* (Copenhagen, 1773).

20. − − − − *Voyage en Arabie et en d'autres pays circonvoisins* (2 vols., Utrecht, 1775–9).

21. Pieter Van Dam, *Beschryving Van de Oostindiche Compagnie*, ed. F.W. Stapped (The Hague, 1939).

22. Sadlier, Captain G.F., *Diary of a Journey across Arabia* (Bombay, 1866).

23. *Selections from State papers, Bombay, regarding the East India Company's connection with the Persian Gulf, with a Summary of Events, 1600–1800*, ed. by J.A. Saldanha (Calcutta, 1908). A list of the precis used in the present work follows:

(a) Precis of Turkish Arabia Affairs, 1801–1905, (Calcutta, 1906).

(b) Precis of Correspondence regarding the Affairs of the Persian Gulf 1801–53 (Calcutta, 1906).

(c) Precis on Commerce and Communication in the Persian Gulf, 1801–1905 (Culcutta, 1906).

24. *Selections from the Records of the Bombay Government*, New Series, no. XXIV; *Historical and other information connected with the Province of Oman, Muscat, Bahrein and other places in the Persian Gulf*, compiled and edited by R. Hughes Thomas (Bombay, 1856).

25. *'Unwān al-Majid*, by Sheikh 'Uthmān b. Bishr (Education Ministry, Saudi Arabia, n.d.).

26. Whitelock, F., 'Notes taken during a journey in Oman along the East Coast of Arabia', *Trans. Bombay Geog. Soc.* i. (1836–8).

Studies

1. Barlett, H. Moyse, *The Pirates of Trucial Oman*, (London, 1966).

2. Belgrave, C., *The Pirate Coast*, (London, 1966).

3. Hawley, D., *The Trucial States*, (London, 1970).

4. Kelly, J.B., *Britain and the Persian Gulf, 1795–1880*, (Oxford, 1968).

5. Longrigg, S.H., *Four Centuries of Modern Iraq*, (Oxford, 1925).

6. Low, C.R., *History of the Indian Navy*, (2 vols. London, 1877).

7. Philips, C.H., *The East India Company, 1784–1834*, (Manchester, 1940).

8. Raychadhuri, T., Habib, I., Kumur, D. and Desai, M., *The Cambridge Economic History of India*, (2 vols. Cambridge, 1982–83).

9. Sutton, J., *Lords of the East: The East India Company and its Ships*, (London, 1981).

Index

'Ababdah tribe 2
Abbas I, Shah 1, 23
Abbas Koly Khan, Nawab 195
'Abdil'azīz, Shaikh (Saudi Chief) 41
Abdul Jalel b. Syud Yas 227
Abdul Rehman b. Rashid, Shaikh 112
Abdulla, Shaikh (brother of Saqr) 34–5
'Abdulla b. Ahmad (Shaikh of Bahrain)
    200, 219, 227
Abdulla b. Croosh, Shaikh 77–81, 146, 147
Abdulla b. Direes 202, 203
'Abdullah b. Rashid (Shaikh of Umm al-
    Qaiwain) 227
'Abdullah b. Sa'ud, Shaikh (Saudi Chief)
    171–3, 178–80 passim, 199–204, 213
Abu Dhabi 4–5, 131, 217
Abū Heyle 5, 225
Abū Musā 162, 164
Africa 7, 8, 13, 14
agreements, inter-Arab 221
    with East India Company see treaties
Ahmad Shah 177–9, 182
Ahmady 215
Ahmed ibn Sa'id, Imam 14
'Ajmān 5, 40, 145, 224
Al 'Alī tribe 2, 5
Al Bu 'Alī iv
Al Bu Said family ii, 9, 27
    see also individual headings
Albediā 6
alliances
    Britain-Oman iii, 40, 54, 79, 84,
        109–19, 122, 151–2, 197
    Joasmees-Muscat 78, 212–13
    Ma'īn 26, 42
    Muscat-Persia 152–3
Americans 117, 196, 197
Antelope (Company cruiser) 48, 215
Arabia 39, 80, 118, 129, 158–9, 198, 219
Arabian Sea iii, 6, 198
Armenians 1, 25, 27, 94
Arthur, Capt. J. (Antelope) 215
'Asilū 3, 13, 216, 217, 225
Aurora (Company cruiser) 197
Ayub Mohamed Mehdi, Khan 72–4

Babcock, Capt. R. (Shannon) 44–9 passim
Babington, S. (Sec., Bombay Govt) 186
Badr, Sayyid 41, 55–9 passim, 61, 62, 65,
    67–72 passim, 74–80 passim, 84

Bahrain iii, iv, 4, 10–14, 34, 40, 112–14,
    145, 200, 212, 215, 219, 221–2
Baluch 1, 115
Bander 'Abbās 1, 8–9, 26, 42, 55, 58, 59,
    61, 62, 71, 72, 115
    see also Gumbroon
Bander Mallām 1, 131, 140, 145
Bander Maqam 3
Bander Rig 3, 16
Bani Yās tribe 4, 5, 221
Bartlett, Lt Col. H. Moyse iv
base, British vii, 38, 39, 89, 121, 134, 145
Basidu 2
Basra vi, 1, 3, 4, 7–8, 11–21 passim, 23,
    25, 27, 33, 41, 62, 109–10, 118, 120,
    132, 213
Bassein (Company snow) 34–5
Batavia 12, 21, 22
Batinah coast 7, 13
Beaumont, John (Res. Bushire) 32, 33
Belgrave, Charles iv
Ben Gabber, Abdulla (Jillama) 111, 115,
    116
Ben Gaith, Hassan 173, 178–82 passim
Ben Ghuss, Hussan 117
Benares (Company cruiser) 158, 165, 167,
    205
Bengal 15, 18, 19, 20, 40
Bennett, Lieut. (Nautilus) 100–1
Bete 103
Bid' 4, 10
Blast, Lieut. (Lively) 103
Bohka 42, 43, 72
Bombay 13, 15, 16, 18–21 passim, 40, 90
    Archives v–vii
    Government i, iii, v–vii, 10, 31, 50,
        57–8, 88, 94, 103, 118, 151, 159,
        186, 189, 191, 219, 221, 229
Bostanah 2
Bridges, Capt. P.H. (Challenger) 198–9,
    211
Briscoe, C.J. 103–6
Britain
    and Muscat/Omanis iii, 27, 31, 33,
        38–41, 50–9 passim, 61, 62, 65, 68,
        69, 75–6, 84, 85, 107–11, 118, 119,
        121, 122, 124, 125, 127–8, 133,
        136, 140–4, 151–4, 159, 164–6,
        197, 205, 207–10, 212, 215, 216,
        219, 222

239